Electing to Fight

Praise for *Electing to Fight*

"Edward D. Mansfield and Jack Snyder argue that **new democracies are often unstable and thus particularly warlike**. . . . They warn that 'unleashing Islamic mass opinion through a sudden democratization could only raise the likelihood of war.' . . . **Their work should give pause**. If democracy is to promise peace—perpetual or otherwise—we must become far better at laying its foundations."
—Gary J. Bass, *New York Times Magazine*

"Mr. Mansfield and Mr. Snyder's lesson is that, depending on the character of the regime and the society that it reflects, democratic elections without democratic institutions might worsen the prospects for real democracy—and they won't do much for American security, either . . . **Their analysis raises profound doubts**—as if enough hadn't already been kicked up—over President George W. Bush's declared policy of spreading democracy across the Middle East."
—Fred Kaplan, *Pittsburgh Post-Gazette*

"[A] **wide-ranging** comparative study. . . . These lessons are **highly topical**, given the various scenarios now under consideration for bringing democracy to north Africa, the Middle East—and China."
—*The Irish Times*

"Mansfield and Snyder are **persuasive**. . . . If Mansfield and Snyder are correct about the bellicose tendencies of young, incompletely democratized states, **the stakes of Iraq's transition are higher than most have supposed**."
—John M. Owen IV, *Foreign Affairs*

"A **timely, intriguing and provocative** analysis of the relationship between democracy and international war . . . **evocative of Samuel Huntington's classic statement in *Political Order and Changing Societies*.**"
—Errol Henderson, *Survival*

"**Provocative** . . . an **excellent** illustration of the way in which scholarship can inform policy in a meaningful way and in a timely fashion."
—Andrew Enterline, *Perspectives on Politics*

"*Electing to Fight* is an **ambitious, fertile, and thought-provoking** book."
—George Lawson, *International Affairs*

"With **notable analytic agility and rigorous empiricism** Mansfield and Snyder dissect the popular policy nostrum that promoting democracy abroad promotes peace in the world. Their **incisive** work will help policymakers steer clear of misleading, facile assumptions and impel scholars to dig deeper and think harder on **a subject of critical contemporary importance**."
—Thomas Carothers, Vice President for Studies—International Law and Governance, Carnegie Endowment for International Peace

"*Electing to Fight* is **an important book**. With **analytical power and historical depth**, Mansfield and Snyder argue for a simple conclusion: democratization can be dangerous, even if democracy, once achieved, is a good thing. **Scholars, journalists, politicians, and citizens all need to hear this message, and to heed it**."
—Joshua Cohen, Leon and Anne Goldberg Professor of the Humanities and Head of the Department of Political Science, Massachusetts Institute of Technology

"*Electing to Fight* is **a must-read** for anyone seriously interested in the theory and practice of democracy."
—Cindy Skach, Associate Professor of Government, Harvard University

"**Mansfield and Snyder tackle one of the most profound foreign policy puzzles of our age:** how to manage the process of political liberalization without creating unnecessary or unacceptable risks for the international community. This work will be of interest to scholars, students, and policymakers alike."
—Allan C. Stam, Daniel Webster Professor of Government, Dartmouth College

Electing To Fight

Why Emerging Democracies Go To War

by Edward D. Mansfield and Jack Snyder

BCSIA Studies in International Security

MIT Press
Cambridge, Massachusetts
London, England

First MIT Press paperback edition, 2007

MIT Press books may be purchased at special quantity discounts for business or
sales promotional use. For information, please email <special_sales@mitpress.mit.edu>
or write to Special Sales Department, The MIT Press, 55 Hayward Street,
Cambridge, MA 02142.

Library of Congress Cataloging-in Publication Data

Mansfield, Edward D., 1962–
Electing to fight : why emerging democracies go to war / Edward D. Mansfield
and Jack Snyder.
p. cm.—(BCSIA studies in international security)
Includes bibliographical references.
ISBN 0-262-13449-7 (hc : alk. paper), 978-0-262-63347-5 (pb : alk. paper)
1. Democratization. 2. War. I. Snyder, Jack L. II. Title. III. Series.

JC423.M354 2005
321.8—dc22
2004057861

Printed in the United States of America.

On the cover: "Siege of Paris 1870–1871" by Ernest Meissonier, painted in 1884.

Parts of Chapter 5 in this volume were previously published in *International
Organization* in 2002. We gratefully acknowledge permission to reprint this material.

10   9   8   7   6   5   4

To our fathers, Edwin Mansfield and Robert Snyder

There is nothing harder than the apprenticeship of freedom.

—Tocqueville, *Democracy in America*

Contents

Preface and Acknowledgments

America's efforts to promote democracy around the globe have all too often been fraught with danger and disappointment. In this book, we seek to explain why. By exploring when and why democratization can lead to war, we seek to understand when—and how—the spread of democracy might be encouraged while avoiding the increased risks of war.

We first began writing on the theme of democratization and war for scholars, policymakers, and the public in 1995, when we published articles in *Foreign Affairs* and *International Security*. Since then, we have benefited immeasurably from suggestions and criticisms, which led us to refine our statistical tests and integrate our case studies better with our statistical results. These improvements in our research design have helped us to sharpen our findings and our prescriptions. Going through the painstaking process of social science, including the incorporation of feedback and criticisms, has led, we believe, to a final product that goes well beyond our initial insights of 1995. We appreciate having the opportunity to thank some of the people who helped us improve our work.

For their comments on the articles that contributed to the development of the ideas in this book, we thank Steve Chan, Miriam Fendius Elman, Erik Gartzke, Peter Gourevitch, Joanne Gowa, Margaret Hermann, Robert Jervis, David Lake, Ned Lebow, Jack Levy, Anthony Mughan, John Oneal, Dan Reiter, Bruce Russett, Randall Schweller, David Spiro, Al Stepan, Randall Stone, William Thompson, Celeste Wallander, and Michael Ward. Karen Ballentine co-authored with Snyder a 1996 article in *International Security*, "Nationalism and the Marketplace of Ideas," which helped to develop part of our argument. For providing valuable comments on the entire book manuscript, we thank Regina

Baker, Dawn Brancati, Robert Kaufman, Dan Reiter, and Etel Solingen. For their contributions to an extremely helpful conference on our manuscript organized by Sean Lynn-Jones and Steve Miller at the Belfer Center for Science and International Affairs at Harvard University, we are grateful to Ivan Arreguín Toft, Scott Bennett, Sarah Buckley, Joshua Cohen, Arman Grigorian, Mike Horowitz, Liu Jianfei, Ha-Won Lee, Neophytos Loizides, Paul MacDonald, Kevin Narizny, Erin Simpson, Cynthia Skach, Stephen Smith, Allan Stam, and Wu Xingzuo. For research assistance, we thank Fiona Adamson, Regina Baker, Christopher Ball, Susan Burgerman, Tim Büthe, George Gavrilis, Arman Grigorian, Colin Kahl, Leyla Karimli, Adrienne LeBas, Kristina Mani, Patrick McDonald, Jon Pevehouse, and Barbora Somogyiova.

The Belfer Center, the Christopher H. Browne Center for International Politics at the University of Pennsylvania, the Harry Frank Guggenheim Foundation, the Hoover Institution at Stanford University, the Mershon Center at Ohio State University, the Pew Charitable Trusts, the United States Institute of Peace, and the Saltzman Institute of War and Peace Studies at Columbia University provided support, financial and logistical, for the project.

Mike Brown showed faith in us by recruiting our book for the BCSIA Studies in International Security. Unfortunately, we were so slow that Mike had moved on to different pastures at Georgetown by the time that we were nearing the finish line. Sean Lynn-Jones spurred us on to completion in his capacity as series editor. He also came up with the title. Teresa Lawson was as always a marvelous editor, who helped us straighten out our ideas as well as our prose. Most important, we would like to thank Charlotte, Katherine, and Liv Mansfield and Anna and Claire Snyder for their encouragement, patience, and support.

—Edward D. Mansfield
Philadelphia

—Jack Snyder
New York

Electing to Fight

Chapter 1

The Perilous Path to the Democratic Peace

No mature democracies have ever fought a war against each other. Consequently, conventional wisdom holds that promoting the spread of democracy will promote world peace and security. President Bill Clinton made this ambition a central theme of his foreign policy.[1] In the wake of the September 11, 2001, terrorist attack, President George W. Bush came to believe that U.S. security might require preventive wars to unseat dangerous despots so as to build the "infrastructure of democracy" abroad and create a "balance of power that favors freedom."[2] Declaring that American security from terrorism depends on the success of democracy in Iraq and its neighbors, Bush argued that "sixty years of Western nations excusing and accommodating the lack of freedom in the Middle East did nothing to make us safe—because in the long run, stability cannot be purchased at the expense of liberty."[3]

Such views strike a resonant chord across the entire spectrum of American opinion. Since the time of Woodrow Wilson, idealists in the United States have envisioned a global transformation in which peace and democracy are mutually reinforcing. The collapse of the Soviet

---

1. 1994 State of the Union address, "Transcript of Clinton's Address," *New York Times,* January 26, 1994, p. A17.

2. Executive Office of the President, *National Security Strategy of the United States* (September 2002), pp. 21, 29.

3. George W. Bush, "Remarks by the President at the 20th Anniversary of the National Endowment for Democracy," Washington, D.C., November 6, 2003, reported in David Sanger, "Bush Asks Lands in Mideast to Try Democratic Ways," *New York Times,* November 7, 2003, p. A1.

Union and the rising danger of global terrorism created conditions in which these longstanding ideals seemed, to some, both achievable and urgent.[4] U.S.-based activist movements have increasingly pressed a transnational agenda in which "all good things go together"—global democratic accountability, global civil society, improved human rights, and peace.[5] Indeed, over the long run, it is probably true that the further spread of democracy will promote global peace and stability.

In the short run, however, the beginning stages of transitions to democracy often give rise to war rather than peace. Since the end of the Cold War, this causal connection between democratization and war has been especially striking, but the fundamental pattern is as old as democracy itself, dating at least to the French Revolution. Not all democratic transitions are dangerous; as we explain in this book, the chance of war arises mainly in those transitional states that lack the strong political institutions needed to make democracy work (such as an effective state, the rule of law, organized parties that compete in fair elections, and professional news media). When these institutions are absent or weak, politicians have incentives to resort to violent nationalist appeals, tarring their opponents as enemies of the nation in order to prevail in electoral competition.

In democratizing states, nationalism is an ideology with tremendous appeal for elites whose privileges are threatened. It can be used to convince newly empowered constituencies that the cleavage between the privileged and the masses is unimportant compared to the cleavages that divide nations, ethnic groups, or races. Nationalism holds that the people as a whole have the right to self-rule, but it does not necessarily promise that the government should be strictly accountable to the average voter through democratic processes governed by the rule of law. Nationalist rhetoric demands government for the people, but not necessarily by the people.

States risk nationalist violence when they attempt to transition to democracy without institutions of public accountability. President Bush claimed that "it is the practice of democracy that makes a nation ready for democracy, and every nation can start on this path."[6] However, our review of the evidence shows that this argument (which most democracy

4. Francis Fukuyama, "The End of History," *The National Interest*, No. 16 (Summer 1989), pp. 3–18; and Charles Krauthammer, "The Unipolar Moment," *Foreign Affairs, America and the World*, 1990/91, Vol. 70, No. 1, pp. 23–33.

5. The term is from Robert Packenham, *Liberal America and the Third World* (Princeton: Princeton University Press, 1973).

6. George W. Bush, "Remarks by the President," November 6, 2003.

activists advocate) is incorrect and dangerously so. In fact, ill-prepared attempts to democratize weak states—such as the recent cases of Yugoslavia, Pakistan, Rwanda, and Burundi—may lead to costly warfare in the short run, and may delay or prevent real progress toward democracy over the long term.

Over thirty years ago, Dankwart Rustow issued a call for an approach to the study of democratization addressing questions of both process and sequence.[7] He complained that existing approaches emphasized the prerequisites for democracy—such as wealth, literacy, and a large middle class—or its functional requirements, such as the rule of law and a free press. These approaches correspond to what Thomas Carothers disparages as the "check-list orientation" of U.S. democracy assistance programs, which holds that democracy will emerge when the full inventory of prerequisites has been installed, regardless of the order in which these factors are put into place.[8]

Rustow argued, in contrast, that the stability of democratic consolidation depends on the sequence in which the requisites appear on the historical stage. The "ingredients [of democracy] must be assembled," he contended, "one at a time, in a manageable sequence of tasks." In Rustow's formulation, democratization typically goes awry when it precedes the emergence of a consensus on national identity. "The hardest struggles in a democracy are those against the birth defects of political community."[9] A number of leading scholars of democratization and political change made similar arguments around the same time: Robert Dahl, Eric Nordlinger, and Samuel Huntington all pointed out that democratic transitions are most successful when strong political institutions are developed before popular political participation increases.[10] Such ideas

---

7.   Dankwart Rustow, "Transitions to Democracy: Toward a Dynamic Model," *Comparative Politics*, Vol. 2, No. 2 (April 1970), pp. 337–363, reprinted in Lisa Anderson, ed., *Transitions to Democracy* (New York: Columbia University Press, 1999), pp. 14–41.

8.   Thomas Carothers, *Aiding Democracy Abroad* (Washington, D.C.: Carnegie Endowment for International Peace, 1999); see also Carothers, "The End of the Transition Paradigm," *Journal of Democracy*, Vol. 13, No. 1 (2002), pp. 5–21.

9.   Rustow, "Transitions to Democracy," pp. 34–35. Juan Linz and Alfred Stepan, *Problems of Democratic Transition and Consolidation* (Baltimore, Md.: The Johns Hopkins University Press, 1996), p. 5, discuss democratic consolidation as the moment when democracy becomes "the only game in town."

10.   Robert A. Dahl, *Polyarchy: Participation and Opposition* (New Haven: Yale University Press, 1971); Eric Nordlinger, "Political Development, Time Sequences and Rates of Change," in James L. Finkle and Robert Grable, *Political Development and Social Change*, 2d ed. (New York: Wiley, 1971), p. 458; and Samuel P. Huntington, *Political Order in Changing Societies* (New Haven: Yale University Press, 1968).

about sequencing have not, however, played a central role in much subsequent scholarship or public policymaking on democratic transitions. We believe they should.

In this book, therefore, we examine the process and sequence of democratization to identify when and how it leads to peace or may instead increase the risk of war. We use statistical evidence to establish general patterns, and we use case studies to trace causal mechanisms. Our research shows that incomplete democratic transitions—those that get stalled before reaching the stage of full democracy—increase the chance of involvement in international war in countries where governmental institutions are weak at the outset of the transition. In such transitional states, as we show in Chapter 5, the risk of war goes up by a factor of four to fifteen. Seven percent of all wars since 1816 are associated with an incomplete democratic transition. Democratic transition is only one of many causes of war, but it is a potent one.

In the rest of this chapter, we discuss some of the many "wars of democratization" that have taken place, especially since the end of the Cold War, but also reaching back as far as the French Revolution. We distinguish the conditions under which wars are most likely: a transition toward democracy that is incomplete; where institutions are too weak to manage the upsurge in the political power of newly enfranchised masses; and where rising or declining elites, or both, play the nationalist card in an attempt to harness that power. We outline the causal mechanisms that we explain more fully in Chapters 2 and 3. We conclude this chapter by stressing why it is crucial to take these dangers into account in devising the foreign policy responses of the United States and the international community to the potential challenges posed by troubled democratizing states.

Wars of Democratization

The decade following the end of the Cold War witnessed some peaceful transitions to democracy, yet a number of turbulent experiments with democratic politics led instead to bloody wars. In 1991, Yugoslavia broke up into separate warring nations within six months of elections in which ethnic nationalism was a powerful factor.[11] In the wake of the Soviet collapse, popular sentiment expressed in the streets and at the ballot box fueled warfare between Armenia and Azerbaijan over the disputed enclave

---

11. Susan Woodward, *Balkan Tragedy* (Washington, D.C.: The Brookings Institution, 1995), p. 17.

of Nagorno-Karabakh.[12] As Peru and Ecuador democratized fitfully during the 1980s and 1990s, troubled elected governments gained popularity
by provoking a series of armed clashes that culminated in a war in the
upper Amazon in 1995.[13] Several years after the collapse of Ethiopia's
Dergue dictatorship, the country's elected government fought a bloody
border war from 1998 to 2000 with Eritrea, which had just adopted,
though not yet implemented, a democratic constitution.[14]

In an especially worrisome case, the nuclear-armed, elected regimes
of India and Pakistan fought the Kargil War in 1999. After the 1988 death
of Pakistani military dictator Zia ul-Haq, a series of revolving-door
elected civilian governments had presided over a rise in militant Islamic
efforts to liberate majority-Muslim Kashmir from Indian control. In Kashmir itself, the restoration of elections after Indira Gandhi's period of
"emergency" authoritarian rule (1975–77) had polarized politics and led
to violent conflict between Muslims and the state. These turbulent processes culminated in the 1999 war, when Pakistani forces infiltrated
across the mountainous frontier in northern Kashmir. The war broke out
as Pakistan was taking steps toward greater democratization, including
constitutional changes in 1997 that were intended to strengthen the powers of elected civilian rulers.[15]

Violence inside some unstable democratizing states also spilled
across borders during the 1990s. Democratization played a catalytic role
in the horrible slaughters that engulfed central Africa. The 1993 elections
in Burundi—even though internationally mandated, free, and fair—
intensified ethnic polarization between the Hutu and Tutsi ethnic groups,
resulting in some 200,000 deaths. In neighboring Rwanda, an internationally orchestrated power-sharing accord, which was intended to usher in
more pluralistic and open politics, instead created the conditions for the
1994 genocide that killed nearly a million Tutsi as well as some moderate

---

12. Stuart Kaufman, *Modern Hatreds: The Symbolic Politics of Ethnic War* (Ithaca, N.Y.:
Cornell University Press, 2001), chap. 3.

13. David R. Mares, *Violent Peace: Militarized Interstate Bargaining in Latin America*
(New York: Columbia University Press, 2001), chap. 7.

14. Tekeste Negash and Kjetil Tronvoll, *Brothers at War: Making Sense of the
Eritrean-Ethiopian War* (Oxford: James Currey, 2000). We discuss these cases from the
1990s in Chapter 8.

15. On India, see Ian Talbot, *India and Pakistan* (London: Arnold, 2000), p. 275; on Pakistan, Hasan-Askari Rizvi, *Military, State and Society in Pakistan* (New York: St. Martin's, 2000), chap. 10. Bruce Russett and John Oneal, *Triangulating Peace: Democracy, Interdependence, and International Organizations* (New York: Norton, 2001), p. 48, discuss
whether the Kargil War should be counted as a war between democracies.

Hutu.[16] The Tutsi exile army based in Uganda invaded to stop the genocide. Its military victory forced Hutu refugees, including many of the genocide's perpetrators, into neighboring Congo, where further fighting involving the troops of several states has led to millions of additional deaths since 1998.

Elsewhere, democratic transitions coincided with renewed or intensified secessionist wars. In East Timor, a favorable vote on independence from Indonesia in an internationally mandated 1999 referendum spurred Indonesian-backed Timorese militias to unleash large-scale backlash violence, creating an international refugee crisis. Newly democratizing Russia fought two wars against its breakaway province of Chechnya. Vladimir Putin won election in 2000 as Russia's president mainly on the popularity of his plan to invade Chechnya to clean out the supposed lair of terrorists and brigands. In all of these varied settings during the 1990s, the turbulent beginning phase of democratization in states with weak political institutions contributed to cross-border violence.

WARS OF DEMOCRATIZATION AS A CHRONIC DANGER IN HISTORY
War-prone transitions to democracy were not just an aberration of the 1990s. Since the origin of modern mass politics around the time of the French Revolution, virtually all of the great powers turned belligerent and fought popular wars during the early phases of their experiments with democracy. In eighteenth-century France, the popular patriotism unleashed by the revolution sustained a mass army that fought the revolution's perceived enemies all across Europe. This tragedy was, as Karl Marx put it, repeated as farce when Louis Napoleon, elected as the French president in 1849, touted his military victories to sustain his power in a constitutional, semi-electoral regime. Even in Britain's relatively painless transition to democracy, the urban middle classes enfranchised by the Reform Bill of 1832 provided the enthusiasm that fueled both Palmerston's policy of commercial imperialism and the Crimean War.[17] Germany's more tortured path toward democracy created the impetus toward its five aggressive wars between 1864 and 1939. As monarchical Prussia transformed itself into the democratizing German Empire, Chancellor Otto von Bismarck forged a war-prone political alliance between the nationalist middle classes and the militarist elites, embodied in a political system that combined a legislature elected by broad suffrage

16.   Gérard Prunier, *The Rwanda Crisis: History of a Genocide* (New York: Columbia University Press, 1995), chaps. 3 and 5.

17.   Kingsley Martin, *The Triumph of Lord Palmerston* (London: G. Allen & Unwin, 1924).

and governments appointed by the Kaiser.[18] Japan's early phase of democratic politics was similarly marked by popular, militarized nationalism. When the Great Depression hit the democratizing Japan of the late 1920s, the democratic, free-trade coalition of workers and capital in export-oriented consumer industries was soon supplanted by an imperialist coalition that was led by the military and had strong electoral support.[19] In the United States of the 1830s and 1840s, the Jacksonian reforms that installed mass democracy by reducing restrictions on suffrage and expanding the direct election of officials coincided with an upsurge of popular support in the slave states for a war to gain territory at Mexico's expense.[20]

As we show in our statistical analyses (presented in Chapters 4, 5, and 6), this historical pattern holds true not only for great powers, but also for states in general. Although mature democracies have never fought a war against each other, incomplete transitions from autocracy toward democracy are fraught with the danger of violent conflict in states whose political institutions are weak.

In this book, we focus on democratization and international war, but other studies have suggested that when institutions in democratizing states are weak, the risks of internal ethnic conflict and civil war also rise.[21] Comprehensive studies of civil wars have found that the regime type most likely to experience civil war is a mixed regime, one that is partly democratic and partly authoritarian, with poorly developed state institutions.[22] The causal mechanisms specified in our theory may also help to account for this finding.

---

18.   Hans-Ulrich Wehler, *The German Empire 1871–1918* (Leamington Spa/Dover, N.H.: Berg, 1985).

19.   Louise Young, *Japan's Total Empire: Manchuria and the Culture of Wartime Imperialism* (Berkeley: University of California Press, 1998).

20.   John M. Owen, "Perceptions and the Limits of Liberal Peace: The Mexican-American and Spanish-American Wars," in Miriam Elman, ed., *Paths to Peace: Is Democracy the Answer?* (Cambridge: MIT Press, 1997), p. 170; for his larger study, see Owen, *Liberal Peace, Liberal War* (Ithaca, N.Y.: Cornell University Press, 1997), pp. 113–124.

21.   Jack Snyder, *From Voting to Violence: Democratization and Nationalist Conflict* (New York: Norton, 2000), applies this theory to both civil wars and international wars. That book, however, presents only case study evidence, not statistical analyses.

22.   Daniel Esty, Jack Goldstone, Ted Robert Gurr, Barbara Harff, Marc Levy, Geoffrey Dalbeko, Pamela Surko, and Alan Unger, "State Failure Task Force Report: Phase II Findings," July 1998; see also James Fearon and David Laitin, "Ethnicity, Insurgency, and Civil War," *American Political Science Review*, Vol. 97, No. 1 (February 2003), pp. 75–90, especially pp. 84–85.

What Conditions Make the Democratization Process Less Dangerous?

Although the process of democratization tends to increase the risk of war, many countries go through the process peacefully. During the 1980s and 1990s, numerous states consolidated their democratic transitions fairly successfully with little if any external or internal violence. These fortunate cases included many in the southern cone of South America, in Northeastern Europe, and in East Asia. South Africa, too, despite some internal violence, experienced a reasonably smooth transition.

These countries had a number of important advantages. They tended to enjoy relatively high per-capita income and literacy; thus, their citizens had the resources and skills to build the institutions and civil society organizations that democracy needs. Before the transition began, many of these success cases had well-developed state institutions, particularly administrative bureaucracies that functioned in a reasonably efficient way to advance state objectives with minimal corruption. Some of these successful states enjoyed the benefit of past experience with independent legal and journalistic institutions that could be adapted for use by the democratizing state. In most of these states, powerful elites did not feel threatened by a successful transition to democracy, in part because trusted state institutions made credible guarantees that elites would have a soft landing, so they were less likely to put up resistance to change.

Where, under such conditions, strong democratic institutions emerged quickly, democracy was fairly easily consolidated, and the transition was largely peaceful, as in Brazil, Chile, Hungary, and Poland. Where institutional groundwork was in place, transitions were peaceful even in geopolitically challenging cases where unresolved national partitions raised the risk of war, as in South Korea and Taiwan. In contrast, where the institutions needed by democracy were weak and democratization remained incomplete, war was more likely, as in Ethiopia, Pakistan, and Peru.

This finding bears out arguments advanced by Dahl, the seminal scholar of democracy and democratization. He argued that the peacefulness of the transition to democracy depended on getting the sequence of the transition right. Where rules, habits, and institutions of competitive politics were well established before holding unfettered mass elections, as in Great Britain after the Second and Third Reform Bills of 1867 and 1884, the transition to democracy went relatively smoothly. In contrast, where mass electoral politics developed before the institutions to regulate political competition were in place, transitions were prone to conflict. In countries that tried to take shortcuts to democracy, Dahl argued,

elites tended to feel threatened by political c
deployed nationalism as a justification for int
We find exactly these causal mechanisms ¿
democratization.

When and How Democratization Increa_

It is possible to imagine several reasons why democratizau.
associated with an increased likelihood of war, other than the argume..
that we advance. Some scholars speculate, for example, that all kinds of
regime change, not just regime change toward democracy, lead to instability and war. Or one might guess that the new democracies are vulnerable and hence targets of attack, but are not aggressors themselves. We explore such alternative explanations in the next chapter and show that
none of them is convincing. Instead, we find that war is most likely during incomplete democratization, when the state also suffers from serious
institutional deficits. Weak institutions *per se* do not increase the chance of
war; they do so only during the early phase of an incomplete democratic
transition.

It is often a strategic mistake for an institutionally weak state that is
handing over power to the mass public to initiate war, and yet such states
often do exactly this. Why? Such states face a gap between rising demands for broad participation in politics and inadequate institutions to
manage those popular demands.[24] Where the institutions of autocratic
authority are crumbling, yet new institutions of democratic accountability have not yet been constructed to take their place, routine institutional
authority is lacking and political leaders frequently turn instead to ideological or charismatic appeals to bolster their rule.

Rallying popular support by invoking threats from rival nations is a
common expedient for hard-pressed leaders who seek to shore up their
legitimacy. During the unraveling of the Yugoslav Communist regime,
for example, Slobodan Milosevic employed demagogic rhetoric about
the alleged danger of Albanian nationalism in Kosovo to gain a popular
following in Serbia's first elections.[25] Institutional weaknesses during
early democratization create both the motive to use this strategy of rule
and the opportunity to dodge accountability for its high costs and biased
rhetoric.

---

23. Dahl, *Polyarchy*, pp. 36–38, 44.

24. Huntington, *Political Order in Changing Societies*.

25. V. P. Gagnon, "Ethnic Nationalism and International Conflict: The Case of Serbia," *International Security*, Vol. 19, No. 3 (Winter 1994–95), pp. 130–166.

contest over national self-determination takes place as the for-
of both elites and mass groups are shifting. Elites left over from the
regime are desperately seeking strategies that will prevent their fall,
hile rising elites are trying to muscle in, and both are scrambling for allies among the newly aroused masses.

Elites often seek to solve these political dilemmas by invoking nationalism, the doctrine that a distinctive people deserve autonomy in a state
that protects and advances their distinctive cultural or political interests.[26] Nationalism helps elites to rally the support of the masses on the
basis of sentiment, rather than seeking their loyalty by providing responsive institutions that protect their interests. Nationalism also helps to
define the people who are exercising self-determination. It thus clarifies
the lines between "the people" and their external foes, who become
scapegoats in a self-fulfilling strategy that rallies support for defense
against external threats.

Nationalism is attractive to rising groups, who use it as a populist
club that can be wielded against elites who are insufficiently zealous in
promoting the interest of "the nation" (that is, "the people"). At the same
time, nationalism can be co-opted as a counter-tactic by elites, old and
new, who want to evade new democratic constraints on their rule. By
claiming to act on behalf of "the people" but not submitting to direct accountability to them, these elites can tar their opponents as "enemies of
the nation" who are in league with external foes, and thus justify curtailing their opponents' political and civil rights. This nationalist club may
be particularly attractive to military elites, economic protectionists, or
ethnic entrepreneurs. The nearly universal emergence of nationalist ideology in the early stages of democratization suggests that its usefulness at
this formative political juncture is generic and can be adapted for use by
almost any would-be ruling group.[27]

In the absence of strong state institutions to knit together the nation,
leaders must struggle for legitimacy in an ill-defined, contested political
arena. A common side effect of state weakness during early democratization is a poorly defined sense of "the nation." Democracy requires national self-determination, but people in weak states who are just emerging into political consciousness often lack a clear, agreed answer to the
question, "who are we; what is our nation?" Although nationalists often

---

26.   For discussions of the definition of nationalism, see Snyder, *From Voting to Violence*, pp. 21–25; and Michael Hechter, *Containing Nationalism* (New York: Oxford University Press, 2000), chap. 1.

27.   Miroslav Hroch, *Social Preconditions of National Revival in Europe* (New York: Columbia University Press, 2000).

believe that the identity of their own nation was fix
ture or culture, on the contrary, it is generally a pe
ence and shared fate in a strong state that solidifies
sense of nationality. Even in a country with a long
such as France, it was only the shared experiences
century—common military service, national railway, -
cation, and mass democracy—that completed the process of forging a
culturally diverse peasantry into self-conscious Frenchmen.[28] Nationalist
appeals in an emerging democracy rally popular support by proposing
answers to these puzzles of self-determination.

War may sometimes result from this potent political brew, as a direct
result of explicitly nationalist political objectives, such as the aim of regaining a lost piece of national territory. War may also result indirectly
from the complex politics of transitional states. It may come as an unintended by-product of belligerent and untrustworthy diplomacy that pro-
vokes a neighbor's fears. Nationalists' mobilizing rhetoric may make war
more likely by distorting the nation's view of the chances of success in a
fight, or of the feasibility of reaching a compromise with the enemy. Political leaders may become entrapped in their own swaggering rhetoric,
their reputations mortgaged to the nationalist commitments they have
made. Heterogeneous political coalitions may become stuck with their
own reckless policies when uncompromising nationalism becomes the indispensable common denominator that binds them together. In short,
it would be misleading to say that nationalistic publics in incompletely
democratizing states simply "want war." Instead, war is often an indirect by-product of the nationalist politics of the transitional regime. In
Chapter 3, we discuss the effect of nationalism on the risk of war in more
detail.

Future Challenges of Democratization and War

There is little reason to believe that the longstanding link between democratization and nationalist war is becoming obsolete. On the contrary,
future transitions may be even more difficult and dangerous. The "third
wave" of democratization in the 1980s and 1990s consolidated democratic regimes mainly in the richer countries of Eastern Europe, Latin
America, Southern Africa, and East Asia.[29] A fourth wave would involve

---

28.   Eugene Weber, *Peasants into Frenchmen* (Stanford: Stanford University Press, 1976).

29.   Larry Diamond, "Is the Third Wave Over?" *Journal of Democracy*, Vol. 7, No. 3 (July 1996), pp. 20–37.

challenging cases: countries that are poorer, more ethnically divided, ideologically more resistant to democracy, with more entrenched authoritarian elites, and with a much frailer base of governmental institutions and citizen-skills.[30] Botched democratizations in such settings could give rise to grave threats to international peace and security. Wars of democratization are therefore likely to remain a central problem of international relations in the coming years.

Since the end of the Cold War, many public intellectuals have speculated on the fundamental nature of the emerging new world order (or disorder). In 1989, Francis Fukuyama foresaw the "end of history," with peaceful, liberal democracy triumphant in all of the most significant countries.[31] History itself soon tarnished this vision with bloody nationalist conflicts in former communist states and in Central Africa. Huntington's counter-prediction of a cultural "clash of civilizations" better captured the mounting anxiety.[32] However, Huntington's image of fixed civilizations locked in struggle did not adequately describe a rapidly changing world in which many of the worst conflicts were within, rather than between, civilizations. Thomas Friedman's *The Lexus and the Olive Tree* did a better job of describing the dual trends of the 1990s—both global liberalization and parochial backlash—but his upbeat conclusions exaggerated the chances of economic success in the developing world and underestimated the degree to which political rivalries could overshadow potential gains from economic liberalization.[33]

Among the contributions of public intellectuals writing recently on global issues, Fareed Zakaria's work on "illiberal democracy" is closest to our own arguments.[34] Zakaria, too, recounts the adverse implications of flawed democracy for peace, minority rights, and social order. He shows how the increasingly ubiquitous notion of electoral legitimacy has sometimes been perverted to serve parochial agendas, including cultural nationalism. In that sense, the themes of Fukuyama and Huntington come together in ironic counterpoint in Zakaria's analysis.

---

30. Adrian Karatnycky, ed., *Freedom in the World: The Annual Survey of Political Rights and Civil Liberties, 2001–2002* (New York: Freedom House, 2002), pp. 11–15, 20–34.

31. Fukuyama, "The End of History."

32. Samuel P. Huntington, *Clash of Civilizations and the Remaking of World Order* (New York: Simon and Schuster, 1996).

33. Thomas L. Friedman, *The Lexus and the Olive Tree: Understanding Globalization* (New York: Farrar Straus Giroux, 1999).

34. Fareed Zakaria, *The Future of Freedom: Illiberal Democracy at Home and Abroad* (New York: Norton, 2003).

Zakaria, like us, implicitly borrows a seminal idea from Huntington. In Huntington's most profound book, *Political Order in Changing Societies*, he showed how rising political participation leads to conflict and instability in states with weak political institutions.[35] Our research shows that this insight is important not only for understanding the stability of democracy within countries but also for understanding international conflict between them. In an era in which troubled, incomplete democratic transitions may engulf such geopolitically salient locations as the Middle East and China, this dynamic could be one of the fundamental determinants of the course of world politics.

Although democratization in the Islamic world might contribute to peace in the very long run, Islamic public opinion in the short run is, in most places, hostile to the United States, reluctant to condemn terrorism, and supportive of forceful measures to achieve favorable results in Palestine, Kashmir, and other disputed areas. Although much of the belligerence of the Islamic public is fueled by resentment of the U.S.-backed authoritarian regimes under which many of them live, simply renouncing these authoritarians and pressing for a quick democratic opening is unlikely to lead to peaceful democratic consolidations. On the contrary, unleashing Islamic mass opinion through a sudden democratization could only raise the likelihood of war.[36] All of the risk factors are there: the media and civil society groups are inflammatory, as old elites and rising oppositions try to claim the mantle of Islamic or nationalist militancy.[37] The rule of law is weak, and existing corrupt bureaucracies cannot serve a democratic administration properly. The boundaries of states are mismatched with those of nations, making any push for national self-determination fraught with peril.

In the Arab world, in particular, states commonly gain their popular legitimacy not through accountability to their own citizens, but by acting demagogically in the purported interests of the Arab nation as whole, which often means taking a belligerent stand on Palestinian issues.[38] As we show in Chapter 7, when Iraq attempted a partial democratic transi-

---

35.   Huntington, *Political Order in Changing Societies*.

36.   Zakaria, *The Future of Freedom*, chap. 4.

37.   Sheri Berman, "Islamism, Revolution, and Civil Society," *Perspectives on Politics*, Vol. 1, No. 2 (June 2003), pp. 257–272, draws parallels to belligerent civil society in the flawed democracy of Weimar Germany and stresses the "Huntingtonian gap" between high demand for political participation and ineffective state institutions; ibid., p. 265.

38.   Michael Barnett, *Dialogues in Arab Politics* (New York: Columbia University Press, 1998).

tion in the late 1940s, the elected leaders of its weak state felt compelled to grant military basing rights to its former colonial ruler, Britain. They then took an inflammatory stance against Israel to try to recoup their diminished nationalist credibility in the eyes of their urban Arab nationalist constituents. This bellicose stance by Iraq's flawed democratic regime pushed the more moderate monarchies in the Arab front-line states to reject compromise over the creation of Israel, opening the door to the 1948 Arab-Israeli war and entrenching the Arab-Israeli rivalry.

We do not argue that Islam is culturally unsuited for democracy, but rather that the institutional preparations for democracy are weak in most Islamic states. Thus, sudden increases in mass political participation are likely to be dangerous. Evidence of this may be found in the theocratic pseudo-democracy established by the Iranian Revolution; it has pressed the offensive in a bloody war of attrition with Iraq and supported violent movements abroad. It took more than two decades for public opinion in revolutionary Iran to moderate. At this point, finally, political liberalization might make Iran more peaceful. But even if moderate democracy eventually takes hold in Iran, the costs of the transition will have been exorbitant.

This does not necessarily mean that all steps toward democracy in the Islamic world would lead to disaster. Etel Solingen argues, for example, that reforms leading toward "democratization from above," combined with economic liberalization, have been consistent with support for peaceful policies in such Arab states as Jordan, Tunisia, Morocco, and Qatar. "The more consolidated democratizing regimes become," she notes, "the less likely they are to experiment with populism and war."[39] Consistent with our argument, these modest success cases indicate that the most promising sequence for democratization in such settings begins with reforms of the state and the economy, together with limited forms of democratic participation, rather than a headlong jump into popular elections before the strengthening of the institutions—such as efficient and even-handed public administration, the rule of law, professional journalism, and political parties—that are needed to make a democratic system work.

Islamic democratization is hardly the only such danger on the horizon. A future democratic opening in China, though much hoped for by advocates of human rights and democratization, could produce a sobering outcome.[40] China's communist rulers have presided over a commer-

---

39.   Etel Solingen, *Regional Orders at Century's Dawn: Global and Domestic Influences of Grand Strategy* (Princeton: Princeton University Press, 1998), p. 213.

40.   For a balanced view that discusses many of the following points, see David Bachman, "China's Democratization: What Difference Would It Make for U.S.-China

cial expansion that has generated wealth and a potentially powerful constituency for broader political participation. However, given the huge socio-economic divide between the prosperous coastal areas and the vast impoverished hinterlands, it seems unlikely that economic development will lead as smoothly to democratic consolidation in China as it has in Taiwan. China's leadership showed its resistance to pressures for democratic liberalization in its 1989 crackdown on the student movement at Tiananmen Square, but party elites know that they need a stronger basis of popular legitimacy to survive the social and ideological changes that economic change has unleashed.

Nationalism is a key element in their strategy. China's demand to incorporate Taiwan into the People's Republic of China, its animosity toward Japan, and its public displays of resentment at U.S. slights are themes that resonate with the Chinese public and can easily be played upon to rally national solidarity behind the regime. At the same time, newly rising social forces see that China's leaders permit more latitude to expressions of nationalism than to liberalism. Thus, some of the same intellectuals who played a role in the Tiananmen pro-democracy protests turned up a few years later as authors of a nationalist text, *China Can Say No*.[41]

Like many other established elites who have made use of popular nationalist rhetoric, China's party leadership has walked a fine line, allowing only limited expressions of popular nationalist outrage after such provocations as the U.S. bombing of the Chinese embassy in Belgrade, anti-Chinese pogroms in Jakarta, or the U.S. spy plane incident of 2001. They realize that criticism of external enemies can quickly become transformed into popular criticism of the government for not being sufficiently diligent in defense of Chinese national interests.

The period of democratization by great powers has always been a moment of particular danger, in part because when states are militarily strong, they may seek to use their force in pursuit of nationalist goals. Vladimir Putin, for example, calculated carefully in using the Second Chechen War to win election as president in Russia in 2000. A similar strategy may appeal to politicians in a transitional China. How should the United States, the international community, or other powerful actors work to avert such dangers?

Relations?" in Edward Friedman and Barrett McCormick, eds., *What If China Doesn't Democratize?* (Armonk, N.Y.: M.E. Sharpe, 2000), pp. 195–223.

41. Song Qiang, Zhang Zangzang, and Qiao Bian, *Zhongguo keyi shuo bu* (China can say no) (Beijing: Zhonghua gongshang lianhe chubanshe, 1996).

Promoting Democracy in the Face of Risk

Our findings about the dangers of war during the process of democratization suggest ways to design strategies for promoting democratization. Admittedly, most transitions to democracy result from a convergence of dynamic social forces, and nobody has full control over their timing and sequence. Nonetheless, a host of powerful actors—the U.S. government, the United Nations, the community of transnational non-governmental organizations (NGOs), and the indigenous pro-democracy movements in various countries—have set for themselves the explicit goal of speeding the transition to democracy and shaping its trajectory. Sometimes their efforts make little difference, but sometimes—as in Burundi in 1993 and in East Timor in 1999—their efforts can be decisive and for the worse. As two great powers, Russia and China, remain at the dangerous early stages of this transition, the international community now has strong incentives to make sure that its influence is part of the solution, not part of the problem.

Our prescriptions stress the importance of getting the sequence right in taking steps toward democracy. Of particular value are the insightful recommendations made in an earlier context by the political scientist Eric Nordlinger: "The probabilities of a political system developing in a non-violent, nonauthoritarian, and eventually democratically viable manner are maximized when a national identity emerges first, followed by the institutionalization of the central government, and then the emergence of mass parties and mass electorate."[42] We examine the extent to which this insight applies not only to the domestic violence that Nordlinger studied, but also to international wars.

Spreading democracy is a worthwhile long-term goal, both as a value in itself and as an eventual means to increasing global peace and stability. Although some democratic transitions are risky, there is no alternative: political change cannot be frozen. In the long run, democratization is an inexorable global trend associated with social and economic development. What democracy promoters must do—whether they are U.S. occupation forces, NGOs, or reform coalitions in transitional states—is try to create favorable institutional conditions in the sequence most likely to foster successful, peaceful democratic transitions. Urging a democratic

---

42. Nordlinger, "Political Development, Time Sequences and Rates of Change," p. 458. We would qualify Nordlinger's sequence by pointing out that the emergence of a national identity is advantageous only if that identity is congruent with the borders of the state.

transition when the necessary institutions are extremely weak risks not only a violent outcome, but also an increased likelihood of a long detour into a pseudo-democratic form of nationalism.

Approaches to promoting democracy, especially by the United States, are often naïve and insufficiently strategic. Carothers argues that activists typically arrive with a shopping list of the ingredients that a mature democracy comprises, such as free speech, the rule of law, a vocal opposition, and a vibrant civil society, and try to mount programs to develop all of these simultaneously, with no strategy for sequencing or integrating these elements in a way that takes into account the dynamics of transition.[43] Yet many of these elements may be counterproductive for democratic consolidation if they are promoted in an institutionally immature setting. Where media are unprofessionalized and dependent on self-serving elites, for example, free speech and vibrant civil society are often hijacked as vehicles for nationalist rhetoric and activism.[44] To avoid this, international democracy promoters and political leaders in transitional states must pay attention to the sequence and pace of democratic experiments.

Our most general rule is to start the process by building the institutions that democracy requires, and then encouraging mass political participation and unfettered electoral competition only after these institutions have begun to take root. Too often, as in Bosnia after the Dayton Accords, elections have come too soon and merely locked in the dominance of illiberal elites who won votes by playing the nationalist card.[45] This is a lesson that seems difficult for some promoters of democracy to learn. During the U.S. occupation of Iraq, for example, the French government called for a quick handover of sovereignty to an elected Iraqi government in 2003.[46]

The first step toward democratic self-determination must be to define the boundaries of the nation in a way that has broad legitimacy. Where

---

43.   Carothers, *Aiding Democracy Abroad*.

44.   Sheri Berman, "Civil Society and the Collapse of the Weimar Republic," *World Politics,* Vol. 49, No. 3 (April 1997), pp. 401–429; and Jack Snyder and Karen Ballentine, "Nationalism and the Marketplace of Ideas," *International Security,* Vol. 21, No. 2 (Fall 1996), pp. 5–41.

45.   For a good analysis of Bosnia's post-Dayton electoral institutions, see Sumantra Bose, *Bosnia after Dayton: Nationalist Partition and International Intervention* (New York: Oxford University Press, 2002).

46.   Foreign Minister Dominique de Villepin, "Irak: Les Chemins de la Reconstruction," *Le Monde,* September 13, 2003, p. 1.

this problem is not already solved by demography or history, national legitimacy can only be achieved by constructing effective state institutions that begin to meet a people's needs for security and create for them a shared fate even if they do not share nationality. In this process, the top priority is to strengthen the ability of the administrative apparatus of the state to act rationally, consistently, and impartially in implementing the policy of the regime. At the same time, the leaders of a would-be pro-democracy coalition, together with its international backers, need to seek out and empower a strong political constituency that anticipates benefits from a successful democratic transition, while neutralizing potential spoilers who might have the power and the motive to wreck it. In many cases, this will involve "center-right" coalitions that include economic and bureaucratic elites left over from the authoritarian regime.[47] Such a solution may be distasteful to some advocates of democratization, but tactical accommodations are sometimes unavoidable in order to achieve idealistic goals in the long run.

Once in power, the pro-reform leadership should work on a broad front to build institutions, and put in place the machinery that is necessary to regulate political participation in a working democracy: institutionalize the rule of law in administrative matters and economic contracting; establish the courts as an independent, reliable guarantor of civil rights; and professionalize objective mass media that reach a broadly inclusive public. Democratic competition is meaningful only once these institutions have begun to take root. At that point, priority can shift to the strengthening of representative institutions and the unleashing of mass political parties.

This process does not necessarily have to go slowly. In the Czech Republic and South Africa, for example, where these preconditions were already in place or could be easily created, democratic consolidation happened quickly and successfully. In the absence of a strong institutional foundation, however, the reform government and its international supporters must get the sequence right to avoid creating the opportunity and motive for illiberal nationalist strategies to subvert the process and turn it toward violence. In these slower-paced transitions, the problem will be to maintain the momentum of democratic institutional development without risking a poorly institutionalized mass politics that could degenerate into a nationalist bidding war. Of course, the international community and their pro-democracy allies may not be able to manage each transition

---

47.   Dietrich Rueschemeyer, Evelyne Huber Stephens, and John D. Stephens, *Capitalist Development and Democracy* (Chicago: University of Chicago Press, 1992), p. 207.

in the optimal way, but if the sequence goes wrong, the world should expect trouble.

In Chapter 2, we place our contribution in the context of the theory of the democratic peace, and we address some alternative explanations for the war-prone nature of democratizing states. In Chapter 3, we lay out more fully the logic behind our argument about incomplete democratization as a cause of nationalism and war. Chapters 4, 5, and 6 present statistical tests of our argument. Chapters 7 and 8 examine a select subset of these historical and contemporary case studies to trace the causal mechanisms in more detail. In Chapter 9, we conclude by discussing the implications of our findings for broader understandings of democratic transitions and prescriptions for how to manage this potentially turbulent process.

Chapter 2

Reconciling the Democratic Peace with Accounts of Democratization and War

War has never happened between mature democracies, yet countries undertaking a transition toward democracy are quite war-prone toward regimes of all types. If the attitudes of publics in mature democracies serve as a prudent constraint on elites' tendencies to wage war, why are the publics in democratizing states apparently more reckless?

Various simple answers to this puzzle do not hold up to scrutiny, as we show in this chapter. The reason that democratizing states are at greater risk for war is not that their voters start off with warlike preferences, not that their weakened states make attractive targets for neighboring countries, and not that transitions from any regime type to any other cause war. There is little if any evidence to support these interpretations.

Rather, as we show in this book, democratizing states are disproportionately war-prone when they lack the coherent political institutions needed to manage intensified domestic political competition and to prevent it from provoking foreign conflicts. Mature democracies behave differently because they have stronger institutions ensuring democratic accountability. Understanding these institutional underpinnings of the democratic peace sheds light on the link between democratization and war. In this chapter, therefore, we show how our arguments about democratization and war are related to the arguments of the many scholars who have tried to explain why mature democracies do not fight each other.

We begin by discussing the puzzle of apparently belligerent voter preferences in democratizing states. We address this through the prism of the three main theories explaining the democratic peace: those based on the effects of institutions, of norms, and of information. Our theory of democratization and war builds on these explanations for the peace among mature democracies. At the end of this chapter, we discuss two other simple, but erroneous explanations for democratization and war—that the democratizing states are simply targets of aggression, and that all regime change makes war more likely. This chapter lays the groundwork for the full elaboration of our own theory in Chapter 3.

Are Voters in Democratizing States Unusually Bellicose?

A relatively simple explanation for the war-proneness of democratizing states might be that the average voter in such states prefers war to peace. In this view, voters knowingly accept the risks and costs of war, thinking that the expected benefits would outweigh them.

However, this explanation begs the question. After all, mature democracies do not fight wars against each other, and research shows that democracies are generally prudent in that they choose to fight only those wars that they can win at relatively moderate cost.[1] If enfranchising the public leads to prudent foreign policies in democracies, how can the public's recklessness explain the war-proneness of democratizing states?

It is true that public opinion sometimes becomes quite warlike in democratizing states, but it rarely starts out that way. More typical is the view, popular at the outset of the French Revolution, that a government responsive to its own people wants no quarrel with neighboring states. War fever took hold of public opinion only through the impact of debates in the free press, among the elected representatives in the National Assembly, and in the Jacobin Clubs of what we would now call "civil society."[2] It is thus not fixed public attitudes of belligerence, but rather something in the political process of the transition itself that turns attitudes and outcomes in a warlike direction.

We do find that belligerent nationalism has been a popular ideology in many incompletely democratizing states, from revolutionary France to the contemporary Balkans. In such countries, the attitude that the state should militantly defend the culture, historical mission, or political principles of the distinctive people that comprise the nation prevails.[3] Public

---

1. Dan Reiter and Allan C. Stam, *Democracies at War* (Princeton: Princeton University Press, 2002).

2. T.C.W. Blanning, *The Origins of the French Revolutionary Wars* (London: Longman, 1986).

3. For a discussion of definitions of nationalism, see Jack Snyder, *From Voting to Violence: Democratization and Nationalist Conflict* (New York: Norton, 2000), pp. 21–25.

opinion is so zealous in demanding that the state vigorously advance the national interest that war becomes more probable. In many cases, however, the average voter is not bellicose at the start of a democratic transition; rather, these attitudes develop during the democratization process itself.

Why should voters in democratizing states become especially inclined toward nationalist bellicosity, and why does this propensity grow as the transition process unfolds? How can this be reconciled with the undoubted predominance of peaceful relations between mature democracies? One conjecture might be that war itself derails the democratization process, and that this explains why incomplete democratization and war go hand in hand. However, our statistical tests and case study narratives show that this cannot account for our findings.

We are left with the puzzle: why do citizens in well-established democratic systems vote for governments that rarely wage war upon each other, while electorates in transitional democracies so often support aggressively nationalist policies, even against democracies?

We start this part of our inquiry by considering the three main lines of explanation that scholars have offered for the democratic peace. These explanations are based, respectively, on institutions, on norms, and on information. Each theory of the democratic peace implies a distinct explanation for why democratizing states might behave differently than mature democracies. While we anchor our own arguments primarily in a version of the institutional approach, we integrate insights from each of the other perspectives as well. Like some leading scholars of the democratic peace, we argue that these perspectives are most useful when viewed as mutually supporting rather than rival explanations.[4]

INSTITUTIONS GUARANTEEING ACCOUNTABILITY TO THE AVERAGE VOTER
The most straightforward explanation for the democratic peace is that effective democratic institutions make the government accountable, through regular elections, to the average voter who bears the costs and risks of war. This is the starting point for our own analysis. The philosopher Immanuel Kant, although he is usually seen as the source of the normative explanation for the democratic peace, grounded his arguments in this institutional explanation. Kings could pass along the costs of war to their powerless subjects, he argued, whereas elected regimes would suffer at the ballot box if they dragged their citizens into needless, costly

---

4. Bruce Russett and John R. Oneal, *Triangulating Peace: Democracy, Interdependence, and International Organizations* (New York: Norton, 2001).

wars. This, he predicted, would make elected governments more prudent in their decisions to go to war.[5]

As a result of this prudence, democracies do not fight each other and are in general more adept at avoiding unsuccessful, costly wars. Although democracies are about as likely to become embroiled in wars as non-democratic regimes,[6] democracies choose their wars more wisely,[7] tend to win them and suffer fewer casualties,[8] are less likely to initiate crises,[9] tend to prevail in the crises that they do initiate,[10] rarely fight preventive wars,[11] and are more astute than their non-democratic counterparts about pulling back from imperial overstretch.[12]

In contrast, states that are only partially democratic do not exhibit the same degree of prudence and cost-consciousness. According to Dan Reiter and Allan Stam, mixed regimes—those that have both authoritar-

---

5.   Another variant of the institutional explanation for the democratic peace centers on legislative checks on executive power that supposedly slow down deliberations on war and thus make them more prudent. In itself, this is a weak argument. A legislature can just as easily stymie peaceful diplomacy as moves for war. The argument gains force only when it is coupled to the more basic argument about the accountability of all government organs to the average voter. For discussion and data, see Bruce Russett, *Grasping the Democratic Peace* (Princeton: Princeton University Press, 1993).

6.   Russett and Oneal, *Triangulating Peace*, pp. 47–50.

7.   Reiter and Stam, *Democracies at War*.

8.   D. Scott Bennett and Allan C. Stam, "The Declining Advantages of Democracy: A Combined Model of War Outcomes and Duration," *Journal of Conflict Resolution*, Vol. 42, No. 3 (June 1998), pp. 344–366; David A. Lake, "Powerful Pacifists: Democratic States and War," *American Political Science Review*, Vol. 86, No. 1 (March 1992), pp. 24–37; and Randolph Siverson, "Democracies and War Participation: In Defense of the Institutional Constraints Argument," *European Journal of International Relations*, Vol. 1, No. 4 (December 1995), pp. 481–489.

9.   David Rousseau, Christopher Gelpi, Dan Reiter, and Paul Huth, "Assessing the Dyadic Nature of the Democratic Peace, 1918–88," *American Political Science Review*, Vol. 90, No. 3 (September 1996), pp. 512–533.

10.   Christopher F. Gelpi and Michael Griesdorf, "Winners or Losers? Democracies in International Crisis, 1918–94," *American Political Science Review*, Vol. 95, No. 3 (September 2001), pp. 633–648.

11.   Randall Schweller, "Domestic Structure and Preventive War: Are Democracies More Pacific?" *World Politics*, Vol. 19, No. 1 (January 1992), pp. 235–269.

12.   Jack Snyder, *Myths of Empire: Domestic Politics and International Ambition* (Ithaca, N.Y.: Cornell, 1991). Raising questions about a number of these findings is Michael Desch, "Democracy and Victory: Why Regime Type Hardly Matters," *International Security*, Vol. 27, No. 2 (Fall 2002), pp. 5–47. For rebuttals to Desch, see the letters by Ajin Choi, David Lake, and Dan Reiter and Allan C. Stam, "Democratic Victory Reconsidered," *International Security*, Vol. 28, No. 1 (Summer 2003), pp. 142–179.

ian and democratic features—have won only 58 percent of the wars they have started, as compared to 93 percent for democracies and 60 percent for dictatorships.[13] Likewise, Hein Goemans found that mixed regimes were more likely to suffer high casualties in their unsuccessful war efforts, and they were more likely to drag out the conclusion of the war.[14] Confirming this pattern, some recent wars have been tremendously costly for the states in transition to democracy that instigated them. For example, notwithstanding some initial Serb victories, many thousands of Serbs lost their lives, homes, or livelihoods in the nationalist wars that Serbia unleashed in the course of its experiment with partially democratic elections in the late 1980s and early 1990s. Likewise, although democratizing Armenia prevailed in its war in the early 1990s against Azerbaijan over the political fate of the Armenian-populated region of Nagorno-Karabakh, it paid the price of a ruined economy, a despoiled environment, and the emigration of 18 percent of its population to Russia and the West despite its "victory" in the war.[15]

Is it possible that the average voter in democratizing states is insensitive to cost and risk? If so, why would such voters be more reckless than voters in mature democracies?

One explanation posits that the early phase of democratization sometimes coincides with a struggle for national self-determination, that is, a nation-in-the-making engages in a battle to free itself from domination by an authoritarian elite or an imperial overlord. Conflict may also ensue from the uncertainties of boundaries and power relations that often accompany the establishment of new states. When state borders are in dispute, incompatible self-determination goals may set intermingled ethnic groups on the path to conflict. Indeed, Ted Gurr's study of ethnic conflict in the late 1980s and 1990s found that democratizing societies in newly established states were especially prone to ethnic violence.[16] If the average voter supports costly conflict in this type of setting, it may not be from a lack of prudence: instead, uncertainty and risk may be inherent in the unsettled situation. Prudence sometimes requires boldness in turbulent times. Nationalities that successfully seize the opportunity to establish a state gain a powerful means of advancing their cultural, economic,

---

13.   Reiter and Stam, *Democracies at War*, p. 29, table 2.1.

14.   Hein E. Goemans, *War and Punishment: The Causes of War Termination and the First World War* (Princeton: Princeton University Press, 2000), chap. 3.

15.   Snyder, *From Voting to Violence*, p. 221.

16.   Ted Robert Gurr, *Peoples versus States: Minorities at Risk in the New Century* (Washington, D.C.: United States Institute of Peace, 2000), p. 163.

and security interests.[17] In contrast, median voters in established democracies have fewer incentives to take risks in pursuit of potentially high-payoff yet high-cost policies.

Notwithstanding the force of this argument, it is insufficient as an explanation for the disproportionate propensity of democratizing states to fight wars. Hardly any of the democratizing initiators of war (which we discuss in Chapter 7) were setting up brand-new states in disputed environments. Although several fought wars to achieve the boundaries to which their nationalists had aspired (such as Prussia in the German wars of unification in 1860s), each of them did so from the relatively secure base of an established state. The 1998–2000 war between Ethiopia and Eritrea likewise broke out in the midst of stability, several years after the collapse of the Dergue regime and the splitting of the Ethiopian state. Thus, this risk-taking was largely optional and not compelled by the press of anarchic circumstances.

Most important, we find that in many cases the public in a democratizing state does not start off desiring war or domination over other nations. Rather, widespread nationalist belligerence arises only later, in the context of the unregulated politics characteristic of early democratization. For example, the Girondin faction in revolutionary France used its control of major newspapers to convince urban readers that Austrian reactionaries were linking up with aristocratic French traitors in a plot against the revolution. The result was the first war of the French revolution in 1792.[18] Half a century later, Napoleon III told his cabinet that a war backing Italian self-determination against Austria would be unpopular until there were victories to report, but that then it would lift the prestige of their semi-democratic regime.[19] Hitler had to play down his belligerent foreign policy views to garner sufficient votes in the Weimar Republic, and even in National Socialist Germany war was not popular with the German public.[20] In that case, nationalism was less effective at whipping up enthusiasm for war than it was at justifying the silencing of liberals, Jews, and socialists. Similarly, V. P. Gagnon argues, Slobodan Milosevic's propaganda warning of ethnic besiegement was designed not so much to

---

17. Barry Posen, "The Security Dilemma and Ethnic Conflict," *Survival*, Vol. 35, No. 1 (Spring 1993), pp. 27–47; and Rogers Brubaker, *Nationalism Reframed* (Cambridge: Cambridge University Press, 1996).

18. Snyder, *From Voting to Violence*, pp. 161–167.

19. Alain Plessis, *The Rise and Fall of the Second Empire, 1852–1871* (Cambridge: Cambridge University Press, 1985), pp. 146–147.

20. Eberhard Jäckel, *Hitler in History* (Hanover, N.H.: University Press of New England, 1984), pp. 21, 34.

create a wave of nationalist enthusiasm as to suppress and discredit liberal reformers as being "anti-Serb."[21]

Even in Armenia's war over Nagorno-Karabakh, which might seem to be a quintessential case of popular national identities in conflict in newly self-determining states, the Armenian electorate never voted recklessly for ultra-nationalist candidates. Levon Ter-Petrossian, the Armenian leader who was the most moderate on this issue, was elected president twice. He had to step down because elite factions, dissatisfied over his proposed concessions to Azerbaijan, forced him out. His more hawkish successor won with a bare plurality over a peace candidate who was handicapped by his past record as the boss of communist-era Armenia.[22]

In many such cases, the median voter in newly democratizing countries did start out as sensitive to the costs of nationalist policies and the risk of war, but the political process frustrated these prudent preferences rather than expressing them. To understand why this happens, we had to study the nature of the political process, not just the initial preferences of the voters, and our results are spelled out in Chapters 7 and 8. Whereas the well-developed institutional structure of mature democracies holds elites accountable to cost-conscious voters, incomplete democratization occurring in states with weak political institutions does not. For reasons that we touched on in Chapter 1 and elaborate in Chapter 3, both rising and declining elites in incompletely democratizing countries—those in which the transition gets stalled before reaching full, consolidated democracy—are likely to use nationalist appeals to attract mass allies and gain the legitimacy needed to rule in the absence of authoritative institutions. This increases public bellicosity and decreases sensitivity to the costs of war.

NORMS AND IDENTITIES

A second explanation for the democratic peace holds that mature democracies do not fight wars against each other because they share a common liberal democratic identity and common norms that govern appropriate political behavior. If this is true, it is conceivable that democratizing states might be warlike because they have not yet developed strong liberal norms.

In the normative view, to make democracy work, a country must have deeply ingrained civic norms such as rule by consent of the gov-

21.   V. P. Gagnon, *The Myth of Ethnic War: Serbia and Croatia in the 1990s* (Ithaca, N.Y.: Cornell University Press, 2004).

22.   We are grateful to Arman Grigorian for discussion of these points.

erned, free speech, due process of law, fair electoral competition, and the settlement of political disputes by peaceful procedures. A people that has internalized such norms, some scholars argue, would consider it illegitimate to use military force against another democracy.[23] Moreover, such peoples expect that other liberal democracies ought to reciprocate the same benign stance. Consequently, these scholars hold that the opportunism and security fears that commonly drive conflict in the anarchic international realm should be replaced by trust between mature democracies.

However, these norms do not mitigate conflict between democracies and non-democracies, which do not share norms and identities. The typical voter in a mature democracy has no qualms about supporting a government that fights non-democracies. As a result, despite the fact that mature democracies do not fight each other, democracies are about as likely to fight wars as non-democracies.[24]

Proponents of the normative explanation of the democratic peace consider this finding to be their main empirical grounds for rejecting the institutionalist argument. A hypothetically amoral, calculating median voter should reward leaders who wage cost-effective wars against democracies and punish leaders who wage cost-ineffective wars against non-democracies. In other words, they contend that the median voter's self-interest, unconstrained by norms of appropriateness, ought to support or oppose the decision to go to war without regard for regime type.

In rebuttal, proponents of the institutional explanation argue that democracies are skilled at using a range of effective bargaining tools, including legal systems and political compromise, to settle their differences with one another without resorting unnecessarily to violent conflict. Thus, politicians who are held strictly accountable to voters have attractive alternatives to war. In addition, institutionalists point out that, even against non-democracies, mature democracies do exhibit a distinct prudence in their decisions to go to war.

Moreover, democracies have certain advantages when facing non-democracies on the field of battle. For one thing, mature democracies have strong militaries and are disproportionately wealthy. Even setting aside the effects of democracies' advantages of wealth and military power, democracies tend to suffer fewer costs while winning their wars against non-democracies. While we think these institutionalist rebuttals

---

23. Michael Doyle, "Liberalism and World Politics," *American Political Science Review,* Vol. 80, No. 4 (December 1986), pp. 1151–1169.

24. Russett and Oneal, *Triangulating Peace,* pp. 49–50, discuss the results of several studies on this point.

are strong ones, we recognize that the debate remains an open and active one.

How might the war-proneness of democratizing states be explained from a normative perspective? States that are beginning a transition to democracy behave differently in international affairs than mature democracies because their citizens have not internalized liberal norms. Some transitional states may behave according to the liberal identity that they aspire to, but this is hardly the usual pattern.[25] Liberal norms are likely to be weak in many newly democratizing states, and so they are not likely to prevent wars with democracies and with other democratizers.[26] Pakistan, for example, fought wars against democratic India in 1965, 1971, and 1999 after making partial moves toward democracy.

As Fareed Zakaria points out, many contemporary "illiberal democracies" hold elections of dubious fairness, lack a strong commitment to liberal civic norms, and tend to become embroiled in military conflicts.[27] In some of these countries, elections are largely window-dressing to cover up the realities of dictatorship. In other countries, elections are genuinely contested, but each of the stalemated factions agrees to hold them only as a temporary expedient to buy time until it can make a bid to establish outright autocratic rule. Sometimes such stalemates lead to democratic consolidation, but when this occurs, the acceptance of liberal norms comes later.[28]

These arguments about the effect of norms are insufficient, however, to explain the puzzling behavior of democratizing states. We find that states in the midst of democratic transitions are the most war-prone type of regime, substantially more so than authoritarian states, which should be even less constrained by norms.

It is not enough just to show why voters in democratizing states are slow to join the liberal peace. We need to explain why they are actually drawn away from it, and are especially attracted to belligerent ideas. We argue that an answer to that question requires a study of institutional weaknesses rather than an enumeration of normative shortfalls.

That said, we think that it is a mistake to treat the institutional and

---

25. John M. Owen, *Liberal Peace, Liberal War* (Ithaca, N.Y.: Cornell University Press, 1997).

26. Russett, *Grasping the Democratic Peace*, pp. 16, 81.

27. Fareed Zakaria, "The Rise of Illiberal Democracy," *Foreign Affairs*, Vol. 76, No. 6 (November/December 1997), pp. 22–43.

28. Adam Przeworski, *Democracy and the Market* (Cambridge: Cambridge University Press, 1991), uses numerous cases in Latin America and elsewhere to illustrate this logic.

normative accounts of the democratic peace as mutually exclusive rivals. As Kant realized, the normative and the institutional explanations are not incompatible. Contemporary proponents of the normative explanation for the democratic peace recognize that democratic norms are inextricably grounded in democratic institutions. They define democracy in terms of institutionalized accountability to voters, and recognize that the normative democratic peace makes no sense outside of that institutional context.[29]

In a mature democracy, norms and institutions are mutually supportive. Fair elections, the rule of law, and other building blocks of democracy depend both on institutions—that is, converging expectations about what conventional behavior is likely to be—and on norms—that is, standards for what behavior ought to be. Some people may adhere to the rules of democratic practice because they think that everyone else will, and thus playing by democratic rules becomes the only way to be effective. This is an institutional reason for adhering to democratic practices.[30] Others may stick to the rules because they believe it is a moral obligation; this is a normative reason. Most people in mature democracies are probably motivated by both kinds of reasons. Zakaria points out that "illiberal democracies" lack not only liberal norms, but also effective democratic institutions.

The starting point for our own analysis is to assess the consequences of incomplete democratic transitions that occur when political institutions are weak. Our statistical analyses are based on measures of institutional change and strength, not on measures of norms, because institutions are the causal point of departure for our argument, and because valid quantitative measures of political norms are unavailable for the vast number of cases that we examine. Our case studies, however, do examine the turbulent normative debates that flourish amid institutional flux.

INFORMATION AND CREDIBILITY IN BARGAINING

A third commonly discussed explanation for the democratic peace argues that democracies are not more pacific, but rather are just better at signaling their intentions credibly to foreign adversaries. Democratic leaders incur costs to their reputation in the eyes of their constituents if they back down after making threats. If foreign leaders anticipate this, they may conclude that democratic leaders are likely to make only threats that they

---

29.   Owen, *Liberal Peace, Liberal War,* p. 15; and Russett and Oneal, *Triangulating Peace,* p. 44.

30.   Juan Linz and Alfred Stepan, *Problems of Democratic Transition and Consolidation* (Baltimore, Md.: Johns Hopkins University Press, 1996), p. 5.

will carry out. Their promises may also be more credible, because democratic leaders are likely to make commitments only if a substantial part of the body politic will back them. More generally, the greater transparency of democratic politics makes it less likely that democratic leaders will bluff or renege on agreements. As a result, bargains will be easier to agree to and stick to, especially if both sides are democratic.[31]

As long as there is some outcome that the parties prefer to war, the dispute should be settled peacefully, whether the aims of the parties are defensive or expansionist. With two-sided transparency about the expected costs and benefits of fighting, there should be little guesswork about which side has the greater resolve, and a bargain can be struck that avoids the costs of fighting it out. Even where each side wants to change the status quo in its favor and neither has scruples about using force to do so, transparency and smart bargaining should lead to a peaceful settlement.

Of course, this logic would break down if the democratic leader had the foreign policy preferences of a Hitler, who was willing to gamble everything on world domination and could imagine no long-term compromise preferable to war. Moreover, the high credibility of democratic commitments can be a double-edged sword. In 1941, the U.S. embargo of oil and steel to Japan did not lack credibility: it was so credible that Japanese leaders concluded that they had no choice but to start the war as soon as possible, while they still had some chance to win it. Where the Japanese went wrong was in their estimate that the United States might fold after sustaining a few initial defeats. This mistake had little to do with U.S. signaling capacity. Rather, Japan's hard-pressed military regime, seeing no alternative but to gamble for resurrection, systematically suppressed analysis of the long odds of success.[32]

In short, democracy goes only so far in making a state transparent, and transparency goes only so far in preventing conflict. It is therefore

---

31.   James Fearon, "Domestic Political Audiences and the Escalation of International Disputes," *American Political Science Review*, Vol. 88, No. 3 (September 1994), pp. 577–592; Kenneth A. Schultz, "Do Democratic Institutions Constrain or Inform? Contrasting Two Institutional Perspectives on Democracy and War," *International Organization*, Vol. 53, No. 2 (Spring 1999), pp. 233–266; G. John Ikenberry, *After Victory: Institutions, Strategic Restraints, and the Rebuilding of Order After Major Wars* (Princeton: Princeton University Press, 2001); and Charles Lipson, *Reliable Partners: How Democracies Have Made a Separate Peace* (Princeton: Princeton University Press, 2003). For a qualification, see Anne Sartori, "The Might of the Pen: A Reputational Theory of Communication in International Disputes," *International Organization*, Vol. 56, No. 1 (Winter 2002), pp. 121–149.

32.   Michael Barnhart, *Japan Prepares for Total War* (Ithaca, N.Y.: Cornell University Press, 1987), pp. 170–171, 240.

implausible that the strong finding that democracies never fight wars against each other could rest principally on transparency and credibility in bargaining. Ultimately, this outcome must rest on the fact that the overwhelming majority of democratic electorates simply do not have preferences like Hitler's, and that democratic leaders do not gamble on political resurrection through war quite so recklessly as did the leaders of Imperial Japan. Effective bargaining may be one mechanism that helps to explain how democracies reconcile their differences so successfully, but a full explanation rests on institutionalized accountability to the cost-conscious median voter.

The lack of credibility in bargaining may play some role in explaining why democratizing states are war-prone. As we explain in Chapter 3, the contradictory and unstable nature of political coalitions in many newly democratizing states is a hindrance to sending clear, credible, and consistent threats or promises. However, this is best understood as one mechanism in a larger syndrome of political dilemmas that confound the diplomacy of the democratizing state, not as the whole explanation.

INFORMATION PROVIDED BY EVALUATIVE INSTITUTIONS
Another explanation based on information stresses the role of evaluative institutions in making democratic accountability work. A few scholars have argued that public-policy analysis is superior in mature democracies compared to other kinds of regimes because a free press and other evaluative institutions effectively scrutinize democratic governments' explanations of their actions. That may be one reason why democracies choose their wars more wisely and tend to win them at lower cost.[33]

In contrast, democratizing states often have weaker press freedoms and evaluative organizations. Even though the publics in democratizing states—like those in democracies but unlike those in autocracies—debate foreign affairs intensely, public rhetoric, although high in energy, is low in quality. This creates the worst of worlds: an information environment in which many politically significant actors base their foreign policy thinking on poor or misleading analysis. This informational shortcoming reflects the institutional deficit of many newly democratizing states as well as the weakness of norms of fair debate and journalistic professionalism. Purveyors of nationalist rhetoric, from Hitler in Weimar Germany to Milosevic in post-Tito Yugoslavia, have thrived in this kind of setting.

---

33. Reiter and Stam, *Democracies at War*, pp. 23–24; and Stephen Van Evera, "Hypotheses on Nationalism and War," *International Security*, Vol. 18, No. 4 (Spring 1994), pp. 32–33.

To sum up, it is far from clear that voters in democratizing states start off with more belligerent attitudes and preferences than those in mature democracies. It seems more likely that publics in both settings start off as cost-conscious seekers of prudent solutions to their political dilemmas. Voters in democratizing states are more likely to turn belligerent not because of the unsettled boundaries of new states or pre-existing nationalist preferences, but rather because of deformations in the institutional and informational environments in which preferences in newly democratizing states are formed and aggregated.

Are Emerging Democracies Disproportionately the Victims of Attacks?

States in the early stages of democratic transitions often undergo a weakening of the organs of the erstwhile authoritarian state, including its military institutions. This military weakness, it might be speculated, could be responsible for the increased risk of war in democratizing regimes, and indeed, we do find that regimes undergoing incomplete democratization with unusually weak political institutions are the ones at the greatest risk for war. As a result, it is logical to ask to what degree the war-proneness of democratizing states might be caused by their temporary weakness and consequent attractiveness as targets of attacks by their neighbors. If the rise of popular political participation makes the state weak in the short run but potentially stronger in the long run, this gives worried neighbors a particular incentive to attack. Stephen Walt shows that this is a common syndrome affecting the war-proneness of revolutionary states. He speculates that other kinds of transitional states may experience similar troubles.[34]

We find, however, that while such dynamics do sometimes occur, they cannot explain the disproportionate propensity of democratizing states to become involved in international wars. In Chapter 5, we present statistical evidence that states undergoing democratic transitions are more likely to be the initiators of these wars than the victims. Moreover, incomplete democratizers are at the greatest risk of war not at the very outset of the transition, when the military institutions of the state might be expected to be in the most chaotic condition, but a few years later, after nationalist politics has succeeded in mobilizing mass adherents. In addition, we find that states with weak institutions are not especially war-prone unless they are at the same time undergoing incomplete democratic transitions. In Chapter 7, we present short narratives of all the

---

34. Stephen M. Walt, *Revolution and War* (Ithaca, N.Y.: Cornell University Press, 1996), pp. 344–349.

cases of democratizing initiators of international wars between 1816 and 1992, showing how the mechanisms specified by our theory explain these outcomes.

That said, it is important to stress that our arguments are not relevant just to democratizing states that initiate large-scale cross-border attacks (which is the way that the database we use classifies the "initiator" of a war). Sometimes belligerent states engage in threatening rhetoric, military posturing, or aiding rebels in neighboring states, which triggers a preventive response with large-scale military force; thus the true initiator of the conflict may not be classified as such in the database. Our statistical results show that states undergoing incomplete democratization are more likely than other states to be responsible for provoking these kinds of militarized interstate disputes: they may thus be the instigators of war even when they are not the initiators of the first large-scale attack. For example, in 1965 Pakistan's military dictator was elected president in a partially free, contested electoral campaign that stressed liberating Kashmir's Muslim majority from supposed oppression by India. Shortly thereafter, the Pakistani army initiated a limited attack on Indian army forces in a disputed swampland, the Rann of Kutch. Our database classifies this as a military dispute, not a war started by Pakistan, because the number of deaths was below the threshold for war. This was followed by Pakistani support for substantially increased infiltration of Kashmir by "volunteer" guerrillas.[35] India responded with a large-scale, cross-border attack and therefore is classified as the initiator of the ensuing war. Even though India, not democratizing Pakistan, was coded as the war's initiator, our theory explains quite well how incomplete democratization in Pakistan led to its outbreak.

Do All Regime Transitions, Whether Democratizing or Not, Increase the Risk of War?

Some scholars speculate that any kind of transition from one regime type to another—not just transitions toward democracy—might make a country more war-prone. They propose a variety of plausible mechanisms that might cause this. Transitional leaders whose hold on power is tentative, including autocratic ones, might try to deflect their subjects' attention from conflicts at home by provoking conflict abroad. Unstable political

---

35. Lawrence Ziring, *The Ayub Khan Era: Politics in Pakistan, 1958–1969* (Syracuse, N.Y.: Syracuse University Press, 1971). For statistical results indicating that incomplete democratization promotes militarized interstate disputes, see Edward D. Mansfield and Jack Snyder, "Incomplete Democratization and the Outbreak of Military Disputes," *International Studies Quarterly*, Vol. 46, No. 4 (December 2002), pp. 529-549.

coalitions, whether democratic or not, might behave erratically abroad. The process of transition, even from a monarchy to a single-party state or a military junta, might cause strategic vulnerabilities that invite attack from abroad.[36]

While these mechanisms may sometimes cause war, they cannot explain our findings. Although we do not have systematic data to evaluate the effects of all kinds of regime changes, we do test whether transitions toward autocracy create as great a risk of war as those toward democracy. They do not. In some preliminary tests, we found that transitions toward autocracy increased the risk of war noticeably, but not nearly as much as transitions toward democracy.[37] More refined tests that take into account differences in states' institutional capacity show that transitions toward autocracy do little, if anything, to increase the risk of war (see Chapter 5). While there may be other causal mechanisms that affect the war-proneness of transitional regimes, they are not as strong as the ones that are distinctive to the transition toward democracy.

Why should transitions toward democracy exert a stronger effect than other kinds of transitions? We argue that the instability of the political elite, which may be characteristic of various kinds of transitions, combines with the expansion of mass political participation in democratizing states in distinctively explosive ways. For reasons that we outline in Chapter 3, this situation creates strong incentives for elites to mobilize popular support through nationalist appeals, which tend to raise the risk of war. This nationalist mobilization may overlap to a degree with some of the dynamics that make states so war-prone when they undergo major social and political revolutions.[38]

In contrast, autocratizing regimes—as well as states that are exchanging one sort of autocracy for another—lack that combustible interaction between insecure elites and energized masses. During autocratization, mass participation is curtailed, so popular nationalism is less needed for political legitimation, and its effects on foreign relations can be better controlled. Insofar as autocratization sometimes increases the risk of war, this may reflect second-order consequences of incomplete democratization. For example, Napoleon I exploited revolutionary France's warlike nationalism to gain autocratic ascendancy over its failed attempt at democratization. In order to legitimate his autocratic rule, he had to con-

---

36. Russett and Oneal, *Triangulating Peace*, p. 51.

37. Edward D. Mansfield and Jack Snyder, "Democratization and the Danger of War," *International Security*, Vol. 20, No. 1 (Summer 1995), pp. 5–38, esp. 34–35.

38. Walt, *Revolution and War*.

tinue his military exploits under the guise of the expansion of a French-led popular revolution across Europe.

In part, our argument shows how general causal mechanisms, such as incentives to provoke "diversionary" conflict, apply with particular force to some kinds of democratizing states. Diversionary theories of war contend that regimes sometimes attempt to use rivalry abroad to strengthen their shaky position at home. Such arguments invoke two rather different causal mechanisms. The first posits a psychological propensity for out-group conflict to increase in-group cohesion. If such a mechanism exists, however, research shows that it is likely to come into play only if the group demonstrates considerable cohesion before the conflict breaks out; if the external threat is seen as endangering the in-group as a whole; and if the instigators of the conflict are seen to be the outsiders, rather than the leadership of the in-group.[39] Our argument suggests how these conditions might be created in newly democratizing states through the development of a nationalist ideology, which constitutes a set of ideas for interpreting conflict with out-groups.

A second set of causal mechanisms is rationalistic. Alastair Smith speculates that international assertiveness helps domestically hard-pressed regimes to demonstrate their competence by achieving foreign policy successes.[40] However, newly democratizing states, unlike mature democracies, are not particularly good at choosing wars that are cheap to fight and easy to win. A more plausible rationalist argument for their wars is that elites in transitional states are gambling for resurrection, that is, taking a risk at long odds that foreign policy confrontations will save them from an otherwise likely fall from power. Deductive arguments of this type propose that elites' informational advantages over their mass audiences may help them carry out such gambles.[41] Empirical research suggests that the strength of the incentive for downwardly mobile elites to make such a gamble depends on the regime type and on the elites' ability to use their influence over the media to make the reckless strategy

39. Jack S. Levy, "The Causes of War: A Review of Theories and Evidence," in Philip E. Tetlock, et al., eds., *Behavior, Society, and Nuclear War*, Vol. 1 (New York: Oxford University Press, 1989); and Arthur Stein, "Conflict and Cohesion: A Review of the Literature," *Journal of Conflict Resolution*, Vol. 20, No. 1 (March 1976), pp. 143–172.

40. Alastair Smith, "Diversionary Foreign Policy in Democratic Systems," *International Studies Quarterly*, Vol. 40, No. 1 (March 1996), pp. 133–153.

41. George W. Downs and David M. Rocke, "Conflict, Agency, and Gambling for Resurrection: The Principal-Agent Problem Goes to War," *American Journal of Political Science*, Vol. 38, No. 2 (April 1993), pp. 362–380.

seem plausible to their constituents.[42] Our argument explains why the motive and opportunity to use this strategy are especially likely to be present when incomplete transitions to democracy occur in states with weak institutions.

Thus, the war-proneness of democratizing states cannot be explained away as an artifact of the supposed war-proneness of all transitional regimes. Even if there may be causal mechanisms that are somewhat conducive to war in a variety of transitional regime types, in the specific context of incomplete democratization with weak institutions, those mechanisms are supercharged with the force of mass politics and nationalism.

Conclusion

It might seem puzzling that mature democratic states never fight each other, yet democratizing states are highly war-prone. The answer to this apparent puzzle is not that democratizing publics have inherently more belligerent preferences, or that democratizing states are disproportionately the vulnerable victims of attack, or that all transitional regimes are war-prone. Rather, the answer lies in mature democracies' strong institutions of democratic accountability to a cost-conscious public, which contrasts to the weak institutions of those incompletely democratizing states that are especially likely to fight wars. The next chapter lays out in more detail the logic underpinning this theory.

---

42. Goemans, *War and Punishment*, pp. 37–51; Levy, "Causes of War," pp. 277–279; Jack S. Levy and Lily Vakili, "Diversionary Action by Authoritarian Regimes," in Manus Midlarsky, ed., *The Internationalization of Communal Strife* (London: Routledge, 1992), pp. 118–146; and Snyder, *From Voting to Violence*, pp. 56–66.

Chapter 3

Explaining Turbulent Transitions

War has never happened between mature democracies, yet democratizing states are disproportionately war-prone toward regimes of all types, when they lack the coherent political institutions that could manage the intensified domestic political competition that characterizes the transition to democracy.

When political institutions are weak, the rising demand for mass participation in politics forces elites to recruit popular allies, yet elites are insufficiently accountable to the average voter.[1] Some groups that are threatened by democratization exploit this chance to evade accountability. They invoke the populist creed of rule *for* the people while simultaneously resisting rule *by* the people. Even those groups that might prefer stable democracy find that nascent democratic institutions are too ineffectual to defend their interests. In this setting, both rising new elites and falling old elites have the motive and the opportunity to resort to the rhetoric of nationalism, which mobilizes mass support through the language of popular sovereignty while evading the accountability that would be provided by free and fair elections and the rule of law. The nationalist politics that this unleashes often embroils the country in military conflicts with other states, for reasons we explain in this chapter.

In the first part of this chapter, we present the logic behind this argument. We begin by laying out the basic building blocks of our scheme for classifying political regimes, first discussing the pure cases: stable au-

---

1. Samuel P. Huntington, *Political Order in Changing Societies* (New Haven: Yale University Press, 1968).

tocracy and mature, consolidated democracy. We then turn to the more complicated cases of regime change, and particularly incomplete democratization. We explain how the pattern of power and interests typical of incompletely democratizing states with weak political institutions increases the likelihood that nationalist ideas and war-prone political coalitions will emerge. We conclude the chapter by recapitulating our main hypotheses and our strategy for testing them.

In the following sections, we lay out our argument in greater detail, beginning with our typology of political regimes and our assumptions about the sources of social power in each of those regimes.

Classifying Regimes: To Whom Are State Authorities Accountable?

We classify regimes into three categories, based on whether the leading state authorities are effectively accountable to the bulk of the state's adult population, to a narrow elite only, or to a mix of these two. By definition, the constituencies to whom state authorities are accountable are those whose assent is needed for them to gain and retain power.[2] These constituencies do not necessarily have the opportunity to accept or reject particular policies relating to questions of war and peace, but they do have the ability to withdraw their support and undermine the power bases of elected officials. (Details of how regime type is coded for the purpose of our statistical tests are found in Chapter 4.)

In an autocracy, state authorities are accountable only to themselves, or at most to a group of elites that maintain unity when dealing with outsiders. No significant political activity—in particular, no contestation for power—is allowed outside the ruling group. Even if some degree of factionalism exists within the ruling group, it is not the basis for political recruitment of allies outside it. High authorities act by means of commands to bureaucratic agents or through patronage relations with dispensable, subordinate clients. Authorities must, of course, devise policies that successfully maintain the compliance of agents and clients, just as they must devise policies that give their subjects incentives to work productively and not flee the country. However, autocratic authorities are not accountable to such agents, clients, and subjects, who are unorga-

---

2. Some political scientists call this constituency the "selectorate." See Bruce Bueno de Mesquita, James D. Morrow, Randolph M. Siverson, and Alastair Smith, "An Institutional Explanation of the Democratic Peace," *American Political Science Review*, Vol. 93, No. 4 (December 1999), pp. 791–808.

nized politically. If the latter do organize to contest power, then the country is no longer an autocracy; it is on its way to becoming a different type of regime.

In a democracy, state authorities are accountable to the bulk of the population (or where female suffrage was lacking, to nearly all households) through fair, regular, and competitive elections. Elected officials set government policy, including foreign and military policy, and act through bureaucratic agents who are subject to the law.

Between autocracy and democracy is the mixed regime, sometimes called *anocracy* by political scientists who study the democratic peace.[3] State authorities in mixed regimes are accountable, formally or informally, to politically organized factions or to groups outside the unified ruling elite. However, political competition falls short of full democracy because of restrictions on who can participate, how they can participate, or what issues they can raise. The state's bureaucratic agents do not necessarily adhere to the rule of law.

The vast majority of mixed regimes hold elections of some kind, although they fall short of the fully democratic standard of competitive and fair elections. In some cases, a mixed regime may not have elections, but its politics are shaped by the anticipation that politically significant elections are likely to be held in the foreseeable future. For example, the growing inevitability of elections, we argue in Chapter 7, decisively influenced the Argentine military junta's launching of the 1982 Falklands War. Our theory about incomplete democratization and war applies to transitions to mixed regimes in countries with weak institutions that either have held meaningful elections or anticipate imminent elections.

In some cases, however, a case classified as a mixed regime in the database we use to conduct our statistical analysis in Chapters 4, 5, and 6 may involve no prospect of politically meaningful elections. For example, some forms of minor political liberalization or factionalization in communist countries qualify as a transition to a mixed regime according to that database. In Chapters 5 and 6, we check to make sure that our statistical results are not distorted by types of regimes that may have been classified in ways that are invalid for our theory. Because the scholars who designed the database did not have our theory or research design in mind, their classification rules do not always match our concepts perfectly. We take this into account by conducting case studies in Chapters 7 and 8 to

---

3.   Ted Robert Gurr, "Persistence and Change in Political Systems, 1800–1971," *American Political Science Review*, Vol. 68, No. 4 (December 1974), pp. 1482–1504; and Bruce Russett, *Grasping the Democratic Peace* (Princeton: Princeton University Press, 1993), pp. 77–79, 86, 121–123.

make sure that the cases driving our analysis do reflect the mechanisms of our theory.

We classify autocracies, democracies, and mixed regimes as stable if they undergo no regime change within a given time period. In the statistical analysis, we examine periods ranging from one to ten years, but focus mainly on five-year periods. Transitions from autocracy to a mixed regime, from autocracy to democracy, or from a mixed regime to a democracy, we call *democratization.* We call a transition from autocracy to a mixed regime that fails to culminate in full democracy in the given time period an *incomplete democratization.* Transitions from democracy to a mixed regime, from democracy to autocracy, or from a mixed regime to autocracy, we call *autocratization.* A transition from democracy to a mixed regime that fails to culminate in full autocracy in the given time period we call an *incomplete autocratization.*

WHAT DETERMINES THE CONSTITUENCY TO WHOM AUTHORITIES ARE ACCOUNTABLE?

How society is organized to accomplish its military, economic, or administrative tasks determines whether power is held by a narrow elite or is widely diffused throughout society.[4] People tend to have political power if their active participation and consent are necessary for political leaders to implement plans and, more broadly, to make society function. Charles Tilly argues, for example, that the politics of mass nationalism and ultimately of democratic accountability arose from the need of rulers to gain popular consent for conscription and war-related taxation.[5] In another variant on this theme, Ernest Gellner and his followers claim that the rise of capitalist commerce and industry created the conditions for mass nationalist politics, once the functioning of the economic system came to depend on the active participation of culturally unified entrepreneurs and workers rather than on the repression of culturally diverse, localized peasants.[6] Along similar lines, Dietrich Rueschemeyer and his co-authors

4. Mancur Olson, "Dictatorship, Democracy, and Development," *American Political Science Review,* Vol. 87, No. 3 (September 1993), pp. 567–576, esp. 573. For a related argument, see Stanislav Andreski, "On the Peaceful Disposition of Military Dictatorships," *Journal of Strategic Studies,* Vol. 3, No. 3 (December 1980), pp. 3–10.

5. Charles Tilly, *Coercion, Capital, and European States, AD 990–1990* (Cambridge: Basil Blackwell, 1990).

6. Ernest Gellner, *Nations and Nationalism* (Ithaca, N.Y.: Cornell University Press, 1983). Note also amendments to Gellner's argument by Michael Mann, "The Emergence of Modern European Nationalism," in John A. Hall and Ian Jarvie, eds., *Transition to Modernity* (Cambridge: Cambridge University Press, 1992), pp. 137–166.

argue that societies become democratic only when support from the urban working class becomes politically indispensable.[7] Benedict Anderson contends that popular nationalism arose when printed vernacular texts (for example, in French) superseded handwritten texts in a transnational language known only to elites (such as Latin), giving the broad population the intellectual resources and perspective needed to play a role in politics.[8] Elections may occur in societies where social power is not diffuse, such as societies with very low per capita income, but such transitions usually fail to become consolidated and tend to revert to autocracy.[9]

We agree with these theorists that mass democracy and nationalism tend to follow the broad diffusion of power that comes with the modernization of society. However, unlike them, we do not posit any single economic, military, or cultural taproot of democratization and nationalism. Rather we argue that interconnected changes in military, economic, and cultural organization jointly shape the concentration or diffusion of social power.

REGIME TYPES: TYPICAL FORMS OF POWER, INTERESTS, INSTITUTIONS, AND IDEAS

In discussing the characteristic political dynamics of particular types of regimes and transitions, we examine in turn the type of power that prevails in the regime, the nature of the empowered interests, the role of institutions in shaping and aggregating interests, and the opportunities for elites to gain support by means of ideology and information.

Whether diffuse or concentrated, the social power that authorities and other political actors wield can be classified into four types, based on the technique that is used to obtain compliance.[10] *Despotic power* is the ability to use physical compulsion to repress opponents and coerce subjects to carry out required tasks. *Patronage power* is the ability to buy compliance or support by offering selective, conditional incentives to

---

7.   Dietrich Rueschemeyer, Evelyne Huber Stephens, and John D. Stephens, *Capitalist Development and Democracy* (Chicago: University of Chicago Press, 1992).

8.   Benedict Anderson, *Imagined Communities* (New York: Verso, 1983).

9.   Adam Przeworski, Michael Alvarez, José Antonio Cheibub, and Fernando Limongi, *Democracy and Development: Political Institutions and Well-Being in the World, 1950–1990* (Cambridge: Cambridge University Press, 2000).

10.   This scheme borrows loosely from Michael Mann, *The Sources of Social Power, vol. I: A History of Power from the Beginning to A.D. 1760* (Cambridge: Cambridge University Press, 1986).

particular groups or individuals. *Infrastructural power* is the ability to gain compliance and support by organizing activity in ways that increase the productivity and efficiency of a group or of society as a whole. *Legitimate power* is the ability to gain compliance and support through appeals to procedural appropriateness, morality, or the sacred. In practice, these types of power always exist in some combination. For example, despotic power over subjects normally must be combined with patronage power or legitimacy to gain the compliance of agents who carry out the coercion.

With respect to the kinds of interests that commonly prevail in a regime type, we follow Mancur Olson in asking first whether the dominant interests are narrowly parochial to some particular sector (e.g., a single-interest group), broadly encompass the health of all assets and sectors (e.g., a secure dynastic ruler), or are diffused more or less equally among all social actors (e.g., voters in a mature democracy).[11] Second, we ask whether the interests of powerful actors give them short time horizons, especially interests that could encourage gambling on war to resurrect the elite's declining domestic political fortunes. Related to that, we ask whether the politically dominant interests would bear substantial costs in the event of failure in war.[12]

The nature of prevailing institutions affects which constituencies' interests are politically decisive and also how effectively the institutions regulate struggles over these interests. We define institutions as patterns of repeated, conventional behavior around which expectations converge. Strong institutions shape expectations and behavior with a high degree of predictability: people know that almost everyone else will conform to the expected pattern and consequently that failure to conform will make it harder to accomplish tasks that require coordination with others. Weak institutions, in contrast, have not become ingrained habits: people know that others may not conform. Consequently, weak institutions do little to shape expectations and regulate behavior. Where the administrative and legal institutions of the state are weak—including those that regulate popular political participation—democratic consolidation and peace are less likely.

Finally, with respect to ideology and information, we ask whether prevailing ideas are based on enemy images of other nations, as in many

---

11. Mancur Olson, *The Rise and Decline of Nations* (New Haven: Yale University Press, 1982), pp. 47–53, 90–93.

12. Hein E. Goemans, *War and Punishment: The Causes of War Termination and the First World War* (Princeton: Princeton University Press, 2000), pp. 39–49.

forms of nationalism, and whether institutions are capable of a rigorous evaluation of international strategies. Does the country enjoy free, critical mass media and independent sources of foreign policy expertise in think-tanks and universities?

Pulling these elements together in the case studies in Chapters 7 and 8, we examine the power resources, interests, institutions, and ideas that were in play on the eve of the collapse of the autocratic regime, taking that as the starting point of our analysis. The trajectory of the transition is influenced by the degree of threat to elite interests and the strength of political institutions at the beginning of that process. The subsequent trajectory is further shaped by the strategies that political actors adopt in the course of the transition, including the coalitions they form, the rules they institutionalize, and the ideologies they promote. Our theory focuses on the typical trajectories that arise from these initial conditions and the actors' strategic choices.

When Autocracies Go to War

Autocratic regimes fight wars with foes of any regime type. Overall, they are as likely to go to war as democracies but they do so less often than democratizers.[13] A variety of the features of autocratic rule permit war, but few strongly encourage it. In particular, autocratic regimes typically have compelling reasons to discourage nationalist mobilization of their subjects, which removes an important cause of war.

THE NATURE OF AUTOCRATIC POWER
The typical formula for autocratic rule rests on despotic repression of the disenfranchised population and distribution of patronage to buy support of the core ruling elite and the agents whose services are necessary to carry out the tasks of ruling. Since repression and patronage are expensive and run the risk of opportunism by agents, autocrats have an incentive to supplement these pragmatic instruments with ideological legitimation of their rule, such as stressing the sacred origins of their right to rule and the procedural correctness of how they come to power.

These features of autocratic power increase the probability of war in a variety of ways. First, an effective autocratic state can repress dissatisfaction on the part of the subjects who pay war's costs in blood and treasure, while distributing the spoils of war to essential constituencies and

---

13. Bruce Russett and John R. Oneal, *Triangulating Peace: Democracy, Interdependence, and International Organizations* (New York: Norton, 2001); and Chapter 5 below.

agents of the state.[14] Second, poor institutionalization of the rule of law creates leeway for agents and clients to set themselves up in opposition to the state, sometimes in collusion with outside powers. Third, and related to the second, disputes over legitimate succession and over the appropriate normative basis for the leader's rule often raise the risk of war.

At the same time, the nature of autocratic power also retards the development of some causes of war, including mass nationalism. Autocracies are frequently ambivalent about mobilizing the energies of their subject populations. On the one hand, pressure to compete militarily against larger or more efficient states may sometimes force autocracies to offer incentives for economic and technical entrepreneurship, grant greater autonomy for social actors outside the ruling clique, encourage a more decentralized economy with a more elaborate division of labor, and motivate the population with nationalist ideas. Moreover, the greater productivity of a mobilized population would create more resources for use in repression and patronage. On the other hand, these incentives for popular mobilization are often far outweighed by the greater need for repression and payoffs in order to maintain rule over social actors who have begun to command more power resources of their own. For that reason, autocracies are sometimes reluctant to unleash the energies of their own people, even in the face in stiff military competition.

Before World War I, for example, some Russian reactionaries argued for peace with Germany at any price rather than risk a military mobilization that would play into the hand of economic reformers, popular nationalists, and patriotic democrats. Even during the war, the tsarist regime was reluctant to tap its society's energies. Like other autocratic Russian regimes, instead of taking the risk of free-wheeling national mobilization, it tried to generate military power through the "advantages of backwardness," using repression to field large, cheap armies of underpaid soldiers.[15] Some of the same considerations hindered military mobilization in Azerbaijan at the beginning of the 1990s: the communist-led regime refused to rouse its society to build an army to defend against Armenian attacks in Nagorno-Karabakh. A popular nationalist movement then demanded elections, which swept this regime away and

14.   David A. Lake, "Powerful Pacifists: Democratic States and War," *American Political Science Review,* Vol. 86, No. 1 (March 1992), pp. 24–37; and Bueno de Mesquita, et al., "An Institutional Explanation of the Democratic Peace."

15.   William C. Fuller, *Strategy and Power in Russia, 1600–1914* (New York: Free Press, 1992).

installed a successor who promised to create a more efficient state to raise taxes, institute conscription, and defeat the national enemy.[16]

In short, autocracies face a mobilization dilemma that makes them less likely to develop belligerently nationalist politics than incompletely democratizing states, where incentives to promote nationalism abound.

THE NATURE OF AUTOCRATIC INTERESTS

Elites empowered by autocracies do not necessarily prevent war, but neither do they strongly encourage war.

CONCENTRATED POWER, BUT ENCOMPASSING INTERESTS. A farsighted autocrat with a firm grip on power has no more incentive to fight unprofitable wars than does the autocrat's average subject. The autocrat controls the whole country and does not need the excuse of a war to extract resources from subjects and shift costs onto them. War makes sense for the autocrat only if it generates a net profit for the country as a whole, thereby increasing the material base from which the autocrat and his cronies extract rents. Agents with parochial interests may have selective incentives to profit from wars with high societal costs, but they can bring this about only if they successfully mislead the autocrat, or if the latter's power is slipping. However, if the autocrat (like Hitler) irrationally embarks on a costly war with dubious prospect of gains, there are few checks and balances to rein him in.

TIME HORIZON AND COSTS OF FAILURE IN WAR. Autocrats who are firmly in power and who care about the condition in which they leave the country for their successors have no reason to take short-term gambles on war. In contrast, hard-pressed autocrats who are facing challenges from traitorous agents or crises of succession or legitimacy may bet on war to bolster their position. Even so, there is no particular reason why autocrats' gambles for political resurrection should take the form of external wars to rally support around them. Unless popular nationalism had already been successfully mobilized in a previous failed effort to democratize, such a gamble would not seem like a good idea. Consistent with this view, Hein Goemans has shown that autocrats with intact powers of repression who lose wars on a moderate scale do not generally fall from power. Thus, as Goemans shows, they lack this incentive to prolong unprofitable wars.[17]

---

16.   Jack Snyder, *From Voting to Violence: Democratization and Nationalist Conflict* (New York: Norton, 2000), pp. 227–228.

17.   Goemans, *War and Punishment;* and Hein Goemans, "Fighting for Survival: The Fate of Leaders and the Duration of War," *Journal of Conflict Resolution,* Vol. 44, No. 5 (October 2000), pp. 555–579.

Overall, the nature of the social interests empowered in autocracies creates no particular barriers to war, but neither does it create any particular incentives for recklessness in war.

INSTITUTIONS OF AUTOCRACY

Two institutional features of certain types of modernized autocracies place them at higher risk of war: the bureaucratized armies at the core of garrison states, and institutionalized nationalism as a surrogate for mass political participation. Both of these features, however, may be found where social power is becoming differentiated and diffuse, indicating that autocracy is becoming unstable. Instability in such societies resembles the disorder in more explicitly transitional states, with similar consequences for their foreign relations.

Both Brian Downing and Charles Tilly, in complementary research, have shown that war made the absolutist state, and the absolutist state made war.[18] Over time, garrison states such as absolutist Prussia developed highly bureaucratized armies that outstripped the institutional development of other components of the state and developed their own ethos and interests. Soldiers took a narrow view of questions of war and peace, and repeatedly recommended preventive war as the all-purpose solution to diplomatic troubles. Although this problem of militarism was nurtured in the womb of autocracy, it affected foreign policy only after Prussia/Germany had begun its incomplete transition toward democracy.[19] (We elaborate on this story in Chapter 7.)

Some autocrats rule literate, mobilized societies that have already experienced social revolution or the beginnings of a democratic transition; this was true of Napoleonic France, Nazi Germany, Imperial Japan and, to some extent, Soviet Russia. Social power is far too diffuse to rule these as if they were inert peasant societies. In order to maintain social control, such governments must resort to institutional expedients and ideological stratagems that go beyond the usual repression and patronage. Typically, these regimes replace grassroots nationalist or patriotic movements with officially controlled ones. Because diffuse social power and strong parochial interests already characterize parts of these modernizing societies, such regimes often create secret police and surveillance or-

---

18. Brian Downing, *The Military Revolution and Political Change* (Princeton: Princeton University Press, 1992); and Tilly, *Coercion, Capital, and European States*.

19. Otto Hintze, *The Historical Essays of Otto Hintze*, edited by Felix Gilbert (New York: Oxford University Press, 1975); and Gerhard Ritter, *The Sword and the Sceptre: The Problem of Militarism in Germany*, vol. 1 (Coral Gables, Fl.: University of Miami Press, 1969), p. 245 and passim.

ganizations in an attempt, usually unsuccessful, to try to keep civil society in check. It is not surprising that such attempts to put the genie of an incomplete democratic transition back in the bottle often share its warlike foreign policy syndrome. Most autocracies are not like this, however, and most do not share this type of regime's high propensity for war.

IDEAS AND INFORMATION IN AUTOCRACY

The environment for ideas and information in autocracies permits war but does not foment it. Most autocracies try to demobilize their population, not whip up political passions. Their first choice is to avoid promoting nationalism, and if that is impossible, their second choice is to tame it through officially sanctioned nationalism. Insofar as effective autocracies monopolize the mass media, they face no need to engage in a bidding war with competitors for the mantle of nationalist legitimacy.

However, an information monopoly does have its costs. Because of the lack of independent evaluative organizations, autocrats often receive inaccurate, unverifiable information from opportunistic toadies and profiteers about the costs, benefits, and probability of success in war. Consequently, they are more likely to stumble into war by miscalculation. Likewise, lacking mechanisms to signal credibly that their threats and promises are truly binding, they are less able to settle conflicts short of war. In short, the ideological and informational environment of autocracy hardly prevents war, but neither does it stoke war.

When Democracies Go to War

Fully democratic regimes have never fought wars against other democracies. Overall, they fight and initiate wars about as often as non-democracies, but they do so more prudently, winning more of their wars at lower cost.[20] This is because strong democratic institutions, backed by civic norms, empower and inform the average voter who bears the costs and risks of war.

THE NATURE OF DEMOCRATIC POWER

Democratic power rests especially on the distinctive ability of democratic institutions and ideology to align private interests with collective purposes. Repression plays a far smaller role in strategies of rule in mature democracies than it does in autocracies. Democracies rarely kill large numbers of their own citizens, although some may use coercion to de-

---

20. Russett and Oneal, *Triangulating Peace*, pp. 66–68.

prive ethnic minorities or other disadvantaged groups of equal political opportunities.[21] Although patronage plays some role in strategies of democratic rule, its influence is checked by the workings of democratic institutions. For example, implicit exchanges of campaign funding for special access to policy-makers are endemic to the American political process, but the risks of publicity and electoral accountability place limits on their abuse. Indeed, groups having special resources of various kinds wield disproportionate influence in all mature democracies, due to their wealth, specialized information, cohesion, the concentrated nature of their interests, or their greater propensity to vote. Arguably, some of these groups may have interests in policies that have the unintended effect of making war more likely. Nonetheless, insofar as the electoral process and a free press reliably empower and inform the average voter, the democratic system has a built-in check on reckless attempts to hijack foreign policy in the service of a parochial agenda. On average, therefore, democracies should be more prudent than other regime types.

THE NATURE OF DEMOCRATIC INTERESTS

Voting is a decision-making system that tends to empower diffuse interests, such as those of taxpayers or of consumers, rather than concentrated interests, such as recipients of subsidies or producers. While special-interest lobbies may achieve some of what they want in a democracy, the fact that they have to convince officials who are accountable to others—to the average voter—makes this more difficult than in non-democratic, pressure-group systems that work mainly though patronage and log-rolling (favor-trading). Not only are leaders more accountable in democracies, their actions and those of special interests are also more transparent. In a democracy, groups must disguise special-interest policies as policies that serve the national interest. This is difficult when politicians are accountable to voters who would suffer from the proposed policy and who have access to alternative sources of information.

On balance, political systems that empower diffuse interests should be less war-prone than those that empower narrowly parochial interests. The latter may derive commercial profits, budget increases, organizational prestige, or ideological legitimation from military adventures while passing the costs to taxpayers.[22] In a political system where diffuse interests do have political power, it would be rare for the median voter to support a war that would not be beneficial for the country as a whole, al-

---

21.   Russett, *Grasping the Democratic Peace,* pp. 81–82.

22.   Jack Snyder, *Myths of Empire: Domestic Politics and International Ambition* (Ithaca, N.Y.: Cornell University Press, 1991), chap. 2.

though this outcome is not unimaginable. For example, if middle-class voters with a commercial interest in imperial expansion were the swing constituency between a pacific, conservative peasantry and a pacific, radical working class, and if the blood cost of a war could be passed on to a small professional army, then decisions made by voting could favor war in ways that are rational for the median voter but might be disadvantageous for the country. Conversely, in some rare cases, a system based on elite "veto-group" politics might be more pacific than a democracy, if a veto-wielding military, for example, were highly averse to risking casualties. In short, empowering diffuse interests does not guarantee prudence in war-making, though on balance doing so is likely to favor it.

TIME HORIZON AND COSTS OF FAILURE IN WAR. In less democratic systems, it is easy to imagine struggling elites using war or the threat of war as part of a strategy of gambling for their own political resurrection in the face of waning prospects, unfavorable trends, or diminishing assets. But since wars are costly in the short run, it is difficult to imagine that a tendency to discount the future would lead the median voter to prefer war. Insofar as the institutional and informational circumstances of mature democracy check elites from maneuvering to use war to stem their own electoral decline, this cause of war should be less common.

Consistent with this view, studies show that democratic rulers are likely to fall from power if they lose wars; therefore, they should be deterred from embarking on risky military adventures. Moreover, democratic leaders lose their jobs, not their heads, when they lose small wars. Consequently, they have little incentive to drag out a failed war in the hope that a long-odds miracle would salvage their position.[23] Both factors favor prudence in democratic war-making.

INSTITUTIONS OF DEMOCRACY

We have argued that a root cause of the democratic peace is that democratic institutions make government authorities accountable to the average voter. In addition, mature democracies also differ from other states in the predictability and continuity with which their institutions function. A statistical study by Adam Przeworski and his collaborators finds that democracies very rarely change their basic constitutional structures, whereas the institutional arrangements of autocracies are highly unstable. This is true despite the fact that autocracies are often long-lived.[24] Autocracies' longevity arises from predictable patterns of repression and patronage,

---

23. Goemans, *War and Punishment*, chap. 3.

24. Przeworski, et al., *Democracy and Development*, pp. 49–50.

rather than the institutionally coordinated expectations of compromise on which democracy depends.[25] Thus democracies tend to have elaborate political institutions whereas autocracies do not. As a result, autocracies that embark upon democratization often do so equipped with institutions that are too weak to be effective.

IDEAS AND INFORMATION IN DEMOCRACY

One of the main reasons that democracies are more prudent in their war-making is that strong evaluative institutions ceaselessly scrutinize the government's foreign policies and make public the information that is needed to weigh the likely consequences of military action in a credible way. In addition, mature democracy resists the most virulent forms of nationalism that lead to reckless choices about war.

Democratic regimes typically enhance their legitimacy by successfully promoting civic nationalism, a form of nationalism that is based on loyalty primarily to political institutions rather than to a distinctive culture. This form of loyalty can only take root where participatory institutions are relatively strong. For example, Britain's development of a free press and parliamentary institutions in the era before mass democracy made possible the emergence of civic nationalism in the eighteenth and nineteenth centuries. Where institutions are initially weak, fledgling democracies may base their nationalism on some degree of ethnic identification and discrimination. As democratic institutions and norms strengthen over time, however, nationalism tends to evolve in a more ethnically neutral or "civic" direction, as the cases of the United States, Germany, and Estonia illustrate. The case of Israel, however, shows that such an evolution is contingent on the strategic environment.

Civic nationalism mitigates one important cause of war: namely, the rivalry of two or more competing ethnic nationalisms that seek to establish ethnically discriminatory states on the territory inhabited by both. However, civic nationalism is hardly pacifist. Even this form of nationalism may be coercive toward internal minorities who prefer to base their political loyalties on ties of ethnicity and culture rather than loyalty to liberal principles and institutions. Civic nationalism can also motivate democracies to try to spread liberal principles abroad, although this is tempered by the liberal tenet that a regime must be established through the consent of the governed, not imposed by force.

---

25. On the tension between the autocratic pattern of patronage politics and the democratic pattern of market society, see Michael Mousseau, "Market Civilization and Its Clash with Terror," *International Security*, Vol. 27, No. 3 (Winter 2002/03), pp. 5–29.

The consequences of nationalism are also tempered in mature democracies by the open debate of policies and ideas, which may call attention to the costs of unchecked nationalism. Here, too, well-institutionalized accountability to the median voter and well-institutionalized scrutiny of policy ideas both tend to moderate deliberations about war and peace in mature democracies.

Mixed Regimes, Incomplete Transitions, and War

When autocratic regimes break up, politics can evolve in a variety of directions. In some cases, the regime may be replaced by another autocratic regime. This is likely when social power remains concentrated in a few hands and mass social mobilization is limited. Recent examples include the replacement of Mobutu Sese Seko by Laurent Kabila in Congo and the replacement of Soviet power by indigenous dictators in Central Asia. In other cases, the regime may make a relatively quick and successful transition to full democracy. This is most likely when social power is quite diffuse, the population already has many of the civic skills that are needed to make democracy work, institutions compatible with democracy are available at the time of the transition or can be quickly constructed, and elites from the old regime expect a relatively soft landing in the new democratic system. Recent examples include the transitions to democracy in the Czech Republic and, to some degree, South Africa.

Often, however, the demise of autocracy precipitates an incomplete democratic transition to a mixed regime that combines some features of autocracy and some of democracy in a distinctly explosive political cocktail. Mixed regimes have a variety of potential fates, some of which do not involve a high likelihood of war. Indeed, some mixed regimes turn out to be stable. Once they reach a certain level of stability, we find, they are no more likely to become embroiled in war than are stable democracies or stable autocracies.[26] Alternatively, they may revert to autocracy. If so, we find that the process of reversion makes them only a little more war-prone than stable regimes. They may also ultimately achieve full democracy. Sometimes they accomplish this through a series of stop-and-go spurts, which may include reversals of democratization. South America,

---

26.   This is based on the results reported in Edward D. Mansfield and Jack Snyder, "Democratic Transitions and War: From Napoleon to the Millennium's End," in Chester A. Crocker, Fen Osler Hampson, and Pamela Aall, eds., *Turbulent Peace: The Challenges of Managing International Conflict* (Washington, D.C.: U.S. Institute of Peace Press, 2001), pp. 113–126.

a relatively peaceful continent, offers numerous examples. We find that regimes making a transition from a mixed regime to full democracy are only slightly more war-prone than stable regimes. The most recent wars in this category have involved militarized, nationalistic regimes locked in enduring rivalries with their neighbors: Turkey and Pakistan.

✱ By far the greatest risk of war stemming from the politics of mixed regimes comes during an incomplete transition from autocracy toward democracy. Generally, the danger is most serious a few years after the transition begins. It is the dynamic of this transition, rather than the steady-state politics of mixed regimes, that causes the problem. The move from autocracy to a mixed regime is most likely to give rise to international war if state institutions are especially weak at the moment of the transition and the fortunes of elites are in flux. Because state institutions are too weak to guarantee elites a soft landing, elites look to their own still-considerable resources to recruit mass allies and manipulate fragile democratic processes. They often do this by provoking nationalist sentiment, and an increased risk of international conflict is a common by-product.

THE NATURE OF POWER DURING INCOMPLETE DEMOCRATIZATION

Typically, a situation in which autocracy is collapsing and demands for popular participation are on the rise is one in which social power has begun to diffuse as a result of increasing literacy, urbanization, or development of a market economy.[27] Old means of legitimating elite rule, such as divine right, inherited succession, or the infallibility of the vanguard party, have lost their force. When this occurs, the instruments of repression and patronage become harder to wield effectively. State elites and established interests nevertheless may still use them to implement their survival strategies. Infrastructural power, especially the power of liberal democratic institutions, is likely to be limited: efficiency and fairness in public administration, professional journalism, and political parties, as well as the rule of law, are likely to be in short supply. New appeals based on some form of popular sovereignty are required, though it may take time and resources to develop, articulate, and exploit them.[28]

What constitutes power and who will have it are up for grabs in this setting. Old elites often retain resources and networks of loyalties that are adaptable to new political tasks, while new elites may find opportunities

---

27. Michael Mann, "The Emergence of Modern European Nationalism," pp. 137–166.

28. For example, consider the stages in the development of nationalism discussed by Miroslav Hroch, *The Social Preconditions of Nationalist Revival in Europe* (New York: Columbia University Press, 2000), pp. 22–30.

to articulate and thus draw power from the aspirations of rising social classes, interest groups, or formerly excluded ethnicities. Outcomes will vary, depending on the institutional circumstances and the competitive landscape of interest groups.

If middle-class and urban working-class groups are fairly strong, and if some participatory institutions are functioning, democratic and peaceful consolidation may prevail fairly quickly. Incorporation of the masses in politics will follow a civic liberal or social democratic path, as in the post-communist transitions in Central Europe. Alternatively, a transition to a stable mixed regime may occur if some remnants of the autocratic state remain fairly cohesive; if they retain some capacity for repression and payoffs; and if the state can generate a degree of popular support among the wealthier segments of society. This was a common historical pattern, and often a fairly peaceful one, in South America during the nineteenth and twentieth centuries. Outcomes are likely to be more volatile, however, where the state is weak, where mass groups are vying for power, and where elite bureaucratic, economic, or ethnic cartels are strong relative to the state but no single cartel dominates the others. Then, conditions are ripe for nationalist mobilization and international war.

THE CALCULUS OF INTERESTS DURING INCOMPLETE DEMOCRATIZATION
When incomplete democratization occurs in a context of weak governmental institutions, the state is hard pressed to manage the rising power of newly politicized mass groups and elite interest groups, including bureaucratic and economic cartels that have split off from the collapsing autocracy. The power of centralized coercive institutions is waning, yet new democratic institutions are not yet powerful enough to replace them effectively. This has several dire consequences that increase the likelihood of international conflict.

PAROCHIAL INTERESTS RATHER THAN DIFFUSE OR ENCOMPASSING ONES.
In these circumstances, the state loses its ability to enforce a coherent set of broad policy priorities. Instead, in what Samuel Huntington describes as the dynamic of "praetorian societies," each parochial group looks to its own devices to make sure that its interests are served: students and ethnic groups riot, workers strike, and the army threatens coups d'état.[29] No one has sufficient power or motive to look out for the coherence of the overall policy outcome. Shortsighted political bargains resulting from the trading of favors in a logroll by concentrated interests can produce conflict with outsiders, especially because imperialist, militarist, and pro-

---

29. Huntington, *Political Order in Changing Societies*, chap. 4.

tectionist interests are often among the most powerful cartels. For example, Germany's incomplete democratization in the late nineteenth century yielded the "marriage of iron and rye," in which increasingly weaker central authorities doled out a fleet-building program to favor the navy and the steel trusts (thus making an enemy of Britain), offered agricultural protection to favor aristocratic rye growers and small farmers (thus angering grain-exporting Russia), and engaged in an arms race and an offensive strategy for land warfare to mollify the general staff (thus driving France further into the arms of Britain and Russia).[30] In Chapter 7, we discuss parallels between the logrolling in Wilhelmine-Germany and in a number of cases of democratizing war initiators, such as Turkey on the eve of the Cyprus invasion in 1974 and Argentina on the eve of the Falklands War in 1982. In some other cases, such as Chile's 1879 War of the Pacific, the logrolled deal was more implicit as central authorities devised policies to neutralize an uncoordinated set of belligerent pressure groups.

Nascent democratic institutions are likely to be too weak and malleable to enable the general populace to counteract dangerous logrolling. Mass politics in weakly institutionalized transitional regimes can, ironically, reinforce the empowerment of concentrated interests, as each elite cartel tries to recruit a mass pressure group to back its piece of the logroll. Thus, in the German case, aristocratic landowners used the Agrarian League to win over small farmers to the cause of agricultural protectionism. Through subsidies to the popular Navy League, the navy won over middle-class leaders to the flashy, high-technology fleet program, which generated a powerful symbolism of modernity as well as attractive employment opportunities for educated youth.

Such outcomes can happen because imperfect democratic institutions are susceptible to agenda control by elites. In Bismarckian and Wilhelmine Germany before World War I, the Kaiser, not the elected Reichstag, appointed government ministers. Elected officials had little expertise about or control over foreign and military policy, other than their power over budgets, and even budgets were set on a multi-year cycle, minimizing their opportunities to exert control. Elections were timed to take advantage of trumped-up national security crises to maximize the electorate's sympathy for pro-military, pro-colonial, and nationalist candidates.[31] Bismarck and his successors used this control of the electoral

---

30.   Eckart Kehr, *Economic Interest, Militarism, and Foreign Policy* (Berkeley: University of California Press, 1977); and Snyder, *Myths of Empire*, chap. 3.

31.   Brett Fairbairn, *Democracy in the Undemocratic State: The German Reichstag Elections of 1898 and 1903* (Toronto: University of Toronto Press, 1997), p. 48.

agenda and nationalist appeals to drive wedges between the workers and the middle classes who might otherwise have joined in a pro-democracy coalition.[32] Control of the legislative agenda also helped fleet proponents arrange a deal by which the Catholic Center Party voted for a huge navy bill in exchange for removal of laws discriminating against Catholics. As a result, the logroll of concentrated interests trumped diffuse interests, setting the stage for the belligerent German policies that led to a series of international crises and then to World War I.[33]

Such conflicts were to a considerable degree an unintended side effect of self-seeking interest-group behavior. Each cartel feared that to give up the part of the policy that benefited it would lead to ruin. Only the brokers of the logrolled package—the state authorities—were in a position to be concerned about the overall consequences, but they were weak and lacked the power to enforce a prudent outcome. At crucial moments narrow interests, such as the military, were able to subvert the efforts of top government leaders to rein in Germany's overextended foreign policy. As Germany's Austrian allies wondered during the July 1914 crisis on the eve of World War I, "Who rules in Berlin, [Chancellor] Bethmann or [Chief of the General Staff] Moltke?"[34]

TIME HORIZON AND THE COSTS OF FAILURE. Incomplete democratization in a context of weak institutions is rife with incentives for elites to engage in reckless gambles to try to achieve their own rise or resurrection. In particular, as downwardly mobile elites of the old regime see their power and privileges slipping away and their ideological legitimacy in shambles, they fear that democratization will end their ability to use state power to serve their own interests, and they fear being punished for crimes of repression and patronage that were business-as-usual in the autocratic system. Given the weakness of emerging democratic institutions, they doubt that a new democratic regime could effectively guarantee an amnesty. For the same reason, they place little trust in offers to secure their property rights or bureaucratic positions in a post-transition system

---

32.   Beverly Heckart, *From Bassermann to Bebel: The Grand Bloc's Quest for Reform in the Kaiserreich, 1900–1914* (New Haven: Yale University Press, 1974); and Snyder, *Myths of Empire*, chap. 3.

33.   In our database, Prussia/Germany initiated or was involved in several wars in the 1860s and 1870 during the decade after its transition to a mixed regime. World War I followed a further crisis of German democratization with the near-victory of the Social Democrats in the 1912 Reichstag election. Though the latter is not coded as a democratic transition in our database, Germany is coded as becoming more democratic in 1890 and in 1908. We discuss the World War I case here because it illustrates a common pattern of incomplete democratizers involved in enduring rivalries.

34.   Ritter, *The Sword and the Sceptre*, vol. 2, pp. 257–263.

in exchange for their agreement to surrender political power. Gambling for the resurrection of their autocratic power looks like a better option. So does adapting a combination of repression, patronage, and a populist sort of legitimacy to conditions in the new mixed regime. Either way, risk-taking to stave off further democratization appears relatively attractive.

Even if the odds are long, international crisis and war may seem like a good way to rally public opinion quickly, enhance the prestige of the regime or of threatened military interest groups, or conquer the resources needed to maintain a patronage strategy. Such strategies may have a fairly low probability of success, but if the declining or threatened elites see that their alternative is to wind up in the dustbin of history, they may find this path attractive nonetheless. As we discuss in Chapters 7 and 8, this strategy worked for Vladimir Putin in Chechnya; it also succeeded temporarily for Slobodan Milosevic, but then failed spectacularly for him in Kosovo. It failed for Ayub Khan and Nawaz Sharif in Pakistan; it failed for the Argentine junta in the Falklands/Malvinas War; and ultimately it failed for the German iron-and-rye coalition.

The costs of such failures tend to be high for incompletely democratized regimes, whether the defeats are small or large. Goemans shows that leaders of mixed regimes are likely to fall from power if they lose even a relatively minor war, because they typically lack the ability to repress opposition. Moreover, in falling from power, they are likely to lose not just their jobs but their lives. One might think that this would make rulers of mixed regimes cautious about starting wars, but as we have seen, other considerations may push them to run these risks. Moreover, Goemans shows, leaders of mixed regimes, knowing that losing a large war is no worse than losing a smaller one, tend to redouble their initial gamble, refusing to terminate wars that are going badly and instead upping the ante. The German decision for unrestricted U-boat warfare in World War I, which led to the fateful sinking of the *Lusitania,* is a classic example.[35]

INSTITUTIONS IN INCOMPLETE DEMOCRATIZATION

The most fundamental problem of societies undergoing incomplete democratization in a context of weak governmental institutions is the gap between rising demands for mass participation and the declining ability

---

35.   Goemans, *War and Punishment,* chap. 3; and Ernest May, "The U-Boat Campaign," in Robert J. Art and Kenneth Waltz, eds., *The Use of Force,* 1st ed. (Boston: Little, Brown, 1971), pp. 298–315.

of political institutions to settle the conflicts of interest that this entails. When autocracies collapse, this gap often opens wide because autocratic institutions lose their effectiveness before strong democratic ones can take their place. However, such an institutional gap is not inevitable. In some instances, a colonial regime or another administratively effective autocracy may leave a useable bureaucratic state that can be adapted to the new conditions. In some especially fortunate cases, such as Britain in the nineteenth century, India after independence, and South Africa in the 1990s, the institutions of representative government for the old elite can be adapted to facilitate the transition to a system of mass suffrage. Some of these institutions may be largely administrative, such as an ethical corps of bureaucrats or a police force that follows the law. Others may pertain more directly to the effective operation of democratic competition, such as impartial and active election commissions, well-organized political parties, competent legislatures, or professional news media.

Both types of institutions—those that regulate administration and those that regulate competition—are needed to make democracy work in a meaningful way. In general, transitions are smoothest when the preconditions of democracy develop in a sequence that begins with the state's construction of an orderly administrative powerbase, followed by development of the rule of law and institutions of public debate. Only after successful completion of the first two steps can the state effectively confront the challenges of integrating the conflicting interests unleashed by universal suffrage.

Such favorable patterns are rare, however, and even harder for aspiring democrats to contrive when they do not occur naturally. The main problem is that elites in transitional societies usually see the weakness of democratic institutions more as an opportunity than as a danger. Their typical strategy is to keep the institutions of mass accountability as weak as possible, either by destroying them entirely or keeping them vulnerable to manipulation, agenda control, and intimidation.[37] Another problem is that the spread of the norm of universal suffrage has made it difficult for transitional states to introduce state-building reforms in the optimal sequence.[38] Peoples who consider themselves deprived of the

---

36.   Huntington, *Political Order in Changing Societies*, chap. 1.

37.   For an analogous argument regarding incomplete economic reforms, see Joel S. Hellman, "Winners Take All: The Politics of Partial Reform in Postcommunist Transitions," *World Politics*, Vol. 50, No. 2 (January 1998), pp. 203–234.

38.   Robert A. Dahl, *Polyarchy: Participation and Opposition* (New Haven: Yale University Press, 1971), p. 39.

right of self-determination, encouraged by the rhetoric of powerful actors in the international community, typically insist on universal suffrage and elections early on. Therefore, states that want to resist full accountability usually have to resort to manipulating votes or preventing strong candidates from running, measures that discredit democracy rather than prepare the groundwork for it.

These institutional deformations raise the risk of international conflict in several ways. They may weaken central authorities and strengthen the power of elite cartels, some of which have a parochial interest in war and expansion, before the median voter has sufficient institutional power to check the cartels. These cartels may include military and economic elites close to the old regime, as well as leaders of irredentist or separatist ethnic groups representing newly rising social forces. Even if some special interests are opposed to war and expansion, the weakness of the central authorities makes it likely that any political compromise will proceed by logrolling in which all groups (including the bellicose ones) get what they want most. This often results in an overcommitted strategy involving some combination of coercive diplomacy, opportunistic aggression, arms races, and support for ethnic irredentism. Even worse, a weak state and inconsistent policy goals hinder the ability of the democratizing state to send clear, credible signals to its foreign adversaries. Neither its threats nor its promises can be trusted. This, too, raises the risk of war.

This process may have second-order effects on institutions that also increase the risk of international conflict. As the democratizing state gets locked into stubborn rivalries abroad, its state institutions and laws become shaped by the demands of international conflict and preparation for war. The military takes a more central role in the workings of the state, and the democratizing state becomes a garrison state. Civil liberties take a back seat to the exigencies of war. Ethnic enmity shapes constitutional provisions and undercuts the emergence of laws and institutions that would guarantee civic equality.

Perhaps most important, however, is the inability of weak institutions to accommodate rising demands for mass political participation. This invites the use of ideology to fill the gap, as we discuss next. The weakness of journalistic and other evaluative institutions allows elites to hijack the public discourse. The result is often an increase in belligerent nationalism.

IDEAS AND INFORMATION DURING INCOMPLETE DEMOCRATIZATION

When an autocratic regime breaks up, there is a dramatic rise in the importance of mass political ideology for legitimating the power of ruling authorities and other elites. The people can no longer simply be repressed or bought off; they must be persuaded. Even in incompletely democratized states, elites must have popular support in order to gain the upper hand against rival elites. Tangible evidence of popular support through voting, demonstrations, pressure group politics, or other means becomes indispensable to demonstrate their political legitimacy.

ALTERNATIVE IDEOLOGICAL APPEALS. In general, elites have several ideological options for making their appeals to a newly awakened mass public. One is liberalism, rooted in the notion that political rivals should compete freely and openly to win the right to govern under the rule of law by attracting votes in a secret ballot of equal citizens. Few elites in poorly institutionalized, newly democratizing states are likely to find this option attractive. First, liberalism is based on true accountability to the average voter. This is likely to be anathema to elites from the old regime, whose privileges and power typically depend on avoiding accountability. It may also conflict with the goals of some newly rising elites, such as ethnic separatist entrepreneurs who want national self-determination in a new state, rather than accountability to the median voter in some existing political unit.

Second, even elites who might prefer liberalism under ideal conditions have to operate in a reality that is not of their own making. The fact that Presidents Eduard Shevardnadze and Levon Ter-Petrossian were philosophically democratic did not prevent post-Soviet Georgia and Armenia from degenerating into strong-arm politics, corruption, and international ethnic strife.

Another potential strategy is an ideological appeal to the class interests of workers or peasants. This strategy may be attractive to some rising radical elites, but its constituency is likely to be short on weapons, money, organizational capacity, and political consciousness when democratization begins. Class appeals are rarely an attractive strategy for old elites, since privileged elites and lower classes almost by definition have opposing class interests.

However, established elites may be able to appeal to lower-class groups by emphasizing common concerns that transcend class. They may, for example, form an alliance based on common sectoral interests, as in the agricultural pressure groups formed by German aristocratic landowners and small farmers. Likewise, conservative cultural and religious values may bind together plutocrats and paupers, as in Bismarck's strategy of extending universal suffrage to the conservative peasantry. Most commonly, however, such cross-class alliances are bound together by nationalism, which holds that cleavages between classes are unimportant compared to the cleavages that divide nations, ethnic groups, or races.

NATIONALISM'S APPEAL FOR ELITES. Nationalism is an ideology with tremendous appeal for elites in democratizing states. Nationalism holds that the people as a whole have the right to self-rule, but it does not necessarily promise that the government should be strictly accountable to the average voter through democratic processes governed by the rule of law. Thus, nationalism is an ideology that allows elites to exploit the rhetoric of popular sovereignty without submitting to its reality. It offers government for the people, but not necessarily by the people.

Nationalism also offers a built-in justification for curtailing the civic rights of potential opponents.[39] This doctrine inherently draws a line between one's own nation and other nations, between the nation's friends and its foes. From there, nationalists and their audiences have found it a short step to fingering and accusing "enemies" and "traitors" whose civic rights must be abridged in order to protect the nation. These enmities often cross international borders, since the most convincing way to tar domestic opponents as traitors is to portray them as the "fifth column" of enemies abroad. Nationalists did this prominently in the French Revolution, and they have been doing it ever since. Indeed, every time the liberal international community sanctions a country for abusing the rights of an ethnic minority, it risks playing into the hands of nationalists who argue that the disloyal minority should be exterminated before they join forces with those powerful outsiders.[40]

Nationalism can be adapted to justify the political exclusion of almost any type of group. Nowadays it is often ethnic enemies who are targeted for political exclusion or even physical expulsion or extermination, as they were in the democratizing states of Yugoslavia in 1990 and Burundi in 1993.[41] In the past, however, class rather than ethnic groups have been targeted as enemies of the nation: aristocrats in the French revolution, or industrial workers and Catholics in Bismarckian and Wilhelmine Germany. Both types of divisions often made enemies at home and abroad, again raising the risk of war.

Nationalism can likewise be adapted to the needs of almost any seller of ideology. Secular revolutionaries such as France's Jacobins, communist

---

39.   Dahl, *Polyarchy*, p. 44.

40.   For theory and evidence on this, see Alan Kuperman, "Tragic Challenges and the Moral Hazards of Humanitarian Intervention: How and Why Ethnic Groups Provoke Genocidal Retaliation" (Ph.D. dissertation, Department of Political Science, MIT, 2002); and the Columbia University dissertation in progress of Arman Grigorian.

41.   Snyder, *From Voting to Violence*, pp. 69–79, 204–220, 300–301.

bureaucrats such as Milosevic, military juntas in Argentina, middle-class pressure groups such as the German Navy League, kings such as Kaiser Wilhelm, aristocrats such as the German Junkers, and religious fundamentalists such as the leaders of the Iranian revolution have all found nationalism to be a useful tool to gain popular legitimacy for a politically exclusionary system of rule.[42]

HOW NATIONALISM IS SOLD. The same circumstances of incomplete democratization that make fomenting nationalism an attractive option for elites also provide opportunities to promote it in public debate. This contrasts with autocracy, where the ruling elite typically has a monopoly over the mass media, but little incentive to use it to spread nationalist ideology. When incomplete democratization occurs in the face of weak institutions, elites have a strong incentive to play the nationalist card, taking advantage of their domination over key news media. In Weimar Germany, for example, Alfred Hugenberg, a board member of Krupp Steel who was also the head of Germany's largest nationalist party, owned the wire service that dominated the supply of news and financial services to many of Germany's smaller cities and towns. Although Jews, liberals, and socialists had strong voices in the press of major urban areas, Hugenberg's partial monopoly fed a steady diet of slanted news to other areas, which were later precisely the ones that voted heavily for Hitler.[43]

Sometimes it is remnants of the waning autocratic ruling class whose residual control of economic assets and specialized information provides them with a partial media monopoly. As Yugoslavia disintegrated, for example, the central Yugoslav leadership sought to promote liberal, multi-ethnic reforms, but found itself with virtually no television at its disposal, because an earlier decentralization had given media jurisdiction to Serbia, Croatia, and the other ethnically-defined republics. Consequently, Milosevic, as Serbia's local party boss, was able to assert near-monopoly control over television news in Belgrade, using it to present an inflammatory picture of Albanian threats to Serbian interests in Kosovo. Franjo Tudjman acted similarly in Zagreb.[44] Even without controlling the media itself, the Wilhelmine German Navy was able to exploit its monopoly over technical and strategic expertise to convince the public that an expanded fleet would thwart the British naval threat without provoking

42. Mark Juergensmeyer, *The New Cold War? Religious Nationalism Confronts the Secular State* (Berkeley: University of California Press, 1993), pp. 50–57.

43. Modris Eksteins, *The Limits of Reason: The German Democratic Press and the Collapse of Weimar Germany* (London: Oxford University Press, 1975), pp. 78–81.

44. Mark Thompson, *Forging War: The Media in Serbia, Croatia, and Bosnia-Herzegovina* (London: Article 19, International Center Against Censorship, May 1994).

an unwinnable arms race, even though its own internal studies showed that this was not the case.[45]

In other instances, it may be newly rising elites that achieve partial media monopolies. The spread of literacy among the disadvantaged minorities of a democratizing population tends to create a booming demand for news media in their vernacular language. Statewide media, in which multiple groups debate ideas in a shared language, may then give way to fragmentary local media dominated by the more parochial perspectives of a single linguistic or ethno-religious community. Often these nascent vernacular media lack professional standards of reporting, pander to the narrow perspectives of their target groups, and are linguistically immune to external scrutiny and rebuttal. Thus, the new literati of the vernacular press are able to push nationalist perspectives from the soapbox afforded by a partial monopoly over a natural media-market niche.[46]

Cultural and historical resonance helps in the selling of a nationalist agenda through the media; over time, determined elites can sometimes create cultural resonance by using systematic divide and rule strategies. Such a top-down approach is associated with European imperialists' tactics of pitting Muslim against Hindu or Tutsi against Hutu, but it is not only a colonial problem. Bismarck accomplished the same outcome in Germany by pitting Catholics against Protestants and middle-class nationalism against working-class socialism.[47]

BIDDING WARS BETWEEN OLD ELITES AND RISING GROUPS. When powerful groups have succeeded in structuring political participation around nationalist issues, other groups have an incentive to try to outflank the nationalists on this very issue. One form that this takes is a mass bidding war for the mantle of elite nationalism. For example, Bismarck and his successors who managed the coalition of iron and rye sought to use nationalism to win votes to keep conservative elites in power in an age of universal suffrage, even though they did not want to unleash nationalism-fueled wars which, they feared, would destabilize the old order. The aristocratic elite running the German army likewise resisted expanding the officer corps to incorporate the middle classes because they feared doing so would undermine the old elite's dominant position. Repeatedly, German diplomats shied away from the use of force in crises that German

---

45.   Paul Kennedy, "Tirpitz, England and the Second Navy Law of 1900: A Strategical Critique," *Militärgeschichtliche Mitteilungen*, Vol. 2 (1970), pp. 33–58.

46.   Snyder, *From Voting to Violence*, pp. 294–295.

47.   Ibid., p. 62.

belligerence provoked. This, however, gave middle-class nationalists the opportunity to flog elite nationalists with their own issue. They declared that if threats to Germany's survival were truly as severe as the established elites described, then the iron-and-rye regime was too weak in its efforts to parry them. The ineffectual select few should therefore stand aside and let the vigorous, numerous middle classes run the state's bureaucracy, army, and diplomatic corps.[48]

CONDITIONAL DANGERS OF INCOMPLETE DEMOCRATIZATION

Thus, incomplete democratization increases the danger of war when political institutions are especially weak and when elites are especially threatened by it. This gives elites the motive and the opportunity to employ strategies of exclusionary nationalism in an effort to survive and prosper despite rising demands for mass political participation. Characteristic symptoms of this syndrome include pressure-group politics, logrolling among elite factions, incapacity of the ruling elite to broker political bargains, contradictory and unconvincing signaling in foreign affairs, the adoption of aggressive foreign policies as part of a gamble for domestic political resurrection, the use of media dominance to promote nationalist ideology, and a nationalist bidding war between old elites and rising mass groups.

Not every one of these symptoms will be present in every case. Differences of institutions, elite configurations, demography, political style, history, strategic choice, and international environment make each case play out somewhat differently. In the cases described in Chapter 7, we show how different patterns of institutional weaknesses and elite interests favor different forms of nationalism, such as the civic versus ethnic varieties, which tend to manifest a somewhat different mix of causal mechanisms and outcomes. Nonetheless, the structural dilemmas of incomplete democratization with weak institutions have sufficiently general effects that enough of these symptoms appear in enough cases to raise the probability of war substantially.

The Risks of War in Cases of Transitions to Complete Democracy

Regimes making a transition from a mixed regime to complete democracy are only slightly more war-prone than stable regimes, and they are much less war-prone than regimes making a transition to incomplete democracy. In this more advanced phase of democratization, the regime

---

48. Geoff Eley, *Reshaping the German Right* (New Haven: Yale University Press, 1980), pp. 322–324.

moves toward a system of unfettered political competition and full governmental accountability to a broad electorate. On the one hand, this phase may create incentives for elites who fear the consequences of democratic consolidation to play the nationalist card in public debate or to gamble for resurrection by provoking a foreign crisis, because they expect no other chance to take back the reins of power. On the other hand, at this more advanced stage of the transition, proponents of democracy are able to wield stronger institutional resources to combat such maneuvers. Moreover, democrats' guarantees about security in the new order may look more credible to both potential supporters and spoilers than in earlier phases of the transition. Forward movement toward democracy no longer looks like a leap into the void. For these reasons, it seems reasonable to expect that although there may be a modest increase in the risk of war at the beginning of the democratic transition, this risk should decline rapidly once the consolidation of democracy begins.[49]

Based on the codings used in our database, the two most recent regimes to initiate war after a transition to full democracy were Turkey in the 1974 Cyprus War and Pakistan in the 1999 Kargil War.[50] Both of these countries are marked by a history of alternating between military regimes and multi-party electoral politics. Over time they developed many of the outward trappings of full democracy, yet the ever-present threat of coups d'état by the country's military prevented consolidation of democracy. In this situation, military elites have an incentive to show that they rule on behalf of the popular will, whereas civilians have an incentive to show that they stand firm on behalf of national security concerns. As a result, both play the game of populist nationalist politics and become embroiled in military rivalries with neighboring states. We expect that transitions to full democracy will be dangerous mainly for states with these characteristics.

Germany between the 1860s and 1945 is another case that echoes this pattern in important respects. Germany's pattern of militarist, nationalist politics arose during early democratization and became embedded in institutions and ideologies. These long-term patterns continued to fuel foreign rivalries through subsequent episodes of democratization, including the nationalist politics of the almost fully democratic Weimar period.

---

49. On the distinction between transition and consolidation, see Juan Linz and Alfred Stepan, *Problems of Democratic Transition and Consolidation* (Baltimore, Md.: Johns Hopkins University Press, 1996), pp. 3–15.

50. Kargil is not included in our statistical analysis because we do not have complete data on war or on the strength of domestic institutions for this period of time. However, see the discussion in Russett and Oneal, *Triangulating Peace*, p. 48.

Later in this volume, we return to the question of the various stages and evolutionary pathways that may follow a state's initial transition from autocracy to a mixed regime. Chapters 7 and 8 use case studies to trace and analyze the logic of some of these pathways that link democratization and enduring international rivalries.

Recapitulating Hypotheses and Testing the Argument

The principal hypotheses that we have offered are, first, that countries undergoing incomplete democratization with weak institutions are more likely than other states to become involved in war. tested in Chp 4

Second, countries undergoing incomplete democratization are more likely than other states to initiate war. tested in Chp 5

Third, incomplete democratization where institutions are weak is especially likely to lead to war when powerful elites feel threatened by the prospect of a democratic transition. tested in Chp 6

Fourth, countries undergoing complete democratization—that is, a transition from either autocracy or a mixed regime to a consolidated democracy—have a moderately higher risk of involvement in war shortly after the transition, but no elevated risk once democracy is consolidated.

Fifth, the increased risk of war for countries undergoing complete democratization mainly applies to states already involved in enduring rivalries whose nationalist and militarist institutions and ideologies were forged in earlier phases of democratization.

Finally, our sixth hypothesis is that the politics of democratizing states that initiate war are likely to exhibit some or all of the following characteristics: exclusionary nationalism, pressure-group politics, logrolling among elite factions, weak brokerage of political bargains by the ruling elite, contradictory and unconvincing signaling in foreign affairs, the use of aggressive foreign policies by declining elites gambling for domestic political resurrection, the use of media dominance to promote nationalist ideology, and nationalist bidding wars between old elites and rising mass groups.

TESTING THE ARGUMENT

Chapters 4, 5, and 6 test the first, second, and fourth hypotheses using statistical techniques to study the war behavior of all states in the international system in the nineteenth and twentieth centuries. (We do not have the quantitative measures and data needed to conduct statistical tests of the remaining hypotheses, so we assess them in the case studies.) Chapter 4 lays out the statistical research design. Chapter 5 presents the core of our statistical findings on the impact of democratic transitions and institutional strength on war. Chapter 6 analyzes statistically the impact of democratization on the likelihood of war between pairs of states, which allows us to take into account specific contextual factors such as dyadic power balances.

The narrative case studies in Chapters 7 and 8 evaluate all six hypotheses. Chapter 7 offers narrative case studies of a subset of the cases analyzed in the statistical chapters—namely, all cases of democratizing states that initiated interstate war—to see whether the causal processes specified in our theory are indeed at work. Chapter 7 also introduces some further conceptual distinctions among different types of nationalism that may emerge in the course of democratization. These distinctions help show how the pattern of institutional strength and weakness shapes the nature and intensity of nationalist politics in the transitional state. Chapter 8 presents case studies that extend beyond the scope of our statistical dataset, examining the consequences of democratization in all international wars between 1991 and 2000. Chapter 9 examines the consequences for war of different paths of democratic transition, and argues for the importance of careful sequencing of the steps toward democracy.

Chapter 4

Data and Measures for Testing the Argument

Having laid out our argument, we now turn to testing it with both quantitative techniques and narrative case studies. This chapter marks the start of our quantitative analysis. To undertake this analysis, we need measures of democratization, the strength of domestic institutions, and war. Here we present the measures and the data used in our statistical tests and we discuss some broad patterns in these factors over time.

Central to our argument is the distinction between the transition from autocracy toward a partially democratic regime and the transition to a fully institutionalized democracy. In this chapter, we develop a variable corresponding to each of these two phases of democratization. We also explain why we measure each of these variables using four distinct indices of regime type.

After addressing the measurement of democratization, we present a measure of the degree to which domestic authority is concentrated in each country's central government. Such a measure is needed to test our argument that the early stages of democratization should have a more pronounced impact on war in countries with less institutional strength and centralization. As we explain further in Chapters 5 and 6, the interaction between this variable and the measure of incomplete democratization is crucial to testing our theory. We conclude this chapter by discussing the data on external wars that are used in these tests.

Measuring Democratization

Throughout this book, we distinguish between two phases in the process of democratization: the transition from autocracy to a partially democratic regime and the shift to a fully institutionalized democracy. As in prior research, we consider the initial stages of democratic transitions to include those cases in which elites conclude bargains involving limited political liberalization, as well as cases in which elites allow voting but merely as a temporary expedient.[1]

As we argued in Chapter 3, hostilities are more likely to break out during the first phase, when old elites threatened by the transition may still be powerful and the institutions needed to regulate mass political participation tend to be very weak. When military, communist, colonial, dynastic, or other authoritarian regimes break down and mass politics begins, democratic procedures are likely to be intermittent, subjected to manipulation by both rising and declining elites, and animated by nationalist or other populist ideologies that give rise to international frictions. Unless the state has the rare luck to inherit fairly strong political institutions at the outset of the transition from autocracy, turbulence is hard to avoid during this first step on the road to democracy.

States that made transitions from an autocracy to a mixed (or anocratic) regime and became embroiled in hostilities soon afterward include Prussia/Germany under Bismarck, France under Napoleon III, Chile shortly before the War of the Pacific in 1879, Serbia's multiparty constitutional monarchy before the Balkan Wars of the late twentieth century, and Pakistan's military-guided pseudo-democracy before its wars with India in 1965 and 1971. Each of these countries experienced an incomplete transition that stalled prior to the establishment of coherent democratic institutions. The rhetoric of popular sovereignty is frequently grandiloquent in such cases, but the power of voters to regulate government policy is weak.

The second distinct phase of democratization occurs when the regime moves to adopt a system of unfettered political competition and full governmental accountability to a broad electorate. This phase may create incentives for elites who fear the consequences of democratic consolidation to play the nationalist card in public debate or gamble for resurrection during a foreign crisis. Democratic institutions may, however, be strong enough to frustrate such maneuvers at this more advanced stage of the transition. Moreover, democrats' commitments may look more credible both to potential backers and to elite skeptics and potential spoilers than in earlier phases of the transition: movement toward democracy no longer looks like a leap into the void. For these reasons, a modest in-

---

1. See Guillermo O'Donnell and Philippe Schmitter, *Transitions from Authoritarian Rule* (Baltimore, Md.: Johns Hopkins University Press, 1986); and Adam Przeworski, *Democracy and the Market* (Cambridge: Cambridge University Press, 1991), p. 52.

crease in the risk of war at the time of the transition to complete democracy, followed by a rapid decline once democracy begins to consolidate, may be expected. In order to test these arguments, it is necessary to construct measures of incomplete and complete democratization. These measures should be monadic—that is, data should be drawn at the level of the individual country—since the hypothesized effect of democratization on conflict arises from the properties of each transitional state and not, for example, from the dyadic properties of country-pairs. This assumption is consistent with research on the democratic peace, which shows that mature democracies are especially peaceful toward each other, and documents a broad range of monadic findings about the distinctive foreign policies of such states.[2]

It seems plausible that these monadic effects are caused by a mutually reinforcing set of institutional, informational, and normative characteristics distinctive to mature democracies—such as accountability to cost-conscious voters, greater transparency with regard to facts and preferences in policy debates, and protection of the civil liberties that make democracy possible. Interactions between mature democracies are moderated by the characteristics of such states, making war very unlikely.[3] The properties of such dyadic relationships may include the effects of shared democratic norms and identities on the legitimacy of conflict, as well as the greater efficiency of inter-democratic bargaining and dispute resolution.[4] It is likely that these dyadic properties emerge in large part

2.   As we noted earlier, democracies choose their wars more wisely, tend to win them and to suffer fewer casualties, rarely fight preventive wars, and are more adept at signaling the credibility of their commitments. See David A. Lake, "Powerful Pacifists: Democratic States and War," *American Political Science Review,* Vol. 86, No. 1 (March 1992), pp. 24–37; Randall Schweller, "Domestic Structure and Preventive War: Are Democracies More Pacific?" *World Politics,* Vol. 44, No. 2 (January 1992), pp. 235–269; James Fearon, "Domestic Political Audiences and the Escalation of International Disputes," *American Political Science Review,* Vol. 88, No. 3 (September 1994), pp. 577–592; Randolph M. Siverson, "Democracies and War Participation: In Defense of the Institutional Constraints Argument," *European Journal of International Relations,* Vol. 1, No. 4 (December 1995), pp. 481–489; D. Scott Bennett and Allan C. Stam, "The Declining Advantages of Democracy: A Combined Model of War Outcomes and Duration," *Journal of Conflict Resolution,* Vol. 42, No. 3 (June 1998), pp. 344–366; and Dan Reiter and Allan C. Stam, "Democracy, War Initiation, and Victory," *American Political Science Review,* Vol. 92, No. 2 (June 1998), pp. 377–390.

3.   Bruce Russett and John R. Oneal, *Triangulating Peace: Democracy, Interdependence, and International Organizations* (New York: Norton, 2001), pp. 47–79.

4.   William J. Dixon, "Democracy and the Peaceful Settlement of International Conflict," *American Political Science Review,* Vol. 88, No. 1 (March 1994), pp. 14–32; John M. Owen, "How Liberalism Produces the Democratic Peace," *International Security,* Vol. 19, No. 2 (Fall 1994), pp. 87–125; and Kenneth Schultz, "Do Democratic Institu-

because democracies are already different in their strategic propensities at the monadic level. Consequently, we see no conceptual dissonance between our monadic argument and the monadic and dyadic democratic peace literatures.

PHASES AND DIMENSIONS OF DEMOCRATIZATION

To test our theory properly, analysis must distinguish the two phases of a democratic transition: first, when mass groups are initially being politically mobilized; and later, when the impending completion of the democratization process may foreclose options for threatened elites. Tests should account for the strength of political institutions during these two phases. They should also be sensitive to the time it may take to carry out a campaign of nationalist mobilization and for such a campaign to promote belligerence abroad.

The influence of other facets of domestic political change on hostilities has been the subject of several recent studies. Some, for example, have examined whether *any* shift in a democratic direction (including shifts *within* autocratic regimes, anocratic [mixed] regimes, and democratic regimes) affects the likelihood of war.[5] These studies do not bear directly on our theory, which is silent on the implications of changes in political openness within a given regime type (for example, an already consolidated democracy that further strengthens the protection of civil liberties, or an autocracy that becomes somewhat less autocratic without becoming an anocracy).

Other research has focused solely on the most pronounced type of democratic transition, where an autocracy is replaced by a coherent democracy.[6] But this focus is too restrictive for our argument, which emphasizes the dangers of transitions from autocracy that fail to produce coherent democratic institutions. None of these studies have used a definition and a measure of democratization that fully captures the institutional changes highlighted in our theory.

Consistent with much existing research, we measure regime type and

---

tions Constrain or Inform?" *International Organization,* Vol. 53, No. 2 (Spring 1999), pp. 233–266.

5.   Andrew Enterline, "Driving While Democratizing," *International Security,* Vol. 20, No. 4 (Spring 1996), pp. 183–196; John R. Oneal and Bruce M. Russett, "The Classical Liberals Were Right: Democracy, Interdependence, and Conflict, 1950–1985," *International Studies Quarterly,* Vol. 41, No. 2 (June 1997), pp. 267–293; and Michael D. Ward and Kristian S. Gleditsch, "Democratizing for Peace," *American Political Science Review,* Vol. 92, No. 1 (March 1998), pp. 51–61.

6.   Oneal and Russett, "The Classical Liberals Were Right."

regime change using the Polity III data and indices developed by Ted Robert Gurr and his colleagues.[7] There are four primary reasons we rely on this data set, which furnishes longitudinal indicators of domestic institutions for 177 countries during the period 1800–1994. First, it provides information on a wide variety of domestic institutions that are emphasized in our argument. Second, a later version of the Polity III data set (referred to as Polity IV) drops a number of useful variables (namely, monocratism, which records whether the ruler is an individual or some sort of committee, and centralization, which measures whether the state is unitary or federal). These variables are especially important for present purposes since we use them to construct our measure of institutional strength and centralization. Third, few other data sets provide the information necessary to distinguish between complete and incomplete regime transitions, a distinction that is central to our argument. Fourth, alternative data sets do not cover as many countries or as long a period of time as the Polity data, and it is important to analyze the broadest sample possible.[8]

Gurr and his colleagues offer measures of the competitiveness of the process through which a country's chief executive is selected, the openness of this process, the extent to which there are institutional constraints on a chief executive's decision-making authority, the competitiveness of political participation within a country, and the degree to which binding rules govern political participation within it. These measures are combined to create 11-point indices of each state's democratic (*Democ*) and autocratic (*Autoc*) characteristics in each year.[9] The difference between

---

7.   Ted Robert Gurr, Keith Jaggers, and Will H. Moore, *Polity II: Political Structures and Regime Change, 1800–1986*, Inter-University Consortium for Political and Social Research Study No. 9263 (1989); and Keith Jaggers and Ted Robert Gurr, "Tracking Democracy's Third Wave with the Polity III Data," *Journal of Peace Research*, Vol. 32, No. 4 (November 1995), pp. 469–482.

8.   For some alternative data on regime type and regime change, see Kenneth A. Bollen, "Issues in the Comparative Measurement of Political Democracy," *American Sociological Review*, Vol. 45, No. 3 (1980), pp. 370–390; Mark Gasiorowski, "An Overview of the Political Regime Change Dataset," *Comparative Political Studies*, Vol. 29, No. 4 (1996), pp. 469–483; Raymond D. Gastil, ed., *Freedom in the World: Political Rights and Civil Liberties* (New York: Freedom House, 1980 and 1990); and Adam Przeworski, Michael E. Alvarez, José Antonio Cheibub, and Fernando Limongi, *Democracy and Development: Political Institutions and Well-Being in the World, 1950–1990* (New York: Cambridge University Press, 2000). For an analysis of these compilations and the Polity data, see Gerardo L. Munck and Jay Verkuilen, "Conceptualizing and Measuring Democracy: Evaluating Alternative Indices," *Comparative Political Studies*, Vol. 35, No. 1 (February 2002), pp. 5–34.

9.   Gurr, Jaggers, and Moore, *Polity II*, pp. 36–39.

these two measures provides a summary measure of regime type ($Reg =$ $Democ - Autoc$) with values ranging from -10 to 10. Keith Jaggers and Gurr define "coherent" democracies as states where $Reg > 6$. Here there is regular, orderly competition for power in the domestic arena involving stable groups, leaders are chosen through competitive elections, the office of chief executive is in principle open to all politically active citizens, and the chief executive is accountable to institutions such as a legislature or a ruling party and depends on the support of these institutions to govern. Jaggers and Gurr define "coherent" autocracies as states where $Reg < -6$, a situation that arises when political participation is restricted and opposition to the ruling regime is suppressed, leaders are selected through hereditary succession or are designated, and the chief executive is subject to few checks. All remaining states (that is, those where $-7 < Reg < 7$) are coded as incoherent.[10] This coding scheme corresponds fairly closely to our complete regime taxonomy (complete democracy, anocracy, complete autocracy).

Jaggers and Gurr's summary measure—which we refer to as the composite index—does a good job of capturing the facets of a state's regime type that we emphasized in Chapter 3. In addition to this index, however, we are also interested in isolating the effects of democratization occurring along some of the specific institutional dimensions that make it up. Particularly important are the competitiveness of political participation, the openness of executive recruitment, and the extent of constraints on the chief executive.

We emphasize these factors and analyze them separately for a number of reasons. First, each is stressed in our argument, but some of them have disproportionately little influence on the value of Jaggers and Gurr's composite index.[11] Second, these factors are not closely related. On average, the correlation between any two of them for a given type of regime change (that is, a complete democratic transition, an incomplete democratic transition, a complete autocratic transition, or an incomplete autocratic transition) is quite modest, indicating that they are not tapping the same institutional characteristics.[12] We will return to this issue shortly. Third, we analyze these factors separately to maintain consis-

10.   Jaggers and Gurr, "Tracking Democracy's Third Wave with the Polity III Data."

11.   Kristian S. Gleditsch and Michael D. Ward, "Double Take: A Re-examination of Democracy and Autocracy in Modern Politics," *Journal of Conflict Resolution*, Vol. 41, No. 3 (June 1997), pp. 361–383.

12.   Edward D. Mansfield and Jack Snyder, "Incomplete Democratization and the Outbreak of Military Disputes," *International Studies Quarterly*, Vol. 46, No. 4 (December 2002), pp. 529–549.

tency with prior research on the relationship between democratization and war.[13] Finally, other than these three factors, the remaining variables that make up *Reg* are coded in a way that makes distinguishing between democracies and autocracies quite difficult.

We assess a state's regime type using specific coding rules for each of the three institutional factors: competitiveness of political participation, openness of executive recruitment, and extent of constraints on the chief executive.

We measure the competitiveness of political participation using the Polity III data set's five-point scale. We code as *autocratic* those states characterized by what Gurr and his colleagues refer to as "suppressed competition," a category that includes totalitarian dictatorships, despotic monarchies, and military dictatorships in which no significant political activity is allowed outside of the ruling regime.[14]

We code as *democratic* the states in which they identify "competitive competition."[15] In such states, competitive political groupings (usually political parties) are stable and enduring, and their competition rarely leads to violence or widespread disruption.

We code as *anocratic* those states falling into any of the three intermediate Polity categories of competitiveness of political participation: restricted/transitional, factional, or transitional competition.

Gurr and his colleagues claim that "transitions to Competitive [i.e., full democracy] are not complete until a national election is held on a fully competitive basis."[16] Based on this variable, distinguishing among autocracies, anocracies, and democracies is fairly straightforward. Since these regime types are characterized by qualitatively different kinds and degrees of political competition, transitions in a democratic direction from one type to another require substantial domestic adjustments. Such domestic change may stimulate turbulence in foreign policy. In this sense, the Polity classifications accurately capture the conceptual underpinnings

---

13.   Edward D. Mansfield and Jack Snyder, "Democratization and the Danger of War," *International Security*, Vol. 20, No. 1 (Summer 1995), pp. 5–38; Mansfield and Snyder, "Democratization and War," *Foreign Affairs*, Vol. 74, No. 3 (May/June 1995), pp. 79–97; Mansfield and Snyder, "Incomplete Democratization and the Outbreak of Military Disputes"; William R. Thompson and Richard M. Tucker, "A Tale of Two Democratic Peace Critiques: The Hypothesized Bellicosity of Democratic Dyads and New Democratizing States," *Journal of Conflict Resolution*, Vol. 41, No. 3 (June 1997), pp. 428–451; and Ward and Gleditsch, "Democratizing for Peace."

14.   Gurr, Jaggers, and Moore, *Polity II*, p. 18.

15.   Ibid., p. 19.

16.   Ibid., p. 19.

of our argument. Thus, our statistical tests based on the competitiveness of political participation bear especially heavily on the merits of our argument.

We measure the openness of executive recruitment using a five-point scale in the Polity III data set. We code as *autocratic* those regimes identified in the data set as having hereditary absolute rulers or rulers who seized power by force.

We code as *anocratic* those regimes with dual executives, in which a hereditary ruler shares authority with an appointed or elected governing minister.

We code as *democratic* those regimes that Gurr and his colleagues classify as having an open system of executive recruitment, whether the executive is popularly elected or rather is selected through some other regularized process.

There are, however, some discrepancies between the scheme Gurr and his colleagues use to code the openness of executive recruitment and our concept of openness. In addition to multiparty regimes, Gurr and his colleagues assign the highest level of openness to some authoritarian systems, such as single-party regimes in which "all the politically active population has an opportunity, in principle, to attain the position [of chief executive] through a regularized process."[17] Consequently, Gurr codes Victorian Britain's dual executive system as anocratic based on this measure, while coding the Soviet Union in the post-Stalin era as an open system. There are other reasons to suspect that patterns of democratization based on Gurr's measure of the openness of executive recruitment will differ in important ways from patterns based on our other measures of regime type, since the procedure for selecting a chief executive is often democratized, at least in theory, well before the other institutional features analyzed here. Our analysis later in this chapter bears out this assessment.

On balance, however, there is no reason to suspect that the underlying characteristics of this variable will bias the results in favor of our hypothesis.[18] For instance, to assess the robustness of our findings, we ran the tests conducted in Chapters 5 and 6 both with and without the communist countries (coded by Gurr et al. as "open") in the sample. The results, as we discuss in these chapters, are quite similar.

---

17. Ibid., p. 11.

18. In fact, the results of one of our earlier studies indicate that this variable may be coded in a way that biases it against our argument about incomplete democratic transitions. See Mansfield and Snyder, "Incomplete Democratization and the Outbreak of Military Disputes."

We measure institutional constraints on the chief executive using a seven-point scale in the Polity III data set. We classify regimes as *autocratic* if the chief executive has unlimited authority, or if the institutional constraints on this individual are less than "slight to moderate."[19]

We classify regimes as *democratic* if "accountability groups [such as legislatures] have effective authority equal to or greater than the executive in most areas of activity" or if the constraints on the executive are more than "substantial," based on the Polity scale.[20] Substantial constraints exist, even where the executive has more effective authority than the legislature, if the legislature can block appointments, funds, or bills proposed by the executive.

We classify as *anocratic* those regimes in which executive constraints are more than "slight" but less than "substantial."

Separately analyzing the effects of the competitiveness of political participation, the openness of executive recruitment, and executive constraints facilitates focused tests of the specific institutional features that are most pertinent to our theory and helps us assess the robustness of the results that are based on the composite index of regime type. These three component indices also provide conceptually clearer divisions between autocracy and anocracy, and between anocracy and democracy, than the composite index.

Although the composite index has been widely employed in studies of the links between regime type and war, it has various limitations. For instance, Jaggers and Gurr offer little theoretical justification for how the various components are aggregated to construct the composite index.[21] Similarly, they provide little rationale for the particular values of *Reg* that they propose to distinguish democracies, anocracies, and autocracies.[22] Whereas the thresholds for regime change as measured by the three component indices correspond closely to the logic of our theory, the thresholds for regime change as measured by the composite index are, conceptually, more arbitrary. Moreover, as the composite index approaches the value demarcating one regime type from another (if, for example, this value is −7, which corresponds to an autocracy but is very close to the lowest value corresponding to an anocracy), a relatively small change in any institutional factor making it up can lead this index to cross the threshold from one type of regime to another.

---

19. Gurr, Jaggers, and Moore, *Polity II*, pp. 14–16.

20. Ibid., p. 16.

21. Munck and Verkuilen, "Conceptualizing and Measuring Democracy."

22. Jaggers and Gurr, "Tracking Democracy's Third Wave with the Polity III Data."

One way to insure that such changes do not have a significant bearing on our results is by varying the values of *Reg* that distinguish between regime types. We have found that setting the thresholds for democracy and autocracy at 5 and −5 and then at 4 and −4, rather than at 6 and −6, produces only modest differences in the following results. Another approach, however, is to compare our findings based on the composite index to those based on the three component indices, since each of the latter indices distinguishes between regime types with greater validity than the composite index, in terms of the logic of our theory.[23]

The sample analyzed throughout this book includes all states coded as members of the interstate system by the Correlates of War (COW) Project during the period from 1816 to 1992.[24] These are the years where we are able to obtain data on regime change, institutional strength, and war. For each measure of regime type (the composite index and the three component indices), we measure democratization over five-year intervals. More specifically, we code each state, i, as democratic, autocratic, or anocratic in every year, t-1. (War, as we explain below, is measured in year t.[25]) We then measure i's regime type in year t-6. Democratization is defined as any fundamental transition in a democratic direction between t-6 and t-1. Three types of regime change constitute a democratic transition: from an autocracy to a democracy, from an autocracy to an anocracy, or from an anocracy to a democracy.

To examine whether the effects of democratization on war depend on the coherence of a country's democratic institutions during and soon after a shift toward democracy, we define two variables. The first, *Complete Demtransition$_i$*, equals 1 if state i changes from either an autocracy or an anocracy to a coherent democracy during the five-year period from t-6 to t-1, and 0 otherwise. The second, *Incomplete Demtransition$_i$*, equals 1 if i

23. Munck and Verkuilen, "Conceptualizing and Measuring Democracy," p. 25.

24. Melvin Small and J. David Singer, *Resort to Arms: International and Civil Wars, 1816–1980* (Beverly Hills, Calif.: Sage, 1982); and Singer and Small, *Correlates of War Project: International and Civil War Data, 1816–1992*, Inter-University Consortium for Political and Social Research Study No. 9905 (1994).

25. Lagging the effects of regime change on war by one year reduces the possibility of simultaneity bias. War's onset, for example, may lead participants to behave in a more autocratic manner or to centralize national authority to prosecute the conflict more effectively. See Arthur Stein and Bruce M. Russett, "Evaluating War: Outcomes and Consequences," in Ted Robert Gurr, ed., *Handbook of Political Conflict: Theory and Research* (New York: Free Press, 1980), pp. 399–422; Ted Robert Gurr, "War, Revolution, and the Growth of the Coercive State," *Comparative Political Studies*, Vol. 21, No. 1 (1988), pp. 45–65; and Edward D. Mansfield and Jack Snyder, "The Effects of Democratization on War," *International Security*, Vol. 20, No. 4 (Spring 1996), pp. 196–207.

changes from an autocracy to an anocracy during this period, and 0 otherwise.

Evaluating democratic transitions over five-year periods has a number of theoretical and methodological advantages. It may take time for the political dynamics touched off by democratization to stimulate the logrolled coalitions and nationalist ideologies that, for reasons we explained in Chapter 3, heighten the likelihood of war. Furthermore, in various cases, the data needed to code a state's regime type are missing for years immediately surrounding a regime change, and thus when very short intervals are analyzed, some instances of democratization are omitted from the sample. This problem is ameliorated by considering the effects of transitions occurring over five-year periods. Five-year periods are not, however, so long that events at the beginning of an interval would be unlikely to influence foreign policy decisions at the interval's end.

It should also be noted that in certain instances (for example, Argentina just before the Falklands War), the Polity data indicate that a transition to a mixed regime occurred before elections were held, based on such developments as increased press freedom and the legalization of political parties prior to elections.[26] Some of these regime changes may not correspond to how other studies have defined democratization. Nonetheless, they are valid for our purposes, insofar as they reflect the causal mechanisms highlighted in our theory, such as the use of nationalist rhetoric to cement a domestic coalition, or gambling for elite resurrection in the face of popular opposition. Further, some cases where shifts from autocracy to a mixed regime based on the Polity coding scheme may not reflect the mechanisms of our theory—in particular, instances involving communist countries and those associated with involvement in world wars—present a challenge for categorization in our coding scheme. We check to make sure that the statistical findings presented in the following two chapters are robust with respect to whether or not we include such cases.

A number of studies have argued that all regime transitions, not just those in a democratic direction, may heighten the likelihood of international conflict.[27] Consequently, we also assess whether transitions toward autocracy foster war. As in our analysis of democratization, we distinguish between autocratic transitions that yield coherent autocracies and those that produce anocracies. This should help indicate whether the ob-

---

26. On the links between democratization and the Falklands War, see Chapter 7.

27. Enterline, "Driving While Democratizing"; Mansfield and Snyder, "Democratization and the Danger of War"; and Ward and Gleditsch, "Democratizing for Peace."

served effect of *Incomplete Demtransition*$_i$ reflects a general tendency for transitions generating an anocracy to promote war, or whether transitions from autocracy to anocracy have a distinct effect. We do not expect a shift toward autocracy to increase the prospects of war. When popular participation in politics is curtailed, elites have less to gain from using nationalist rhetoric to maintain their rule and are less likely to become trapped in nationalist bidding wars. Our analysis of autocratization depends on two variables. First, *Complete Auttransition*$_i$ equals 1 if state i undergoes a transition from either democracy or anocracy to autocracy during the period from t-6 to t-1, and 0 otherwise. Second, *Incomplete Auttransition*$_i$ equals 1 if i changes from a democracy to an anocracy during that period, and 0 otherwise.

THE DISTRIBUTION OF DEMOCRATIZATION

It is useful to get a sense of how frequently democratic transitions have occurred, whether the incidence of democratization has varied over time, and whether patterns of democratization depend on which measure of regime type is analyzed.

Based on our sample, democratization has been a rare event, and incomplete democratic transitions have tended to occur more frequently than complete democratic shifts. To begin addressing these issues, we count the number of discrete instances of democratization in our sample. As shown in Table 4.1, there have been 90 instances in which a country experienced an incomplete democratic transition based on the composite index, 100 instances based on the competitiveness of political participation, 104 cases based on the constraints on the chief executive, and just 22 cases based on the openness of executive recruitment. Some of these cases include countries that made more than one such transition during the nineteenth and twentieth centuries. Nonetheless, sixty countries underwent incomplete democratization at least once during the nineteenth and twentieth centuries by each of the first three measures. The 22 instances of incomplete democratization found when we focus on the openness of executive recruitment involve eighteen countries.

In general, transitions culminating in a coherent democracy have been rarer events than those producing an anocracy. When counting is based on the composite index, the competitiveness of political participation, or the constraints on the chief executive, complete democratization has taken place only about half as often as incomplete democratization, and it has occurred in far fewer countries. This pattern is reversed when the measure is the openness of executive recruitment: complete democratization has occurred more than three times as frequently as incomplete democratization, and it has involved twice as many countries.

Table 4.1. The Frequency of Democratization, 1816–1992.

	Composite Index	Competitiveness of Participation	Executive Constraints	Openness of Executive Recruitment
		Incomplete Democratization		
Number of transitions	90	100	104	22
Number of countries	64	68	68	18
Number of country-years	290	298	357	90
Mean—overall	.031	.033	.038	.010
Mean—19th century	.022	.020	.040	.019
Mean—20th century	.034	.038	.037	.006
		Complete Democratization		
Number of transitions	50	50	55	73
Number of countries	35	43	32	36
Number of country-years	167	177	168	243
Mean—overall	.016	.020	.018	.026
Mean—19th century	.005	.012	.012	.015
Mean—20th century	.019	.022	.020	.030

As another way to get a sense of the overall frequency of democratization, we analyze country-years of democratization. Recall that regime change is measured between years t-6 and t-1. If a country is coded as autocratic from 1960 to 1965 and as anocratic from 1966 to 1970, for example, it would have undergone a single, discrete episode of incomplete democratization. Yet *Incomplete Demtransition$_i$* would equal 1 in 1971, 1970, 1969, 1968, and 1967, since for each of these years, t, a regime change occurred between t-6 and t-1. As Table 4.1 reports, there have been 357 country-years of incomplete democratization based on the constraints on the chief executive, 298 based on the competitiveness of political participation, 290 based on the composite index, and just 90 based on the openness of executive recruitment. Here again, complete democratization occurs only about 50 to 60 percent as often as incomplete democratization when the first three indices of regime type are analyzed, but almost three times as frequently when the openness of executive recruitment is examined.

The rarity of democratization becomes even more apparent when we consider that the mean number of incomplete democratic transitions per country-year is .010 using the openness of executive recruitment. The corresponding means for the other three measures are much larger in relative terms, but they are still quite small, ranging from .031 to .038. Except for the openness of executive recruitment, the mean number of complete democratic transitions per country-year is even lower than the mean number of incomplete democratic transitions, varying from .016 to .026.

Although democratization has occurred infrequently, there have been noticeable differences in its incidence over time. Figures 4.1, 4.2, 4.3, and 4.4 present the total annual country-years of both incomplete and complete democratization throughout the nineteenth and twentieth centuries, based on the composite index and on each of the three component indices, respectively. Table 4.1 reports the mean number of transitions per country-year for the nineteenth and the twentieth centuries (1816–1992). The results indicate that the tendency for incomplete democratic transitions to occur more frequently than complete democratization does not vary over time. In seven out of eight cases, the mean number of incomplete democratic transitions per year exceeds the mean number of complete transitions in the same century.[28] Furthermore, complete democratic transitions occurred with greater frequency in the twentieth than the nineteenth centuries, regardless of which measure of regime type is analyzed. The nature of the variation over time in cases of incomplete democratization, however, depends greatly on which measure of regime type is used. Based on the composite index and the competitiveness of political participation, incomplete democratic transitions occurred more frequently in the twentieth than in the nineteenth century. In contrast, incomplete democratization based on the openness of executive recruitment yields the opposite finding, while there is virtually no difference between the nineteenth century and the twentieth century when the measure is the constraints on the chief executive.

These results reinforce our earlier point that key differences exist between the measures of regime type used in this book. So too does the fact

---

28. The exception is when the openness of executive recruitment is used to measure democratization in the twentieth century.

Figure 4.1. Frequency of Democratic Transitions, Incomplete and Complete, Based on the Composite Index, 1816–1992.

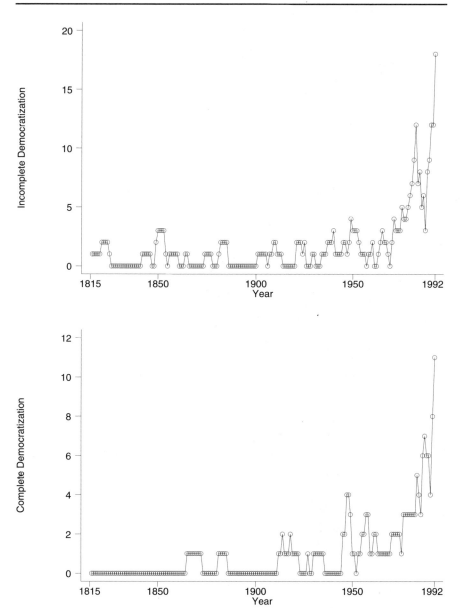

Figure 4.2. Frequency of Democratic Transitions, Incomplete and Complete, Based on Competitiveness of Political Participation, 1816–1992.

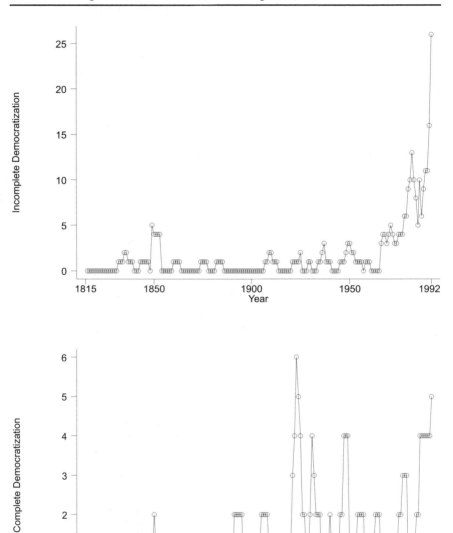

Figure 4.3. Frequency of Democratic Transitions, Incomplete and Complete, Based on Constraints on the Chief Executive, 1816–1992.

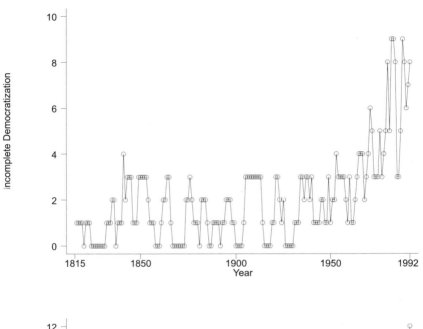

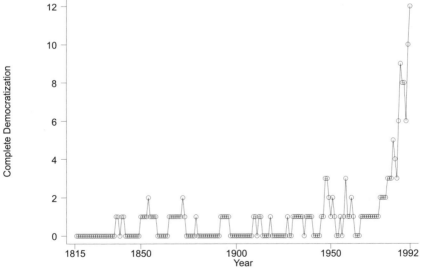

Figure 4.4. Frequency of Democratic Transitions, Incomplete and Complete, Based on Openness of Executive Recruitment, 1816–1992.

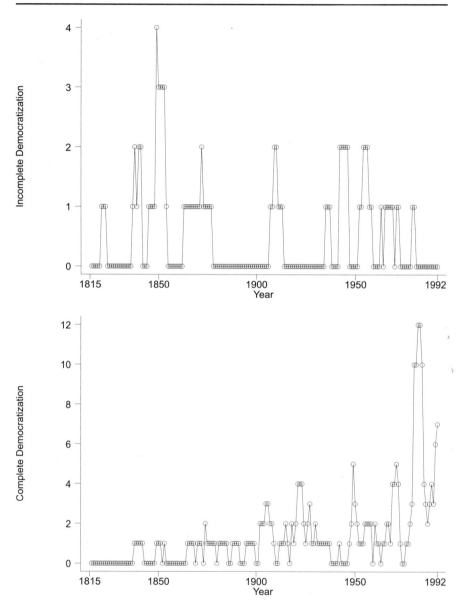

that transitions rarely occur in unison across the three component indices. Taken together, there are 590 country-years where an incomplete democratic transition took place (from year t-6 to t-1) based on at least one of these three indices.[29] Incomplete democratization took place by all three indicators of regime change in only 3 percent of these cases, whereas it occurred by just one of these indicators 77 percent of the time. Similarly, there are 488 country-years where a complete democratic transition occurred based on at least one of the three component measures of regime type, but in only 1 percent of these country-years did such a transition occur based on all three indicators. In 80 percent of these instances, complete democratization is signaled by only a single institutional indicator. The competitiveness of political participation, the openness of executive recruitment, and the constraints on the chief executive clearly do not change in lockstep. Since our argument emphasizes each of these factors, it is important to consider each of them separately in our empirical analysis.

Measuring the Strength of Domestic Institutions

Our theory predicts that the effects of democratization on war will be stronger and more pronounced in countries having less institutional strength and centralization. As we explained in Chapter 3, incomplete democratization occurring in a context of weak governmental institutions undermines the state's ability to manage elite interest groups and newly politicized mass groups. Political institutions are unable to resolve or suppress the conflicts of interest stemming from growing demands for political participation, thereby creating various dynamics that encourage belligerence abroad. Incomplete democratization is not, of course, always accompanied by institutional weakness. In some instances, autocracies leave behind a useable bureaucratic state that can be adapted to the new anocratic regime, helping to regulate the effects of incomplete democratization and dampen its adverse consequences for foreign policy.

For purposes of our theory, the most important institutions are administrative, such as a non-corrupt bureaucracy and a police force that follows the law, and those that regulate political competition, such as impartial election commissions, well-organized political parties, competent legislatures, and professional news media. Direct measures of these institutional features are scarce. Almost none cover the broad range of countries during the past two centuries that we analyze in our tests. However,

---

29. In this analysis, we exclude country-years where data are missing for any of these three measures of regime change.

Gurr and his colleagues have created a measure that meets our needs and that is used throughout this book. Their measure, *DomConcentration$_i$*, is an 11-point index—ranging from 0 to 10—of the degree to which domestic authority is concentrated in state *i*'s central government in year *t-1*. The measure rises in countries where political participation is regulated or restricted in accordance with institutionalized procedures, executive recruitment is regulated, the chief executive is either designated in accordance with institutionalized procedures or chosen via competitive elections, there are few constraints on the chief executive's authority, this executive does not depend on some group (like a junta or cabinet) for authority, and authority is concentrated in the central government with local and regional governments having little independent authority.[30] Thus, this index measures several institutional features that, we argue, affect a regime's ability to manage the foreign-policy consequences of rising political participation.

The value of *DomConcentration$_i$* increases if a regime has more clearly established rules regulating political competition and if it enjoys a more centralized grip on the reins of domestic power. Under these conditions, the regime should be better able to manage the rivalry of elite factions and minimize the adverse consequences of interest-group logrolling. For example, the regulation of political participation through an institutionalized process helps to ensure that parochial interest groups do not dominate domestic politics. The absence of significant constraints on the chief executive helps this individual to manage rivalries between competing interest groups and to head off potentially dangerous logrolling between such groups. That the executive's power does not depend on a particular group allows this individual to avoid becoming enmeshed in interest-group politics and parochial stances on foreign policy. Moreover, with the stronger institutional resources of a more centralized and better regulated state at its disposal, the regime is likely to have less reason to rely on reckless nationalist appeals to consolidate its authority.

The argument we advanced earlier therefore suggests that stalled democratic transitions are more likely to stimulate involvement in war when states are marked by a low value of *DomConcentration$_i$*. To test this hypothesis, we analyze *DomConcentration$_i$* and its interaction with *Incomplete Demtransition$_i$*. We also analyze the interaction between *DomConcentration$_i$* and *Complete Demtransition$_i$*, *Complete Auttransition$_i$*, and *Incomplete Auttransition$_i$*, respectively, to determine whether the effects of

---

30.　Gurr, Jaggers, and Moore, *Polity II*, pp. 39–40.

other types of regime change depend on the concentration of domestic authority.

As shown in Table 4.2, the distribution of $DomConcentration_i$ is roughly normal, with a mean of 5.7 and a standard deviation of 1.8. Furthermore, maximally dispersed and maximally concentrated polities almost never appear in our data set: $DomConcentration_i$ equals 0 in only 0.11 percent of the country-years analyzed here, and never equals 10. Similarly (but not shown in the table), the average level of concentration has been quite stable over time: in the nineteenth century, its mean was 6.0, while in the twentieth century, its mean dipped only slightly to 5.6.

In addition to describing some general patterns in the concentration of domestic authority, it is useful to analyze this variable's relationship to democratization. Our argument is that they are conceptually distinct. A preliminary statistical analysis indicates that these factors are empirically distinct as well. For each measure of regime type analyzed in this book, the bivariate correlation between $DomConcentration_i$, on the one hand, and both $Complete\ Demtransition_i$ and $Incomplete\ Demtransition_i$, on the other, rarely exceeds .10, and usually is much lower.

Table 4.3 shows that the mean value of domestic concentration for countries undergoing an incomplete democratic transition is very similar to the mean for the sample as a whole, regardless of which measure of regime type is analyzed. The mean value for states engaged in a complete democratic transition tends to be somewhat lower than the mean for the entire data set. However, the extent of this tendency depends on which index of regime type is examined. For example, average concentration is slightly higher for states making a complete democratic transition than for the sample as a whole as measured by the competitiveness of political participation, whereas it is almost a full standard deviation less than the mean for the entire sample when we focus on the constraints on the chief executive. In sum, then, there is no systematic evidence that the level of concentration of authority is much lower for democratizing countries than for other states.

Still another issue that merits attention is whether, regardless of whether they have undergone a regime change, anocratic countries are marked by lower levels of concentration than other states. There is reason to expect this since, as Gurr notes, an "essential quality of the 'anocratic polity' is its relative lack of political power and institutionalization."[31] We therefore compute the mean level of domestic concentration for all states

31. Ted Robert Gurr, "Persistence and Change in Political Systems, 1800–1971," *American Political Science Review,* Vol. 68, No. 4 (December 1974), p. 1487.

Table 4.2. The Distribution of Domestic Concentration of Authority, 1816–1992.

Level of Concentration	Frequency (country-years)	Percentage
0	11	0.11%
1	78	0.77%
2	247	2.44%
3	557	5.51%
4	1,679	16.62%
5	1,974	19.53%
6	2,457	24.31%
7	1,191	11.79%
8	1,243	12.30%
9	668	6.61%
10	0	0.00%
Total	10,105	100.00%

Mean level = 5.7
Standard deviation = 1.8

Table 4.3. Mean Level of Domestic Concentration of Authority for Democratizing Countries and Anocracies, 1816–1992.

	Composite Index	Competitiveness of Participation	Executive Constraints	Openness of Executive Recruitment
Incomplete Democratization*	5.2	5.5	5.2	5.6
Complete Democratization*	4.5	5.8	4.3	5.1
Anocracy**	5.0	5.0	4.9	5.1

* Incomplete Democratization and Complete Democratization are measured from year t-6 to year t-1.
** Anocracy is measured in year t-1.

that are anocracies in a given year. As shown in the final row of Table 4.3, however, mean is only .6 to .8 less (depending on which measure of regime type is analyzed) than the overall sample mean of 5.7, providing no indication that concentration is markedly lower for anocracies than for other countries.

Measuring War

Like most quantitative studies of war, we rely on the COW Project's definition of war and its data on war.[32] The COW Project defines two types of external wars, which are conflicts in which a state (or group of states) actively fights a foreign enemy. International wars are hostilities between members of the interstate system that generate at least one thousand battle fatalities. A state that suffers at least one hundred fatalities or sends at least one thousand troops into combat is considered a participant. Extra-systemic wars are imperial or colonial actions in which a nation-state engages in military conflict against a non-state actor, leading to at least one thousand battle deaths. A state is not considered a participant in such wars unless it (together with any allies) sustains at least one thousand deaths in battle during each year of the conflict. Since we argue that democratization has an effect on the onset of external war, regardless of whether a democratizing state's opponent is also sovereign, we consider all external wars—interstate and extra-systemic combined—in the monadic tests of our argument conducted in Chapter 5.[33] As we explain later, however, the dyadic tests conducted in Chapter 6 address relations within pairs of countries. Consequently, we focus just on interstate wars in that analysis. In both chapters, we are concerned with explaining the outbreak of war for each state (Chapter 5) or pair of states (Chapter 6) in each year, t, during the nineteenth and twentieth centuries.

Throughout the period covered in this book (1816–1992), there have been 79 interstate wars and 108 extra-systemic wars, involving a total of 88 different countries. In our data set, there have been 398 country-years in which an external war began and 262 country-years in which an interstate war broke out. The total annual incidence of the onset of external war for the countries included in our analysis is shown in Figure 4.5.

Fortunately, war is a relatively rare event. The mean number of external wars beginning per country-year is only .037; it was roughly twice

---

32. Small and Singer, *Resort to Arms;* and Singer and Small, *Correlates of War Project.*

33. The results based on interstate wars are very similar to those based on all external wars, presented in Chapter 5.

Figure 4.5. Number of Countries Experiencing the Outbreak of War, by Year, 1816–1992.

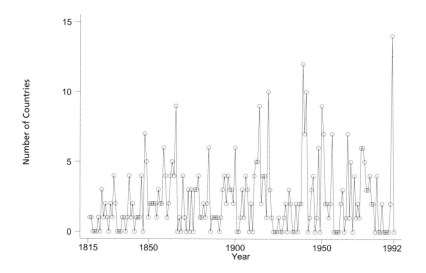

as large in the nineteenth century (.061) as in the twentieth century (.030). This difference stems almost solely from the greater number of imperial and colonial wars waged during the earlier era, since the mean number of interstate wars breaking out does not vary much between these centuries.[34]

Our argument centers on the effect of democratization on the onset of war, but various studies have addressed the influence of democratic transitions on a much wider array of external conflicts. Many of them have analyzed militarized interstate disputes (MIDs), a broad class of conflicts ranging in intensity from wars to disputes that involve threats to use force but no actual fatalities.[35] Disputes that do not escalate to war constitute the vast majority of MIDs.[36] States' propensity to engage in low-level

34. For a more extensive analysis of the distribution of wars over time, see Singer and Small, *Resort to Arms;* and Edward D. Mansfield, *Power, Trade, and War* (Princeton: Princeton University Press, 1994), especially chap. 2.

35. See, for example, Oneal and Russett, "The Classical Liberals Were Right"; and Enterline, "Driving While Democratizing."

36. For descriptions of the MIDs data, see Charles S. Gochman and Zeev Maoz, "Militarized Interstate Disputes, 1816–1976: Procedures, Patterns, and Insights," *Journal of Conflict Resolution*, Vol. 28, No. 4 (December 1984), pp. 585–616; and Daniel M.

disputes cannot be directly extrapolated from their propensity to fight wars. Even mature democracies, which have not fought wars against each other, have engaged each other in various MIDs.[37] Since our argument emphasizes the links between democratization and war, we focus on explaining wars (not MIDs) in the following analysis. It is important to recognize, however, that a number of studies have found that democratization also promotes MIDs as well as other aspects of conflict short of war.[38]

In addition, several scholars have argued that tests of the relationship between democratization and war should address whether it is the states experiencing a democratic transition that tend to initiate the hostilities.[39] Indeed, if democratizing states were almost always the targets of aggression and virtually never the instigators, then one might conclude that democratization promotes war because it undermines a country's political-military capacity, rather than because it increases nationalism or belligerence. To address this concern, we examine the relationship between democratization and the initiation of war in Chapter 5. However, because of conceptual ambiguities in measuring initiation, our analysis of war initiation should be viewed as a supplement to rather than a substitute for our analysis of the links between democratic transitions and the outbreak of war.

In the COW data set, the initiator of each war is coded based on "whose battalions made the first attack in strength on their opponents' armies or territories." The architects of this data set stress that "we are not labeling any government the 'aggressor' in these wars, or trying to reach a firm data-based conclusion as to which participant 'caused' the war,

---

Jones, Stuart A. Bremer, and J. David Singer, "Militarized Interstate Disputes, 1816–1992: Rationale, Coding Rules, and Empirical Patterns," *Conflict Management and Peace Science*, Vol. 15, No. 2 (1996), pp. 163–213.

37. Dixon, "Democracy and the Peaceful Settlement of International Conflict"; and Joanne Gowa, *Ballots and Bullets: The Elusive Democratic Peace* (Princeton: Princeton University Press, 1999).

38. See, for example, Christopher Gelpi and Joseph Grieco, "Attracting Trouble: Democracy, Leadership Tenure, and the Targeting of Militarized Challenges, 1918–1992," *Journal of Conflict Resolution*, Vol. 45, No. 6 (December 2001), pp. 794–815; Mansfield and Snyder, "Incomplete Democratization and the Outbreak of Military Disputes"; and Patricia A. Weitsman and George E. Shambaugh, "International Systems, Domestic Structures, and Risk," *Journal of Peace Research*, Vol. 39, No. 3 (May 2002), pp. 289–312. See also Lars-Erik Cederman, "Back to Kant: Reinterpreting the Democratic Peace as a Macrohistorical Learning Process," *American Political Science Review*, Vol. 95, No. 1 (March 2001), p. 27.

39. See, for example, Enterline, "Driving While Democratizing," p. 185.

whether by action, threat, or provocation."[40] Thus, wars may be launched by status-quo states in an effort to weaken an increasingly belligerent rival who may, therefore, reasonably be seen as the real instigator of the war. For example, neighboring governments frequently fear states undergoing revolutionary transformations—including those in the early stages of democratization—and respond by striking out at them militarily.[41] In the same vein, a nationalistic democratizing state may become a lightning rod for attacks because its neighbors expect its temporary weakness to be followed by rising strength and belligerence. If there are cases in which countries experiencing a democratic transition are targets of attack, this may support our theory just as well as instances in which such countries initiate wars. For that reason, we consider patterns of war involvement—and not simply patterns of war initiation—when testing our argument.

Having explained the key variables in our study, in the next chapter we conduct a set of statistical analyses that address whether democratization actually promotes belligerence.

40. Small and Singer, *Resort to Arms*, p. 194.

41. Stephen M. Walt, *Revolution and War* (Ithaca, N.Y.: Cornell University Press, 1996).

Chapter 5

Democratization and War: Statistical Findings

In this chapter, we analyze the relationship between democratization and war using the data and measures described in Chapter 4. Consistent with our argument, we find that transitions from an autocratic regime to a partly democratic regime are a potent impetus to war when governmental institutions, including those regulating political participation, are especially weak. In contrast, transitions that quickly culminate in a fully coherent democracy are much less perilous. Further, our results refute the view that transitional democracies are simply inviting targets of attack due to their temporary weakness: in fact, they tend to be the initiators of war. We also refute the view that any regime change is likely to precipitate the outbreak of war by showing that incomplete democratization is significantly more likely to generate hostilities than any form of autocratization. Finally, by showing that war has very little bearing on the occurrence of democratic transitions and on whether such transitions yield coherent democratic institutions, we exclude the possibility that the effect of democratization on war actually reflects the influence of war on democratization.

The Research Design

As we discussed in Chapter 4, the sample used in our statistical analysis includes all states coded as members of the interstate system during the nineteenth and twentieth centuries by the Correlates of War (COW) Project.[1] Since our argument pertains to the effects of democratization on the

---

1. See Melvin Small and J. David Singer, *Resort to Arms: International and Civil Wars, 1816–1980* (Beverly Hills, Calif.: Sage, 1982); and Singer and Small, *Correlates of War*

onset of external war, regardless of whether a democratizing state's opponent is also sovereign, we analyze all external wars identified by the
COW Project.[2] These include, in addition to wars between sovereign
states, wars between a state and a non-state actor, such as imperial and
colonial wars. For each year, t, we assess whether every state, i, that was a
member of the interstate system became involved in an external war. Various studies have addressed the effects of democratic transitions on the
subset of external wars that comprises interstate wars.[3] It should be noted
that the results for interstate wars are very similar to those presented below. We specifically address interstate wars later in this chapter and in
Chapter 6.

Recall that each state's regime type is measured using four different
indices: the composite index, the competitiveness of political participation, the openness of executive recruitment, and the extent of the constraints placed on the chief executive. For each index, we measure
democratization over five-year periods. Each state, i, is coded as democratic, autocratic, or anocratic in year t-6 and then again in year t-1, using
the coding rules laid out in Chapter 4. Democratization occurs if country
i's regime type changes from an autocracy to either a democracy or an
anocracy, or from an anocracy to a democracy, between t-6 and t-1. To address whether incomplete democratization is a more potent impetus to
war than transitions culminating in coherent democratic institutions, we
define two dummy variables. *Complete Demtransition$_i$* indicates whether
state i undergoes a transition from either an autocracy or an anocracy

---

Project: International and Civil War Data, 1816–1992, Inter-University Consortium for
Political and Social Research No. 9905 (1994).

2. A recent study has updated and amended the COW Project's data on external
wars. See Meredith Reid Sarkees, "The Correlates of War Data on War: An Update to
1997," *Conflict Management and Peace Science,* Vol. 18, No. 1 (2000), pp. 123–144. Our results are very similar regardless of whether we use Singer and Small's original COW
data or Sarkees's updated data. However, we focus on Singer and Small's data since
they are used in most quantitative studies of war.

3. See Edward D. Mansfield and Jack Snyder, "Democratization and the Danger of
War," *International Security,* Vol. 20, No. 1 (Summer 1995), pp. 5–38; Mansfield and
Snyder, "The Effects of Democratization on War," *International Security,* Vol. 20, No. 4
(Spring 1996), pp. 196–207; William R. Thompson and Richard M. Tucker, "A Tale of
Two Democratic Peace Critiques: The Hypothesized Bellicosity of Democratic Dyads
and New Democratizing States," *Journal of Conflict Resolution,* Vol. 41, No. 3 (June
1997), pp. 428–441; Mansfield and Snyder, "A Reply to Thompson and Tucker," *Journal
of Conflict Resolution,* Vol. 41, No. 3 (June 1997), pp. 457–461; and D. Scott Bennett and
Allan C. Stam, *The Behavioral Origins of War* (Ann Arbor: University of Michigan Press,
2003).

to a coherent democracy; *Incomplete Demtransition$_i$* indicates whether *i* changes from an autocracy to an anocracy.

In Chapter 3, we argued that the impact of democratization on war should be stronger and more pronounced in countries marked by little institutional strength and centralization. In Chapter 4, we discussed *DomConcentration$_i$*, which is a measure of these institutional factors. More specifically, it is an 11-point index, ranging from 0 to 10, of the degree to which domestic authority is concentrated in state *i*'s government in year *t*-1. To test our argument that stalled democratic transitions are likely to stimulate involvement in war when states have weak domestic institutions, we include *DomConcentration$_i$* and its interaction with *Incomplete Demtransition$_i$*. Since the effects of complete democratization also might depend on domestic concentration, we analyze *Complete Demtransition$_i$* × *DomConcentration$_i$* as well.

Our argument implies that the coefficient of *Incomplete Demtransition$_i$* should be positive and the coefficient of *Incomplete Demtransition$_i$* × *DomConcentration$_i$* should be negative. Taken by itself, the estimate of *Incomplete Demtransition$_i$* represents the effect of incomplete democratization on the outbreak of war when *DomConcentration$_i$* equals 0. We expect the likelihood of war to be greatest under these conditions. The coefficient of *Incomplete Demtransition$_i$* × *DomConcentration$_i$* reflects the change in the effect of incomplete democratization on the likelihood of war stemming from a one-unit change in domestic concentration. We expect this coefficient to be negative because as the extent of institutional strength and centralization rises, yielding an increase in the value of *DomConcentration$_i$*, the conflict-promoting effects of an incomplete democratic transition should be dampened.[4]

We also assess whether transitions toward autocracy precipitate war, in order to determine whether any observed effects of democratization might actually stem from a more general tendency whereby regime change of any type stimulates conflict. *Complete Auttransition$_i$* indicates whether state *i* began its transition to autocracy as either a democracy or an anocracy, and *Incomplete Auttransition$_i$* indicates whether *i* changes from a democracy to an anocracy. Finally, we include the interactions be-

---

4. On the interpretation of interaction terms, see Robert J. Friedrich, "In Defense of Multiplicative Terms in Multiple Regression Equations," *American Journal of Political Science,* Vol. 26, No. 4 (November 1982), pp. 797–833; and William H. Greene, *Econometric Analysis,* 2d ed. (Englewood Cliffs, N.J.: Prentice Hall, 1993), p. 239. For a discussion of interaction terms in models, like ours, with a dichotomous dependent variable, see James Jaccard, *Interaction Effects in Logistic Regression* (Thousand Oaks, Calif.: Sage, 2001).

tween *DomConcentration$_i$* and each of these variables to assess whether any influence of autocratization on war depends on the concentration of domestic authority.

The Statistical Model

Initially, we estimate the following model for the period from 1816–1992, the years (*t*) that the data sets used to measure regime type and war have in common.[5]

(5.1) $War_i = \beta_0 + \beta_1$ *Complete Demtransition$_i$* + β_2*Incomplete Demtransition$_i$* + β_3*Complete Auttransition$_i$* + β_4*Incomplete Auttransition$_i$* + β_5*DomConcentration$_i$* + β_6(*Complete Demtransition$_i$* × *DomConcentration$_i$*) + β_7(*Incomplete Demtransition$_i$* × *DomConcentration$_i$*) + β_8(*Complete Auttransition$_i$* × *DomConcentration$_i$*) + β_9(*Incomplete Auttransition$_i$* × *DomConcentration$_i$*) + β_{10}*Majpower$_i$* + β_{11}*Civwar$_i$* + β_{12}*Concap* + e_i

The dependent variable is the log of the odds that state *i* experiences the outbreak of an external war in year *t*, where we observe 1 if *i* enters a war in *t* and 0 otherwise. As discussed earlier, *Complete Demtransition$_i$*, *Incomplete Demtransition$_i$*, *Complete Auttransition$_i$*, and *Incomplete Auttransition$_i$* are dummy variables indicating whether *i* engages in a democratic or an autocratic transition between years *t*-6 and *t*-1. *Dom-*

---

5.   The Polity III data set covers the period from 1800 to 1994 and the COW data set covers the period from 1816 to 1992. The years that are common to these compilations are 1816–1992. As mentioned above, for each year, *t*, only those countries listed by the COW Project as members of the interstate system are included in our sample. But for any country listed as a member of the system in *t*, we use all available information on its regime type and changes in this type during the period from *t*-6 to *t*-1, even if it was not a member of the system during all or a part of this interval (including, for example, data prior to 1816). In addition, some countries were formed and others dissolved during the nineteenth and twentieth centuries. There is usually agreement between the Polity III and COW data about the occurrence and date of a state's formation and dissolution, but in four cases a disagreement exists. Gurr, Jaggers, and Moore consider Sardinia and Italy, Prussia and Germany, the Ottoman Empire and Turkey, and Serbia and Yugoslavia to be separate countries, whereas the COW Project views each pair as a single country. Like previous studies on this topic, we code each pair as two distinct polities. See Ted Robert Gurr, Keith Jaggers, and Will H. Moore, *Polity II: Political Structures and Regime Change, 1800–1986*, Inter-University Consortium for Political and Social Research No. 9263 (1989); and Mansfield and Snyder, "Democratization and the Danger of War."

Concentration$_i$ measures the degree to which authority is concentrated in the hands of *i*'s national officials in year *t*-1. Equation 5.1 is estimated separately using the composite index, the competitiveness of political participation, the openness of executive recruitment, and executive constraints to measure *Complete Demtransition$_i$*, *Incomplete Demtransition$_i$*, *Complete Auttransition$_i$*, and *Incomplete Auttransition$_i$* (and their respective interactions with *DomConcentration$_i$*).

In addition, we include three other variables that previous studies have linked to the onset of war. First, *Majpower$_i$* is a dummy variable that equals 1 if state *i* is a major power in year *t*-1 and 0 otherwise. There is evidence that major powers are more likely to become involved in wars than weaker states. Further, various cases in which democratization led to war involved a major power.[6] Including this variable helps to distinguish the tendency for states to enter wars because of their political-military strength from their tendency to do so because of a democratic transition. Second, *Civwar$_i$* is a dummy variable that equals 1 if *i* is involved in a civil war in year *t*-1 and 0 otherwise. Since democratization can promote domestic as well as international violence and some studies have found that internal violence affects the onset of external wars, it is important to control for the effects of civil war.[7]

Third, while our primary focus is on the domestic influences on war, international factors have contributed to the outbreak of hostilities too. The concentration of capabilities (*Concap*) has had a particularly potent effect on international war during the nineteenth and twentieth centuries, and is defined as follows:[8]

---

6. See Stuart A. Bremer, "National Capabilities and War Proneness," in J. David Singer, ed., *The Correlates of War II: Testing Some Realpolitik Models* (New York: Free Press, 1980), pp. 57–82; Edward D. Mansfield and Jack Snyder, "Democratization and War," *Foreign Affairs*, Vol. 74, No. 3 (May/June 1995), pp. 79–97; and Mansfield and Snyder, "Democratization and the Danger of War."

7. See Arthur Stein and Bruce M. Russett, "Evaluating War: Outcomes and Consequences," in Ted Robert Gurr, ed., *Handbook of Political Conflict: Theory and Research* (New York: Free Press, 1980), pp. 399–422; and Jack Snyder, *From Voting to Violence: Democratization and Nationalist Conflict* (New York: Norton, 2000).

8. On the relationship between the concentration of capabilities and war, see J. David Singer, Stuart Bremer, and John Stuckey, "Capability Distribution, Uncertainty, and Major Power Wars, 1820–1965," in Bruce M. Russett, ed., *Peace, War, and Numbers* (Beverly Hills, Calif.: Sage, 1972), pp. 37–74; Edward D. Mansfield, *Power, Trade, and War* (Princeton: Princeton University Press, 1994); and Bennett and Stam, *The Behavioral Origins of War*.

$$(5.2) \quad Concap = \sqrt{\frac{\sum_{i=1}^{N}(S_i^2) - 1/N}{1 - 1/N}}$$

In Equation 5.2, N is the number of major powers in the system in year t-1, and S_i is the proportion of the total capabilities possessed by the major powers in t-1 that major power i controls. As in many previous studies, S_i is an unweighted average of the proportion of major power i's national population, urban population (in cities having more than 20,000 residents), energy consumption, iron and steel production, military personnel, and military expenditures.[9] Since various scholars—particularly realists—claim that the distribution of power in the international system is a central influence on the outbreak of war, it is useful to compare its effect directly with that of democratization. Moreover, such scholars might be concerned that the existence of a highly concentrated system dominated by democratic states could affect both the likelihood of democratization and the prospects that these transitions will promote war. Including the concentration of capabilities helps to address these issues. We use COW Project data to code major powers and civil wars and to measure the concentration of capabilities.[10] Finally, e_i is a stochastic error term.

The parameters in Equation 5.1 are estimated using logistic regression. The tests of statistical significance reported below are based on robust (Huber) standard errors, which correct for any panel heteroskedasticity and account for the grouped nature of our data (by country). In addition, to address any problems of temporal dependence in our model, we follow Nathaniel Beck, Jonathan N. Katz, and Richard Tucker in introducing, for each country in every year, a natural spline function (with three knots) of the number of years that have elapsed since that country last experienced the onset of war.[11] (Note, however, that the estimates of these parameters are not shown in the tables.)

---

9. For the original derivation of this index, see James Lee Ray and J. David Singer, "Measuring the Concentration of Power in the International System," *Sociological Methods and Research*, Vol. 1, No. 1 (1973), pp. 403–437. Data used to measure these variables are taken from J. David Singer and Melvin Small, *National Material Capabilities Dataset*, Inter-University Consortium for Political and Social Research No. 9903 (1993). Where data are missing for a major power, we interpolate between existing values of the variable for this country, if it is possible to do so.

10. See Small and Singer, *Resort to Arms;* Singer and Small, *National Material Capabilities Dataset;* and Singer and Small, *Correlates of War Project.*

11. See Nathaniel Beck and Richard Tucker, "Conflict in Space and Time: Time-Series-Cross-Section Analysis with a Binary Dependent Variable" (paper presented at the annual meeting of the American Political Science Association, San Francisco, Calif., 1996); Nathaniel Beck and Jonathan N. Katz, "The Analysis of Binary Time-

The Statistical Results

The results that are reported in the first columns of Tables 5.1, 5.2, 5.3, and 5.4 (labeled base model) indicate that incomplete democratic transitions—that is, those from autocracy to anocracy—promote the outbreak of war when a state's institutions are weak and fragmented. By contrast, there is only scattered evidence that transitions culminating in a coherent democracy influence war, and there is very little indication that autocratic transitions—from democracy to anocracy, from democracy to autocracy, or from anocracy to autocracy—precipitate hostilities. A list of the cases in our data set where democratization (either complete or incomplete) led to the outbreak of war is presented in the Appendix to this book.

In addition, major powers are more likely to become involved in military conflict than other states: each estimate of $Majpower_i$ is positive and statistically significant. Civil wars, however, have a weaker influence on external wars: the estimate of $Civwar_i$ is never significant and is relatively small.[12] Finally, a strong, inverse relationship exists between the concentration of capabilities and the likelihood of conflict. The estimate of $Concap$ is always negative and statistically significant, indicating that external wars are more likely to begin when there exists a relatively uniform distribution of capabilities among the major powers.[13] Equally important is the size of these effects. Holding constant the remaining variables in Equation 5.1, major powers are, on average, three to four times more likely to become involved in wars than other states. A change in the concentration of capabilities from its highest to its lowest observed

Series-Cross-Section Data and/or the Democratic Peace" (paper presented at the annual meeting of the Political Methodology Group, Columbus, Ohio, 1997); and Nathaniel Beck, Jonathan N. Katz, and Richard Tucker, "Taking Time Seriously: Time-Series-Cross-Section Analysis with a Binary Dependent Variable," *American Journal of Political Science,* Vol. 42, No. 4 (October 1998), pp. 1260–1288.

12. Note, however, that many of these estimates would have been significant at the .10 level had we conducted one-tailed rather than two-tailed tests. Note also that civil wars appear to spur greater involvement in international wars than in extra-systemic or colonial wars. Additional tests indicate that each estimate and t-statistic of $Civwar_i$ is considerably larger when only interstate wars rather than all external wars are analyzed. See also Chapter 6.

13. A recent study found evidence of a quadratic relationship between the concentration of capabilities and the frequency all international wars during the nineteenth and twentieth centuries. See Mansfield, *Power, Trade, and War,* chap. 3. However, we found little evidence of this type of relationship, which is probably due to differences in the dependent variable and the level of analysis between our study and this earlier analysis.

Table 5.1. Estimates of the Parameters in Equation 5.1, Based on the Composite Index of Regime Type.

Variable	Base Model	Country Specific Fixed Effects[a]	Controlling for Regime Type (Anoc/Autoc)	Controlling for Regime Type (Reg)	Excluding Major Wars[b]
Intercept	-1.383***	—	-.918	-1.357**	-1.489***
	(.507)		(.613)	(.546)	(.573)
Complete Demtransition	.445	1.111	.105	.427	-.143
	(1.151)	(1.414)	(1.212)	(1.157)	(1.248)
Incomplete Demtransition	2.683**	2.090**	2.427**	2.644**	2.979**
	(1.343)	(1.050)	(1.210)	(1.270)	(1.326)
Complete Auttransition	-1.589	-.965	-1.793	-1.659	-.625
	(1.630)	(2.221)	(1.643)	(1.574)	(1.732)
Incomplete Auttransition	2.146	3.172	1.898	2.097	—c
	(1.330)	(2.522)	(1.296)	(1.400)	
DomConcentration	.005	.072	-.051	-.004	.017
	(.039)	(.047)	(.054)	(.050)	(.046)
Complete Demtransition × DomConcentration	-.124	-.325	-.051	-.115	-.071
	(.278)	(.338)	(.288)	(.280)	(.281)
Incomplete Demtransition × DomConcentration	-.515**	-.396*	-.464**	-.510**	-.585**
	(.259)	(.210)	(.234)	(.250)	(.256)
Complete Auttransition × DomConcentration	.193	.092	.239	.201	.028
	(.230)	(.311)	(.225)	(.223)	(.256)
Incomplete Auttransition × DomConcentration	-.460**	-.635	-.406*	-.450**	—c
	(.201)	(.519)	(.209)	(.216)	
Majpower	1.304***	1.315***	1.293***	1.309***	1.257***
	(.216)	(.392)	(.219)	(.211)	(.224)

Table 5.1. Continued.

Variable	Base Model	Country Specific Fixed Effects[a]	Controlling for Regime Type (Anoc/Autoc)	Controlling for Regime Type (Reg)	Excluding Major Wars[b]
Civwar	.312	.264	.355	.306	.394
	(.250)	(.309)	(.258)	(.254)	(.247)
Concap	-4.766***	-5.596***	-5.489***	-4.690***	-4.385***
	(1.565)	(1.469)	(1.729)	(1.504)	(1.595)
Anocracy			-.119		
			(.209)		
Autocracy			.251		
			(.259)		
Reg				-.004	
				(.015)	
Log Likelihood	-1339.96	-1092.73	-1337.81	-1339.89	-1128.80
N	9229	6387	9229	9229	8417

NOTE: Entries are logistic regression estimates, with robust standard errors in parentheses. Each model is estimated after including a natural spline function with three knots.

[a] Entries are fixed-effects logit estimates.

[b] Entries are derived after excluding the years during which World War I, World War II, and the Korean War took place.

[c] This parameter is not estimated because there is no case in which a transition from democracy to anocracy led to a war.

*** $p \leq .01$; ** $p \leq .05$; * $p \leq .10$ (two-tailed tests are conducted for all estimates).

Table 5.2. Estimates of the Parameters in Equation 5.1, Based on the Competitiveness of Political Participation.

Variable	Base Model	Country Specific Fixed Effects[a]	Controlling for Regime Type (Anoc/Autoc)	Controlling for Regime Type (Reg)	Excluding Major Wars[b]
Intercept	-1.498***	—	-1.529*	-1.376**	-1.633***
	(.549)		(.823)	(.577)	(.645)
Complete Demtransition	.462	.665	.477	.391	1.223
	(1.378)	(2.483)	(1.412)	(1.366)	(1.425)
Incomplete Demtransition	2.639**	2.071**	2.657**	2.571**	2.798**
	(1.280)	(1.008)	(1.117)	(1.213)	(1.277)
Complete Auttransition	-1.321	-.478	-1.304	-1.504	-.594
	(1.539)	(2.601)	(1.550)	(1.521)	(1.620)
Incomplete Auttransition	-.094	.772	-.073	-.078	.051
	(1.408)	(1.935)	(1.422)	(1.359)	(1.091)
DomConcentration	.015	.071	.001	-.009	.034
	(.041)	(.048)	(.058)	(.049)	(.051)
Complete Demtransition × DomConcentration	-.088	-.152	-.074	-.060	-.275
	(.230)	(.432)	(.231)	(.226)	(.239)
Incomplete Demtransition × DomConcentration	-.571**	-.415**	-.557***	-.566**	-.583**
	(.239)	(.212)	(.214)	(.231)	(.237)
Complete Auttransition × DomConcentration	.109	-.003	.123	.128	-.025
	(.215)	(.368)	(.217)	(.214)	(.229)
Incomplete Auttransition × DomConcentration	.148	-.007	.162	.151	.062
	(.265)	(.367)	(.273)	(.257)	(.240)
Majpower	1.287***	1.346***	1.296***	1.274***	1.230***
	(.211)	(.393)	(.229)	(.206)	(.225)

Table 5.2. *Continued.*

Variable	Base Model	Country Specific Fixed Effects[a]	Controlling for Regime Type (Anoc/Autoc)	Controlling for Regime Type (Reg)	Excluding Major Wars[b]
Civwar	.275	.277	.264	.246	.345
	(.251)	(.312)	(.247)	(.253)	(.256)
Concap	−4.609***	−5.631***	−4.582**	−4.388***	−4.284**
	(1.654)	(1.486)	(2.031)	(1.598)	(1.736)
Anocracy	—	—	.089	—	—
			(.197)		
Autocracy	—	—	.170	—	—
			(.261)		
Reg	—	—	—	−.011	—
				(.015)	
Log Likelihood	−1301.07	−1060.42	−1300.71	−1297.24	−1096.86
N	8901	6250	8901	8854	8188

NOTE: Entries are logistic regression estimates, with robust standard errors in parentheses. Each model is estimated after including a natural spline function with three knots.

[a] Entries are fixed-effects logit estimates.

[b] Entries are derived after excluding the years during which World War I, World War II, and the Korean War took place.

*** $p \leq .01$; ** $p \leq .05$; * $p \leq .10$ (two-tailed tests are conducted for all estimates).

Table 5.3. Estimates of the Parameters in Equation 5.1, Based on the Openness of Executive Recruitment.

Variable	Base Model	Country Specific Fixed Effects[a]	Controlling for Regime Type (Anoc/Autoc)	Controlling for Regime Type (Reg)	Excluding Major Wars[b]
Intercept	-1.406***	—	-1.476***	-1.319**	-1.507***
	(.472)		(.472)	(.497)	(.542)
Complete Demtransition	-1.132	-.981	-1.118	-1.127	-.627
	(.933)	(1.242)	(.874)	(.928)	(.886)
Incomplete Demtransition	5.388***	3.247**	5.409***	5.320***	5.522***
	(1.589)	(1.445)	(1.563)	(1.545)	(1.471)
Complete Auttransition	.167	.451	.167	.218	.137
	(1.364)	(2.547)	(1.384)	(1.371)	(1.365)
Incomplete Auttransition	3.209	3.020	3.235	3.221	—[c]
	(2.621)	(3.257)	(2.570)	(2.604)	
DomConcentration	.000	.052	-.001	-.009	.015
	(.037)	(.046)	(.048)	(.046)	(.045)
Complete Demtransition × DomConcentration	.292*	.253	.293**	.288*	.190
	(.154)	(.214)	(.149)	(.153)	(.159)
Incomplete Demtransition × DomConcentration	-1.109**	-.690**	-1.107**	-1.100**	-1.101**
	(.469)	(.337)	(.462)	(.463)	(.440)
Complete Auttransition × DomConcentration	-.105	-.168	-.102	-.116	-.070
	(.231)	(.432)	(.235)	(.233)	(.228)
Incomplete Auttransition × DomConcentration	-.731	-.796	-.729	-.736	—[c]
	(.479)	(.753)	(.477)	(.477)	
Majpower	1.323***	1.344***	1.318***	1.297***	1.276***
	(.211)	(.393)	(.229)	(.206)	(.219)

Table 5.3. *Continued.*

Variable	Base Model	Country Specific Fixed Effects[a]	Controlling for Regime Type (Anoc/Autoc)[c]	Controlling for Regime Type (Reg)	Excluding Major Wars[b]
Civwar	.285	.286	.288	.263	.348
	(.256)	(.310)	(.256)	(.258)	(.259)
Concap	-4.689***	-5.995***	-4.474***	-4.612***	-4.437***
	(1.435)	(1.464)	(1.300)	(1.408)	(1.467)
Anocracy	—	—	.079	—	—
			(.268)		
Autocracy	—	—	.049	—	—
			(.217)		
Reg	—	—	—	-.005	—
				(.014)	
Log Likelihood	-1334.90	-1090.51	-1334.77	-1331.46	-1126.62
N	9229	6387	9229	9178	8456

NOTE: Entries are logistic regression estimates, with robust standard errors in parentheses. Each model is estimated after including a natural spline function with three knots.

[a] Entries are fixed-effects logit estimates.

[b] Entries are derived after excluding the years during which World War I, World War II, and the Korean War took place.

[c] This parameter is not estimated because there is no case in which a transition from democracy to anocracy led to a war.

*** $p \leq .01$; ** $p \leq .05$; * $p \leq .10$ (two-tailed tests are conducted for all estimates).

Table 5.4. Estimates of the Parameters in Equation 5.1, Based on the Constraints on the Chief Executive.

Variable	Base Model	Country Specific Fixed Effects[a]	Controlling for Regime Type (Anoc/Autoc)	Controlling for Regime Type (Reg)	Excluding Major Wars[b]
Intercept	-1.319***	—	-.907*	-1.250**	-1.474**
	(.505)		(.518)	(.540)	(.581)
Complete Demtransition	-6.191***	-7.664	-6.699***	-6.167***	-6.128***
	(1.426)	(4.947)	(1.409)	(1.426)	(1.509)
Incomplete Demtransition	2.384**	2.316**	1.935**	2.353**	2.841***
	(1.041)	(.926)	(.979)	(.979)	(1.074)
Complete Auttransition	-.056	.377	-.489	.016	.347
	(1.439)	(1.559)	(1.454)	(1.437)	(1.679)
Incomplete Auttransition	.494	1.796	.029	.448	-1.243
	(1.674)	(2.300)	(1.703)	(1.781)	(1.609)
DomConcentration	-.005	.059	-.073	-.008	.014
	(.041)	(.048)	(.064)	(.050)	(.050)
Complete Demtransition × DomConcentration	1.130***	1.314	1.205***	1.127***	1.066***
	(.275)	(.826)	(.272)	(.274)	(.278)
Incomplete Demtransition × DomConcentration	-.389*	-.362**	-.323*	-.386*	-.470**
	(.209)	(.185)	(.191)	(.202)	(.219)
Complete Auttransition × DomConcentration	.044	-.027	.108	.032	-.028
	(.214)	(.227)	(.217)	(.213)	(.259)
Incomplete Auttransition × DomConcentration	-.137	-.356	-.069	-.131	.090
	(.331)	(.429)	(.339)	(.351)	(.297)
Majpower	1.312***	1.316***	1.337***	1.282***	1.268***
	(.216)	(.390)	(.190)	(.209)	(.226)

Table 5.4. *Continued.*

Variable	Base Model	Country Specific Fixed Effects[a]	Controlling for Regime Type (Anoc/Autoc)	Controlling for Regime Type (Reg)	Excluding Major Wars[b]
Civwar	.246	.248	.217	.229	.297
	(.272)	(.310)	(.282)	(.276)	(.278)
Concap	−5.007***	−5.914***	−5.043***	−4.983***	−4.621***
	(1.536)	(1.479)	(1.403)	(1.491)	(1.540)
Anocracy	—	—	−.482**	—	—
			(.189)		
Autocracy	—	—	.196	—	—
			(.291)		
Reg	—	—	—	−.002	—
				(.015)	
Log Likelihood	−1337.03	−1089.38	−1329.07	−1333.70	−1127.91
N	9229	6387	9229	9178	8473

NOTE: Entries are logistic regression estimates, with robust standard errors in parentheses. Each model is estimated after including a natural spline function with three knots.

[a] Entries are fixed-effects logit estimates.

[b] Entries are derived after excluding the years during which World War I, World War II, and the Korean War took place.

*** $p \leq .01$; ** $p \leq .05$; * $p \leq .10$ (two-tailed tests are conducted for all estimates).

level yields an increase in the likelihood of war of similar magnitude.[14] These effects are considerable, which accords with the views of realists and others. Considerable, too, are the effects of incomplete democratic transitions. These effects are considered below.

RESULTS BASED ON THE COMPOSITE INDEX OF REGIME TYPE

The results based on the composite index, which are presented in the first column of Table 5.1, indicate that transitions from autocracy to anocracy increase the likelihood of external war if little authority is concentrated in the hands of national government officials. As our theory suggests, the coefficient of *Incomplete Demtransition$_i$* is positive and the coefficient of *Incomplete Demtransition$_i$* × *DomConcentration$_i$* is negative. Moreover, the estimates of both of these coefficients are sizeable and statistically significant.

These estimates indicate that incomplete democratic transitions are increasingly likely to precipitate war as the level of domestic concentration falls. Based on the results in Table 5.1, incomplete democratization increases the odds of war by $e^{(2.683\ -\ .515\ \times\ DomConcentration)}$. When domestic concentration equals 1, countries undergoing a transition from autocracy to anocracy are almost nine times more likely to become involved in hostilities than other countries. As concentration rises, however, the effect of incomplete democratization is mitigated. When the level of concentration reaches 5, the odds of war for states making such a regime change are only about 10 percent higher than for other countries. In countries marked by considerable institutional strength and therefore a level of concentration that exceeds its sample mean of 5.7, incomplete democratization actually reduces the probability of war.

Incomplete democratic transitions occurring in the face of institutional weakness and fragmentation are not only dangerous, they are more dangerous than any other set of domestic political conditions analyzed here. To compare the effects of these transitions to other ones, we calculate the predicted probability of war for each type of regime change included in our model, using the logit estimates in the first column of Table 5.1. For each type of regime change, the predicted probability of war is derived only for the range of values of domestic concentration that ac-

---

14. It is useful to keep in mind that, while *Concap* can range from 0 to 1, it only ranges from .18 to .43 in our data set. Consequently, the magnitude of its effect is somewhat smaller than might be expected in light of the size of its coefficient (see Tables 5.1, 5.2, 5.3, and 5.4).

tually appear in the data.[15] For the purpose of calculating these probabilities, we hold constant the concentration of capabilities at its mean and assume that state i is neither experiencing a civil war nor is a major power. As shown in Figure 5.1, incomplete democratization coupled with a level of concentration below 5 is more likely to stimulate war than any other set of conditions that we consider.

Our results also provide some indication that incomplete autocratic transitions promote war, although they have a weaker and smaller influence on hostilities than incomplete democratic transitions. The estimate of *Incomplete Auttransition$_i$* is positive, but it is not statistically significant, whereas the estimate of *Incomplete Auttransition$_i$ × Dom-Concentration$_i$* is both negative and significant. Hence, like incomplete democratic transitions, the effects of incomplete autocratic transitions are heightened when authority is less highly concentrated in the hands of public officials. But unlike incomplete democratic transitions, there is no case in which an incomplete autocratic transition actually leads to war for a country where the value of domestic concentration is less than 5. Moreover, as shown in Figure 5.1, the predicted probability of war for states with relatively low levels of concentration is greater if they undergo an incomplete democratic transition than if they experience an incomplete autocratic transition.

Finally, there is no evidence that transitions culminating in either a coherent democracy or a coherent autocracy have a strong effect on war. The estimate of *Complete Demtransition$_i$* is positive, but it is not statistically significant. Furthermore, the effect of transitions generating a coherent democracy does not seem to depend on the extent of domestic concentration. The estimate of *Complete Demtransition$_i$ × DomConcentration$_i$* is not statistically significant and the predicted probability of war does not change much with variations in the level of domestic concentration (see Figure 5.1). In addition, the estimate of *Complete Auttransition$_i$* is negative and the estimate of *Complete Auttransition$_i$ × DomConcentration$_i$* is positive. Both of them, however, are small and neither one is statistically significant.

Nor does the level of domestic concentration affect whether countries that are not experiencing a regime change become involved in hostilities.

---

15. Thus, for example, we do not present the predicted probability of war for any type of regime change when the level of concentration equals zero because there is no case in the data where a regime change took place and concentration was equal to zero. We do present the predicted probability of war when no regime change takes place and concentration equals zero, since there are some cases of this sort in the data.

Figure 5.1. Predicted Probability of War by Transition Type, Based on the Composite Index of Regime Type.

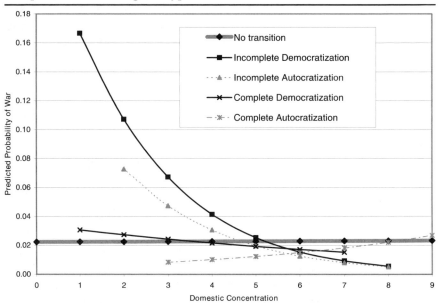

The estimate of *DomConcentration$_i$* is positive, but it is not statistically significant and it is quite small.

RESULTS BASED ON THE COMPONENT MEASURES OF REGIME TYPE

The results based on the competitiveness of political participation, the openness of executive recruitment, and the constraints on executive power are shown in the first columns of Tables 5.2, 5.3, and 5.4, respectively. They provide even stronger evidence that transitions from autocracy to anocracy are a potent impetus to war when the level of domestic concentration is low. In each case, the estimate of *Incomplete Demtransition$_i$* is positive, that of *Incomplete Demtransition$_i$* × *DomConcentration$_i$* is negative, and both are significant.

Moreover, the quantitative effects of incomplete democratization and domestic concentration on hostilities continue to be quite large when we focus on these three component measures of regime type. If domestic concentration equals 1, for example, countries undergoing a transition from autocracy to anocracy are between seven and eight times more likely to become involved in hostilities than other countries, based on both the competitiveness of political participation and the constraints on the chief executive. Based on these two component measures, this type of regime change generates about a five-fold rise in the probability of war when concentration increases to 2, about a three-fold rise when concentration increases to 3, and a rise of roughly 45 percent (for the competitiveness of political participation) to 130 percent (for executive constraints) when concentration equals 4.

The effect of an incomplete democratic transition coupled with a low level of domestic concentration is even greater when regime change is measured using the openness of executive recruitment (see Table 5.3).[16] Furthermore, like our earlier results based on the composite index of regime type, Figures 5.2, 5.3, and 5.4 show that in general the predicted probability of war is greater for states experiencing incomplete democratic transitions in the face of institutional weakness than under any of the other circumstances we examine.[17] Moreover, for lower levels of concentration—that is, levels less than 5—incomplete democratic transitions generally yield a greater predicted probability of war than other types of regime change.

Unlike the results based on the composite index, there is also some evidence that transitions culminating in a coherent democracy influence war when regime change is assessed by reference to the constraints on the chief executive and the openness of executive recruitment. The estimate of *Complete Demtransition$_i$* is statistically significant if we focus on executive constraints (see Table 5.4), and the estimate of *Complete Demtransition$_i$ × DomConcentration$_i$* is significant when we focus either on the openness of executive recruitment or on executive constraints (see Tables 5.3 and 5.4). There is no indication, however, that transitions leading to a coherent democracy precipitate war when the competitiveness of political participation is the measure of regime change (see Table 5.2). Hence, we find only scattered evidence that transitions yielding a coherent democracy heighten the prospect of conflict. But the evidence point-

---

16. Based on the competitiveness of political participation (Table 5.2), incomplete democratization increases the odds of war by $e^{(2.639 - .571 \times DomConcentration)}$; based on the openness of executive recruitment (Table 5.3), incomplete democratization increases the odds of war by $e^{(5.388 - 1.109 \times DomConcentration)}$; and based on executive constraints (Table 5.4), incomplete democratization increases the odds of war by $e^{(2.384 - .389 \times DomConcentration)}$.

17. As in our analysis of the composite index, the predicted probabilities of war in Figures 5.2, 5.3, and 5.4 are computed using the logit estimates in the first columns of Tables 5.2, 5.3, and 5.4, respectively. For each type of regime change, we again present the predicted probability of war only for the range of values of domestic concentration that are actually found in the data. To generate these probabilities, we continue to hold constant the concentration of capabilities at its mean and assume that state i is neither experiencing a civil war nor is a major power.

Figure 5.2. Predicted Probability of War by Transition Type, Based on the Competitiveness of Political Participation.

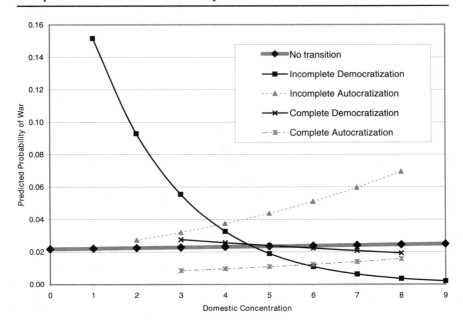

Figure 5.3. Predicted Probability of War by Transition Type, Based on the Openness of Executive Recruitment.

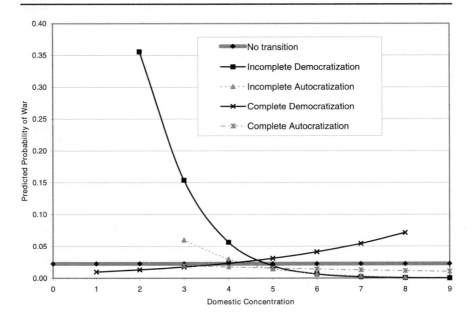

Figure 5.4. Predicted Probability of War by Transition Type, Based on the Constraints on the Chief Executive.

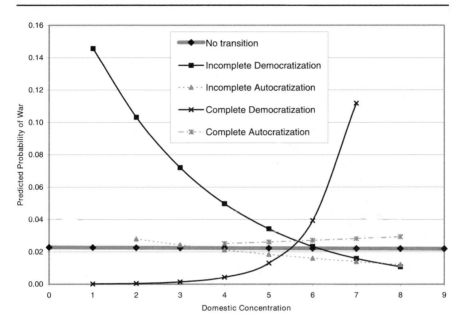

ing in this direction suggests that these transitions are unlikely to foment armed conflict when the level of domestic concentration is low; they are more likely to stimulate hostilities as authority becomes more highly concentrated in the hands of national officials (see Figures 5.3 and 5.4). This finding does not conform to our expectations, and we address it below in an analysis of the robustness of these results.

In contrast to the effects of democratization, there is little indication that the process of autocratization influences the onset of war when the component measures of regime type are analyzed. None of the estimates of *Incomplete Auttransition$_i$, Complete Auttransition$_i$, Incomplete Auttransition$_i$ $\times$ DomConcentration$_i$,* or *Complete Auttransition$_i$ $\times$ Dom-Concentration$_i$* in Tables 5.2, 5.3, and 5.4 are statistically significant. Similarly, the magnitude of the impact of complete autocratization is quite small based on each of these measures. It is only when we measure regime type using the competitiveness of political participation that incomplete autocratization has a noticeable quantitative effect on war (see Figure 5.2). The direction of this effect, however, runs counter to that based on the composite index (see Figure 5.1). Taken as a whole, therefore, we find no evidence that autocratization has a systematic bearing on the outbreak of hostilities. Finally, as we found based on the composite index, there is no evidence that the extent of domestic concentration in stable regimes influences war. The estimate of $DomConcentration_i$ is positive in two cases and negative in one; it is never significant, and the size of its effect is quite modest.

To assess the substantive effects of regime change on war, Figures 5.5, 5.6, 5.7, and 5.8 present the "relative risk" of state i becoming involved in a war based on the composite index and the three component measures of regime type. For each category of regime change, this risk is the probability of war when that type of change occurs, divided by the probability of war when no regime change takes place, holding constant the remaining variables in the model. In these figures, we report the relative risk of war for each type of regime change under two conditions: first, when $DomConcentration_i$ is set to 5—which is just below its sample mean of 5.7—and second, when this variable is set to 2—which is about two standard deviations below its sample mean.[18]

Regardless of which measure of regime type is analyzed, it is clear that the relative risk of war stemming from an incomplete democratic transition rises considerably when the value of $DomConcentration_i$ is reduced from 5 (the situation, for example, in Pakistan during the late 1980s, after the death of Zia ul-Haq, or in Argentina during the early 1980s) to 2 (the situation, for example, in the Ottoman Empire prior to the Balkan Wars and similar to that in Yugoslavia during the early 1990s).[19] As we pointed out earlier, incomplete democratization has little bearing on war when domestic concentration is close to its mean: the relative risk of war tends to be about 1 when $DomConcentration_i$ equals 5. By contrast, states experiencing incomplete democratic transitions are (depending on the measure of regime type that is evaluated) roughly four to fifteen times more likely to go to war than states that do not undergo a regime change when the level of domestic concentration is reduced to 2.

---

18. For a discussion of the summary statistics for $DomConcentration_i$ see Chapter 4. Note that like our earlier analyses, we hold $Concap$ constant at its mean and the dichotomous variables—$Majpower_i$ and $Civwar_i$—at 0, which is the modal value of each one.

19. To be more precise, Pakistan experienced an incomplete democratic transition based on the composite index, the constraints on the chief executive, and the competitiveness of political participation. The level of domestic concentration was 5 in 1988 and 1989 (years t-1). Argentina made such a transition based on the competitiveness of political participation; its level of concentration was 5 in 1981 (year t-1). The Ottoman Empire experienced incomplete democratization across all four measures analyzed here. Its level of domestic concentration was 2 from 1909 to 1912 (years t-1). Yugoslavia underwent an incomplete democratic transition based on the competitiveness of political participation; its level of domestic concentration was 1 in 1990 and 1991 (years t-1).

Figure 5.5. Relative Risk of War by Transition Type, Based on the Composite Index of Regime.

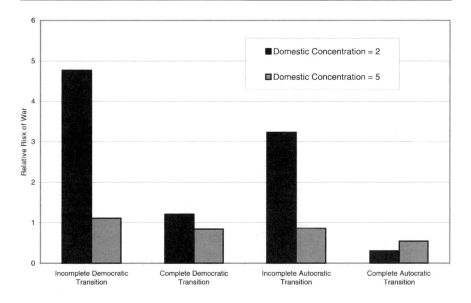

Figure 5.6. Relative Risk of War by Transition Type, Based on the Competitiveness of Political Participation.

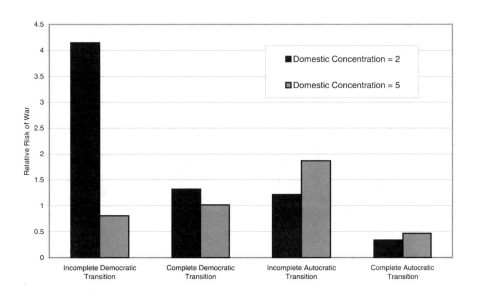

Figure 5.7. Relative Risk of War by Transition Type, Based on the Openness of Executive Recruitment.

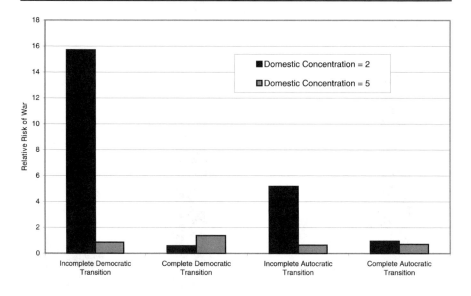

Figure 5.8. Relative Risk of War by Transition Type, Based on the Constraints on the Chief Executive.

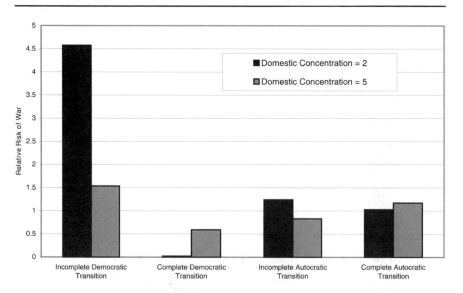

Furthermore, the relative risk of war is much lower for every other type of regime change. Neither complete democratization nor complete autocratization has a strong influence on war, regardless of whether the level of domestic concentration is set to 2 or 5.[20] In addition, although there is some evidence that incomplete autocratization leads to war when domestic institutions are weak, the magnitude of this effect varies a great deal across the four measures of regime type. Compared to the absence of regime change when $DomConcentration_i$ equals 2, such transitions yield about a three-fold increase in the probability of war when the composite measure is analyzed, and roughly a five-fold increase when the openness of executive recruitment is evaluated, but only about a 20 to 25 percent rise in the likelihood of hostilities when the constraints on the chief executive or the competitiveness of political participation are examined. Each of these increases is far smaller than the corresponding increase in the likelihood of war stemming from an incomplete democratic transition.

COMBINING THE COMPONENT MEASURES OF REGIME TYPE

The preceding analysis addressed the separate effects on war of changes in the competitiveness of political participation, the openness of the process through which a chief executive is selected, and the institutional constraints on that executive. Now we examine such shifts in combination. Changes in these three institutional features rarely move in unison, as we discussed in Chapter 4. Moreover, democratic (and autocratic) transitions occurring over multiple institutional dimensions are likely to be more pronounced than those occurring over a single dimension. One implication of our argument is that countries experiencing a democratic transition may be more likely to go to war if the transition affects a wide range of institutional features than if it affects relatively few features.

To address this issue, we redefine *Complete Demtransition_i* as the sum of the transitions occurring across the competitiveness of political participation, the openness of executive recruitment, and the constraints on the chief executive that culminate in a coherent democracy for each state, *i*, between years *t*-6 and *t*-1.

Likewise, we redefine *Incomplete Demtransition_i* as the sum of the transitions that *i* experiences from an autocracy to an anocracy based on these three institutional factors. Finally, *Complete Auttransition_i* and *Incomplete Auttransition_i* are the number of transitions culminating in a coherent

---

20. Note, however, that the risk of war stemming from a complete democratic transition would be fairly sizable if we set concentration at a very high level and focused on either the competitiveness of political participation or the constraints on the chief executive. See Figures 5.3 and 5.4.

autocracy and from a democracy to an anocracy, respectively, that i undergoes from t-6 to t-1. Thus, each variable pertaining to regime change takes on values ranging from 0 to 3.[21]

The results based on these variables are reported in the first column of Table 5.5 (again labeled "Base Model"). Consistent with our earlier findings, the estimate of *Incomplete Demtransition$_i$* is positive, that of *Incomplete Demtransition$_i$* × *DomConcentration$_i$* is negative, and each one is statistically significant. Not only is there strong evidence that incomplete democratic transitions occurring in a context of weak political institutions raise the risk of war, but hostilities become increasingly likely as the number of such transitions increases.

Consider, for example, the case where the level of domestic concentration is 2, the concentration of capabilities is evaluated at its mean, and state i is nether a major power nor involved in a civil war. Figure 5.9 shows the relative risk of war under these conditions when this state undergoes a transition across one, two, or all three indicators. War is roughly three times more likely to break out if this state undergoes a transition from autocracy to anocracy along a single institutional dimension than if it does not undergo any such transition. If an incomplete democratic transition occurs across two dimensions rather than one, then the relative risk of war is about two and one-half times as high; the risk is more than twice as high if such a transition takes place across all three dimensions rather than two. Furthermore, holding constant the number of regime transitions, the relative risk of war is higher for incomplete democratization than for any other type of regime change.

It is also noteworthy that, holding constant the number of incomplete

---

21. By analyzing the sum of the transitions across these institutional features, we are assuming that the likelihood of war is a monotonic function of the number of such changes. An alternative would be to include a dummy variable corresponding to each number of institutional shifts for *Incomplete Demtransition$_i$*, for *Complete Demtransition$_i$*, for *Incomplete Auttransition$_i$*, and for *Complete Auttransition$_i$*. However, our argument suggests that the relationship between the number of democratic transitions and war is likely to be monotonic, and indeed, this alternative procedure yields results that are similar to those reported below. Note that, for each type of regime change, we code the sum of the transitions as missing if data on any of the three institutional features used to derive this sum are missing. We do so because institutional shifts might occur during periods when data are missing. If so, summing the number of transitions across only those features where data exist could distort our findings. However, we also conducted a separate set of tests after defining each measure of regime change (*Incomplete Demtransition$_i$*, *Complete Demtransition$_i$*, *Incomplete Auttransition$_i$*, and *Complete Auttransition$_i$*) as the number of regime shifts that take place, treating missing data for any of the three institutional factors that make up this summary measure as though no transition took place. Again, the results based on this alternative coding procedure are similar to those discussed in this chapter.

Figure 5.9. Relative Risk of War by Transition Type, Based on the Sum of Transitions, Setting Domestic Concentration Equal to 2.

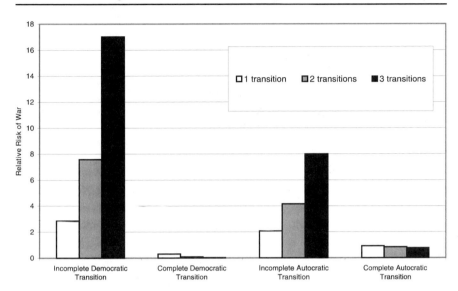

democratic transitions, the likelihood of conflict increases steadily as the level of domestic concentration is reduced. This finding conforms to our earlier findings. So does the fact that an incomplete democratic transition, as measured by all three features, combined with the lowest observed value of concentration yields a higher predicted probability of war than any other set of domestic political conditions we analyze.

Our results also indicate that transitions culminating in a coherent democracy influence the outbreak of war. The estimate of *Complete Demtransition$_i$* is negative, the estimate of *Complete Demtransition$_i$ × DomConcentration$_i$* is positive, and both are statistically significant. Holding concentration constant, the likelihood of conflict declines as the number of indicators showing a transition to a complete democracy increases. Indeed, based on our sample, there have been no instances of war when such transitions occurred as measured by all three dimensions. Further, holding constant the number of transitions to democracy, the likelihood of conflict increases as authority becomes more highly concentrated.

In contrast to democratic transitions, there is relatively little evidence that autocratic transitions affect the likelihood of war. The estimates of *Incomplete Auttransition$_i$, Incomplete Auttransition$_i$ × DomConcentration$_i$, Complete Auttransition$_i$,* and *Complete Auttransition$_i$ × DomConcentration$_i$* are never statistically significant. While some evidence suggests that

Table 5.5. Estimates of the Parameters in Equation 5.1, Based on the Sum of the Transitions Occurring across the Competitiveness of Political Participation, the Openness of Executive Recruitment, and the Constraints on the Chief Executive.

Variable	Base Model	Country Specific Fixed Effects[a]	Controlling for Regime Type (Anoc/Autoc)	Controlling for Regime Type (Reg)	Excluding Major Wars[b]
Intercept	-1.500***	—	-1.028	-1.383***	-1.657***
	(.513)		(.672)	(.537)	(.624)
Complete Demtransition	-1.973***	-1.593	-2.071***	-1.950***	-1.623**
	(.738)	(1.054)	(.730)	(.715)	(.787)
Incomplete Demtransition	1.772***	1.251***	1.710***	1.732***	1.823***
	(.269)	(.436)	(.239)	(.253)	(.268)
Complete Auttransition	-.101	.310	-.350	-.135	.177
	(.591)	(.826)	(.632)	(.586)	(.644)
Incomplete Auttransition	1.070	2.296	.933	.997	.708
	(1.105)	(1.425)	(1.152)	(1.131)	(1.221)
DomConcentration	.014	.076	-.058	-.007	.033
	(.041)	(.050)	(.079)	(.051)	(.052)
Complete Demtransition × DomConcentration	.377***	.293	.399***	.379***	.293**
	(.124)	(.180)	(.126)	(.122)	(.134)
Incomplete Demtransition × DomConcentration	-.340***	-.221**	-.316***	-.338***	-.339***
	(.060)	(.092)	(.062)	(.060)	(.059)
Complete Auttransition × DomConcentration	-.101	-.052	.034	-.135	-.041
	(.591)	(.123)	(.092)	(.586)	(.100)
Incomplete Auttransition × DomConcentration	-.160	-.406	-.115	-.145	-.168
	(.242)	(.294)	(.252)	(.247)	(.262)
Majpower	1.320***	1.358***	1.347***	1.303***	1.261***
	(.203)	(.393)	(.194)	(.201)	(.218)

Table 5.5. *Continued.*

Variable	Base Model	Country Specific Fixed Effects[a]	Controlling for Regime Type (Anoc/Autoc)	Controlling for Regime Type (Reg)	Excluding Major Wars[b]
Civwar	.317	.298	.312	.288	.366
	(.249)	(.314)	(.256)	(.253)	(.250)
Concap	-4.746***	-5.825***	-5.116***	-4.581***	-4.347***
	(1.530)	(1.487)	(1.488)	(1.515)	(1.586)
Anocracy	—	—	-.086	—	—
			(.094)		
Autocracy	—	—	.101	—	—
			(.129)		
Reg	—	—	—	-.009	—
				(.015)	
Log Likelihood	-1297.05	-1057.70	-1294.99	-1293.59	-1093.96
N	8901	6250	8900	8854	8188

NOTE: Entries are logistic regression estimates, with robust standard errors in parentheses. Each model is estimated after including a natural spline function with three knots.

[a] Entries are fixed-effects logit estimates.

[b] Entries are derived after excluding the years during which World War I, World War II, and the Korean War took place.

*** $p \leq .01$; ** $p \leq .05$; * $p \leq .10$ (two-tailed tests are conducted for all estimates).

incomplete autocratization increases the likelihood of war in countries marked by weak political institutions, Figure 5.9 shows that these effects are much smaller than those stemming from incomplete democratization.

Assessing the Robustness of the Results

The results in this chapter provide considerable support for our central argument: incomplete democratic transitions are especially likely to promote wars in countries where government institutions are weak and where little power is concentrated in the hands of national officials. At this point, it is important to assess the robustness of these results.

First, there are various cultural, social, and historical factors specific to the countries in our sample that are not included in Equation 5.1, but that might influence the outbreak of war. A well-known way to account for such unmeasured heterogeneity across countries is to include country-specific fixed effects in the model.[22] Various observers, however, argue that this solution creates more problems than it resolves and recommend eschewing fixed-effects specifications, especially in situations like ours where a dichotomous dependent variable is analyzed and the distribution of that variable is highly skewed.[23] Nonetheless, to assess the robustness of our results, we estimate Equation 5.1 using a fixed-effects specification.[24] The results—which are shown in the second columns of Tables 5.1, 5.2, 5.3, 5.4, and 5.5—continue to indicate that incomplete democratic transitions precipitate war in states with little institutional strength or centralization. As before, each estimate of *Incomplete Demtransition$_i$* is positive, each estimate of *Incomplete Demtransition$_i$ × DomConcentration$_i$* is negative, and all of them are statistically significant. However, there is no evidence that any other type of regime transition influences war, including transitions culminating in a coherent democracy. Recall that our earlier analyses yielded some indication that transi-

---

22. See Donald P. Green, Soo Yeon Kim, and David H. Yoon, "Dirty Pool," *International Organization*, Vol. 55, No. 2 (Summer 2001), pp. 441–468.

23. See Beck and Tucker, "Conflict in Space and Time"; and Nathaniel Beck and Jonathan N. Katz, "Throwing Out the Baby with the Bath Water: A Comment on Green, Kim, and Yoon," *International Organization*, Vol. 55, No. 2 (Summer 2001), pp. 487–495. On this issue, see also Gary King, "Proper Nouns and Methodological Propriety: Pooling Dyads in International Relations Data," *International Organization*, Vol. 55, No. 2 (Summer 2001), pp. 497–507.

24. See Greene, *Econometric Analysis*, chap. 16.

tions producing a coherent democracy are more likely to stimulate hostilities as authority becomes more highly concentrated domestically (see the first columns of Tables 5.3, 5.4, and 5.5). The results based on the fixed-effects logit specification suggest that this unexpected finding may be an outgrowth of heterogeneity in the data, that is, of country-specific factors not included in Equation 5.1 that might influence the outbreak of war.

Second, our previous tests treated all stable regimes as homogeneous, rather than distinguishing among stable autocracies, anocracies, and democracies. To determine whether making this distinction influences our results, we include two dummy variables: $Autocracy_i$ equals 1 if state i is autocratic at both the beginning and end of the period from year t-6 to year t-1, and 0 otherwise. $Anocracy_i$ equals 1 if i is anocratic at both the beginning and end of this period, and 0 otherwise. We arbitrarily establish stable democracy as the reference category.

As shown in the third columns of Tables 5.1, 5.2, 5.3, 5.4, and 5.5, the estimate of $Autocracy_i$ is positive in each case but is never statistically significant. The estimate of $Anocracy_i$ is negative in three cases, positive in two instances, and significant in only one. Moreover, including these variables in the model has virtually no bearing on the sign, size, or statistical significance of any of the variables in Equation 5.1. To address this issue further, we replace these two dummy variables with Reg_i. As we explained in Chapter 4, this variable is Jaggers and Gurr's summary measure of state i's regime type in year t-1, which takes on values ranging from -10 to 10. The fourth columns of Tables 5.1, 5.2, 5.3, 5.4, and 5.5 present our findings. The estimate of Reg_i is never statistically significant and including it in the model has very little influence on our other results. This continues to be the case if we replace Reg_i with dummy variables pertaining to the regime type of i in t-1. In sum, then, we find no evidence that distinguishing among different types of stable regimes or controlling for regime type affects our findings.

Third, there are a number of cases in which states undergoing democratic transitions became involved in World War I, World War II, or the Korean War. Some of these states were only nominal participants in the extensive hostilities of those wars, so it is important to ensure that our results are not being driven by them. To this end, we exclude all observations in the years during which World War I (1914–1918), World War II (1939–1945), and the Korean War (1950–1953) took place. The results generated after doing so, presented in the final columns of Tables 5.1, 5.2, 5.3, 5.4, and 5.5, indicate that omitting these years has little influence on the observed relationship between democratization and the outbreak of armed conflict. Interestingly, however, once these years are excluded, there are no instances of an incomplete autocratic transition precipitating war when regime change is measured either by the composite index or by the openness of executive recruitment.

Fourth, we mentioned in Chapter 3 that certain countries emerging from communist rule made a transition from autocracy to anocracy according to our coding criteria, but these might not be valid instances of incomplete democratization and might not reflect the mechanisms underlying our theory. In some of these cases, for example, countries coded as having a mixed regime do not have any prospect of politically meaningful elections. Instead they underwent only minor political liberalization or factionalization. It is important to ensure that our results are not being driven by these cases. Consequently, we re-estimate Equation 5.1 for each measure of regime type after removing all communist countries from the sample.[25] The results are very similar to those shown in the first columns of Tables 5.1, 5.2, 5.3, 5.4, and 5.5. Hence, there is no evidence that our results are affected by the breakdown of communist regimes.

Fifth, we have measured regime change over five-year intervals thus far. There are sound theoretical and empirical reasons to do so, but it is useful to determine whether our results would differ if longer or shorter intervals were analyzed. We therefore measure *Complete Demtransition$_i$*, *Incomplete Demtransition$_i$*, *Complete Auttransition$_i$*, and *Incomplete Auttransition$_i$* over intervals ranging from one year to ten years in length. More specifically, we measure these variables from year t-$(n+1)$ to year t-1, where n takes on values ranging from 1 to 10 (inclusive). For each value of n, separate estimates are generated using the composite index, the competitiveness of political participation, the openness of executive recruitment, the executive constraints, and the sum of the transitions occurring across the latter three measures. These results are much the same as those reported earlier: the estimate of *Incomplete Demtransition$_i$* is positive in each case, the estimate of *Incomplete Demtransition$_i$* × *Dom-Concentration$_i$* is always negative, and both estimates are statistically significant in all but a small handful of cases.

Based on the composite index, the estimate of *Complete Demtransition$_i$* is positive and quite large when regime type is evaluated over one-year and two-year intervals, and it is statistically significant in the latter case. The corresponding estimates of *Complete Demtransition$_i$* × *Dom-*

25. The communist countries excluded from the sample are Albania (1946–1991), Bulgaria (1947–1989), Cambodia (1976–1990), China (1949–1992), Cuba (1961–1992), Czechoslovakia (1948–1989), East Germany (1954–1989), Hungary (1948–1989), Laos (1975–1991), Mongolia (1924–1990), North Korea (1948–1992), Poland (1948–1989), Rumania (1948–1988), the Soviet Union (1917–1991), Yugoslavia (1946–1991), and Vietnam (1954–1992).

Concentration$_i$ are large, but neither one is significant. Obviously these results are not terribly strong; nonetheless, they do conform to the logic of our argument. It seems reasonable to expect that nationalist ideologies and movements would already be present in the pluralistic setting of an anocratic regime and therefore might quickly be energized by the opening to unfettered mass democracy. Furthermore, at longer intervals after a transition to democracy, the likelihood of democratic consolidation should increase, yielding a state that is more stable and less war-prone than one in the throes of democratization. Finally, we continue to find little evidence that autocratic transitions precipitate war.

Sixth, several recent studies have analyzed the influence on hostilities of *any* shift in a democratic direction, including shifts *within* autocratic regimes, anocratic regimes, and democratic regimes.[26] As we mentioned in Chapter 4, these studies do not bear directly on our theory, which is silent on the implications of changes in political openness within a given regime type. However, it is useful to analyze whether our results hold up after accounting for such changes. To this end, we supplement the model by including ΔReg_i. This variable is the change in the value of the summary measure of regime type developed by Gurr and his colleagues (and described in the previous chapter) for each state, *i*, from year *t*-6 to year *t*-1. Including this variable has no effect on the earlier results in the first columns of Tables 5.1, 5.2, 5.3, 5.4, and 5.5. Moreover, the estimate of ΔReg_i is always small and is never close to being statistically significant. Thus, taking account of a broader range of institutional change has no bearing on the relationship between democratization and interstate conflict.

Seventh, it is useful to account for any selection effects that could arise if the same factors that contribute to the onset of conflict short of war also contribute to the conflict's escalation to war.[27] To this end, we estimate a censored probit model.[28] In the selection equation, we model the probability of state *i* becoming involved in a militarized interstate dispute

---

26.   See Andrew Enterline, "Driving While Democratizing," *International Security*, Vol. 20, No. 4 (Spring 1996), pp. 183–196; John R. Oneal and Bruce M. Russett, "The Classical Liberals Were Right: Democracy, Interdependence, and Conflict, 1950–1985," *International Studies Quarterly*, Vol. 41, No. 2 (June 1997), pp. 267–293; Michael D. Ward and Kristian S. Gleditsch, "Democratizing for Peace," *American Political Science Review*, Vol. 92, No. 1 (March 1998), pp. 51–61; and Bennett and Stam, *The Behavioral Origins of War*.

27.   See William Reed, "A Unified Statistical Model of Conflict Onset and Escalation," *American Journal of Political Science*, Vol. 44, No. 1 (January 2001), pp. 84–93.

28.   On this technique, see Greene, *Econometric Analysis*, pp. 660–663.

(MID) in year t.[29] As we discussed in Chapter 4, MIDs are events in which one state threatens, displays, or uses force against another state. We include all of the variables in Equation 5.1, plus a natural cubic spline function of the length of time since the last outbreak of a MID involving state i. We simultaneously estimate Equation 5.1 after redefining War_i as the probability that state i experiences the outbreak of an interstate war in year t, since MIDs do not involve non-state actors. The null hypothesis being tested is that these equations are independent or, more technically, that $\rho = 0$. Under these circumstances, there is no selection bias and each of these two models can be estimated separately.

We estimate a censored probit model for each of the five measures of regime type used earlier in this chapter: the composite index, the competitiveness of political participation, the openness of executive recruitment, the extent of the constraints placed on the chief executive, and the sum of the transitions as indicated by the latter three measures. In no case do we even come close to rejecting the null hypothesis that $\rho = 0$. Therefore, it is entirely appropriate to estimate Equation 5.1 as we did earlier, since this equation is independent of the equation for MIDs.

Moreover, it is interesting that the effects of the variables in Equation 5.1 that are generated using the censored probit model of interstate wars are quite similar to the results in Tables 5.1, 5.2, 5.3, 5.4, and 5.5 generated using a single-equation model of all external wars. Hence, not only can we dismiss the possibility that our results are adversely affected by non-random selection, there is also little difference in the effects of regime change on all external wars and wars between nation-states.

Eighth, we mentioned in Chapter 4 that both wars and episodes of incomplete democratization are rare events. It is useful to make sure that our results are not unduly influenced by any single instance where incomplete democratization led to war. There are a total of 47 such instances in our data set (see Appendix). We therefore eliminate each of these cases, one at a time, and then re-estimate the model. In all 47 cases, the estimate of *Incomplete Demtransition$_i$* remains positive and statistically significant. Furthermore, the estimate of *Incomplete Demtransition$_i$* × *Dom-Concentration$_i$* is always negative, and it is statistically significant in 46 out

---

29. For descriptions of the MIDs data, see Charles S. Gochman and Zeev Maoz, "Militarized Interstate Disputes, 1816–1976: Procedures, Patterns, and Insights," *Journal of Conflict Resolution*, Vol. 28, No. 4 (December 1984), pp. 585–616; and Daniel M. Jones, Stuart A. Bremer, and J. David Singer, "Militarized Interstate Disputes, 1816–1992: Rationale, Coding Rules, and Empirical Patterns," *Conflict Management and Peace Science*, Vol. 15, No. 2 (1996), pp. 163–213.

of 47 instances.[30] From a statistical standpoint, this one case out of 47 could be due to chance alone. Hence, no single episode of incomplete democratization and war seems to be driving our results.

Finally, Gary King and Langche Zeng contend that using logistic regression to analyze rare events can lead to biased estimates.[31] They have developed a procedure to address any bias of this sort. However, re-estimating Equation 5.1 using their rare-event logit procedure yields estimates that are quite similar to our earlier findings, indicating that our results do not suffer from a rare event bias.

Democratization and War Initiation

The preceding results demonstrate that states in the initial stages of democratization are especially prone to become involved in wars. Our theory leads us to expect that such states, spurred by rising nationalism and logrolled overcommitments, will be the initiators of a significant number of these conflicts. If democratizing states were always the targets of attack and never the initiators of hostilities, we might suspect that the political or military weakness of democratizing states was the main reason for their war involvement. However, we do not expect that democratizing countries will always be the attackers: there may be many cases in which they are the targets of an attack, yet the conditions precipitating the war accord with our theory. For example, a nationalistic democratizing state might provoke fears among status-quo neighbors; these neighbors, in turn, may attempt to contain its power by forceful means.

Moreover, the democratizing state might appear weakened in the short run, yet dangerous in the long run, both because of its belligerence and because of the prospect that its power will rise once its popular energies are harnessed to its nationalist aims. If so, countries neighboring this state would have a strong motive for a preventive strike. As Stephen M. Walt shows, this is commonly the case with revolutionary states, such as Iran in 1980 and Bolshevik Russia; these are among the instances in which states engaging in a transition from autocracy to anocracy were targets of attack.[32] In addition, in some states, such as the Ottoman Em-

---

30. The p-value of this estimate is .13 when Chile is removed from the sample in 1879 and constraints on the chief executive is the measure of regime change.

31. Gary King and Langche Zeng, "Explaining Rare Events Bias in International Relations," *International Organization*, Vol. 55, No. 3 (Summer 2001), pp. 693–715.

32. Stephen M. Walt, *Revolution and War* (Ithaca, N.Y.: Cornell University Press, 1996).

pire after the Young Turks' revolution on the eve of the Balkan War of 1912, an incomplete democratic transition may encourage the political mobilization of ethnic minorities, which may contribute to the weakening of the state and entice outside powers to attack it.[33]

Thus, not all cases of an attack on a democratizing state are at odds with our theory. Nor do all cases in which democratizing states initiate war confirm our theory, since such states may sometimes attack their neighbors for reasons of rational opportunism that have nothing to do with nationalism, prestige strategies, or logrolling. For these reasons, analyses of war initiation are not in themselves adequate tests of our theory. Nonetheless, such analyses do help to assess the argument that it might be the military weakness of democratizers, rather than their turbulent domestic politics, that draws them into wars. With these cautions in mind, we now turn to a preliminary statistical treatment of the relationship between democratization and the initiation of war.

Here, we focus on explaining the initiation of interstate wars. We do so in order to address the possibility that democratization is associated with the outbreak of war because it undermines states' political-military capacity, thereby rendering them especially susceptible to attack by rival countries. (It should be noted, however, that the following results are much the same as those based on analyses of the initiation of all external wars.) For the purpose of conducting the following tests, we therefore define War_i as the log of the odds that state i initiates an interstate war in year t, based on data compiled by the COW Project.[34] As in Table 5.5, we define each measure of regime change (*Complete Demtransition_i*, *Incomplete Demtransition_i*, *Complete Auttransition_i*, and *Incomplete Auttransition_i*) as the number of transitions state i experiences, based on the measurements of the competitiveness of political participation, the openness of executive recruitment, and the constraints on the chief executive during the period from year t-6 to year t-1. However, since there are significant differences in the results when we vary the length of time over which regime change is measured, we present the results for intervals ranging from one year to ten years long.[35]

---

33.   George Gavrilis, "Revolution, Democratization, and War in a Declining, Multinational Empire: The Ottoman Case," unpubl. ms. Columbia University, August 1997.

34.   See Small and Singer, *Resort to Arms;* and Singer and Small, *Correlates of War Project.*

35.   As in the previous section, we measure *Complete Demtransition_i*, *Incomplete Demtransition_i*, *Complete Auttransition_i*, and *Incomplete Auttransition_i* from year t-$(n+1)$ to year t-1, where n takes on values ranging from 1 to 10, inclusive. A separate set of estimates is then generated for each value of n.

In contrast to our prior analyses, we find no evidence that the level of domestic concentration influences the relationship between either democratization or autocratization and war initiation. As we explain more fully in Chapter 7, there is an important path to war initiation that may be followed by democratizing states with highly concentrated domestic political authority, as well as significant paths to war taken by states with little concentration of authority.

When, for example, incompletely democratizing Prussia attacked Denmark in 1864 and Austria in 1866, its level of domestic concentration was 6, slightly higher than average for our sample. States like Prussia that have relatively strong administrative institutions but poorly developed institutions regulating democratic participation are likely to use their bureaucratic clout to promote counterrevolutionary nationalism.

The more usual path, however, is exemplified by Chile. On the eve of its decision to initiate the War of the Pacific, Chile's level of domestic concentration was just 3. In that case, the state's institutional weakness left it unable to overcome diverse pressures for war exerted by political parties and economic interests.

Among the democratizing states in our sample that became involved in war, the "low-concentration" paths to hostilities have predominated. Among the smaller group of democratizing states that were the initiators of war, however, the high and low concentration paths are more equally represented. Consequently, we omit *Complete Demtransition$_i$ × DomConcentration$_i$, Incomplete Demtransition$_i$ × DomConcentration$_i$, Complete Auttransition$_i$ × DomConcentration$_i$,* and *Incomplete Auttransition$_i$ × DomConcentration$_i$* in our analysis of war initiation.[36] Since there is no evidence that the terms in the natural spline function are either jointly or individually significant, they too are omitted.

The results of that analysis, presented in Table 5.6, show that states tend to launch wars soon after transitions to a coherent democracy and some time after incomplete democratic transitions. The estimate of *Complete Demtransition$_i$* is positive and statistically significant when regime change is measured over one-year and two-year intervals. However, such transitions have little bearing on war initiation over the longer run as democratic institutions become consolidated, because none of the remaining estimates of *Complete Demtransition$_i$* are significant.

---

36. More specifically, for each value of n, the results of a likelihood ratio test provide no indication that *Complete Demtransition$_i$ × DomConcentration$_i$, Incomplete Demtransition$_i$ × DomConcentration$_i$, Complete Auttransition$_i$ × DomConcentration$_i$,* or *Incomplete Auttransition$_i$ × DomConcentration$_i$* should be included in our model of war initiation.

Table 5.6. Effects of Democratization and Autocratization on the Initiation of Interstate War, Based on the Sum of the Transitions Occurring Across the Competitiveness of Political Participation, the Openness of Executive Recruitment, and the Constraints on the Chief Executive.

Variable	Number of years (n) over which regime change is measured				
	1	2	3	4	5
Intercept	-4.408***	-4.336***	-4.211***	-4.148***	-4.483***
	(.932)	(.931)	(.886)	(.898)	(.902)
Complete Demtransition	1.258***	.777**	.190	-.089	-.245
	(.333)	(.344)	(.425)	(.442)	(.433)
Incomplete Demtransition	-.407	.127	.114	.358	.334
	(.925)	(.451)	(.338)	(.304)	(.258)
Complete Auttransition	-.201	-.536	-.371	-.507	-.611
	(.539)	(.609)	(.423)	(.444)	(.456)
Incomplete Auttransition	a	a	a	a	a
DomConcentration	.014	.013	.003	.007	.015
	(.073)	(.073)	(.071)	(.072)	(.074)
Majpower	1.908***	1.932***	1.869***	1.872***	1.937***
	(.262)	(.278)	(.272)	(.273)	(.273)
Civwar	.265	-.046	.372	.381	.443
	(.558)	(.711)	(.563)	(.568)	(.568)
Concap	-3.829	-4.306	-4.244	-4.609	-3.621
	(2.917)	(2.985)	(2.899)	(2.940)	(2.886)
Log Likelihood	-399.00	-373.97	-384.63	-377.23	-365.78
N	9420	9217	9049	8894	8747

Table 5.6. Continued.

Variable	\multicolumn{5}{c}{Number of years (n) over which regime change is measured}				
	6	7	8	9	10
Intercept	-4.234***	-4.207***	-4.093***	-4.199***	-4.061***
	(.907)	(.954)	(.964)	(.982)	(.976)
Complete Demtransition	-.428	-.272	-.030	.135	-.078
	(.445)	(.366)	(.300)	(.324)	(.292)
Incomplete Demtransition	.398	.464**	.565**	.571***	.534**
	(.288)	(.234)	(.223)	(.221)	(.213)
Complete Auttransition	.063	.286	.203	.159	.232
	(.238)	(.183)	(.186)	(.223)	(.213)
Incomplete Auttransition	——[a]	——[a]	——[a]	.502	.410
				(.403)	(.420)
DomConcentration	.003	-.005	-.001	.009	-.005
	(.072)	(.076)	(.078)	(.081)	(.079)
Majpower	1.917***	1.905***	1.877***	1.873***	1.897***
	(.274)	(.277)	(.275)	(.269)	(.270)
Civwar	.411	.390	.344	.319	.343
	(.571)	(.572)	(.584)	(.575)	(.568)
Concap	-4.328	-4.550	-5.136*	-5.148*	-5.260*
	(3.002)	(3.058)	(3.091)	(3.113)	(3.107)
Log Likelihood	-370.11	-356.24	-354.11	-354.19	-357.28
N	8599	8466	8342	8444	8330

NOTE: Entries are logistic regression estimates, with robust standard errors in parentheses.

[a] There are no cases in which a state undergoing an incomplete autocratic transition initiated a war. Instances where Incomplete Auttransition is greater than or equal to 1 are dropped from the analysis.

*** $p \leq .01$; ** $p \leq .05$; * $p \leq .10$ (two-tailed tests are conducted for all estimates).

Moreover, there is evidence that states undergoing incomplete democratic transitions are disproportionately prone to initiate war, especially over the longer run. The estimate of *Incomplete Demtransition_i* is positive in nine out of ten cases, and it is positive and statistically significant in four cases. Furthermore, this estimate would be statistically significant (at the .10 level) in six instances if we conducted one-tailed rather than two-tailed significance tests. States making the transition from autocracy to anocracy become more likely to initiate a war as the period over which regime change is measured grows longer. The lag between the demise of an authoritarian regime and the initiation of war by its anocratic successor may reflect the time needed for interest groups, coalition leaders, and politicians to promote and disseminate belligerent ideologies in reaction to the political dilemmas arising from the transition. If democratizing states were simply the weak prey of their exploitative neighbors, we would be more likely to see attacks sooner after the transition.

A separate set of tests confirms that democratizing states are not especially likely to be the targets of attack. To address this issue, we follow Dan Reiter and Allan C. Stam in coding as a target each participant in a given interstate war that did not initiate the war.[37] We then estimate the same model used to generate the results in Table 5.6, after restricting the sample to states participating in interstate wars. The results of this analysis indicate that the estimate of *Complete Demtransition_i* is positive and statistically significant only when one-year and two-year periods are analyzed; there is no other case in which the estimate of either *Complete Demtransition_i* or *Incomplete Demtransition_i* is significant. These findings therefore provide no evidence that states undergoing transition toward democracy are disproportionately prone to being attacked.[38]

Also noteworthy is that autocratization has little bearing on the initiation of war. Neither the results in Table 5.6 nor the results of the tests focusing on states engaged in interstate wars described in the preceding

---

37. Dan Reiter and Allan C. Stam, "Democracy, War Initiation, and Victory," *American Political Science Review*, Vol. 92, No. 2 (June 1998), pp. 377–390.

38. Furthermore, we continue to find virtually no case in which the estimate of any of these variables is statistically significant when we amend the COW Project's list of interstate war initiators in the ways recommended by Reiter and Stam and when we focus only on what they refer to as "core dyads," which are pairs involving the initiator of a war and its primary target or targets. Reiter and Stam, "Democracy, War Initiation, and Victory."

paragraph yield a single case in which the estimate of *Complete Aut-transition_i* or *Incomplete Auttransition_i* is statistically significant.

In sum, our results strongly suggest that states undergoing democratization are more likely to initiate wars than stable regimes or autocratizing countries. Moreover, democratizing states that become involved in wars are not especially likely to have been targets of attack. Consequently, a realist explanation focusing on the supposed military weakness of democratizing states cannot provide the main reason for their heightened risk of war.

Does War Influence Democratization?

In this chapter, we have provided considerable evidence that incomplete democratization raises the risk of war. It is also important, however, to ensure that our results are not threatened by any simultaneity bias that might arise if war also affects democratization. In fact, existing research offers little reason to suspect that this sort of problem will arise. Previous studies have found little evidence that war influences either democratization or the extent of democracy in any given country.[39] Furthermore, we have already addressed this issue in a preliminary way by lagging the effects of regime change, since it is measured from year t-6 to year t-1 and war's onset is measured in year t. Similarly, by including the spline function of war, our earlier tests controlled for any effects of war during and prior to the period in which regime change occurs.

Nonetheless, to more fully address this issue, we undertake two additional analyses. First, we directly examine whether war influences the occurrence of either complete or incomplete democratization. To do so, we measure both incomplete and complete democratization from $t+1$ to $t+6$ and war in t. Then sixteen logistic regressions are estimated.

In the first four, incomplete democratization is regressed on war, using the composite index and each of the three component measures of regime type, respectively. In the next four, we do likewise but add a natural spline function with three knots of the length of time since country i last experienced an incomplete democratic transition, to account for any temporal dependence in the data. The final eight regressions are set up in the same way as the first eight, except that the dependent variable is the oc-

39.   See Michael Mousseau and Yuhang Shi, "A Test for Reverse Causality in the Democratic Peace Relationship," *Journal of Peace Research*, Vol. 36, No. 6 (1999), pp. 639–663; and Jon C. Pevehouse, *Democracy from Above? Regional Organizations and Democratization* (New York: Cambridge University Press, 2005).

currence of a complete democratic transition. Taken together, these sixteen regressions produce only two instances where war has a statistically significant effect (at the .10 level) on democratization.[40]

Second, it is important to analyze whether war influences the trajectory of democratic transitions once they are underway. Some of these transitions yield coherent democracies within five years, whereas others do not.[41] To find out whether the outbreak of war bears on whether democratization becomes complete or remains incomplete, we focus on countries that are autocratic in year t-6 and make a change to either anocracy or democracy by t-1.

We define a variable, the observed value of which is 1 if state i undergoes an incomplete transition (that is, if i is anocratic in t-1) and 0 if it makes a complete transition (that is, if i is democratic in t-1). This variable is then regressed on a variable indicating whether a war involving i broke out at any point from t-6 to t-1. Four separate logistic regressions are estimated, using the composite index, the competitiveness of political participation, the constraints on the chief executive, and the openness of executive recruitment, respectively, to measure democratization. In no case is the effect of war even close to statistically significant. Further, its influence is virtually unchanged when we control for the existence of a civil war during the interval from t-6 to t-1 and the value of Reg_i in t-6, factors that also might affect whether transitions from autocracy culminate in an anocracy or a democracy.

In sum, then, these analyses provide very little evidence that war influences whether a democratic transition occurs and absolutely no indication that war influences whether those transitions that do take place are complete or incomplete. Consequently, there is no reason to worry that our earlier results are threatened by problems of endogeneity.

---

40.   The two instances are when the dependent variable is the occurrence of a complete democratic transition based on the openness of executive recruitment, with and without the spline function. It should also be noted that war has little effect on domestic concentration. We regressed the value of domestic concentration in year $t+1$ on the outbreak of war in year t, both with and without a lagged endogenous variable. In neither case was the estimate of war statistically significant.

41.   Democratic transitions that are incomplete after five years usually remain incomplete for some time; they are rarely followed soon thereafter by transitions to full-fledged democracy. Of the 316 discrete cases of incomplete democratization in our data set—based on all four indices of regime change combined (see Table 4.1)—there are only 23 instances in which an incomplete transition over a given five-year period was followed by a transition to coherent democracy over the following five-year interval.

Conclusion

The many democratic transitions occurring in recent years have been greeted with substantial enthusiasm. However, transitions to democracy can be treacherous processes. Those that become stalled prior to the establishment of a coherent democracy in states where little authority is centralized in the hands of public officials create conditions ripe for external war.

The results of our statistical analyses bear out this argument. Tests conducted using each of five measures of regime type yield considerable evidence that, during the nineteenth and twentieth centuries, states with weak institutions that experience transitions from an autocracy to an anocracy have been more likely to become involved in a war than states experiencing either other types of regime change or no change.

Chapter 6

Democratizing Dyads and the Outbreak of War: Statistical Findings

The results presented in the previous chapter provide considerable support for our argument that incomplete democratization is a potent impetus to war when domestic institutions are fragmented and weak. These tests were based on a monadic research design: the individual nation-state was the unit of analysis.

However, much of the existing research on the links between regime type and hostilities is cast at the dyadic level of analysis, particularly the extensive and influential body of literature on the democratic peace. Whereas many studies have concluded that mature democracies do not fight each other, the bulk of the evidence indicates that they are about as likely as autocracies to fight states that are not democratic. This difference between the dyadic democratic peace and the monadic impact of democratization raises a conceptual question about how to join the two sets of findings. It also highlights the need to control for dyadic attributes when analyzing the monadic influence of democratization on military conflict.

This chapter addresses these issues by extending the analysis conducted in Chapter 5. The results from our investigation of country-pairs indicate that the likelihood of interstate war rises markedly if either state in a dyad undergoes an incomplete democratic transition when its political institutions are weak. Furthermore, these findings hold up even after accounting for the static regime characteristics emphasized in research on the democratic peace, various aspects of power relations stressed in realist theories of international relations, and other factors.

The Research Design

Almost all of the existing work on the relationship between democratization and international conflict has been cast at the monadic level of analysis. This is consistent with our argument that states undergoing incomplete democratic transitions are likely to become drawn into conflicts with all types of regimes: stable democracies, anocracies, and autocracies, as well as transitional states. The effect of incomplete democratization on conflict arises from the monadic properties of the transitional state, not the dyadic properties stemming from this state's relationship with another country.

However, some observers have argued that it is also important to address the effects of democratization on war using a dyadic research design, since doing so helps to account for a wide range of factors that influence political-military relations between states.[1] Such factors cannot be included in a strictly monadic analysis and could affect the relationship between incomplete democratization and war that we observed in Chapter 5. Only a few dyadic studies have addressed the effects of democratic transitions on hostilities and they have focused on explaining classes of conflict that, like militarized interstate disputes (MIDs), range in intensity from wars to disputes involving threats to use force but no actual fatalities.[2] But MIDs rarely escalate to war. Since our argument emphasizes the links between democratization and war, it is important to conduct a set of tests using a dyadic research design that directly examines these links.

At the outset, however, it is important to recognize that these tests are limited in a number of important ways. As in Chapter 5, our sample in-

1. See, for example, John R. Oneal and Bruce M. Russett, "The Classical Liberals Were Right: Democracy, Interdependence, and Conflict, 1950–1985," *International Studies Quarterly*, Vol. 41, No. 2 (June 1997), pp. 267–293; Zeev Maoz, "Realist and Cultural Critiques of the Democratic Peace: A Theoretical and Empirical Re-assessment," *International Interactions*, Vol. 24, No. 1 (1998), pp. 3–89; and D. Scott Bennett and Allan C. Stam, *The Behavioral Origins of War* (Ann Arbor: University of Michigan Press, 2003).

2. Oneal and Russett, "The Classical Liberals Were Right"; Christopher Gelpi and Joseph Grieco, "Attracting Trouble: Democracy, Leadership Tenure, and the Targeting of Militarized Challenges, 1918–1992," *Journal of Conflict Resolution*, Vol. 45, No. 6 (December 2001), pp. 794–815; Bruce Russett and John R. Oneal, *Triangulating Peace: Democracy, Interdependence, and International Organizations* (New York: Norton, 2001); Edward D. Mansfield and Jack Snyder, "Incomplete Democratization and the Outbreak of Military Disputes," *International Studies Quarterly*, Vol. 46, No. 4 (December 2002), pp. 529–549; and Shuhei Kurizaki, "Dyadic Effects of Democratization on International Disputes," *International Relations of the Asia-Pacific*, Vol. 4 (2004), pp. 1–33.

cludes all countries identified as members of the interstate system by the Correlates of War (COW) Project during the nineteenth and twentieth centuries (specifically, 1816–1992).[3] But the tests in the previous chapter addressed the outbreak of all external war, since our argument is that democratization promotes imperial and extra-systemic wars against non-state actors as well as belligerence against sovereign states. By contrast, the dyadic nature of the current analysis requires us to restrict attention to interstate wars, since non-state actors are not members of the international system. Because various states in the throes of democratization have launched extra-systemic wars that are excluded from this analysis, these tests of our argument will be especially demanding.[4] Furthermore, while the outbreak of war is a relatively rare event for any given state, war between a given pair of states is even more rare. With such sparse data, the results of our analysis must be interpreted cautiously. Nonetheless, in light of the fact that many recent studies of conflict are based on a dyadic research design and of the various calls that have been issued for tests of the relationship between democratization and war that account for dyadic factors, it is useful to get some sense of whether our previous results hold up in a dyadic setting.

As in Chapter 5, we rely on the COW Project's data on war to conduct this analysis. For each year, t, we code whether a war broke out between every pair of states, s and l, in the global system. We observe 1 if a war began and 0 otherwise. We measure regime change using the same five indices that were analyzed in Chapter 5: the composite index, the competitiveness of political participation, the openness of executive recruitment, the extent of the constraints placed on the chief executive, and the sum of the number of transitions occurring across the last three of these indices. For each index, we continue to measure regime change over five-year periods, using the coding rules described in Chapter 4. We also continue to distinguish between complete and incomplete regime transitions. But because each observation contains information on two states, s and l, two variables are included for each type of re-

---

3. Melvin Small and J. David Singer, *Resort to Arms: International and Civil Wars, 1816–1980* (Beverly Hills, Calif.: Sage, 1982); and Singer and Small, *Correlates of War Project: International and Civil War Data, 1816–1992*, Inter-University Consortium for Political and Social Research No. 9905 (1994).

4. Edward D. Mansfield and Jack Snyder, "Democratization and the Danger of War," *International Security*, Vol. 20, No. 1 (Summer 1995), pp. 5–38; and Mansfield and Snyder, "Democratization and War," *Foreign Affairs*, Vol. 74, No. 3 (May/June 1995), pp. 79–97.

gime change, rather than one variable as was the case in the monadic analysis.

To distinguish between states s and l, we rely on the composite measure of regime type (*Reg*) developed by Ted Robert Gurr and his colleagues and described in Chapter 4.[5] Recall that Gurr's measure ranges from −10 to 10, where higher (lower) values correspond to more democratic (autocratic) polities. Since it has been used extensively in empirical studies of the democratic peace, we include the value of this variable for each country in each dyad in the following statistical tests.[6] We define country s as the state with the smaller value of *Reg* in year t-1 (that is, the least democratic state) and country l as the state with the larger value of *Reg* (that is, the most democratic state) in that year.[7]

We also use *Reg* to distinguish between the two variables corresponding to each type of regime change. More specifically, to address the effects of incomplete democratization on war, we define two dummy variables, *Incomplete Demtransition*$_s$ and *Incomplete Demtransition*$_l$. The former variable indicates whether state s undergoes a shift from autocracy to anocracy between year t-6 and year t-1. The latter variable indicates whether state l undergoes such a shift. Similarly, *Complete Demtransition*$_s$ and *Complete Demtransition*$_l$ measure whether states s and l, respectively, change from either autocracy or anocracy to democracy between years t-6 and t-1. *DomConcentration*$_s$ and *DomConcentration*$_l$ are the levels of institutional strength and centralization in countries s and l in year t-1. To test within a dyadic framework the argument that stalled democratic transitions are more likely to precipitate the outbreak of war if states have weak domestic institutions, we include *DomConcentration*$_s$ and its interaction with *Incomplete Demtransition*$_s$ as well as *DomConcentration*$_l$ and its interaction with *Incomplete Demtransition*$_l$. We also analyze the interaction between each measure of complete democratization and domestic con-

---

5.   Ted Robert Gurr, Keith Jaggers, and Will H. Moore, *Polity II: Political Structures and Regime Change, 1800–1986*, Inter-University Consortium for Political and Social Research No. 9263 (1989); and Keith Jaggers and Ted Robert Gurr, "Tracking Democracy's Third Wave with the Polity III Data," *Journal of Peace Research*, Vol. 32, No. 4 (November 1995), pp. 469–482.

6.   See, for example, Erik Gartzke, "Preferences and the Democratic Peace," *International Studies Quarterly*, Vol. 44, No. 2 (June 2000), pp. 191–212; and Russett and Oneal, *Triangulating Peace*.

7.   In cases where the value of *Reg* is the same for two states, we arbitrarily define country s as the state with the lower COW country code and country l as the state with the higher COW country code. For these codes, see Small and Singer, *Resort to Arms*; and Singer and Small, *Correlates of War Project*.

centration (*Complete Demtransition$_l$* × *DomConcentration$_l$* and *Complete Demtransition$_s$* × *DomConcentration$_s$*).

As in Chapter 5, our argument suggests that the coefficient of incomplete democratization should be positive for both the most and least democratic state in each pair (*Incomplete Demtransition$_l$* and *Incomplete Demtransition$_s$*) and that their associated interaction terms (*Incomplete Demtransition$_l$* × *DomConcentration$_l$* and *Incomplete Demtransition$_s$* × *DomConcentration$_s$*) should be negative. By themselves, the estimates of *Incomplete Demtransition$_l$* and *Incomplete Demtransition$_s$* indicate the influence of an incomplete democratic transition on war for, respectively, the most and least democratic state in each pair when domestic concentration equals 0. We expect that such a transition will be especially dangerous in countries with virtually no institutional strength or centralization. The coefficients of *Incomplete Demtransition$_l$* × *DomConcentration$_l$* and *Incomplete Demtransition$_s$* × *DomConcentration$_s$* indicate the change in the impact of incomplete democratization on the likelihood of interstate war due to a one-unit change in domestic concentration. We expect these coefficients to be negative. As we explained in Chapter 3, countries undergoing an incomplete democratic transition are less prone to war if they are marked by greater institutional strength and centralization, and hence a higher level of domestic concentration.

Finally, we continue to assess whether regime change in an autocratic direction influences the use of force. *Incomplete Auttransition$_s$* and *Incomplete Auttransition$_l$* indicate whether states s and l experience a change from democracy to anocracy between year t-6 and year t-1; *Complete Auttransition$_s$* and *Complete Auttransition$_l$* measure whether these states undergo a transition from either democracy or anocracy to autocracy. As in Chapter 5, we analyze the interaction between each of these variables and the level of domestic concentration as well.

CONTROL VARIABLES

In addition to the variables described in the previous section, it is important to account for the effects of factors operating at various levels of analysis that might underlie any observed relationship between democratization and war. To begin, we include the control variables that were analyzed in Chapter 5: major power status, civil violence, and the international distribution of power.

To assess the effects of major powers on the outbreak of interstate wars using a dyadic research design, we define two variables. *Majpower$_1$* is a dummy variable that equals 1 if one state in the dyad is a major power in year t-1, and 0 otherwise. *Majpower$_2$* equals 1 if both states are major powers. In addition, we account for the effects of civil violence on external war by including *Civwar$_{sl}$*, which equals 1 if either state s or state l experienced a civil war in year t-1 and 0 otherwise.[8] We also include *Concap*, the concentration of capabilities among the major powers in year t-1.

We supplement these variables with a set of factors that are associated with political-military relations between states and that have been analyzed repeatedly in dyadic studies of conflict. A number of them are emphasized by realists, who might speculate that democratization promotes war by undermining the political-military power of states undergoing regime change, rather than for the reasons advanced in Chapter 3. To address this concern, we include *Capratio$_{sl}$*, a measure of the distribution of capabilities between states s and l in year t-1. Following existing statistical studies of regime type and conflict, we measure each state's capabilities by averaging its share of the international system's total population, urban population, military expenditures, military personnel, iron and steel production, and energy consumption, using data taken from the COW Project.[9] *Capratio$_{sl}$* is the ratio of the share of these capabilities controlled by the more powerful state to the share controlled by the weaker one.

To further capture the nature of political-military relations, we analyze the effects of alliances. *Allies$_{sl}$* equals 1 if s and l are political-military allies in t-1, and 0 otherwise, based on the COW Project's data.[10] Including this variable is important because it is widely argued that wars are less likely to occur between allies than between other states.

Equally well known is the fact that antagonism is more frequent between states in relatively close proximity.[11] Consequently, we include two

---

8. Note that we do not define a second variable for cases in which both states experienced a civil war, since there are no cases in the data where this occurred and an interstate war broke out.

9. Such studies include Gartzke, "Preferences and the Democratic Peace"; Russett and Oneal, *Triangulating Peace;* Mansfield and Snyder, "Incomplete Democratization and the Outbreak of Military Disputes"; and Bennett and Stam, *The Behavioral Origins of War.* Data on these capabilities are taken from J. David Singer and Melvin Small, *National Material Capabilities Dataset,* Inter-University Consortium for Political and Social Research No. 9903 (1993).

10. J. David Singer and Melvin Small, "Alliance Aggregation and the Onset of War, 1816–1965," in J. David Singer, ed., *Quantitative International Politics: Insights and Evidence* (New York: Free Press, 1968), pp. 247–268; and Correlates of War Project, *Alliances Data* (University of Michigan, 1993).

11. Stuart A. Bremer, "Dangerous Dyads: Conditions Affecting the Likelihood of In-

measures of the geographic distance between the states making up each dyad. First, *Contiguous$_{sl}$* is a dummy variable that distinguishes between dyads that are geographically contiguous and those that are not. Second, *Distance$_{sl}$* is the distance (in miles) between the capital cities of states *s* and *l*. It equals 0 if these countries are contiguous.

As in Chapter 5, our statistical analysis covers the period from 1816–1992, the era for which comprehensive data on regime type, the centralization and strength of domestic institutions, and war are available. We continue to run separate analyses using the composite index, the competitiveness of political participation, the openness of executive recruitment, executive constraints, and the sum of the transitions occurring across the last three of these indices to measure regime change. Logistic regression is used to estimate the effects of the aforementioned variables on the onset of interstate war, after including a natural spline function (with three knots) of the number of years that have elapsed since each dyad last experienced the outbreak of war.[12] (Note, however, that the estimates of these parameters are not shown in the tables.) We also continue to conduct tests of statistical significance using robust (Huber) standard errors, which correct for any panel heteroskedasticity and account for the grouped nature of our data (by dyad).

The Statistical Results

The results of this analysis are shown in Table 6.1. They provide additional evidence that incomplete democratization promotes war in the face of low levels of domestic concentration. As predicted by our theory, the estimates of *Incomplete Demtransition$_s$* and *Incomplete Demtransition$_l$* are positive, the estimates of *Incomplete Demtransition$_s$* × *DomConcentration$_s$*

terstate War, 1816–1965," *Journal of Conflict Resolution*, Vol. 36, No. 2 (June 1992), pp. 309–341; John Vasquez, *The War Puzzle* (Cambridge: Cambridge University Press, 1994); Paul Huth, *Standing Your Ground: Territorial Disputes and International Conflict* (Ann Arbor: University of Michigan Press, 1996); Russett and Oneal, *Triangulating Peace*, pp. 86–87; and Bennett and Stam, *The Behavioral Origins of War*.

12.   Nathaniel Beck and Richard Tucker, "Conflict in Space and Time: Time-Series-Cross-Section Analysis with a Binary Dependent Variable" (paper presented at the annual meeting of the American Political Science Association, San Francisco, Calif., 1996); Nathaniel Beck and Jonathan N. Katz, "The Analysis of Binary Time-Series-Cross-Section Data and/or the Democratic Peace" (paper presented at the annual meeting of the Political Methodology Group, Columbus, Ohio, 1997); and Nathaniel Beck, Jonathan N. Katz, and Richard Tucker, "Taking Time Seriously: Time-Series-Cross-Section Analysis with a Binary Dependent Variable," *American Journal of Political Science*, Vol. 42, No. 4 (October 1998), pp. 1260–1288.

Table 6.1. Logit Estimates of the Effects of Democratization on War Between States.

Variable	Composite Index	Competitiveness of Political Participation	Openness of Executive Recruitment	Constraints on the Executive	Sum of the Transitions
Intercept	-3.465***	-3.127***	-3.790***	-3.583***	-3.366***
	(.690)	(.692)	(.659)	(.672)	(.661)
Complete Demtransition$_l$	-0.503	-1.138	-2.744**	-7.259***	-3.026***
	(0.588)	(1.375)	(1.218)	(1.074)	(.701)
Complete Demtransition$_s$	—a	-1.770	-1.882*	—a	-2.907***
		(1.291)	(1.012)		(.914)
Incomplete Demtransition$_l$	2.902***	2.468**	5.088***	3.153***	1.514***
	(.955)	(1.050)	(1.707)	(.791)	(.324)
Incomplete Demtransition$_s$	3.393**	2.949***	3.659***	2.386**	1.431***
	(1.448)	(.867)	(.878)	(1.129)	(.295)
Complete Auttransition$_l$	-4.004*	-1.855**	-.083	-1.376	-1.012
	(2.246)	(.911)	(1.976)	(2.708)	(1.093)
Complete Auttransition$_s$	2.306***	1.666**	-3.462***	.590	.297
	(.753)	(.785)	(1.089)	(2.036)	(.423)
Incomplete Auttransition$_l$	4.993***	3.425***	4.215***	4.539***	3.774***
	(.753)	(.684)	(.868)	(.816)	(.450)
Incomplete Auttransition$_s$	4.180***	3.384***	4.430***	.971	1.869*
	(1.117)	(1.168)	(1.727)	(1.260)	(.960)
DomConcentration$_l$	.080	.086	.081	.083	.089
	(.054)	(.054)	(.052)	(.055)	(.055)
DomConcentration$_s$	.016	-.015	-.007	.004	-.017
	(.056)	(.054)	(.053)	(.056)	(.054)

Table 6.1. *Continued.*

Variable	Composite Index	Competitiveness of Political Participation	Openness of Executive Recruitment	Constraints on the Executive	Sum of the Transitions
Complete Demtransition$_l$	—[b]	.064	.406**	1.097***	.419***
		(.223)	(.201)	(.088)	(.106)
× DomConcentration$_l$					
Complete Demtransition$_s$	—[a]	.298**	.384***	—[a]	.536***
		(.132)	(.148)		(.127)
× DomConcentration$_s$					
Incomplete Demtransition$_l$	−.447**	−.486**	−1.150**	−.520***	−.266***
	(.187)	(.225)	(.521)	(.166)	(.075)
× DomConcentration$_l$					
Incomplete Demtransition$_s$	−.907**	−.839***	−.573***	−.461*	−.309***
	(.423)	(.240)	(.180)	(.242)	(.072)
× DomConcentration$_s$					
Complete Auttransition$_l$	.681**	.324***	.091	.320	.206
	(.287)	(.108)	(.314)	(.367)	(.154)
× DomConcentration$_l$					
Complete Auttransition$_s$	−.364***	−.270**	.279***	−.177	−.091
	(.109)	(.111)	(.057)	(.290)	(.064)
× DomConcentration$_s$					
Incomplete Auttransition$_l$	−.831***	−.632***	−.639***	−.734***	−.691***
	(.082)	(.108)	(.141)	(.090)	(.089)
× DomConcentration$_l$					
Incomplete Auttransition$_s$	−.877***	−.496***	−.764***	.051	−.197
	(.079)	(.181)	(.214)	(.219)	(.179)
× DomConcentration$_s$					
Reg$_l$	.069***	.061***	.062***	.070***	.070***
	(.017)	(.017)	(.016)	(.017)	(.017)
Reg$_s$	−.064***	−.064***	−.072***	−.073***	−.071***
	(.021)	(.021)	(.021)	(.023)	(.021)
Majpower$_l$	1.691***	1.623***	1.669***	1.688***	1.643***
	(.189)	(.187)	(.182)	(.187)	(.182)

Table 6.1. *Continued.*

Variable	Composite Index	Competitiveness of Political Participation	Openness of Executive Recruitment	Constraints on the Executive	Sum of the Transitions
Majpower$_2$	.592**	.704***	.619**	.579***	.752***
	(.256)	(.263)	(.257)	(.256)	(.264)
Civwar	.820***	.749***	.807***	.713***	.868***
	(.228)	(.233)	(.231)	(.233)	(.231)
Concap	−17.793***	−17.960***	−16.321***	−17.529***	−17.607***
	(2.287)	(2.299)	(2.106)	(2.218)	(2.183)
Capratio$_{sl}$	−.011***	−.010***	−.011***	−.011***	−.010***
	(.003)	(.003)	(.003)	(.003)	(.003)
Allies$_{sl}$	.144	.076	.126	.120	.116
	(.221)	(.228)	(.224)	(.225)	(.232)
Contiguous$_{sl}$	1.657***	1.674***	1.660***	1.671***	1.662***
	(.241)	(.242)	(.240)	(.240)	(.243)
Distance$_{sl}$	−.00003	−.00004	−.00003	−.00003	−.00004
	(.00004)	(.00004)	(.00004)	(.00004)	(.00004)
Log Likelihood	−1503.63	−1474.45	−1502.37	−1500.15	−1458.53
N	339,302	321,539	339,302	339,302	321,539

NOTE: Entries are logistic regression estimates, with robust standard errors in parentheses. Each model is estimated after including a natural spline function with three knots.

[a] This parameter is not estimated because there is no case in which a complete democratic transition led to war.

[b] This parameter is not estimated due to collinearity.

*** $p \leq .01$; ** $p \leq .05$; * $p \leq .10$ (two-tailed tests are conducted for all estimates).

and *Incomplete Demtransition$_l$* × *DomConcentration$_l$* are negative, and each one of them is statistically significant, regardless of which measure of regime type is considered.

In contrast, complete democratization has a less consistent effect on the outbreak of war, differing markedly across the various measures of regime type. When focusing on the openness of executive recruitment and the sum of transitions, the estimates of *Complete Demtransition$_s$* and *Complete Demtransition$_l$* are negative, their associated interaction terms are positive, and all of these estimates are statistically significant. Measuring regime change using the constraints on the chief executive also yields a negative and significant estimate of *Complete Demtransition$_l$* and a positive and significant estimate of *Complete Demtransition$_l$* × *DomConcentration$_l$*. However, there is no case where state *s* (the less democratic of the pair) entered a war in the wake of a complete democratic transition. Further, the effects of complete democratization are relatively weak based on the competitiveness of political participation and quite weak based on the composite index.

Even more inconsistent is the influence of complete autocratization. For the most democratic state in each pair (state *l*), the estimate of *Complete Auttransition$_l$* is always negative and the estimate of *Complete Auttransition$_l$* × *DomConcentration$_l$* is always positive; however, each set of estimates is statistically significant only when the composite index and the competitiveness of political participation are analyzed. Conversely, for the least democratic state in each pair (state *s*), the estimate of *Complete Auttransition$_s$* is positive in four out of five cases. It is positive and significant in two cases and it is negative and significant in one. The estimate of *Complete Auttransition$_s$* × *DomConcentration$_s$* is negative in four instances. It is negative and significant in two cases and it is positive and significant in one. Clearly, neither complete democratization nor complete autocratization exerts a uniform effect on war, a finding that corresponds with our earlier results presented in Chapter 5.

Incomplete autocratization, however, does appear to have a strong influence on the outbreak of belligerence, a result that differs from our previous findings. Each estimate corresponding to this type of transition is positive, each estimate of the interaction between incomplete autocratization and domestic concentration is negative, and all but three of them are statistically significant. In other words, like incomplete democratization, incomplete autocratic transitions seem to spur the onset of interstate wars as the level of concentration declines. The following analysis, however, reveals that these results are misleading; they stem from the spurious association between Greece's incomplete autocratization in 1915 and its subsequent entrance into World War I.

Results When the World Wars are Excluded

As we mentioned in Chapter 5, there are a number of cases in which states undergoing a regime transition became involved in World War I, World War II, or the Korean War. Since many of these countries were only nominal participants in the hostilities, it is important to assess the robustness of the results in Table 6.1 by re-estimating our models after excluding those years during which World War I (1914–1918), World War II (1939–1945), and the Korean War (1950–1953) were waged.[13]

The results presented in Table 6.2 indicate that omitting these years has virtually no bearing on the effect of incomplete democratic transitions. In each case, the estimate of incomplete democratization is positive and the estimate of the interaction between incomplete democratization and domestic concentration is negative. In every case except one, both of these estimates are statistically significant.[14] Further, the results continue to provide little indication that either complete democratization or complete autocratization exerts a systematic influence on the outbreak of interstate war.

In stark contrast to our earlier results, however, there is also little evidence that incomplete autocratization promotes hostilities. In Table 6.2, two estimates of *Incomplete Auttransition$_l$* and three estimates of *Incomplete Auttransition$_s$* are positive; their associated interaction terms are negative in three cases and positive in two. But only four of these ten estimates are statistically significant. Five coefficients associated with incomplete autocratization (and their corresponding interaction terms) cannot be estimated because there is no instance where such a transition was followed by the outbreak of war once we exclude the years during which World War I, World War II, and the Korean War were under way.

What accounts for the considerably weaker influence of incomplete autocratization when these war-years are excluded? There is only one case where a state making this type of transition subsequently became involved in a world war.[15] Based on all of our measures of regime type,

---

13. We noted in Chapters 4 and 5 that, in certain cases, countries that make a shift from autocracy to anocracy while emerging from communist rule may not be valid instances of incomplete democratization and may not reflect the mechanisms underlying our theory. We re-estimated the model for each measure of regime type after removing the communist countries from the sample. The results are much the same as those shown in Table 6.1. For a list of these countries, see Chapter 5, fn. 25.

14. The one exception is when state *l*—the more democratic of the two—is analyzed and regime type is measured using the competitiveness of political participation.

15. Here and elsewhere in this chapter, we refer to World War I, World War II, and the Korean War as the world wars.

Table 6.2. Logit Estimates of the Effects of Democratization on War Between States, Excluding Years in which World War I, World War II, and the Korean War were Fought.

Variable	Composite Index	Competitiveness of Political Participation	Openness of Executive Recruitment	Constraints on the Executive	Sum of the Transitions
Intercept	-7.022***	-6.884***	-7.926***	-7.354***	-7.811***
	(.973)	(1.021)	(1.042)	(.984)	(1.052)
Complete Demtransition$_l$	—a	2.677**	-2.739**	—a	-3.066***
		(1.153)	(1.153)		(.712)
Complete Demtransition$_s$	—a	.542	-.694	—a	-2.315**
		(1.378)	(1.009)		(.938)
Incomplete Demtransition$_l$	3.295***	2.120*	6.097***	3.809***	1.885***
	(1.165)	(1.284)	(1.755)	(.906)	(.329)
Incomplete Demtransition$_s$	4.438***	3.608***	5.831***	3.858***	2.085***
	(1.592)	(.954)	(.783)	(1.363)	(.286)
Complete Auttransition$_l$	-13.492***	—a	.630	-2.141	-1.070
	(1.991)		(1.606)	(2.985)	(1.409)
Complete Auttransition$_s$	3.548***	2.435**	-2.181*	2.327	.881*
	(.836)	(1.127)	(1.191)	(2.523)	(.493)
Incomplete Auttransition$_l$	—a	1.601	—a	—a	1.617*
		(1.015)			(.913)
Incomplete Auttransition$_s$	—a	2.786*	—a	.324	1.469
		(1.435)		(.927)	(1.086)
DomConcentration$_l$	.085	.095	.090	.088	.103
	(.068)	(.072)	(.069)	(.069)	(.073)
DomConcentration$_s$	.156**	.109	.146*	.142*	.138*
	(.078)	(.075)	(.077)	(.081)	(.077)

Table 6.2. Continued.

Variable	Composite Index	Competitiveness of Political Participation	Openness of Executive Recruitment	Constraints on the Executive	Sum of the Transitions
Complete Demtransition$_l$	—[a]	-.708***	.495***	—[a]	.440***
		(.124)	(.191)		(.105)
× DomConcentration$_l$					
Complete Demtransition$_s$	—[a]	.220	.296**	—[a]	.523***
		(.180)	(.142)		(.128)
× DomConcentration$_s$					
Incomplete Demtransition$_l$	-.575**	-.407	-1.268**	-.664***	-.330***
	(.255)	(.267)	(.560)	(.201)	(.083)
× DomConcentration$_l$					
Incomplete Demtransition$_s$	-.943**	-.797***	-.755***	-.582**	-.324***
	(.441)	(.204)	(.163)	(.284)	(.067)
× DomConcentration$_s$					
Complete Auttransition$_l$	1.720***	—[a]	-.127	.404	.163
	(.239)		(.261)	(.418)	(.207)
× DomConcentration$_l$					
Complete Auttransition$_s$	-.569***	-.385**	.151	-.426	-.177**
	(.109)	(.156)	(.079)	(.376)	(.084)
× DomConcentration$_s$					
Incomplete Auttransition$_l$	—[a]	-.433***	—[a]	—[a]	-.543***
		(.142)			(.115)
× DomConcentration$_l$					
Incomplete Auttransition$_s$	—[a]	-.230	—[a]	.265	.007
		(.160)		(.176)	(.172)
× DomConcentration$_s$					
Reg$_l$	.048**	.045**	.048**	.055**	.050**
	(.022)	(.022)	(.021)	(.023)	(.022)
Reg$_s$	-.086**	-.104***	-.098***	-.110**	-.111***
	(.034)	(.032)	(.038)	(.044)	(.037)
Majpower$_l$	1.130***	1.058***	1.153***	1.182***	1.076***
	(.265)	(.269)	(.259)	(.256)	(.255)

Table 6.2. *Continued.*

Variable	Composite Index	Competitiveness of Political Participation	Openness of Executive Recruitment	Constraints on the Executive	Sum of the Transitions
Majpower$_2$	-.404	-.247	-.397	-.419	-.219
	(.547)	(.562)	(.541)	(.544)	(.561)
Civwar	1.363***	1.275***	1.324***	1.204***	1.396***
	(.273)	(.286)	(.275)	(.282)	(.277)
Concap	-8.178***	-7.485***	-6.170**	-7.791***	-6.438**
	(2.869)	(2.848)	(2.702)	(2.739)	(2.708)
Capratio$_{sl}$	-.020***	-.019**	-.020***	-.021**	-.018**
	(.008)	(.008)	(.008)	(.008)	(.008)
Allies$_{sl}$	-.156	-.228	-.130	-.185	-.152
	(.283)	(.293)	(.281)	(.291)	(.290)
Contiguous$_{sl}$	2.001***	1.982***	1.964***	1.993***	1.953***
	(.341)	(.350)	(.340)	(.343)	(.353)
Distance$_{sl}$	-.00028***	-.00032***	-.00029***	-.00029***	-.00033***
	(.00009)	(.00009)	(.00009)	(.00009)	(.00009)
Log Likelihood	-804.53	-778.08	-795.06	-796.81	-762.46
N	321,255	305,563	321,255	321,255	305,563

NOTE: Entries are logistic regression estimates, with robust standard errors in parentheses. Each model is estimated after including a natural spline function with three knots.
a This parameter is not estimated because there is no case in which a complete democratic transition led to war.
b This parameter is not estimated due to collinearity.
*** $p \leq .01$; ** $p \leq .05$; * $p \leq .10$ (two-tailed tests are conducted for all estimates).

Greece shifted from democracy to anocracy before entering World War I in 1917. This case alone is responsible for the observed effects of incomplete autocratic transitions in Table 6.1. Further analysis, however, reveals that regime change had little bearing on the Greek decision to go to war.

In 1913, King George I died and Constantine assumed the Greek throne. Constantine advocated Greek neutrality in World War I. However, Eleftherios Venizelos, the leader of the Greek Liberal Party, forcefully advocated entering the war in support of the Entente, convinced that the Entente would emerge victorious and that fighting alongside this alliance would enable Greece to realize its territorial ambitions in Eastern Thrace, the Aegean, northern Epirus, and Asia Minor.[16] This "National Schism" between the royalists and Venizelists "split the country into two rival, and sometimes warring, camps."[17]

The transition to anocracy began at the end of 1915, when Venizelists boycotted the national elections, setting the stage for the establishment of a provisional government by Venizelos in the summer of 1916. At this point, Greece had two governments, one led by Constantine and a second led by Venizelos. The members of the Entente, anxious to have Greece enter the war on their behalf, recognized the provisional government and began placing intense pressure on the monarch to relinquish the throne.[18] In June 1917, Constantine was forced by the Entente to leave Greece and the country soon joined the Entente's war effort.

Although this was a situation in which an incomplete autocratic transition was followed by hostilities, the transition itself was hardly the root cause of Greece's decision to enter the war. The regime change occurred in 1915, when Constantine was still the head of state and committed to the policy of Greek neutrality. It was the leadership change orchestrated by the Entente and its recognition of Venizelos' provisional government—not the earlier regime change—that precipitated Greece's involvement in World War I.

Thus, the far weaker influence of incomplete autocratization that emerges when we exclude the world wars grows out of a spurious case

---

16.   D. George Kousoulas, *Modern Greece: Profile of a Nation* (New York: Charles Scribner's Sons, 1974), p. 106.

17.   Richard Clogg, *A Concise History of Greece*, 2d ed. (New York: Cambridge University Press, 2002), p. 83.

18.   George B. Leontaritis, *Greece and the First World War: From Neutrality to Intervention, 1917–1918* (New York: Columbia University Press, 1990); Clogg, *A Concise History of Greece*, pp. 88–89; and John S. Koliopoulos and Thanos M. Veremis, *Greece: The Modern Sequel from 1831 to the Present* (New York: New York University Press, 2002), p. 285.

of regime change and involvement in World War I. Since the other types of regime change we analyze have a fairly consistent effect regardless of whether we include or exclude the years when world wars were conducted, the results in Table 6.2 seem to provide a more reliable picture than the results in Table 6.1 of the relationship between regime change and the outbreak of hostilities.

To interpret the findings in Table 6.2 more fully, Figures 6.1, 6.2, 6.3, and 6.4 show the relative risk of war between state s and state l, based on the composite index and the three component measures of regime type. Recall from Chapter 5 that, for each regime change analyzed here, the relative risk is the probability of war when that type of change takes place, divided by the probability of war in the absence of regime change. To conduct this analysis, we hold constant each continuous variable (Reg_s, Reg_l, $Concap$, $Capratio_{sl}$, and $Distance_{sl}$) at its mean and set each dichotomous variable ($Majpower_1$, $Majpower_2$, $Civwar$, $Allies_{sl}$, and $Contiguous_{sl}$) to 0, since that is the modal value of each. As in Chapter 5, we present the relative risk of war associated with each type of regime change when $DomConcentration_s$ and $DomConcentration_l$ are both set to 5 and then again when they are both set to 2. Doing so helps illustrate the effects of incomplete democratization on war as the domestic level of concentration declines.

The results provide strong support for our argument. Depending on the index used to measure regime type, the relative risk of interstate war due to incomplete democratization increases by roughly four-fold to forty-five-fold when domestic concentration dips from 5 to 2. Moreover, for each measure of regime type except the competitiveness of political participation, the relative risk of hostilities is greatest when state s—the less democratic state in each pair—makes an incomplete democratic transition and its level of concentration equals 2.

Clearly, there is some scattered evidence that other types of regime change also influence the use of force. It is particularly interesting that a complete autocratic transition by state s leads to a sizeable increase in the risk of war when domestic concentration is relatively low based on each measure of regime type other than openness of executive recruitment. However, transitions of this sort by state l—the more democratic state —have no such effect. Notwithstanding this evidence, our central argument holds: incomplete democratic transitions combined with low levels of domestic concentration create a much more potent impetus to belligerence than any other set of conditions analyzed here.

To analyze the results in Table 6.2 further, Figure 6.5 presents the relative risk of war based on the number of component measures that indicate a transition (competitiveness of political participation, openness of

Figure 6.1. Relative Risk of War for Each Type of Regime Change, Based on the Composite Index and Excluding Years in which World Wars were Fought.

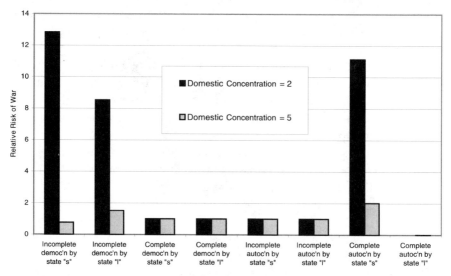

NOTE: State s is the less democratic country in each dyad and state l is the more democratic country.

Figure 6.2. Relative Risk of War for Each Type of Regime Change, Based on the Competitiveness of Political Participation and Excluding Years in which World Wars were Fought.

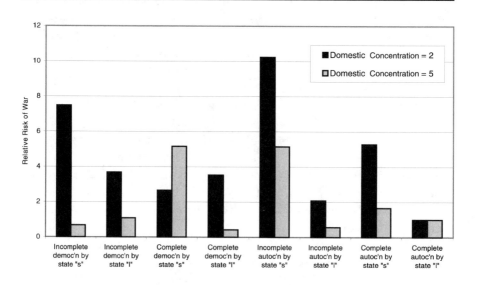

NOTE: State s is the less democratic country in each dyad and state l is the more democratic country.

Figure 6.3. Relative Risk of War for Each Type of Regime Change, Based on the Openness of Executive Recruitment and Excluding Years in which World Wars were Fought.

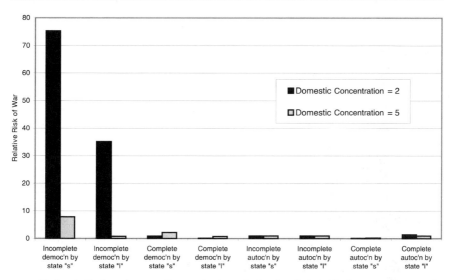

NOTE: State s is the less democratic country in each dyad and state l is the more democratic country.

Figure 6.4. Relative Risk of War for Each Type of Regime Change, Based on the Constraints on the Chief Executive and Excluding Years in which World Wars were Fought.

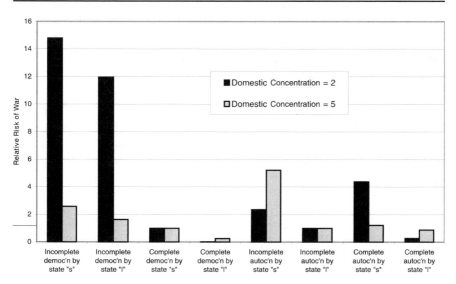

NOTE: State s is the less democratic country in each dyad and state l is the more democratic country.

Figure 6.5. Relative Risk of War for Each Type of Regime Change, Based on the Sum of Transitions, Excluding Years in which World Wars were Fought, and Setting Domestic Concentration Equal to 2.

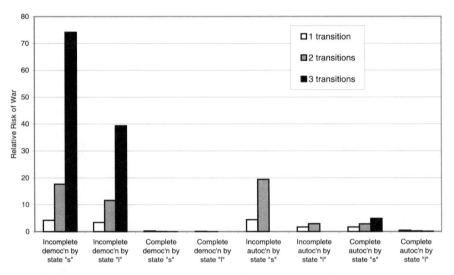

NOTE: State s is the less democratic country in each dyad and state l is the more democratic country.

executive recruitment, and extent of the constraints placed on the chief executive). As in Chapter 5, we set the level of domestic concentration at 2 to compute the relative risks shown in Figure 6.5, but we only present the relative risk for a given number of transitions if this number actually occurred in our data set.[19] The results show that the risk of war rises substantially as an increasing number of measures indicate that an incomplete democratic transition took place. The probability of war is over four times greater if state s (the less democratic state of the pair) undergoes a transition by one such measure than if it does not make such a change by any measure; the probability is about 18 times greater if state s makes an incomplete democratic transition by two measures rather than none; and it is almost 75 times larger if state s experiences a transition by all three

---

19. Thus, we do not consider the relative risk of war associated with three incomplete autocratic transitions because there is no case where a state made three such transitions in the data set analyzed here. There are a few cases of this sort in the monadic data set analyzed in Chapter 5, but they are not included in this chapter due to missing data for some of the control variables.

measures. The corresponding values for state l—the more democratic of the pair—are somewhat smaller, but quite sizeable nonetheless.

Effects of the Control Variables

Of course, regime change is not the only cause of war. Our results point to various other factors that promote hostilities too. Given how few dyadic studies of war have been conducted (compared to the number of studies of broader classes of political conflict, such as MIDs), the effects of our control variables should be of interest.

First, power relations have a strong influence on the outbreak of war. Consistent with various previous studies, we find that major powers are more likely to become embroiled in antagonism than weaker states.[20] However, since most belligerence involving major powers occurred during World War I, World War II, and the Korean War, it is not surprising that the effects of major powers are reduced when we exclude the years when these wars were waged. The estimate of $Majpower_1$ is always positive and statistically significant, but it is about 50 percent larger in Table 6.1, which includes those years, than in Table 6.2, which excludes them. Based on the results in Table 6.1, pairs including a major power are more than five times more likely to become involved in a war than dyads without a major power. In contrast, when the world-war years are excluded, hostilities are only about three times more likely to break out between states that include a major power than between other states, as shown in Table 6.2. Furthermore, each estimate of $Majpower_2$ in Table 6.1 is less than half the size of the corresponding estimate of $Majpower_1$, and in Table 6.2, $Majpower_2$ has a negative but statistically insignificant effect. These results indicate that, in general, major powers are only about 35 to 40 percent as likely to go to war with each other as they are to become involved in hostilities with weaker states. Moreover, excluding the years during which World War I, World War II, and the Korean War took place, major powers are actually somewhat less likely to fight each other than non-major powers are to come to blows.

In addition, both the international distribution of power and power relations between the states composing each dyad influence the prospects that they will resort to force. The international distribution of power is rarely included in quantitative research cast at the dyadic level of analy-

20. Small and Singer, *Resort to Arms*; Joanne Gowa, *Ballots and Bullets: The Elusive Democratic Peace* (Princeton: Princeton University Press, 1999), pp. 60–61; and Russett and Oneal, *Triangulating Peace*.

sis. We find strong evidence, however, that the probability of war dips as the distribution of capabilities among the major powers becomes increasingly skewed.[21] However, while the estimate of *Concap* is negative and statistically significant in both Tables 6.1 and 6.2, it is more than twice as large (in absolute value) when we consider all interstate wars than when we exclude the years during which world wars were ongoing.[22] When they are included, as shown in Table 6.1, an increase in the mean level of international concentration by one standard deviation reduces the predicted probability of war by about 50 percent (holding constant the remaining independent variables). When those war-years are excluded, as shown in Table 6.2, such an increase yields a reduction in the likelihood of conflict of roughly 30 percent. Thus, highly concentrated international systems are more likely to inhibit the onset of world wars than to discourage the onset of other interstate hostilities.

We also find considerable evidence that war is less likely to break out between a pair of countries, the more skewed the distribution of power between them becomes. In every case, the estimate of $Capratio_{sl}$ is negative and statistically significant, a result that accords with most previous research on interstate conflict.[23] The absolute value of this estimate, however, is twice as large when World War I, World War II, and the Korean War are excluded as when all interstate wars are analyzed, indicating that an asymmetric distribution of capabilities does far less to discourage participation in world wars than in lesser hostilities. This finding is hardly surprising: various small states entered the world wars and were willing to fight against stronger adversaries because they were fighting alongside sizeable allies. Some small states were only nominal participants in the world wars and thus did not actively wage war against much more powerful foes. But regardless of which set of results we emphasize, the bilateral distribution of power has a very substantial impact on war. Increasing the mean value of this variable by one standard deviation reduces the predicted probability of war when all interstate hostilities are analyzed by about 90 percent; the figure grows to more than 98 percent when we omit the years during which World War I, World War II, and the Korean War were fought.

---

21. For exceptions, see Zeev Maoz, *Domestic Sources of Global Change* (Ann Arbor: University of Michigan Press, 1996); and Bennett and Stam, *The Behavioral Origins of War*.

22. As we mentioned in the previous chapter, *Concap* can range from 0 to 1, but it only ranges from .18 to .43 in our data set. Therefore, its effect is smaller than might be expected in light of the size of its coefficient in Tables 6.1 and 6.2.

23. Maoz, *Domestic Sources of Global Change*; Gartzke, "Preferences and the Democratic Peace"; and Russett and Oneal, *Triangulating Peace*.

Second, although power relations have a very strong effect on the outbreak of hostilities, alliances do not. Various studies have found that allies are less likely to become involved in MIDs than other states.[24] By contrast, we find no evidence that allies are less likely to become involved in wars. The effects of alliances are substantively small and statistically weak.

Third, there is considerable evidence that contiguity increases the likelihood of interstate war. The estimate of $Contiguous_{sl}$ is always positive and statistically significant; and contiguous countries are roughly five to eight times more likely to become embroiled in hostilities than states that do not share a common border. These findings are in agreement with most of the existing literature on interstate conflict.[25] Whether geographic distance influences the outbreak of war, however, depends on whether World War I, World War II, and the Korean War are excluded. Including the years during which these wars were waged produces estimates of $Distance_{sl}$ that are small and statistically insignificant. Excluding these years yields estimates that are large and highly significant. These results reflect the fact that the world wars involved many antagonists across the globe, whereas lesser wars are usually fought by a few states in close proximity.[26]

Fourth, we find strong evidence that internal violence promotes the outbreak of interstate war. Each estimate of $Civwar_{sl}$ in Tables 6.1 and 6.2 is positive, statistically significant, and relatively large. These results may stem from a tendency for civil violence to weaken states, rendering them attractive targets of aggression. Alternatively, civil conflict may bring nationalist sentiment to a boil, prompting states to pursue belligerent foreign policies for some of the same reasons outlined in Chapter 3. Regardless, civil wars clearly have had little influence on the onset of the world wars: the estimates of $Civwar_{sl}$ are about 50 percent larger if we omit the years when these wars were fought. They also have had little bearing on external wars involving a state and a non-state actor: recall from Chapter 5 that civil wars did not have a large or statistically significant effect on all external wars.[27]

---

24. See, for example, Gartzke, "Preferences and the Democratic Peace"; and Russett and Oneal, *Triangulating Peace.*

25. See, for example, Gowa, *Ballots and Bullets;* Gartzke, "Preferences and the Democratic Peace"; Russett and Oneal, *Triangulating Peace;* and Bennett and Stam, *The Behavioral Origins of War.*

26. Vasquez, *The War Puzzle;* and Huth, *Standing Your Ground.*

27. However, civil wars had a much stronger effect on the outbreak of interstate wars. See Chapter 5, fn. 12.

Nonetheless, these results are interesting since no dyadic study of international war of which we are aware has addressed the effects of civil war. Indeed, while a great deal of ink was spilled over links between external and internal violence a few decades ago, this relationship has generated very little attention of late.[28] Our results suggest that it merits further analysis.

While we have emphasized the effects of regime change, the regime type of countries at a given point in time also has a potent influence on the outbreak of war.[29] As the least democratic state in each dyad becomes more democratic (that is, as the value of Reg_s increases), the specter of war is reduced; this finding is emphasized in much of the work on the democratic peace.[30] Consistent with John Oneal and Bruce Russett's research on MIDs, the estimate of Reg_s is always negative and statistically significant.[31] Furthermore, increasing the mean value of this variable by one standard deviation produces about a 30 to 40 percent decline in the likelihood of antagonism, holding constant the remaining independent variables. As the most democratic state in each dyad (state l) becomes more democratic, however, the likelihood of war increases, since the estimate of Reg_l is always positive and significant.[32] In fact, a rise of one standard deviation in the mean value of this variable increases the predicted probability of war by roughly 40 to 65 percent. This result reflects the tendency for fully democratic states to become embroiled in hostilities with

---

28. Arthur Stein and Bruce M. Russett, "Evaluating War: Outcomes and Consequences," in Ted Robert Gurr, ed., *Handbook of Political Conflict: Theory and Research* (New York: Free Press, 1980), pp. 399–422; Daniel S. Geller and J. David Singer, *Nations at War: A Scientific Study of International Conflict* (Cambridge: Cambridge University Press, 1998); and Jack Snyder, *From Voting to Violence: Democratization and Nationalist Conflict* (New York: Norton, 2000).

29. As in Chapter 5, we also analyze whether our results hold up after accounting for other changes in domestic institutions that do not yield a regime change. More specifically, we include the change in both Reg_s and Reg_l from year t-6 to year t-1 in the model. Doing so, however, has no influence on our results—including the effects of democratization—and these variables do not exert a consistent or systematic impact on the outbreak of interstate war.

30. The argument that the regime type of the least democratic state in each dyad is central to influencing the prospects of conflict between the dyad members has come to be known as the "weak link hypothesis." See Bruce Bueno de Mesquita and David Lalman, *War and Reason: Domestic and International Imperatives* (New Haven: Yale University Press, 1992); and Russett and Oneal, *Triangulating Peace*.

31. Oneal and Russett, "The Classical Liberals Were Right"; and Russett and Oneal, *Triangulating Peace*.

32. For a similar finding based on an analysis of MIDs, see Oneal and Russett, "The Classical Liberals Were Right."

autocracies. Holding regime change constant, the most dangerous dyads are those composed of a democracy and an autocracy (that is, where $Reg_s = -10$ and $Reg_l = 10$). Furthermore, the absolute value of each coefficient of Reg_s in Table 6.1 is strikingly similar to the value of the corresponding coefficient of Reg_l. Thus, country-pairs that are highly autocratic at a given point in time are about as unlikely to become embroiled in wars as their highly democratic counterparts (that is, the probability of war is roughly the same if $Reg_s = Reg_l = -10$ or if $Reg_s = Reg_l = 10$).[33]

Finally, we have attempted to account for the tenor and history of political-military relations between the states comprising each dyad by analyzing whether they are allies, the distribution of power between them, and the length of time since a war last broke out between them (the spline function). Another key aspect of these relations is whether states are political-military rivals. It seems quite likely that competitors of this sort would be more likely to go to war than other states. Furthermore, some studies suggest that a rivalry can influence domestic politics in the belligerents.[34] Thus, it is useful to determine whether political-military rivalries affect the observed relationship between incomplete democratization and war.

To address this issue, we analyze three different measures of rivalry: Paul Diehl and Gary Goertz's measure of "enduring" rivalries, Scott Bennett's measure of "interstate" rivalries, and William Thompson's measure of "strategic" rivalries.[35] These studies define rivals somewhat differently, but they generally agree with Thompson that such states "regard each other as (a) competitors, (b) the source of actual or latent threats that pose some possibility of becoming militarized, and (c) enemies."[36] However, these studies operationalize the concept of rivalry very

---

33.   On this issue, see also Suzanne Warner, "The Effects of Political Similarity on the Onset of Militarized Disputes, 1816–1985," *Political Research Quarterly*, Vol. 53, No. 2 (June 2000), pp. 343–374; Mark Peceny and Caroline C. Beer, with Shannon Sanchez-Terry, "Dictatorial Peace," *American Political Science Review*, Vol. 96, No. 1 (March 2002), pp. 15–26; and Bennett and Stam, *The Behavioral Origins of War*, especially pp. 128–130.

34.   See, for example, William R. Thompson, "Identifying Rivals and Rivalries in World Politics," *International Studies Quarterly*, Vol. 45, No. 4 (December 2001), p. 562.

35.   Paul F. Diehl and Gary Goertz, *War and Peace in International Rivalry* (Ann Arbor: University of Michigan Press, 2000); D. Scott Bennett, "Measuring Rivalry Termination," *Journal of Conflict Resolution*, Vol. 41, No. 2 (April 1997), pp. 227–254; Bennett, "Integrating and Testing Models of Rivalry," *American Journal of Political Science*, Vol. 42, No. 4 (October 1998), pp. 1200–1232; and Thompson, "Identifying Rivals and Rivalries in World Politics."

36.   Thompson, "Identifying Rivals and Rivalries in World Politics," p. 560.

differently, yielding a substantial amount of variation across their three data sets. Consequently, we create a separate measure of rivalry based on each data set. Each of these three variables equals 1 if states s and l are rivals in year t-1, and 0 otherwise. Rather than report the results when each of these variables is included in every model estimated in this chapter, we focus on the model where the composite index is used to measure regime change and World War I, World War II, and the Korean War are excluded (the first column of Table 6.2).[37]

Not surprisingly, the results shown in Table 6.3 indicate that rivalry promotes the outbreak of war. Regardless of which measure is used, the estimate of this variable is positive, large, and statistically significant. In fact, based on our findings, rivals are between seven and one-half times (interstate rivalries) and twenty-six and one-half times (strategic rivalries) more likely to go to war than other country-pairs. Most important for our purposes, however, is that accounting for rivalries has very little influence on the effects of incomplete democratization (although doing so does influence the size and strength of the effects of certain control variables). When analyzing each measure of rivalry, the estimates of *Incomplete Demtransition$_s$* and *Incomplete Demtransition$_l$* are positive, the estimates of *Incomplete Demtransition$_s$* $\times$ *DomConcentration$_s$* and *Incomplete Demtransition$_l$* $\times$ *DomConcentration$_l$* are negative, and all of them are statistically significant. Furthermore, the size of these estimates does not depend much on which, if any, measure of rivalry is included in the model. Thus, our results are not being driven by political-military rivalries.

Conclusion

Almost all of the existing research on democratization and war has been cast at the monadic level of analysis. In this chapter, we have presented the results of one of the first studies of this topic using a dyadic research design.[38] Consistent with the quantitative analysis in Chapter 5, the re-

---

37.   Note, however, that the results derived using the other measures of regime type and including the world wars also do not change much when we include these measures of rivalry.

38.   Bennett and Stam also analyze the effects of democratization on war using a dyadic design, although they define and operationalize democratization much differently than we do here. See Bennett and Stam, *The Behavioral Origins of War*. As we noted earlier, various studies have analyzed the relationship between democratization and broader categories of interstate conflict, such as MIDs. See, for example, Oneal and Russett, "The Classical Liberals Were Right"; Gelpi and Grieco, "Attracting Trouble"; Russett and Oneal, *Triangulating Peace;* Mansfield and Snyder, "Incomplete Democratization and the Outbreak of Military Disputes"; and Kurizaki, "Dyadic Effects

Table 6.3. Logit Estimates of the Effects of Democratization on War Between States, Excluding Years in which World War I, World War II, and the Korean War were Fought, and Controlling for the Effects of Enduring Rivalries.

Variable	Enduring Rivalries	Interstate Rivalries	Strategic Rivalries
Intercept	−7.179***	−7.375***	−9.039***
	(.976)	(.957)	(.924)
Complete Demtransition$_l$	___ a	___ a	___ a
Complete Demtransition$_s$	___ a	___ a	___ a
Incomplete Demtransition$_l$	2.919**	2.938**	2.803***
	(1.237)	(1.150)	(.977)
Incomplete Demtransition$_s$	4.117***	4.347***	5.077***
	(1.478)	(1.435)	(1.598)
Complete Auttransition$_l$	−14.720***	−13.799***	−15.389***
	(1.646)	(1.821)	(1.442)
Complete Auttransition$_s$	3.674***	3.793***	3.850***
	(.936)	(.917)	(.966)
Incomplete Auttransition$_l$	___ a	___ a	___ a
Incomplete Auttransition$_s$	___ a	___ a	___ a
DomConcentration$_l$	.083	.080	.076
	(.068)	(.067)	(.071)
DomConcentration$_s$	.175**	.203**	.205**
	(.086)	(.084)	(.093)
Complete Demtransition$_l$ × DomConcentration$_l$	___ a	___ a	___ a
Complete Demtransition$_s$ × DomConcentration$_s$	___ a	___ a	___ a
Incomplete Demtransition$_l$ × DomConcentration$_l$	−.497*	−.507**	−.450**
	(.270)	(.251)	(.219)
Incomplete Demtransition$_s$ × DomConcentration$_s$	−.900**	−.937**	−1.082**
	(.412)	(.400)	(.453)
Complete Auttransition$_l$ × DomConcentration$_l$	1.848***	1.749***	1.994***
	(.172)	(.208)	(.148)
Complete Auttransition$_s$ × DomConcentration$_s$	−.584***	−.601***	−.612***
	(.123)	(.120)	(.126)
Incomplete Auttransition$_l$ × DomConcentration$_l$	___ a	___ a	___ a
Incomplete Auttransition$_s$ × DomConcentration$_s$	___ a	___ a	___ a

Table 6.3. *Continued.*

Variable	Enduring Rivalries	Interstate Rivalries	Strategic Rivalries
Reg_l	.029	.035*	.042*
	(.020)	(.021)	(.022)
Reg_s	−.053	−.066**	−.054
	(.033)	(.032)	(.037)
$Majpower_1$	.842***	.983***	1.183***
	(.291)	(.261)	(.279)
$Majpower_2$	−.558	−.566	−1.861***
	(.533)	(.530)	(.551)
Civwar	1.162***	1.263***	1.147***
	(.303)	(.283)	(.284)
Concap	−8.981***	−9.404***	−5.599**
	(2.558)	(2.592)	(2.610)
$Capratio_{sl}$	−.014**	−.017**	−.007**
	(.006)	(.007)	(.003)
$Allies_{sl}$	.101	−.032	.118
	(.284)	(.275)	(.302)
$Contiguous_{sl}$	1.403***	1.725***	.471
	(.346)	(.337)	(.428)
$Distance_{sl}$	−.00027***	−.00027***	−.00025***
	(.00008)	(.00008)	(.00007)
$Rivalry_{sl}$	2.325***	2.026***	3.278***
	(.382)	(.378)	(.414)
Log Likelihood	−766.67	−784.42	−732.71
N	321,255	321,255	321,255

NOTE: Entries are logistic regression estimates, with robust standard errors in parentheses. Each model is estimated after including a natural spline function with three knots. In each model, regime change is measured using the composite index.

[a] This parameter is not estimated because there is no case in which a regime change of this sort led to war.

*** $p \leq .01$; ** $p \leq .05$; * $p \leq .10$ (two-tailed tests are conducted for all estimates).

sults provide considerable support for our argument that when domestic institutions are weak and fragmented, incomplete democratization promotes war.

Although these tests have required us to restrict our focus to interstate wars, which is a drawback since our argument applies to all external wars, they have allowed us to control for a wide variety of dyadic attrib-

of Democratization on International Disputes." Our results are in agreement with the only previous study of this sort that has distinguished between incomplete and complete democratization. See Mansfield and Snyder, "Incomplete Democratization and the Outbreak of Military Disputes."

utes that are emphasized in the literature on international conflict. Realists, for example, might speculate that fluctuations in the relative military strength or the alliance relations of a democratizing state encourage aggression for reasons that are only incidental to regime type.

However, our results show that the relationship between incomplete democratization and armed conflict holds even when controlling for these factors. Likewise, we show that states' static regime characteristics at a given point in time—a key feature of various liberal theories—do not account for the belligerence of democratizing countries. Nor do factors such as geographic proximity, civil violence, or political-military rivalries influence the relationship between democratic transitions and war. Furthermore, despite the rarity with which interstate war occurs in our dyadic research design, the effects of the control variables generally conform to the findings of previous dyadic studies addressing more frequently occurring aspects of interstate conflict.

The results in this and the preceding chapter are in accord with the argument advanced in this book, but quantitative tests cannot directly address whether the underlying causal mechanisms emphasized in our theory are responsible for the observed relationship between democratization and the use of force. Thus, it is important to supplement these tests with carefully constructed case studies that assess the reasons why regime change in a democratic direction has often been such a combustible process. We turn to that task in the next two chapters.

Chapter 7

Democratizing Initiators of War: Tracing Causal Processes

The statistical findings presented in the previous chapters provide strong evidence that incomplete democratization is associated with an increased chance of war when political institutions are weak. These statistical results also rule out some hypothetical alternative explanations for the effects of democratization and weak institutions on war.

Nonetheless, these statistical tests do not directly measure some of the key causal factors and processes that are pertinent to our argument. They include no direct measure of nationalism. They do not directly measure the extent of threats to elites posed by democratization. Nor can they trace the coalition processes that unfold during the early phase of democratization. And although we do measure the state's institutional strength, the statistical results do not in themselves show that the institutions worked—or failed to work—in the ways that our theory would expect.

In order to assess whether these causal mechanisms conform to our expectations, we survey ten case studies that comprise all of the democratizing states in our data set that initiated interstate wars, except for the few questionable communist cases that, as we have shown, do not affect the statistical results. These democratizing initiators of war ought to be the easiest cases for our theory to explain. If the causal mechanisms in a large proportion of these instances fail to conform to the expected pattern, our argument would be weakened.

We find that the expected causal mechanisms are very clearly manifest in most of these cases. Some cases offer only ambiguous support for the theory, because the causal mechanisms are only weakly present, or because the war lies beyond the five-year time lags after democratization that we use for many of our statistical tests, or because the case stretches our definition of democratization.[1] A small number of cases are false positives, where the expected mechanisms were not present in a country that was coded as democratizing or where unrelated causes of the war seem more significant. Overall, however, we find that our causal argument helps to explain the outcome in the bulk of these cases.

The case studies highlight two broader patterns that are not fully captured in our statistical research, which takes historical trajectory and strategic interaction into account only to a limited degree. The first pattern, found in several instances, consists of a country that initiates a series of wars during the course of a long and tortuous trajectory of democratization. A second pattern, found in a few instances, involves a durable and even institutionalized rivalry with another state that shapes the politics of a pair of competing democratizing states. Our statistical tests in Chapter 6 showed that the relationship between democratization and war holds independently of the existence of a long-term rivalry between two states, but they could not examine directly the potential for causal interplay among enduring rivalry, democratization, and war. We take note of some of these patterns in this chapter and pursue them further in Chapters 8 and 9.

Conditional Predictions and Mechanisms

To recapitulate our basic predictions: countries undergoing incomplete democratization—that is, stalled transitions from autocracy to democracy that result in anocracy within approximately five years—are more likely to be involved in war than other regime types. Incomplete democratization is especially likely to lead countries with weak political institutions to start wars. Such weakness may occur in the general institutions that underpin central state authority as well as those that regulate political participation. These conditions are especially likely to lead to war when powerful elites feel threatened by the prospect of a democratic transition. Countries undergoing complete democratization—that is, a transition from either autocracy or anocracy to democracy—have a moderately higher risk of involvement in war shortly after the transition, but no elevated risk once democracy is consolidated. Once that stage is reached, the risk rises mainly for states with enduring rivalries and whose nationalist

---

1. On the problem of concept-stretching in studies of democratization, see David Collier and Steven Levitsky, "Democracy with Adjectives: Conceptual Innovation in Comparative Research," *World Politics*, Vol. 49, No. 3 (April 1997), pp. 430–451.

or militarist institutions and ideologies were forged in earlier phases of democratization.

The politics of democratizing states that initiate war are likely to exhibit at least some of the following causal mechanisms: exclusionary nationalism that generates enemy images or perceptions of conflicts of interest with other states; pressure-group politics by military, ethnic, or economic groups that seek a parochial benefit from policies that raise international tensions; logrolling among elite factions that include such groups; persuasion and outreach by such groups to garner mass allies; ineffectual brokerage of political bargains by the ruling elite; contradictory and unconvincing signaling in foreign affairs; the use of aggressive foreign policies by groups gambling for domestic political resurrection; the use of partial or complete media domination to promote nationalist ideology; and nationalist bidding wars between old elites and rising mass groups. We do not expect that all of these mechanisms will be present in every democratizing state that fights a war, but we do expect at least a few of them.

Which mechanisms are expected to be present in a particular case depends on two factors: the adaptability of elite interests and the strength of the country's political institutions during early democratization.[2] Together, these two factors determine the intensity of the democratizing country's nationalism and the form that nationalist exclusions are likely to take. Representing the resulting possibilities as a schematic simplification, this yields four types of nationalism, which are portrayed in Table 7.1: counterrevolutionary, revolutionary, ethnic, and civic nationalism. Each type of nationalism is likely to reflect a somewhat different mix of causal mechanisms that affect the chance of war.

Three of the four types of nationalism entail severe exclusions of different kinds of "enemies of the nation" and are likely to lead to intense nationalist conflicts. *Counterrevolutionary nationalism* is likely to emerge when powerful elite interests are not readily adaptable to a potentially democratic system, and when administrative institutions are strong, but representative institutions are weak. In that situation, attempts at nationalist persuasion are likely to be intense and effective. As in Germany before World War I, threatened ruling elites will justify excluding political opponents from power by portraying them as revolutionary enemies of the nation. Any and perhaps all of the causal mechanisms mentioned

---

2. The following section on types of nationalism is based on Jack Snyder, *From Voting to Violence: Democratization and Nationalist Conflict* (New York: Norton, 2000), chaps. 1 and 2.

Table 7.1. Relationship of Political Institutions and Elites' Interests to the Type of Nationalism during the Early Phase of Democratization.

	Strength of the Nation's Political Institutions	
Nationalist Elites' Interests	Strong	Weak
Adaptable	Civic—strong representative institutions (Britain)	Revolutionary (Revolutionary France)
Unadaptable	Counterrevolutionary—strong administrative institutions (pre–World War I Germany)	Ethnic (pre–World War I Serbia)

above are likely to be present, including elite logrolling, pressure-group politics, gambling for resurrection, and nationalist bidding wars.

Revolutionary nationalism will emerge when state institutions have already collapsed, and opportunistic elites seek to establish a popular basis for restoring power to the state. As in the French Revolution, nationalist persuasion will be used to rally support in the name of the revolution against foes at home and abroad. Predominant mechanisms will be elite outreach to mass groups, ideological persuasion, and nationalist bidding wars. Mechanisms that involve entrenched elite groups and logrolling may be absent.

Ethnic nationalism is likely when democratization begins in a setting where the basic building blocks of political or administrative institutions have never been laid down. In this institutional desert, elites will tend, by default, to base appeals to loyalty on the only available alternative, traditional popular culture. As in nineteenth-century Serbia, an intensely exclusionary nationalism will take an ethnic form. Predominant mechanisms are likely to include ethnic pressure-group politics and ethnic nationalist bidding wars.

These three types of exclusionary nationalism—counterrevolutionary, revolutionary, and ethnic—are likely to produce violent nationalist conflicts with the excluded groups inside the country and with any foreign allies of these groups.

The fourth variant, civic nationalism, is inclusive. Nationalism will take this form when elites are not particularly threatened by democratization, and when representative and journalistic institutions are already well established before the mass of the populace gains political power. Under those conditions, as in Britain in the eighteenth and nineteenth centuries, nationalists lack both the motive and the opportunity to promote divisive doctrines. While civic nationalisms are not predicted to be pacifistic, they have far less reason to fall prey to the kind of reckless, ideologically driven conflicts characteristic of the other three types. Most of the causal mechanisms leading to war will be weak or absent.

Criteria for Evaluating the Cases

In principle, what process-tracing evidence would count against our argument?[3] In the case studies, we need to see whether the political changes captured in the Polity data were valid indicators of democratization, whether nationalism played a prominent role, and whether democratization, nationalism, and war were linked by the causal mechanisms specified in our theory.

EVIDENCE THAT THE CODING OF DEMOCRATIZATION IS INVALID

In some cases, Polity may have coded a country as making a transition across one of our thresholds of democratization, yet when we go into the details of the case we find that the political change has little or nothing to do with a move toward opening up an electoral process. In particular, one of the Polity indices that we use in the statistical analysis—the openness of executive recruitment—captures changes that sometimes do not involve meaningful popular voting. This is true in particular for some communist countries undergoing modest reforms implemented from above. Such cases are false positives and do not count for our argument. We have chosen not to get into the *ad hoc* quagmire of recoding cases piecemeal, which could introduce bias into our results. Instead, we have carried out statistical tests that show that our findings hold up even when communist countries are removed. Thus, false positives in that category are not a problem for our overall argument. If we find a substantial number of false positives among non-communist cases, this could raise questions. However, as we explain below, we also know of a number of false negatives—cases that fit our theory and embody our causal mechanisms, but are not counted in our database. Consequently, as long as the number of false positives is small, our overall results are not substantially undermined.

---

3. On process-tracing methods, see Alexander George and Timothy McKeown, "Case Studies and Theories of Organizational Decision Making," *Advances in Information Processing in Organizations*, vol. 2 (Greenwich, Conn.: JAI Press, 1985), pp. 21–58.

THERE IS DEMOCRATIZATION AND WAR, BUT NO NATIONALISM

A case would cast doubt on our argument if there were democratization and war, but no belligerent nationalism and no nationalist bidding war. For example, it might be that poorly institutionalized democratizing states are simply inept at diplomacy and strategic decision-making, because their bureaucracies are unprofessional and their public opinion is fickle, even though the states are not especially belligerent or nationalist. Thus, they might send out confused signals that unintentionally invite challenges or provoke fears, and as tension rises, the democratizing states might rashly decide to mount preventive attacks.

THERE IS DEMOCRATIZATION, WAR, AND NATIONALISM, BUT NOT LINKED BY OUR MECHANISMS

It is possible that some democratizing states fight frequently because their citizens simply prefer to incur the costs and risks of war rather than forgo national objectives that might be achieved by war. These nationalist preferences might be of long standing, merely unleashed by democratization, and not, as we argue, forged by nationalistic rhetoric in the course of the democratization process. Moreover, it is possible that newly democratizing states are disproportionately likely to have such preferences because of the unsettled status of their historical claims to national self-determination. In such a case, one might observe nationalism, but one would see few if any of the other mechanisms that our argument stresses: no manipulative use of media monopolies for mass persuasion, no perverse dynamics of competitive outbidding, and no gambling for resurrection. If widespread belligerent nationalist preferences clearly preceded democratization, the case might count in favor of a different theory of democratization and war, but not ours.

THERE IS DEMOCRATIZATION AND WAR, BUT STRATEGIC EXPLANATIONS ACCOUNT FOR THE OUTCOME

In the preceding statistical analysis, we tried to control for alternative causes of war that might correlate with democratization, especially strategic factors. For example, we designed statistical tests to make sure that democratizers were not fighting more wars because they were particularly attractive targets nor, conversely, because they were particularly good at picking on weak opponents. Case studies allow us to check those findings and also ask a more general counterfactual: does it seem plausible that if the country had had a different domestic system, it would have been able to avoid the war? If the answer to that question were "no" for a substantial number of our democratizing initiators, it would raise questions about our argument.

DEMOCRATIZATION SEEMS COMPLETELY UNRELATED TO THE WAR
Since war has many causes, it is possible that in some cases a democratizing country might fight a war for reasons that are totally unrelated to its domestic political changes. For example, it might be that an autocratic country concludes a mutual defense pact with an ally, and then shortly after the autocracy undergoes a democratic transition, the ally is attacked and the new democracy honors its predecessor regime's commitment to attack the aggressor. Since these kinds of random influences should lead to false negatives just as often as to false positives, such cases would not bear on the validity of our argument unless there were an unusually high proportion of them.

Deciding Which Sets of Cases to Examine

The database used in our statistical analyses includes over 9,000 country-years; 316 incomplete democratic transitions and 221 complete democratic transitions based on at least one of the four indices of regime change; and 79 interstate wars and 108 extra-systemic wars. Thus, any narrative reconstruction of cases to trace causal processes must be selective.

First, we look at all of the cases of democratizing states that initiated war (except for the communist states which, as we have shown, do not affect our statistical findings). We include all war initiators that were democratizing according to any of the four indices of regime type. These indices are based on Polity codings, our thresholds for complete and incomplete democratization, and time lags of one to ten years. These are crucial cases for our argument. If the domestic politics of democratizing states is especially likely to lead to belligerent, nationalist foreign policies, these dynamics ought to appear in this set of cases. If our mechanisms rarely appeared among these cases, our argument would be seriously undermined. In contrast, it would be less damaging if our mechanisms appeared more rarely in cases where democratizers were merely involved in war, but did not initiate it, since any state can get caught up in war for a variety of reasons.

This set of democratizing initiators comprises ten countries (some of which were involved in multiple wars): eight cases of incomplete democratization and two cases of complete democratization. This set of ten countries, though technically including all of the cases of war-initiating democratizers, nonetheless leaves out quite a few noteworthy cases of democratizing states that instigated wars. In some cases, such as the Indo-Pakistan War of 1965, this is because the democratizing side that provoked the fighting was not the first one to attack with substantial forces on the opponent's territory.

Some cases with democratizing initiators occurred too late to appear in our database; for example, incompletely democratizing Ethiopia as initiator of the 1999 war with Eritrea, and Pakistan as the initiator of the 1999 Kargil War. Similarly, the Correlates of War (COW) Project database that we used considers the 1992 Karabakh War to be an interstate war between Armenia and Azerbaijan. Although Armenia was a democratizing state that initiated the use of substantial forces in Azerbaijan's territory, our research design, which lags the effects of democratization on war, does not include wars between brand-new states.[4] Although Serbia and Croatia were both incompletely democratizing states in the early 1990s, COW does not classify the fighting between their armies and members of opposing ethnic groups as an international war.[5] Another democratizing war-initiator, Serbia in its 1885 attack on Bulgaria, is not in the database of interstate wars because Bulgaria was not recognized as a fully sovereign state at the time. In some great-power wars, aggression that was arguably a long-term consequence of democratization gone awry was initiated after the ten-year cut-off point for our statistical tests.

Many of these cases embody the causal mechanisms specified in our theory, yet they do not appear among the ten initiators. Moreover, many of them include contemporary cases of considerable intrinsic interest. Consequently, in addition to the ten democratizing initiators that we discuss in this chapter, we examine in the following chapter all interstate wars between 1991 and 2000.

Incompletely Democratizing War Initiators

Eight countries appear in our database as incompletely democratizing initiators of interstate war. A few of them underwent transitions to complete democracy, as measured by the openness of executive recruitment,

---

4. Armenia is coded as a democracy at the time of the war based on the composite index and the openness of executive recruitment, and as an anocracy based on executive constraints and competitiveness of political participation. Azerbaijan is coded as a democracy based on the openness of executive recruitment, and as an anocracy based on the other measures. Note that some argue that this is not an interstate war.

5. On the relevance of democratization to the origins of this war, see Snyder, *From Voting to Violence*, pp. 204–220.

around the same time as they shifted from autocracy to a mixed regime on other indicators; overall, however, their democracy was far from consolidated, so we discuss them in the context of incomplete democratization. A few of these countries fought multiple wars during or after the transitions that our database identifies. Due to the time lags of the regime changes, some of the wars in these series may not appear as wars of democratization in our statistical results, and in some cases, the incompletely democratizing state may not be coded by the COW Project as the initiator. Nonetheless, we discuss the whole series of relevant wars because of our interest in trajectories of regime change and wars, including some that extend over longer time periods. We discuss the wars of the eight countries in roughly chronological order.

FRANCE, 1849–1870

Starting with the French revolution of 1848, France fought five international wars in just over two decades: a war against the new Roman Republic in 1849, the Crimean War against Russia from 1854 to 1856, a war against Austria in Italy in 1859, the Franco-Mexican War from 1862 to 1867, and the Franco-Prussian War of 1870. All of these wars were fought under Louis Napoleon Bonaparte, the nephew of the first Napoleon. The Roman war followed his election in December 1848 as President of the Second Republic, and he waged the rest as Emperor Napoleon III following the coup d'état and confirmatory plebiscite of December 1851.

In an era of rising demands for mass political participation, these wars played a central role in Napoleon's search for a formula of rule that would be widely popular without submitting to truly democratic procedures of accountability. Consciously echoing the political strategies of the first Napoleon, his nephew sought to use the rhetoric of progressive nationalism to reconcile republicans seeking social change and conservative classes seeking the maintenance of social order. His foreign policy served as a tool to validate those domestic principles and to satisfy the ideological interests of his key constituencies. Napoleon III repeatedly used military force abroad on behalf of limited constitutional regimes that rejected both radicalism and reaction, and more generally to advance the national prestige of France. His strategy of rule captures most of the key mechanisms of our theory of democratization and war. In terms of our typology of nationalisms, this case is primarily an example of the counterrevolutionary type, though its rhetoric sometimes borrowed revolutionary and civic themes. A brief review of democratization and war in the time of the French Revolution and Napoleon I will provide necessary background for its reprise under his nephew, Napoleon III.

PRECURSORS: THE FRENCH REVOLUTION AND NAPOLEON I. The wars of the French Revolution (1792–1802) and of Napoleon I (1803–1815) constitute the seminal examples of the phenomenon we are studying. Although they lie outside of the timeframe of our statistical database, together they constituted a touchstone explicitly invoked by later practitioners of the art of nationalist war in transitional states, including Napoleon III.

Revolutionary France democratized prematurely in an environment that was institutionally ill-prepared for mass politics. This experience established a pattern of popular, militarized nationalism that continued to plague France's subsequent transitions. These struggles revealed the full potential of belligerent mass nationalism for the first time in history. This was hardly foreseeable at the beginning of the French Revolution in 1789, when the Constituent Assembly voted to renounce the use of military force in foreign affairs.[6] Yet within three years, France had declared war on Austria, to be followed shortly by war with Britain, the Netherlands, and Spain. Wars of expansion were waged almost ceaselessly by a parade of French post-revolutionary regimes: the republican Girondins in 1792–93, the guillotine-wielding Committee on Public Safety led by the revolutionary Jacobin faction in 1793–95, the somewhat more stable regime ruled by the Directory beginning in 1795, and regimes dominated by Napoleon after 1799.

After two decades of nearly constant fighting against a series of coalitions of European states, the overextended French armies briefly occupied Moscow in 1812, only to collapse in defeat by 1814. French revolutionary nationalism extinguished itself in a last gasp at the Battle of Waterloo in 1815, and the pre-revolutionary Bourbon dynasty returned to rule in Paris.

This nationalism was not ethnic. Citizenship was based on criteria of territorial residence and loyalty to French political principles, not on language or the ethnic culture of the Île de France. French nationalism also differed from the British style of civic nationalism. The French variant was collectivist, not individualist, and derived from participation in the community, not from individual liberties. "In England," explains Liah Greenfeld, "it was the liberty of the individuals who composed it that made the nation free. In France, it was the liberty of the nation that constituted the freedom of the individuals."[7] Thus, nationalism in France

---

6. Jeremy Popkin, *Revolutionary News: The Press in France, 1789–1799* (Durham, N.C.: Duke University Press, 1990), p. 153.

7. Liah Greenfeld, *Nationalism: Five Roads to Modernity* (Cambridge: Harvard University Press, 1992), pp. 167–168; see also Beatrice Hyslop, *French Nationalism in 1789 ac-*

took the revolutionary form, basing its appeals for collective action on the defense of a political revolution that had brought to power a regime that governed in the name of the nation, and violently opposing those who were seen as trying to undo that change.

What accounts for this sudden outburst of self-defeating, revolutionary nationalist aggression? Like many subsequent instances of nationalist belligerence, the French nationalism of the Revolutionary Wars coincided with early steps toward democratic elections and an avalanche of political commentary from a newly free press. After the storming of the Bastille prison in 1789, the monarchy's relatively tight press censorship collapsed, as did state control of publications through regulation of the printers' guild. The number of newspapers exploded from 60 in 1789 to over 500 in 1792 in Paris alone, where combined circulation could reach as high as 300,000.[8] With adult male literacy reaching 50 percent nationwide and over 90 percent in some districts in Paris, middle-class citizens of the new France read avidly and discussed what they read in ubiquitous political clubs. What we would now call "civil society" was at its most vibrant and spontaneous.[9]

Journalists were among the leading political figures in the revolution, among them the leader of the war party in the assembly, Jacques Pierre Brissot, who had been a "hack writer and police spy in the 1780s." Brissot used his control over a popular newspaper to assume leadership of the Girondists, one of the leading political factions opposing the king.[10] The uncontrolled hubbub of revolutionary discourse did not, however, guarantee a full airing of major policy issues. Not one Paris newspaper voiced opposition to the escalation of war fever in January 1792. Not one Paris newspaper objected when Napoleon declared war on monarchical Austria in April 1792.[11]

cording to the General Cahiers (New York: Octagon, 1968; orig. ed. New York: Columbia University Press, 1934), p. 98.

8.   Simon Schama, Citizens (New York: Knopf, 1992), pp. 176–178, 525; and Popkin, Revolutionary News, pp. 32, 62, 82.

9.   Popkin, Revolutionary News, p. 24; Michael Kennedy, The Jacobin Clubs in the French Revolution, 2 vols. (Princeton: Princeton University Press, 1982 and 1988); Schama, Citizens, p. 180; and Hugh Gough, The Newspaper Press in the French Revolution (London: Routledge, 1988), p. 214.

10.   The phrase is used by Schama, Citizens, pp. 582–583; see also Gary Kates, The Cercle Social, the Girondins, and the French Revolution (Princeton: Princeton University Press, 1985), p. 34; and Popkin, Revolutionary News, p. 41.

11.   T.C.W. Blanning, The Origins of the French Revolutionary Wars (London: Longman, 1986), p. 113; see also Sydney Seymour Biro, The German Policy of Revolutionary France, vol. I (Cambridge: Harvard University Press, 1957), p. 62.

What made militant nationalism so attractive and persuasive in this era of burgeoning mass politics? Why was it part of every successful faction's program? Since the policy of war was costly, only intermittently successful, and ultimately disastrous for revolutionary France, why was it so successful in political debates?

The lack of effective institutions to channel the explosion of mass politics forced elites into an intense ideological competition for authority, according to the prevailing consensus of historians. In this contest of ideas, the easiest and cheapest shot was the scapegoating of enemies of the nation at home and abroad. War hawks exploited flaws in the marketplace of ideas, which hindered an objective evaluation of these charges.

After the autocracy collapsed, there was no fixed system for deciding who should rule and how policy should be made. The French elite was united against absolutism, but deeply split about what to put in its place. Thus the king, the ministries, the deputies, the political clubs and factions, and a variety of free-lancing political entrepreneurs contended for power amid fluid institutions. Although there were elections for the assembly, the "average voter" provided no stable reference point for political authority: suffrage rules were constantly changing, there were no organized political parties, local issues dominated electoral campaigns, and changing circumstances rapidly left electoral promises outdated.[12]

The Girondin regime's constitution of 1793 provided for universal-suffrage elections for local officials, but after the rival Jacobins came to power, this promise went unfulfilled.[13] Lacking an institutionalized mandate, the contending factions reached out to urban popular groups via the press and the political clubs to create popular support through ideological appeals.[14] With political power utterly insecure from one moment to the next, the factions had no choice but to evaluate foreign policy almost entirely on the basis of its short-run consequences for the ideological power struggle.[15]

---

12. Popkin, *Revolutionary News*, p. 4.

13. Vivien Schmidt, *Democratizing France: The Political and Administrative History of Decentralization* (Cambridge: Cambridge University Press, 1990), pp. 12–25.

14. François Furet, *Interpreting the French Revolution* (Cambridge: Cambridge University Press, 1981), p. 49; and Theda Skocpol, *States and Social Revolutions* (Cambridge: Cambridge University Press, 1979), pp. 65–66.

15. This interpretation is advanced most clearly by Furet, *Interpreting*, pp. 47, 53–56, but the detailed diplomatic histories by Blanning and Schroeder also invoke this argument. Blanning, *The Origins of the French Revolutionary Wars*; and Paul Schroeder, *The Transformation of European Politics, 1763–1848* (Oxford: Clarendon, 1994).

The trump card in this political struggle was to portray one's opponents as tainted by treasonous threats to the nation emanating from enemies at home and abroad. Like most nationalisms, French popular nationalism asserted the right of the people to rule themselves in their own state. But since stable democratic rule was far from institutionalized, who truly represented the nation was always in doubt. Ernest Renan's famous characterization of nationalism as a "daily plebiscite" on popular loyalties was never truer than at this stage of the French revolution.[16] In these circumstances, one dramatic way to establish one's popular credentials was to take the vanguard in the fight against the nation's enemies. Factions that played this card won; factions that did not play it lost.[17] "If the Girondins, from late 1791, were the most eloquent advocates of war with the Austrian Emperor," says historian François Furet, "it was because they were convinced that it was the only way they could come to power."[18]

In short, the post-revolutionary French case illustrates the belligerent form that nationalism can take when political institutions have collapsed, a newly free press is unsophisticated, and opportunistic elites are willing to exploit any issue to win public support.

The first Napoleon made French revolutionary nationalism routine and harnessed it to the revitalization of the French state. After the revolution had destroyed the institutional basis of authority, nationalism played a large role in this reconstruction of state power. When the inefficient old regime collapsed, political entrepreneurs from Brissot to Napoleon struggled to build a new state capable of mobilizing collective action to meet modern military and economic challenges. All of them used nationalist ideology to overcome this institutional deficit. Nationalism, tied to conspiracy theories linking purported domestic traitors with foreign foes, was used to do away with factional rivals, to motivate military enlistment in the new mass army, and to provide populist ideological cover for the construction of Napoleon's absolutist state.[19]

---

16.   Quoted in E. J. Hobsbawm, *Nations and Nationalism since 1780* (Cambridge: Cambridge University Press, 1990), p. 88.

17.   Schroeder, *Transformation,* p. 126; see also Blanning, *Origins,* pp. 106, 111–112.

18.   Furet, *Interpreting,* p. 65; see also pp. 47, 53–55.

19.   Barry Posen, "Nationalism, the Mass Army, and Military Power," *International Security,* Vol. 18, No. 2 (Fall 1993), pp. 80–124; John Lynn, *The Bayonets of the Republic* (Urbana: University of Illinois Press, 1984); and Jean-Paul Berthaud, *The Army of the French Revolution* (Princeton: Princeton University Press, 1988).

THE WARS OF NAPOLEON III.   The society that Louis Napoleon sought to govern was deeply divided in the wake of the 1848 revolution that deposed the Orléans monarchy. Urban lower classes were prepared to fight in the streets for social justice. Monarchists and the conservative military were equally prepared to use force to defend the social order and were more effective in doing so. The Catholic Church, which provided an ideological rallying point for these conservative groups, was anathema to the radicals. Commercial classes and professionals demanded constitutional government that would give them a share of power and privilege while keeping socialism at bay. Masses of peasants in a predominantly agrarian populace were skeptical of the political programs espoused by all these urban groups. The problem, as Louis Napoleon put it, was finding a way to "satisfy the instinct of the most numerous classes" and at the same time "attach oneself to the upper classes."[20]

Militant nationalism cloaked in popular rhetoric proved to be an effective means of accomplishing this difficult task. Louis Napoleon declared that the people, not the monarch, were sovereign, and that the state served the interests of the people.[21] To symbolize this, he promoted universal manhood suffrage, counting on the conservative peasantry to act as a check on the votes of urban radicals. But to serve the people as a whole, Louis Napoleon argued, the state had to be above party, and therefore he utilized plebiscites rather than competitive elections to ratify his imperial authority and to endorse his policies at key junctures in 1851, 1852, and 1870.[22] According to Napoleon, authoritarian power was not the antithesis of rule by the people, but its instrument and savior. "Order is the maintenance of what has been freely elected and agreed to by the people," he said in 1850, "it is the national will triumphant over all factions."[23] Thus, he portrayed his coup in 1851 as saving the Republic from the faction-ridden, careerist Assembly.[24] Because Napoleon's rhetoric and policies sought to assuage the sensibilities of all factions except the most

---

20.   Roger Price, *The French Second Empire: An Anatomy of Power* (Cambridge: Cambridge, 2001), p. 44.

21.   J.A.S. Grenville, *Europe Reshaped, 1848–1878* (Ithaca, N.Y.: Cornell University Press, 1980 edition; orig. 1976), p. 117.

22.   Theodore Zeldin, *The Political System of Napoleon III* (New York: Norton, 1971, orig. ed. 1958), p. 2; and Price, *The French Second Empire*, pp. 33–36, 397–400.

23.   Zeldin, *The Political System of Napoleon III*, p. 7.

24.   Grenville, *Europe Reshaped, 1848–1878*, p. 117.

uncompromising radicals and socialists, his Empire was the form of rule that divided Frenchmen least.[25]

This grand coalition of opposites could not be easily maintained through normal democratic procedures. When competitive politics ran free under the Second Republic in 1848–51, the Assembly was divided into factions, and the contest of interests was sometimes carried out by struggle in the streets. Under Napoleon III's subsequent Empire, elite solidarity against the urban lower-class threat held together the core of his coalition and approved coercive measures of social control. After the coup, over 25,000 political prisoners were arrested, though most of those were soon released, since massive repression would have undercut Napoleon's claim to rule by popular consent.[26]

Government success in legislative elections was initially guaranteed by having centrally appointed mayors stand guard over the ballot boxes where voting papers for officially sanctioned candidates were a different color from those of opposition candidates.[27] In the 1850s, press censorship was tight, and the supply of news was managed through the quasi-governmental *Havas* news agency, though by the 1860s a freer progressive press prevailed in Paris.[28] Over time, aversion to revolution lost effectiveness as a reliable binding agent.[29] In each election, the government's ability to control the results declined, until it was near zero by 1869.[30]

Although Napoleon deployed many high-handed tactics to rule over his heterogeneous coalition, his most indispensable stratagem of rule was to call upon the progressive nationalist prestige of his famous namesake and the policies of military glory that he embodied. Citing his uncle's commentaries on Julius Caesar, Napoleon III noted that in the aftermath of revolution an external war was "necessary . . . to amalgamate the remains of all the parties."[31] He stressed the need to throw off the restrictions of the 1815 treaties and to restore France's former glories. These appeals resonated across the political spectrum, not least among the mass of

---

25.   Ibid., p. 331.

26.   Ibid., p. 170.

27.   Zeldin, *The Political System of Napoleon III*, pp. 84–85, 91–94, 135; and Price, *The French Second Empire*, p. 95.

28.   Price, *The French Second Empire*, pp. 171–178.

29.   Ibid., p. 127.

30.   Ibid., p. 127.

31.   Ibid., p. 406.

voters in rural France, where "the only decoration on so many walls was the lithograph illustrating the military triumphs of Napoleon I or his nephew."[32]

This strategy succeeded even though the average citizen was not consistently bellicose: Napoleon first had to stimulate the public's appetite for military glory and national honor before he could use it to legitimate his rule. Just as after the revolution of 1789, French public opinion was not especially warlike in the immediate aftermath of the revolution of 1848. Napoleon was well aware of this, and proclaimed in 1852 that "the Empire means peace."[33] The public was not keen to enter the Crimean War when it began in January 1854, and after sustaining 100,000 war-related deaths by 1855, the public's war-weariness led Napoleon to make concessions to Russia at the bargaining table. Similarly, the French public was initially opposed to participation in the Italian and Austro- Prussian Wars, fearing a disruption of the economy.[34]

Nonetheless, Napoleon learned that military victories heightened the prestige of his regime despite this reluctant public. The Crimean victory created the conditions for what is acknowledged to be the height of Napoleon's authority, notwithstanding the war-weariness that accompanied it.[35] He tried to recapitulate this success when he saw his popularity waning in January 1859. On the eve of French military intervention in the Italian struggle with Austria, Napoleon told his cabinet, "On the domestic front, the war will at first awaken great fears; traders and speculators of every stripe will shriek, but national sentiment will [banish] this domestic fright; the nation will be put to the test once more in a struggle that will stir many a heart, recall the memory of heroic times and bring together under the mantle of glory the parties that are steadily drifting away from one another day after day."[36] In this way, Napoleon tried to use military struggle for a supposedly glorious goal to rally a wary, divided public and thus strengthen his rule. By 1870, Napoleon and his

---

32. Ibid., p. 264.

33. Ibid., p. 405.

34. William E. Echard, *Napoleon III and the Concert of Europe* (Baton Rouge: Louisiana State University Press, 1983), pp. 31, 37, 49; and Lynn M. Case, *French Opinion on War and Diplomacy during the Second Empire* (Philadelphia: University of Pennsylvania Press, 1954), pp. 54–56, 64–65, 71, 273.

35. J. M. Thompson, *Louis Napoleon and the Second Empire* (New York: Columbia University Press, 1983), pp. 144–145.

36. Alain Plessis, *The Rise and Fall of the Second Empire, 1852–1871* (Cambridge: Cambridge University Press, 1985), pp. 146–147.

ministers found that militant opinion had become all too easy to rally and that it helped sweep them not to glory, but into a disastrous war.

THE ROMAN REPUBLIC. The war against the Roman Republic illustrates particularly clearly how Louis Napoleon catered to the ideological interests of France's factions in his foreign policy and how his formula for waging war straddled the positions of his coalition of opposites. Amid the turbulence of 1848, radicals in the Papal States, including Rome, overthrew the temporal power of the Pope and set up a constitutional republic with an elected Assembly. The Pope fled to the Kingdom of Naples and called upon the Catholic powers of Europe to reinstate him.

French opinion was sharply divided. Conservative Catholics were appalled at the ouster of the Pope, whereas French radicals sympathized with the revolutionaries. Indeed, Louis Napoleon's radical cousin, Carlo Bonaparte, was one of the leaders of the Roman revolution.[37] In November 1948, General Louis Cavaignac, a leading presidential candidate who had become the darling of the conservatives by using force against socialist demonstrators in Paris, responded to the Pope's plea by sending a naval squadron to try to intimidate Rome's republicans. Though the French Assembly endorsed the measure by 480 to 63, Louis Napoleon, a member of the assembly at the time and an aspiring presidential candidate, was loath to alienate either the Catholics or the radicals, and so abstained.[38] The French fleet accomplished nothing. However, the Austrians geared up for a land invasion to put down the rebellion and restore the Pope.

To forestall this action, Louis Napoleon, then newly-elected president, decided to send French troops to occupy Rome and prevent the success of both the radical socialist revolution and an Austrian-sponsored restoration of reactionary papal authority in April 1849. The extreme left in the Assembly opposed this, but the moderate republicans approved, and a vote of 395 to 283 authorized financial credits for the expedition.[39] The French hoped that the Romans, now led by the Italian nationalist Giuseppe Mazzini, would not oppose the expeditionary force and would instead welcome it as a bulwark against the impending Austrian invasion. However, the wary Romans insisted that the French remain outside of the city, and placarded their march route with posters quoting the provision in the new French constitution that France would never threaten the liberty of any foreign nation. This hopeful reminder of the principles of the democratic peace was to no avail. At the outskirts of the city, the

---

37. Jasper Ridley, *Napoleon III and Eugénie* (London: Constable, 1979), p. 228.

38. Ibid., pp. 228–229.

39. Ibid., p. 249.

Roman defenders under Giuseppe Garibaldi opened fire and routed the French, who were commanded by the reactionary General Nicholas Oudinot.[40]

After this setback, Louis Napoleon promised to send reinforcements to redeem France's "military honor." While these military preparations were unfolding, Mazzini agreed with a French envoy that French troops should stay outside of the city, the elected assembly of the Roman Republic should stay in office, and the Pope should return to the Vatican. Meanwhile, however, the conservative Party of Order won a landslide in France's May 1849 elections, gaining an absolute majority in the Assembly and consequently a dominating position in the cabinet. As a result, the French government reneged on the agreement with Mazzini, and Oudinot launched a surprise attack that killed a thousand of Garibaldi's defenders. Following up this victory, Oudinot bombarded the civilian population of the city, Garibaldi and Mazzini fled, and the victorious French dissolved the Assembly and reinstated the temporal power of the Pope. Although Louis Napoleon urged the Pope to appoint a moderately liberal, constitutional government, this advice was ignored, and reactionary politics were resumed. Napoleon publicly washed his hands of this unwanted outcome, which violated his principle of backing neither conservative reaction nor radicalism, but moderate constitutionalism. This left him at odds with the press and his conservative cabinet, which he dismissed on October 31 in defiance of the notion that the government should be responsible to the majority in the Assembly.[41]

Was this a war between two democracies? Polity III codes France as moving from an autocracy score of 4 (our variable *Autoc*) and a democracy (*Democ*) score of 3 under the Orléans constitutional monarchy in 1847, to an *Autoc* score of 0 and a *Democ* score of 6 under the Second Republic in 1848–50. On the composite index of regime type, this constitutes a move from mid-ranking anocracy to the very threshold of a democratic regime, but not across it. Although the Roman Republic briefly had a freely elected regime in 1848–49, Polity codes this simply as "missing data" (i.e., too confusing to categorize). Bruce Russett argues that democracy in both states was too fleeting for this to count seriously against the democratic peace hypothesis.[42] Judging by the component indices of our data set, this war counts as an interstate war initiated by democratizing

---

40.   Ibid., pp. 249–250.

41.   Ibid., pp. 251–261; and Alphonse Balleydier, *Histoire de la Révolution de Rome*, vol. 1 (Geneva: Librairie Européenne, 1851).

42.   Bruce Russett, *Grasping the Democratic Peace* (Princeton: Princeton University Press, 1993), p. 18.

France, which completed its democratic transition in 1848 (as measured by openness of executive recruitment).

The Franco-Roman war illustrates several of the causal mechanisms of our theory. Under conditions of weakly institutionalized mass electoral politics, state leaders used force abroad in order to pander to the ideological concerns of elite and mass constituencies. The diplomatic and military strategy was the product of a logroll of opposites, using force in a way that would satisfy the demands of antithetical interest groups simultaneously. Prestige was invoked as a reason for escalating the conflict. The war was hardly forced upon France, and its outcome served only to deepen the crisis of governability of the democratizing state. In all of these ways, the case conforms to the logic of our theory.

CRIMEA. Napoleon's overall diplomatic strategy was aimed at disrupting the Concert of Europe's great powers and the Vienna settlement of 1815, which blocked France from regaining its lost territories and, equally important for him, its former prestige. His means for accomplishing this were to align himself with liberal Britain against the powers that stood for old-style monarchical legitimacy, especially Austria and Russia, and to harness the rising power of nationalism to disrupt the Vienna settlement. An opportunity to set this design in motion came in 1850, when France sharply protested Russia's arrogation of the right to oversee the Christian Holy Places in the Ottoman Empire, including Catholic churches in Jerusalem.

Although Russia eventually conceded to France's demands on the Holy Places, this dispute nonetheless helped embroil Russia in an ongoing conflict with Turkey and Britain that set the stage for the start of the Crimean War in 1854. This dispute also had the side-benefit for Napoleon that it was reasonably popular both with France's conservative Catholics and with its radicals, who hated Russia for intervening with military force to stamp out popular liberalism and nationalism in several countries. Although the cost of the war in blood and treasure dismayed France's business community and its peasantry, the limited Franco-British victory over Russia contributed substantially to solidifying Napoleon's position at home and abroad.[43]

In our database, France counts as a democratizing participant in the Crimean War (as measured by openness of executive recruitment). However, when measured in terms of the competitiveness of participation and constraints on the executive, the war followed changes in the direction of

43. Norman Rich, *Why the Crimean War? A Cautionary Tale* (Hanover: University Press of New England, 1985), pp. 6–7, 18–22; and Plessis, *The Rise and Fall of the Second Empire*, pp. 140–142.

greater autocracy. This reflects Napoleon's attempts to bridge the gap between populist and authoritarian politics, which is symptomatic of the incomplete transition.

ITALY. In July 1858, Napoleon met with Count Camillo Cavour, the prime minister of Piedmont, and plotted how to lure Austria into a war that would eject it from Northern Italy.[44] This plan came to partial fruition the following year when Austria attacked Piedmont, and France intervened militarily on the Italians' behalf, prevailing at the battles of Solferino and Magenta, and making territorial gains that helped prepare Italy for unification. Though Napoleon sought territorial concessions for France, his main objective was to gain prestige as an effective military power coercing reactionary states on behalf of progressive, constitutional nationalism.

Whereas the main opposition to Napoleon's government-backed candidates in the French parliamentary election of 1852 had come from monarchists, opposition came almost entirely from republicans in 1857.[45] This heightened Napoleon's incentives to employ a strategy of backing progressives abroad while resisting their increasing influence at home. Emile Ollivier, then a leader of the republican opposition, supported Napoleon's Italian policy, but felt that "Italian independence is only a pretext. . . . Basically the Emperor is only concerned to strengthen his dynasty and silence the slowly emerging internal opposition."[46] This entailed a complicated political strategy, however, since the threat to Papal power from anti-clerical radicalism in the Italian nationalist movement alienated French conservatives and clergy. Moreover, French business interests opposed the war on economic grounds. Napoleon mounted a press campaign to sell the war to the reluctant French population, but above all counted on victories to rally support. He realized, however, that this support was thin and negotiated a quick end to the conflict, forgoing his anticipated territorial concessions.[47] The prestige of military victory just barely made possible the success of a foreign policy that straddled a coalition of nearly opposite domestic interests, but this was a high-wire act that required repeated lunges and balancing corrections.

---

44.   Grenville, *Europe Reshaped, 1848–1878*, pp. 181–182.

45.   Plessis, *The Rise and Fall of the Second Empire*, pp. 143–144.

46.   Price, *The French Second Empire*, p. 409; see also Plessis, *The Rise and Fall of the Second Empire*, p. 142.

47.   Price, *The French Second Empire*, pp. 409–410; Case, *French Opinion on War and Diplomacy during the Second Empire*, pp. 54–56, 64–78; Plessis, *The Rise and Fall of the Second Empire*, pp. 145–147; and Grenville, *Europe Reshaped, 1848–1878*, pp. 182–183, 252.

MEXICO.   In 1861, with the United States distracted by its Civil War, three European creditor states—Britain, France, and Spain—intervened militarily in Mexico to seize the customs house in Vera Cruz to pay the debts of the bankrupt, anti-clerical, radical republican regime of Benito Juarez. The next spring, French troops marched toward Mexico City to overthrow the Juarez regime, but were defeated in battle by Mexican forces. Massively reinforced, the French installed the liberal Austrian Archduke Maximilian as Mexico's Emperor in 1864. The turbulent conditions there blocked any confirmation by referendum. With the end of the U.S. Civil War, France was compelled to pull its troops out of Mexico and left Maximilian to be executed by Juarez's forces in 1867.[48]

While economic motives and a desire to appease France's Catholics may have played a small role, this debacle was above all an astonishingly misguided attempt to advance the French position by bestowing enlightened, moderate constitutional leadership upon a young nation of the Latin world.[49] In a sense, this was a disastrous replay of the main elements of the war against the Roman Republic: avenge a minor setback to military prestige at all costs, crush radical republicanism, install a liberal Catholic ruler, oppose the reactionary policy of the Pope, and gain prestige as an enlightened great power that spreads progress and civilization.[50] While the outcome strayed far from this intention, Napoleon made many of these themes explicit in his advice to Maximilian: "A country torn by anarchy cannot be regenerated to *parliamentary* liberty. What is needed in Mexico is a *liberal* dictatorship; that is to say, a strong power which shall proclaim the great principles of modern civilization, such as equality before the law, civil and religious liberty, an upright administration, an equitable judicial procedure, etc."[51] In other words, Napoleon sought to apply his formula for ruling post-revolutionary France to post-revolutionary Mexico, where its success would validate its continuing legitimacy in France itself.

Nothing in the politics of 1862 France compelled Napoleon to adopt such reckless strategies of legitimation. Nonetheless, the gradual waning of the propertied classes' fear of revolution was placing continued pressure on Napoleon to liberalize the regime. In 1860, he allowed greater freedom of speech in the Assembly and permitted press reports of these

---

48.   Ridley, *Napoleon III and Eugénie*, pp. 498–517, 523, 532.

49.   Plessis, *The Rise and Fall of the Second Empire*, p. 150.

50.   Ridley, *Napoleon III and Eugénie*, p. 498; and Thompson, *Louis Napoleon*, p. 215.

51.   September 19 and October 2, 1863, quoted in Ridley, *Napoleon III and Eugénie*, p. 515.

debates.[52] Reflecting this trend, Polity records a two-point increase in constraints on the executive between 1859 and 1862. In this context, Napoleon started to become increasingly reckless in employing his tried-and-true tactic of seeking to legitimate his domestic regime through exemplary foreign adventures.

THE FRANCO-PRUSSIAN WAR. In a dispute over the candidacy of a relative of the Prussian king for the throne of Spain, France attacked Prussia in July 1870 and suffered a decisive defeat that ended Napoleon III's rule. Although the Prussians had withdrawn this candidacy, the French felt affronted by the Prussians' unwillingness to guarantee that no other Hohenzollerns would be put forward in the future. This showdown occurred just a year after freely contested parliamentary elections in France, which led to substantial electoral successes by the liberal opposition and dramatic changes in the composition of the cabinet. Our database codes this as a change from autocracy to a mixed regime as measured by constraints on the executive, a jump from 1 to 3 between 1859 and 1862 followed by a jump from 3 to 5 in 1869. France, by this component measure, was a country undergoing incomplete democratization, and it was the initiator of the war. The composite index of regime type, however, records only a limited change within the mixed regime category: for 1869 France's *Autoc* score declined from 6 to 5, and its *Democ* score moved from zero to 2.

It would be going too far to say that liberal successes in the 1869 elections forced Napoleon III to gamble on political resurrection by recklessly trumping up a pretext for war with powerfully armed Prussia, the decisive winner of the 1866 war with Austria for hegemony in Germany. Despite the opposition's electoral successes, the government had held onto a majority in the Assembly by backing liberals to prevent radicals from winning.[53] In the spring of 1870, Napoleon held a referendum in which more than twice as many voters endorsed the Empire and its self-styled "liberal" policy as opposed it or abstained.

As a result, some historians and contemporary observers argue that any heightened risk of war would have stemmed from the overconfidence of the Empire's elite rather than their desperate fear of collapse.[54] Insofar as the electoral setback did give rise to fears, its initial ef-

---

52. Zeldin, *The Political System of Napoleon III*, pp. 100–110; Ridley, *Napoleon III and Eugénie*, p. 474; and Plessis, *The Rise and Fall of the Second Empire*, pp. 150–151.

53. Zeldin, *The Political System of Napoleon III*, pp. 135, 139.

54. Price, *The French Second Empire*, pp. 400–401; and David Wetzel, *A Duel of Giants: Bismarck, Napoleon III, and the Origins of the Franco-Prussian War* (Madison: University of Wisconsin Press, 2001), p. 30.

fect was to make the regime more cautious in foreign affairs, not bolder. After the election, the foreign minister wrote to his ambassadors that "our policy is to preserve the status quo. . . . Every European country has enough to do at home without whipping up external quarrels."[55] Emile Ollivier, a Germanophile former republican oppositionist, became prime minister with a peace agenda in January 1870.[56]

Napoleon, however, longed for a bolder response to the political onslaught of the liberal and radical opposition. Less than two weeks after the 1869 vote, he wrote to a minister that "what is missing . . . is the occasion to strike a major blow which will rouse the public's spirits."[57] In May 1870, Napoleon appointed as France's foreign minister the Duke of Gramont, who could be counted on to seize—or even create—any such opportunity.

Relations had been tense between France and Prussia since the Prussians' victory over Austria in 1866. Napoleon had demanded territorial compensation for France, but had not mobilized the French Army to back the demand, and so was rebuffed in a humiliating fashion. Although the timidity of French public opinion had been a factor in Napoleon's decision not to mobilize, the public nonetheless blamed him for having missed the best chance to contain rising Prussian power.[58] Despite these competitive tensions, Prussia's Minister-President Otto von Bismarck expected that Ollivier's government would pursue a peace policy that would allow Prussia to gradually unify Germany without war. But once the appointment of Gramont was announced, Bismarck, like other keen observers, was sure this would mean war.[59] Since Bismarck was confident that the well-oiled Prussian military machine could defeat the French army, whose half-hearted reforms had barely begun, he set about promoting the Hohenzollern candidacy as a provocation to lure the French to attack and thus put them in the wrong in the eyes of Europe.

Why was Gramont so keen to fall into this trap? Ignorance of the perilous state of the French army was only part of it.[60] "I will be the French Bismarck," he said upon leaving his ambassadorial post for the ministry in Paris. Just as Bismarck had used forceful diplomacy to shore up the hard-pressed authoritarian regime in Prussia, Gramont would attempt

---

55. Price, *The French Second Empire*, p. 426.

56. Wetzel, *A Duel of Giants*, p. 28.

57. Price, *The French Second Empire*, p. 425.

58. Case, *French Opinion on War and Diplomacy during the Second Empire*, pp. 216–218.

59. Wetzel, *A Duel of Giants*, pp. 33–34, 83.

60. Price, *The French Second Empire*, pp. 432–433.

the same in France.[61] Gramont belonged to a faction of authoritarian Bonapartists, including the owners of some of Paris's largest newspapers, who promoted the use of force abroad as a way to wrest the political initiative from liberals. For them, says historian Roger Price, "the war would represent a displacement of internal into external politics."[62] In the liberal opposition, Adolphe Thiers ruefully agreed with this assessment, fearing that either a defeat at Prussia's hands or a victory won by Gramont's faction would "take our liberty away."[63]

When the Prussian king withdrew Leopold's candidacy for the Spanish throne, Gramont remained unsatisfied. Seeking a humiliation that would give him the upper hand in diplomacy toward Prussia and in domestic politics toward the liberals, Gramont insisted that the king pledge never to renew a Hohenzollern claim on Spain's crown. Somewhat disingenuously, Gramont claimed that incensed French public opinion, which "has burst into flames and threatens to overwhelm us," demanded this pledge.[64] "The government will not survive in the Chamber tomorrow unless it is able to present definite Prussian concessions."[65] Historians generally agree, however, that Gramont, his newspaper cronies, and like-minded government officials whipped up this public outcry and interpreted it to justify their preferred tactics.[66]

Notwithstanding the partially manufactured nature of the belligerent clamor, even the liberal and relatively pacific Ollivier was swept along with the frenzied mood. "Any cabinet—any government—that acquiesced in this affair would be overthrown," he told a British diplomat in justifying the demand for further guarantees. "The very honor, the very greatness, of France is at stake."[67] As early as January 1870, at the outset of his term in office, Ollivier expressed the same view in a more general context, telling the same diplomat that "a rebuff [from Germany] would mean war. . . . We who have to render account to parliament and to the country are less than the former government able to put up with any

---

61. Wetzel, *A Duel of Giants*, p. 34.

62. Price, *The French Second Empire*, p. 431; see also p. 429.

63. Ibid., p. 434.

64. Wetzel, *A Duel of Giants*, p. 120.

65. Price, *The French Second Empire*, pp. 427–428; see also Wetzel, *A Duel of Giants*, p. 116.

66. Price, *The French Second Empire*, pp. 432–433; Wetzel, *A Duel of Giants*, p. 120; but for some qualifications, see Case, *French Opinion on War and Diplomacy during the Second Empire*, p. 267.

67. Wetzel, *A Duel of Giants*, p. 119.

wound to the national pride. Our main object is peace, but we must show firmness and spirit or we shall not be able to cope with revolution abroad and socialism at home."[68]

In fact, the government almost certainly had more leeway than that in the crisis, if it chose to make use of it. Thiers had argued in favor of accepting the Prussian king's initial disavowal of the Hohenzollern candidacy, no questions asked. The Assembly was divided on Gramont's speech.[69] But instead of taking yes for an answer, Napoleon's government blundered into Bismarck's trap: King Wilhelm declined to discuss further guarantees with the French envoy, and Bismarck published an edited version of a telegram from Wilhelm that appeared insulting to France. This led speedily to a French mobilization, legislative approval of war credits, and the ill-fated attack.

The Franco-Prussian clash, the most consequential European war between 1815 and 1914, fits our theory well both in terms of its coding in our database and in terms of the causal mechanisms that are revealed in a narrative account. Napoleon III's five wars from 1849 to 1870 support our theory when viewed individually and also when considered in light of the development of Napoleon's strategy of rule as a whole. One distinctive feature of this trajectory, however, is that the expected patterns of foreign policy under incomplete democratization remained prominent even during the period of Napoleon's regression into a largely autocratic system of government between 1852 and 1859. This pattern endured because popular nationalism, heightened during the early phase of the incomplete democratic transition, continued to serve as the ideological cover for the subsequent retreat into autocracy.[70] Overall, the era of Napoleon III shows the value of viewing cases not just singly, but in their long-run trajectory, a theme to which we will return.

PRUSSIA/GERMANY, 1848–1870 AND AFTER
Between 1848 and 1945, Prussia and its successor state Germany were the instigators of six interstate wars, including four great-power wars that

---

68.   Ibid., p. 30.

69.   Ibid., pp. 108, 119.

70.   Before leaving the French case, it is necessary to mention a false positive case that affects one of our tests of war initiation. Polity III codes France as having made a transition in 1814 from Napoleonic autocracy to a mixed-regime constitutional monarchy, based on the constraints on the executive. Therefore, in testing the effects of transitions over ten-year periods, we find France to be an incompletely democratizing state initiating war to overthrow the Spanish republican regime in 1823. However, the Bourbon regime that invaded Spain had just undergone a rightward shift in its policies, if not its institutions, and none of our causal mechanisms is relevant to the case.

fundamentally reshaped international politics: the First and Second Schleswig-Holstein Wars against Denmark in 1848–49 and 1862, the Austro-Prussian War of 1866, the Franco-Prussian War, World War I, and World War II. All of these wars arose out of the social stresses of incomplete democratization and the long-term consequences of German elites using war and nationalism to manage that turbulent transition.[71]

As in the France of Napoleon III, Prussia's Revolution of 1848 took place in a society in which an extraordinarily broad range of social groups contended for power, including an absolutist monarch, a strong administrative and military apparatus linked to the landed aristocracy, increasingly assertive urban professional classes, incipient capitalist and working classes on the brink of explosive growth, and a numerically preponderant peasantry. Prussia faced the further complication that Germany's boundaries and political identity were in flux during this formative moment of rising demands for mass political participation. German speakers were divided among Prussia, multiethnic Austria, and some thirty-five smaller sovereign units in western and southern Germany.

Prussia's traditional ruling elites faced a double challenge in revolutionary 1848 and the following two decades.[72] Liberals argued that the German people deserved to rule themselves in their own national state. Linking popular self-rule and nationalism in this way, they demanded both a constitutional state that would limit the powers of the old elites and also a national state that would unify German-speakers. Notwithstanding the popularity of their political message, the German liberals faced two barriers to assuming political power and achieving their objectives. First, the urban professional and commercial classes that were the liberals' core constituency had no desire to open the floodgates to a mass democracy that would empower peasants and urban laborers. Second, they found that the achievement of their program of national unification was blocked at every turn by autocracies or by rival national states, and thus could make no progress without the support of the German state's powerful military force.

Ironically, this situation allowed Otto von Bismarck, who became minister-president of autocratic Prussia in 1862, to co-opt the issues of both national unification and universal manhood suffrage from the liber-

---

71. For a fuller discussion, see Snyder, *From Voting to Violence*, chap. 3.

72. Thomas Nipperdey, *Germany from Napoleon to Bismarck, 1800–1866* (Princeton: Princeton University Press, 1996; orig. German ed. 1983); and David Blackbourn, *Fontana History of Germany, 1780–1918: The Long Nineteenth Century* (New York: Fontana, 1997).

als. In his series of lightning wars against Denmark, Austria, and France, Bismarck created a unified, national German state and granted the vote to the conservative peasantry and the urban working class. At the same time, the new German empire retained the authority of the king to name ministers who were not responsible to the national legislature. In this way, Bismarck subordinated the liberal parties and urban middle classes by taking over their political agenda, using the votes of conservative peasants against them, and protecting them from the rising working class by allying them to an authoritarian state and hereditary aristocracy. Economically, this arrangement was reinforced by a protectionist alliance of "iron and rye" after 1879, logrolling the interests of aristocratic grain-growers and heavy industrialists.

Bismarck's successors entrenched this system of rule through the ideology of militarized nationalism, which glorified the military virtues of the state, recruited the middle classes into political life through militarist and imperialist pressure groups, and branded the socialist workers as anti-national "enemies of the Reich." Whenever possible, the elite cartel fought elections on "national" issues, such as the military budget, colonial policy, or purported cultural threats from minority groups such as the Poles or Catholics. When the government parties did this, voter turnout increased, the parties were more cohesive in their electoral strategy, and their share of votes and seats went up.[73] The manufacturing of international crises and arms races helped to extend the life of this strategy, even as the inexorable rise of the urban working population was making obsolete Bismarck's old strategy of relying on the votes of easily manipulated conservative peasants.

An unintended consequence of the state's strategy of threat exaggeration and prestige diplomacy strategy was that middle-class pressure groups such as the Navy League insisted that the old elites should either stand firm on behalf of threatened German national interests, or else allow the more vigorous middle classes greater access to power. Some historians have argued that Germany's decision for war in 1914 was a direct consequence of its elites' need to escape from the contradictions of the use of nationalism to maintain their rule under conditions of incomplete democratization.[74] At a minimum, however, it is fair to say that Germany's belligerent diplomacy and military strategy, which was integral

73. Brett Fairbairn, *Democracy in the Undemocratic State: The German Reichstag Elections of 1898 and 1903* (Toronto: University of Toronto Press, 1997), p. 48.

74. See, for example, Fritz Fischer, *War of Illusions* (New York: Norton, 1973; orig. German ed. 1969).

to its elites' domestic political strategy, helped cause the war as an unintended consequence.[75]

Overall, this series of cases strongly supports our theory and reflects almost all of its causal mechanisms. The type of nationalism was counterrevolutionary, which fits our expectations for a country that has strong administrative institutions but relatively weak institutions regulating democratic participation. In our database, Prussia/Germany shows up as a war initiator undergoing incomplete democratization only for the wars of 1864 and 1866, but the causal processes set in motion by Germany's pattern of incomplete democratization left their mark on all of the wars between 1848 and 1945.

THE FIRST SCHLESWIG-HOLSTEIN WAR. In 1848–49, amid the revolutionary nationalist tide in Germany, Prussia invaded Schleswig and Holstein, two independent duchies that formed a part of the Danish monarchy, in support of rebellious German-speaking subjects. Holstein was a mainly German-speaking area and a member of the German Confederation. The Danish king would have been willing to release Holstein from Danish sovereignty upon his death. Schleswig, however, was demographically divided between its Danish-speaking north and its German-speaking south; both the Danish king and the German nationalists wanted all of it. When the Danish state attempted to annex Schleswig formally in March 1848, rebellious German-speaking Schleswigers proclaimed a provisional government of the two duchies and announced that "we will join in the movement for German unity and freedom with all our might."[76] When the Danes attacked rebel detachments, pushing them back to the border between Schleswig and Holstein, the Prussian army counterattacked into Schleswig.

Although the Prussian king held to monarchist rather than nationalist principles, the revolutionary politics of 1848 made it prudent for him to act forcefully on behalf of this hugely popular national cause.[77] Russia, however, was unwilling to sanction this forceful action on behalf on national interests against monarchical rights. Neither nationalists nor monarchists liked Britain's sensible proposal to divide Schleswig along demographic lines, so Britain weighed in with Russia in favor of a Prussian withdrawal and a temporizing return to the status quo ante, which Prus-

75. Steven E. Miller, ed., *Military Strategy and the Origins of the First World War* (Princeton: Princeton University Press, 1985); and Snyder, *Myths of Empire*, chap. 3.

76. W.E. Mosse, *The European Powers and the German Question, 1848–71* (New York: Octagon, 1969, orig. ed. 1958), p. 18.

77. Nipperdey, *Germany from Napoleon to Bismarck*, pp. 531, 554.

sia accepted. The Frankfurt National Assembly, a self-styled pan-German "parliament," denounced the retreat as "treason" and a violation of "national honor"; but lacking a state or an army, this toothless talking shop eventually voted to approve the ceasefire.[78]

Despite the rhetorical rabble-rousing of 1848, Polity records only a minuscule increase in the competitiveness of political participation in Prussia. The king remained in power at all times, the army remained intact and loyal to the monarchy, and concessions to constitutionalism were at best fleeting. Consequently, the Prussian attack on Danish Schleswig does not count in our database as a war initiated by an incompletely democratizing state. Nonetheless, this was the opening move in a longer-term process that supports our theory in terms both of its causal mechanisms and our statistical measures.

THE SECOND SCHLESWIG-HOLSTEIN WAR. When the Danish king died in 1863, a dispute about the right of succession in the duchies led in the following year to military intervention by Prussia and Austria, which defeated the Danes and agreed to administer the duchies jointly. Bismarck's strategy for creating and exploiting this victory demonstrates how he used militarized nationalism to weather the storms of Germany's incomplete democratization.

Prussia, coded as an incompletely democratizing initiator, had recently undergone transitions from autocracy to a mixed regime as measured by the openness of executive recruitment, the competitiveness of political participation, and the constraints on the executive. In 1858, Crown Prince Wilhelm became regent, replacing the incapacitated King Friedrich Wilhelm IV. Though mainly interested in military reforms, the crown prince instituted some broader political reforms that allowed a relatively tame group of liberals to win the majority of seats in the lower house of the Prussian legislature.[79]

This tentative opening toward constitutional government reached a crisis point in 1862, when the legislature refused to ratify Wilhelm's plan to rationalize the Prussian army by extending the term of conscription to three years and integrating the civilian Landwehr reserve into the organizational framework of the regular army. Bismarck, considered too much of a reactionary to hold high office in a reformist regime, was now called back from a diplomatic post to become Prussia's minister-president and to implement Wilhelm's plans without a legislatively authorized budget.[80]

---

78. Ibid., pp. 555, 632.

79. Ibid., p. 622.

80. Ibid., pp. 64–67.

Already in 1858 Bismarck had written a long memorandum on the foreign policy issues facing the new regime. Predicting a diplomatic offensive by Austria to gain hegemony in Germany, Bismarck argued that the only source of power to buttress Prussia's position was the moral pressure of German nationalist public opinion which, he argued, dovetailed with Prussia's state interest.[81] Once in office in Berlin, Bismarck set about the task of harnessing German mass nationalism to Prussian state goals. Bismarck thought that this strategy would allow him not only to stymie Austria, but also to win over the liberals, break the constitutional deadlock between the king and the legislature, and fend off the neofeudal conservatives, who longed to renounce the constitution and return to absolute monarchical rule.[82] Moving to implement this strategy in 1862, Bismarck called for the creation of a parliament for the German Confederation to be elected by universal manhood suffrage, a proposal popular with German liberals and nationalists that Bismarck knew Austria would have to reject.[83] Bismarck's gains from this gambit were limited, however, since the liberal nationalist audience viewed it as yet another Machiavellian ploy by this cynical reactionary.[84]

The war with Denmark increased Bismarck's credibility with the liberal nationalists, showing that Prussian state power could deliver what they wanted. Bismarck was highly attuned to the public relations opportunities of war; for example, he ordered the dramatic storming of Danish entrenchments against the objections of Prussian field commanders.[85] Even so, in order to insure the neutrality of the great powers, the victory had to be shared with Austria, an impediment that Bismarck soon set about to remove.

THE AUSTRO-PRUSSIAN WAR. Despite the victory over Denmark, Bismarck had still been unable to break the budget deadlock with Prussia's legislature. In February 1866 Bismarck told King Wilhelm that he would have to choose among three options: accepting a government with liberal ministers, allowing a coup to overturn the constitution, or going to war with Austria to co-opt the liberal nationalists by unifying Germany under the authority of the monarchical Prussian state. The next week, Wilhelm

---

81. Otto Pflanze, *Bismarck and the Development of Germany*, vol. I: *The Period of Unification, 1815–1871* (Princeton: Princeton University Press, 1963), pp. 122–125.

82. Nipperdey, *Germany from Napoleon to Bismarck*, p. 608.

83. Ibid., pp. 630–631, and for other examples, pp. 681–682.

84. Ibid., p. 646.

85. Ibid., p. 688.

authorized an alliance with Italy to open up a second front by attacking Austrian-held Venice.[86]

In April, to provoke Austria and create a pretext for war, Bismarck revived his proposal to remake the German Confederation through a universal-suffrage federal assembly, which he insisted Austria had to accept or else withdraw from the Confederation.[87] Bismarck anticipated that conjuring up the liberal nationalist hexing power of universal suffrage, "the strongest of freedom's arts," would have the additional effect of deterring the great powers from "sticking their fingers into our national pie."[88]

Even so, there was little public enthusiasm for war. Liberals feared that a war managed by Bismarck would become a pretext for repression, not an opportunity for national liberation.[89] Acting on a prudent instinct for self-preservation, most of the smaller German states sided with Austria.[90]

This all changed, however, when the reformed Prussian army led by the military genius Helmuth von Moltke won a quick, decisive victory in July 1866, innovatively using railroad mobility to encircle the outclassed Austrians at the battle of Sadowa (Königgrätz). The progressive and left-center parties now lined up to cooperate with Bismarck, seeking to gain a voice in forming the new North German Confederation, which incorporated the recalcitrant small German states that Prussian armies had also defeated. Out of the remnants of the old liberal groupings, a new party was formed, the National Liberals, with the emphasis now on the "national" rather than the "liberal."[91] Within two months of the battle, the Prussian legislature voted budgetary credits to cover the government's expenses during its four-year breach of the constitution.[92]

Historians agree that domestic and foreign policy were intimately interrelated in Bismarck's strategy. It would be going too far, however, to argue that Bismarck sought military conquests only for the sake of their

---

86. James J. Sheehan, *German History, 1770–1866* (Oxford: Clarendon, 1989), p. 900.

87. Nipperdey, *Germany from Napoleon to Bismarck*, pp. 689–690.

88. Ibid., p. 693; and John Breuilly, *Nationalism and the State*, 2d ed. (Chicago: University of Chicago, 1993), pp. 110–111.

89. Sheehan, *German History, 1770–1866*, p. 900; and Nipperdey, *Germany from Napoleon to Bismarck*, p. 697.

90. Blackbourn, *Fontana History of Germany, 1780–1918*, p. 243.

91. Nipperdey, *Germany from Napoleon to Bismarck*, p. 711.

92. Blackbourn, *Fontana History of Germany, 1780–1918*, p. 244.

domestic political benefits. Rather, he sought both domestic and foreign gains as mutually reinforcing means to strengthen the Prussian state in a time of both domestic and international crisis. As Thomas Nipperdey puts it, the domestic benefits were "a calculated and desired effect of such [foreign] policies."[93]

THE FRANCO-PRUSSIAN WAR. The victory over Austria left many loose ends to be gathered up before the project of German unification would be fulfilled. Bavaria and the German states south of the Main River stayed outside of the North German Confederation, which remained something less than a cohesive state. Napoleon III, embarking on military reform after the sharp lesson of Sadowa, still nursed hopes for territorial compensation on the west bank of the Rhine, which Bismarck had denied him in 1866. On Prussia's domestic front, progress on German unification would help Bismarck fend off the need to compromise with the parliamentary liberals.[94]

Although neither domestic nor international conditions compelled Bismarck to embark on a war with France, when the belligerence of France's Gramont ministry convinced him that he could use the Hohenzollern candidacy to provoke France into a foolhardy attack, Bismarck seized the opportunity to speed up the timetable for accomplishing his grand design in international and domestic politics. This was not a war of democratization according to our Polity codings, because more than a decade had elapsed since Wilhelm's constitutional changes. Nonetheless, it marks a culminating point in Bismarck's overall strategy of deploying popular nationalism to co-opt demands for broadened political participation and thus to weather a crisis of incomplete democratization.

WORLD WARS I AND II. After the victory of 1870, Bismarck established the German Reich, or Empire, with its Reichstag, or Parliament, elected by universal suffrage. Nonetheless, he continued to use his considerable powers as chancellor to rule subject only to limited democratic constraints. After the new Kaiser, Wilhelm II, forced Bismarck from office in 1890, the relatively liberal Caprivi government introduced changes that, according to Polity codings, increased constraints on the executive and enhanced the competitiveness of participation. For the first time, Germany's democracy score is higher than its autocracy score. As our theory would expect, the decades following this loosening of the grip of

---

93. Nipperdey, *Germany from Napoleon to Bismarck*, pp. 681–682; see also Breuilly, *Nationalism and the State*, p. 115.

94. Pflanze, *Bismarck and the Development of Germany*, pp. 435–437; and Wetzel, *A Duel of Giants*, pp. 69–72.

state power witnessed a burst of elite competition to mobilize support among mass groups. Junker landed aristocrats organized small farmers into the protectionist Agrarian League, while industrialists and the military organized the middle-class Navy and Army Leagues.[95] The Polity score for constraints on the executive increased again in 1908 with mounting pressures for ministerial accountability to the Reichstag.

Despite these incremental changes, Germany remained a mixed regime until the collapse of the Reich and the establishment of Weimar democracy in 1919. Therefore, Germany's attack on France in August 1914 was not a war of democratization in our data set, even though it illustrates many of the causal mechanisms of our theory.[96] Bismarck's pattern of co-opting pressures to democratize through a militarized, nationalist foreign policy had become ingrained in German institutions and ideology. Given this legacy, additional incremental pressures for democratization simply deepened the polarization between middle class nationalists and the growing working class, whose socialist votes prevented a government majority in the 1912 election.[97]

Even after the establishment of the Weimar democracy, German politics remained marked by many of the factional divisions, institutional legacies, and ideological presuppositions of the pre-1914 era. In particular, Nazi nationalist thinking can trace a direct lineage to the ideas and political alignments of the Wilhelmine era. We do not claim that nationalist ideas played the same functional role in the Nazi political system as they did in that of Bismarck or Kaiser Wilhelm. Once in power, Hitler's decisions to act on his aggressive agenda reflected his own internalization of a belligerent, nationalist world view, not mass pressure for nationalist political movements. But insofar as those ideas arose through blowback from earlier nationalist rhetoric, the legacy of Germany's incomplete democratization continued to exert its lethal power in World War II.[98]

---

95. Geoff Eley, *Reshaping the German Right* (New Haven: Yale University Press, 1980); H.J. Puhle, *Agrarische Interessenpolitik und preussischer Konservatismus im wilhelminischen Reich, 1893–1914* (Hanover: Verlag fur Literatur und Zeitgeschehe, 1966); and David Blackbourn and Geoff Eley, *The Peculiarities of German History* (New York: Oxford, 1984), pp. 272–275.

96. For a detailed discussion of those causal mechanisms, see Snyder, *From Voting to Violence*, chap. 3.

97. Konrad Jarausch, *The Enigmatic Chancellor* (New Haven: Yale, 1973), p. 90.

98. Blowback occurs when manipulators are captured by their own propaganda; see Snyder, *Myths of Empire*, pp. 41–42, 49, 92–95, 105–108.

CHILE: THE WAR OF THE PACIFIC

Chile's role as initiator of the War of the Pacific against Peru and Bolivia in 1879, fought over nitrate deposits, demonstrates the dangers of coalition politics in weakly institutionalized states undergoing an incomplete democratic transition. Following the extension of suffrage to all male property owners in 1874,

well-defined political parties began to press their divergent views upon the executive branch and to seek the support of a larger electorate. The Chilean leadership had to be more responsive to Congress, and had to defend its policies in a broader public arena. . . . The debates produced heated and often intemperate expressions of opinion, expressions that the government found it difficult to ignore.[99]

These political developments yielded a transition from autocracy to a mixed regime, as measured by the constraints on the executive. The transition occurred under conditions of relatively weak governmental institutions and fragmented political power.[100]

In 1879, a severe economic downturn, which drove a surge of unemployed workers into the capital, coincided with a diplomatic dispute between Chile and Argentina over control of the Straits of Magellan. Mobs in Santiago protested against truculent public statements by the Argentine negotiator. Members of Chile's Conservative opposition party referred to President Aníbal Pinto's foreign policy as craven. Meanwhile, the Bolivians decided that Chile's preoccupation with its dispute against Argentina would give them a free hand to increase the taxes they levied on Chilean nitrate firms operating in Bolivian-held disputed territory in the Atacama Desert. This further heightened the politically motivated war fever in Santiago. At the same time, nitrate mining interests were planting pro-war stories in Chile's press. "With Congressional elections scheduled for 1879, the various parties desperately needed an issue to use against the Pinto regime," says historian William Sater.

Earlier these elements had manipulated the Argentine crisis to discredit Pinto's Liberal Party and to galvanize public opinion against the govern-

---

99. Robert N. Burr, *By Reason or Force: Chile and the Balancing of Power in South America, 1830–1905* (Berkeley: University of California Press, 1965), p. 115; see also William F. Sater, *Chile and the War of the Pacific* (Lincoln: University of Nebraska Press, 1986). We are grateful to Susan Burgerman and Kristina Mani for research and analysis of this case.

100. During this episode, the level of domestic concentration in Chile was only 3 on the 11-point scale, far below the mean of 5.7. See Ted Robert Gurr, Keith Jaggers, and Will Moore, *Polity II: Political Structures and Regime Change, 1800–1986* (Ann Arbor: Inter-University Consortium for Political and Social Research, 1989).

ment. Unfortunately for Pinto, the Bolivian crisis overlapped the Argentine situation and many Chileans feared that Santiago would humble itself as shamelessly before La Paz as it had groveled before Buenos Aires.[101]

A prominent legislator, telling Pinto of an enthusiastic pro-war demonstration outside of his window, predicted: "Either we occupy all Antofagasta [in the nitrate region] or they will kill you and me."[102] Pinto hoped to avoid war with Bolivia and its ally, Peru, just as he had with Argentina, but "driven by an inflamed public," Sater concludes that he "had no choice but to declare war if he wished to remain president."[103]

Although Chile succeeded in gaining control over valuable nitrates that were in high demand in Europe and the United States for use in fertilizers and explosives, the war was hardly a coolly calculated, premeditated decision by Chile's leaders. The Chilean army was unprepared to wage war against two states that together had twice Chile's population. It took five years to achieve victory in a costly struggle that led to far higher taxation on Chilean nitrate firms than the Bolivians had imposed. Historians argue that a naval blockade of Bolivia's nitrate ports could have accomplished Chile's economic objectives far more quickly and cheaply.[104] Thus, the decision for war can be fully understood only in light of the political dynamics that are characteristic of incomplete democratization with weak institutions.

But which of these dynamics were most important to the outcome, and what light do they shed on the causal mechanisms in our theory? In the cases of Napoleon III and Bismarck, the central leadership of the state played the key role in seizing upon the national aspirations of the people and turning them toward war in order to legitimate their own rule in an era of mass politics. These leaders, ruling states with strong administrative institutions but weak participatory ones, were in a position to shape the nationalist agenda in ways that helped them maintain their authoritarian style of rule. In contrast, in the Chilean case, the state leadership was dragged into war by elite and mass groups that had already formulated belligerent demands: the nitrate interests, the jingo press, the opposition parties, and the mob in the streets.[105] With weaker institutional le-

---

101. Sater, *Chile and the War of the Pacific*, p. 15.

102. Ibid., p. 16.

103. Ibid., p. 16; see also p. 9

104. Bruce W. Farcau, *The Ten Cents War: Chile, Peru, and Bolivia in the War of the Pacific, 1879–1884* (Westport, Conn.: Praeger, 2000), p. 45.

105. Ibid., p. 40.

vers at his disposal, Pinto had to respond to interest-group jockeying rather than shape it. Elite interest groups and factions, rather than the central state, took the lead in using belligerent nationalist appeals to mobilize mass support for their parochial objectives. Though these causal mechanisms differed because of the difference in institutional setting, they are both consistent with the overall logic of our theory.

Bruce Farcau's recent examination of the war stresses the role of the opposition press in generating war fever. The governments of all three states, he says, were "prisoner to the whims of the crowd. While only Chile had a functioning democracy at the moment even in the broadest definition of the term, all recognized freedom of the press, to a certain degree, and opposition political groups could make their wishes known. None of the regimes had a firm enough grasp on power to risk taking the wildly unpopular stand that conciliation would have entailed."[106]

The media campaign had the perverse effect of making leaders seem spineless to their counterparts abroad, yet too rigid to compromise. The Chilean press campaign about Pinto's shameless lack of resolve helped convince the Bolivian president that the tax on nitrate exports could be safely restored.[107] Subsequently, Pinto used the intransigence of Chilean public opinion as a reason for not backing down in the negotiations, claiming that his government would fall if he made concessions.[108] This example contrasts with mature democracies, which may be able to bargain efficiently because of their transparency and ability to make credible commitments; here a government in the throes of an incomplete democratic transition lacked the authority to make either concessions or threats credible.

GUATEMALA: THE CENTRAL AMERICAN WARS OF 1885 AND 1906
According to our database, Guatemala was a democratizing initiator of war with El Salvador in 1885 (based on constraints on the executive and the openness of executive recruitment), and again in 1906 (based on the openness of executive recruitment). These wars occurred a few years after presidential elections and, in the earlier case, a momentous regime change that established the "Liberal" modernizing faction in power. Nonetheless, we find that these wars are false positives for our theory.

With backing from the Mexican Liberal regime of Porfirio Diaz, in

---

106. Ibid., p. 45.

107. Ibid., p. 41.

108. Ibid., p. 44.

1871 Guatemalan Liberals overthrew an authoritarian Conservative regime, run by a landowning oligarchy that had largely ignored the country's sham constitution. The Liberals were bent on modernizing the Guatemalan economy and society, building roads and railroads, seizing the lands of the oligarchy and the church, banning religious orders, planting vast plots of coffee, exporting it to the United States, and thereby, they hoped, generating the capital needed to develop the country. Taking Napoleon III and Porfirio Diaz as models, they embarked on extensive institutional and cultural changes, suppressing economic guilds, introducing modern civil law codes and civil marriage, creating a National Ministry of Development, proclaiming free and compulsory public education, and professionalizing the military with the help of foreign experts. The Constitution of 1879 introduced habeas corpus for the first time, but also included clauses permitting emergency rule by the president.[109]

This reform succeeded in spurring a twenty-fold increase in international trade between 1870 and 1900. However, it did little to stimulate the development of an internal market, because of capital flight and the use of cheap coerced labor in producing export crops. The military—whose budget increased ten-fold between 1870 and 1910—provided an avenue of upward mobility for the middle class, but was an instrument of repression and coup-plotting that largely left the constitution politically irrelevant. Just 3 percent of the population voted in the presidential election of 1880, won by the Liberal Justo Ruffino Barrios in a landslide, and only 4 percent voted in 1904. Barrios ruled with a rubber-stamp assembly in what is sometimes called a "republican dictatorship" until 1885, when he died in battle during the attack on El Salvador.[110]

Liberals such as Barrios struggled against the old oligarchies throughout Central America in their attempts to remake the society and economy. Barrios hoped to spread his system of modernization through a confederation of Honduras, El Salvador, Nicaragua, and Costa Rica. When several states resisted this, Barrios tried to use military force to ac-

---

109. Brian Loveman, *The Constitution of Tyranny: Regimes of Exception in Spanish America* (Pittsburgh: University of Pittsburgh Press, 1993), p. 105; Ralph Lee Woodward, *Central America: A Nation Divided* (New York: Oxford, 1976), pp. 168–170; Wayne Clegern, *Origins of Liberal Dictatorship in Central America: Guatemala, 1865–1873* (Boulder: University Press of Colorado, 1994), pp. 147, 154; and Thomas Karnes, *The Failure of Union: Central America, 1824–1960* (Chapel Hill: University of North Carolina Press, 1961), p. 152.

110. Woodward, *Central America*, pp. 163, 170; and Deborah Yashar, *Demanding Democracy: Reform and Reaction in Costa Rica and Guatemala, 1870s–1950s* (Stanford: Stanford University Press, 1997), pp. 37, 43.

complish his goal of unification, citing the successes of modernizing nationalism in Germany and Italy.[111]

However, this is hardly the whole story, since wars were common in Central America both before and after the Liberal revolution. A deeper reason for these wars was that all of these states were weak, and state boundaries were highly permeable to political intrigues. Initially joined in a federation, the states never fully achieved independent political identities during the nineteenth century. Rulers of all the states harbored rebels who sought to unseat their neighbors' regimes. This set of sub-state actors created a security dilemma in which the destabilization of neighboring states became an indispensable form of self-defense.

This pattern continued in transborder squabbles among Liberal factions even after the Conservatives were gone from the scene. The 1906 war, for example, started when El Salvador supported an incursion by Guatemalan rebels, and Guatemala responded by invading.[112]

Thus, dramatic social, economic, and political change is likely to cause war within and between poorly institutionalized societies. Sometimes this may be accompanied by social modernization, voting, and lip service to a constitution, but as in this case, that does not mean that the process is necessarily one of democratization, nor one in which our theory's causal mechanisms apply.

SERBIAN ETHNIC NATIONALISM AND THE BALKAN WARS

Serbia's incomplete democratization in the late nineteenth and early twentieth centuries coincided with the mobilization of popular nationalism and contributed to Balkan wars in 1877, 1885, 1912, 1913, and most devastatingly in 1914. Serbia's role in this series of wars is paradigmatic of the ethnic nationalist pattern that we expect when weakly institutionalized democratizing states seek legitimacy through appeals to ties of popular culture. Serbia appears in our database as an incompletely democratizing initiator of one of these conflicts, the First Balkan War of 1912, in which Serbia, Bulgaria, and Greece attacked and defeated Turkey. In 1903, Serbia underwent a transition from autocracy to a mixed regime as measured by constraints on the executive, but a transition to democracy when measured by the openness of executive recruitment.

The nationalism that fueled these wars was not simply—as has sometimes been said—a reflection of primordial feelings of ethnic rivalry. In fact, Serbian nationalism emerged through the processes of state-building

111. Karnes, *The Failure of Union*, pp. 153–162.

112. Woodward, *Central America*, pp. 153–155, 171, 191.

and democratization in the nineteenth century. Serbia achieved a status of virtual independence from the Ottoman Empire through a series of revolts and negotiations between 1804 and 1830. Almost all modern scholars discount the notion that this rebellion was motivated by Serbian nationalism. Rebelling peasants sought ownership of their own land and relief from arbitrary taxation. Small-scale pig merchants sought a decentralized system that would give them local autonomy, whereas the rival leaders of the two largest merchant dynasties, Karageorge and Milos Obrenovic, vied to establish a more centralized system with themselves as the new overlords of the region. It is true that the Ottoman Turks were viewed as alien oppressors, but before about 1840 this grievance was not framed in national terms. Serb leaders lived as Turks did, and aspired to the status of favored, autonomous lords loosely integrated at the margins of the Ottoman system. Some Muslim merchants, no less inconvenienced than the Serbs by the chaos of Ottoman decline, fought alongside Karageorge for Serbian autonomy.[113]

After the expulsion of Ottoman officialdom, Serbia had no traditional aristocratic or bureaucratic elite of its own. The dynasties of Karageorge and Milos Obrenovic in 1815 ruled over a highly undifferentiated society of illiterate peasants with very little state apparatus. Thus, Prince Milos confronted the problem of establishing his rule in an institutional vacuum while competing with two empires, a rival dynasty, and local notables, ruling over a population with minimal organizational experience. In an attempt during the 1830s to institutionalize more fully the rule of the Obrenovic dynasty, Milos brought in educated Serbs from Austrian lands to staff government bureaucracies and schools.

The first glimmerings of truly national goals and consciousness came only with these efforts to build a modern Serbian state in the 1830s. At this time, Milos sought to gain the support of peasants against local notables by reviving the tradition of the *skupstina,* a mass outdoor assembly of the armed men of a clan or locality. This served as the basis for periodic popular assemblies to ratify the prince's decisions. At this stage, the peasantry typically aligned with Milos and the bureaucracy against the local notables, who sought to impose a local patriarchy. Thus, a populist alliance between the central state and the peasantry began to take shape.[114]

Nationalism was the natural ideology to cement this alliance. Throughout the nineteenth and early twentieth centuries, the Serbian

---

113. Barbara Jelavich, *History of the Balkans* (Cambridge: Cambridge University Press, 1983).

114. Charles Jelavich and Barbara Jelavich, *The Establishment of the Balkan National States, 1804–1920* (Seattle: University of Washington Press, 1977), pp. 56, 60.

state used the public school system, which it controlled, to inculcate the historical lesson that only a strong, unified state could protect the Serbian nation from foreign domination.[115] Nationalism was an advantageous ideology for Serbia's state-building elites in part because it helped to cement central authority over local elites. It also helped to rationalize steep taxes to support hugely expensive railroad projects and military programs, which fed the growth of the state bureaucracy and provided a steady flow of cash for kickback schemes.[116] Popular nationalism also helped mobilize volunteers for the state's repeated wars through the universal conscription law of 1861.[117]

This nationalism took an ethnic form in part because Serbia's democratizing civic institutions were too transient and weak to serve as a stable basis for popular loyalty. As early as 1869, all taxpayers could vote (including most of the peasantry) and political parties recruited electoral support from all sectors of society. Elections were often rigged, however.[118] Western-sounding laws existed, but the rule of law did not. Government ministries instructed judges not to apply laws literally, but to make their rulings instead "according to conscience and conviction with regard for popular justice and customs."[119]

SERBIAN PARTY POLITICS AND THE WAR OF 1877.   In the Serbian context, liberalism was not an alternative to ethnic nationalism, but a promoter of it. Self-styled liberals were among the most committed ethnic nationalists. The more democratic the party and the more popular its appeal, the more belligerent was its nationalism.

Liberal militants often prevailed in public debate, despite the dubiousness of their arguments. For example, the Liberal Party defeated the Conservatives in the 1875 elections on the strength of its clamor for Ser-

---

115.   Charles Jelavich, *South Slav Nationalism: Textbooks and Yugoslav Union before 1914* (Columbus: Ohio State University Press, 1990), p. 191; and Michael Petrovich, *A History of Modern Serbia, 1804–1918* (New York: Harcourt Brace Jovanovich, 1976), pp. 502, 583–584.

116.   Gale Stokes, "The Social Origins of East European Politics," in Daniel Chirot, ed., *The Origins of Backwardness in Eastern Europe: Economics and Politics from the Middle Ages until the Early Twentieth Century* (Berkeley: University of California Press, 1989), pp. 236–237; Jelavich, *History of the Balkans*, vol. 1, 379–380; and Jelavich and Jelavich, *Establishment*, p. 141.

117.   Jelavich and Jelavich, *Establishment*, p. 65.

118.   Petrovich, *History of Modern Serbia*, p. 367; Gale Stokes, *Legitimacy through Liberalism: Vladimir Jovanovic and the Transformation of Serbian Politics* (Seattle: University of Washington Press, 1975); and Jelavich and Jelavich, *Establishment*, p. 190.

119.   Petrovich, *History of Modern Serbia*, p. 402.

bian support for the popular Bosnian uprising against the Ottomans. In contrast, conservative proponents of a more prudent style of power politics, including the reigning monarch, Milan Obrenovic, were wary of triggering an Austrian military occupation of Bosnia; however, such caution was swept aside. Two thousand Belgrade volunteers, primed by nationalist poetry readings at public rallies, signed up within days to fight in the Bosnian resistance movement.[120] Reinforcing emotional appeals with the usual panoply of pseudo-strategic justifications, Liberal interventionists claimed that Russia, Austria's rival, would deter Austrian countermoves against the Serbs. They also predicted that all Balkan Christians would support Serbia, and that war would counter the internal threats from Serbia's socialists and restore internal unity. Furthermore, they contended that economic growth would be spurred by military expansion and heightened military expenditures. The Liberals also contended that Serbia would get no spoils if it refused to fight. In fact, none of these assertions was borne out. When Russia attacked the Ottoman army in the Balkans in 1877, the Serbian military intervened against Ottoman forces, which were already reeling from the Russian offensive. However, Serbia's efforts failed to impress the great powers. Much of the territory occupied by Serb forces had to be ceded to Bulgaria. Austria occupied Bosnia. Inside Serbia, the intervention failed to stem Liberal criticism of Milan's government, which was vilified as incompetent.[121]

THE ATTACK ON BULGARIA IN 1885. Liberal reforms continued in 1883 with modest measures to increase the freedom of the press and the independence of the judiciary. Despite these concessions, the liberal nationalist Radical Party trounced the ruling party by a two-to-one margin in the 1883 election, but Milan refused to offer the Radicals a chance to govern. Seeing that militant nationalism worked as a potent rhetorical tool for the opposition, Milan once again tried to adapt nationalism as a popular basis for a government dominated by conservative parties. Milan saw an opportunity for nationalist posturing when, in 1885, Bulgaria annexed Rumelia, a formerly Ottoman region populated by Bulgarians. Though Serbia had no claim to Rumelia, Milan argued that the increase in Bulgaria's size would upset the balance of power to Serbia's disadvantage. Consequently, he insisted, Bulgaria should cede some territory to Serbia as compensation. Rebuffed, Milan launched a disastrous offensive into Bulgarian territory. This stratagem worked no better in domestic politics than it did on the battlefield. Serbs could mount little enthusiasm for a

---

120. Ibid., pp. 381–382, 536.

121. Ibid., pp. 384, 392, 394–401.

war against fraternal Slavs, from whom they felt little ethnic differentia-tion. Radicals and liberals wanted compensation from the Ottomans, not war against Bulgaria.[122] Thus, nationalist manipulations were attempted, but their effectiveness was constrained by the underlying ethnic sympa-thies and enthusiasms of the people, which the state itself had done so much to encourage.

FURTHER STEPS IN DEMOCRATIZATION AND THE BALKAN WARS OF 1912–1914. Serbia's political system became more democratic under the short-lived Constitution of 1888, which established the secret ballot, banned emergency rule by the executive branch, gave the elected Assem-bly power over the budget, and barred censorship of the press. In 1889, the Radical Party, a populist nationalist movement led by Nikola Pasic, came to power through a relatively free and fair election. Far from consol-idating rule by law, however, the Radical victory was taken as a signal that the law and order imposed by more conservative regimes was a thing of the past. Banditry, arson, political murders, and riots increased, even under the eye of the police. Losing some support in the 1893 elec-tions, the Radicals were maneuvered out of power when the king re-voked the 1888 Constitution.[123] Thus, politics was populist, but not insti-tutionalized in a way that might root civic loyalty in effective democratic practices.

After an interlude of relatively authoritarian rule, the corrupt Obrenovic dynasty was overthrown in 1903 in a military coup that put the Karageorgevic dynasty, the scions of Karageorge, back in power.[124] One of the charges against the deposed ruler, Alexander Obrenovic, was that he had done little to advance Serbian national goals in the Balkans and had aligned with Austria, the occupier of Serb lands in Bosnia. In contrast, the new king, Peter Karageorgevic, was a patriot who had fought as a volunteer in the 1875 Bosnian Serb uprising against Ottoman rule. Karageorgevic was also a liberal who had translated John Stuart Mill's *On Liberty* into Serbo-Croatian.

A modified version of the relatively democratic 1888 Constitution was reinstated in 1903. Though this made Serbian politics more open and competitive, it did not guarantee stability. Five different governments held office between 1904 and 1906, when Pasic's Radicals established a working majority and remained in power through 1918.

---

122. Jelavich and Jelavich, *Establishment*, pp. 188–189; and Petrovich, *History of Mod-ern Serbia*, pp. 430–431.

123. Petrovich, *History of Modern Serbia*, pp. 441, 448–450, 460.

124. Ibid., pp. 504–505, see also 371.

One of the keys to the Radicals' electoral appeal was their ability to capitalize on Serbian nationalist sentiment through their confrontational foreign policy. Under the Radicals, the Serbian government embarked on a tariff war with Austria (the "pig war") and joined an offensive military alliance with Greece and Bulgaria to seize Turkish territory in the Balkans in 1912. After defeating Turkey, the nationalistic victors fell to squabbling over the territorial spoils. Rather than surrender some of its gains, Bulgaria attacked Serbia and Greece, but was quickly defeated.

In these projects, Serbia's Radical government had to run hard to keep up with militant nationalist groups like the Black Hand, warlike factions in the military, and legislators who needed to be responsive to public opinion. After Austria's 1908 move to formally annex occupied Bosnia, the reaction of the Serbian public to the subjugation of the Bosnian Serb populations was so violent that the police had to intervene. Opinion in the Assembly was similarly belligerent.[125]

Journalistic freedom under the 1903 Constitution provided an effective platform for promoting militant views. Like party politics, journalism was freewheeling, but poorly institutionalized, contentious, and unprofessional. The reading public was intensely interested in politics; by 1904 Belgrade alone supported seventy-two newspapers. Only one, however, the newly established *Politika*, was a truly professional paper, not tied to any party, offering news, features, reports from foreign correspondents and wire services, and a sports section. Virtually all of the other newspapers were bitterly polemical mouthpieces for political parties, featuring personal attacks instead of real news reports.[126]

This press, especially the populist Radical organs, was stridently nationalistic. The Carnegie Commission, in its 1914 examination of the origins of the Balkan Wars of 1912 and 1913, laid a great deal of the blame on strident nationalist propaganda in the press and from official institutions.[127] Leon Trotsky, later to become a Russian Bolshevik leader, but then a war correspondent in the Balkans, reported that "agitation for war—never mind with whom: Austria, Bulgaria, Turkey, even the Concert of Europe—has furnished the uniform political keynote of the entire

---

125. Jelavich, *History of the Balkans*, vol. 2, pp. 108–111; and Petrovich, *History of Modern Serbia*, p. 558.

126. Petrovich, *History of Modern Serbia*, pp. 585–586. This situation remained unchanged in interwar Yugoslavia. See Rothschild, *East Central Europe*, pp. 237, 277.

127. Carnegie Endowment for International Peace (CEIP), *The Other Balkan Wars* (Washington, D.C.: CEIP, 1993), reprinting CEIP, *Report of the International Commission to Inquire into the Causes and Conduct of the Balkan Wars* (Washington, D.C.: CEIP, 1914), pp. 19, 50–51.

'independent' press of Belgrade."[128] Similar nationalist outpourings came from the press of the partially democratized states of Bulgaria and Greece.[129] In 1914, following the assassination of Austrian Archduke Franz Ferdinand in Bosnia by a Serbian nationalist, Austria insisted that the Serbian government clamp down on anti-Austrian diatribes in the Serbian press and on the teaching of militant nationalism in Serbian public schools.[130]

In short, Serbian institutions created outlets for mass political energies and pluralistic debate, but they did not provide a stable framework for democratic politics or the coherent assessment of public arguments. In this setting, loyalties could not attach themselves to civic processes as a basis for nationalism. Rather, civic and state institutions, such as dynasties, parties, and newspapers, gained legitimacy by cloaking themselves in the mantle of an extra-institutional loyalty to the Serbian ethnic group. A weak but modernizing bureaucratic state grafted on elements of premodern folk democracy to legitimize its rule in an era of mass politics.[131]

It might be argued that some of Serbia's wars can be explained in terms of the more or less rational pursuit of geopolitical opportunities for expansion, which any vulnerable but reasonably ambitious state might have seized, regardless of its regime type. Serbia more than doubled its territory through its victories in 1878 and 1913, preying on the Turks' weakness and the Bulgarians' errors in judgment.[132] Arguably, however, the bill for Serbia's multi-directional nationalist belligerence came due in August 1914, when Austria ran out of patience with Serbia's fomenting of anti-Habsburg violence. While not ignoring the role of strategic opportunism in some of Serbia's wars, we argue that the Serbian case clearly shows our theory's causal mechanism at work.

FRANCO-THAI WAR OF 1940–1941

In November 1940, Thailand's military-dominated constitutional regime attacked territories in Laos and Cambodia held by the Vichy French regime after the fall of France to the Nazis. The Thais sought to take advan-

---

128.   Leon Trotsky, *The War Correspondence of Leon Trotsky: The Balkan Wars, 1912–1913* (New York: Monad, 1980).

129.   Petrovich, *A History of Modern Serbia*, p. 601.

130.   Petrovich, *History of Modern Serbia*, pp. 492–493, 614; and Jelavich, *History of the Balkans*, vol. II, p. 33.

131.   Petrovich, *History of Modern Serbia*, p. 443.

132.   E. C. Helmreich, *The Diplomacy of the Balkan Wars* (Cambridge: Harvard University Press, 1938).

tage of France's dire circumstances to regain land lost to France between 1893 and 1907, and to preempt a possible Japanese seizure of those areas. After sharp fighting, the Thai army achieved its objectives, and a settlement was reached under Japanese mediation.[133]

Our database considers Thailand an incompletely democratizing initiator of this war, based on transitions from autocracy to a mixed regime in 1932 as measured by the openness of executive recruitment, constraints on the executive, and competitiveness of participation. This is hardly a perfect case for our theory, since opportunities for meaningful democratic mass political participation were at best minimal in Thailand in 1940, and because geopolitical incentives for action were salient in Thai decision-making. Nonetheless, the case illustrates a number of our theory's causal mechanisms and overall seems quite consistent with our arguments.

Before 1932, Siam was an autocratic monarchy with the beginnings of a modern, Western-educated bureaucracy and military. A modernizing faction of the army mounted a coup in June 1932 with support among some high-level state elites. In December the new leaders promulgated a constitution that established a national Assembly, half of whose members were to be appointed and half indirectly elected. After a second coup solidified the modernizers' control, elections were held in November 1933 in which 10 percent of the population participated. Over time, the Assembly began to play a more significant role in political decision-making. In September 1934, the Assembly forced the resignation of the government over its scheme for an international rubber cartel, leading to a reshuffling of cabinet ministries. In November 1937, 26 percent of the population voted in direct elections of half of the Assembly's members. This popular mandate was sufficient to allow representatives to raise objections to high military budgets and the placement of military officers in senior civil posts. In September 1938, the Assembly forced the government to resign over a budget issue.[134]

The winner of the new elections in November 1938 was Luang Phibunsongkram (also known as Phibun), the military mastermind of the 1932 and 1933 coups. While maintaining constitutional forms, Phibun's regime embarked on an authoritarian nationalist campaign to modernize Thai society. Arresting some forty key rivals after his electoral victory, Phibun deftly used the government's monopoly over radio and its con-

---

133.   David Wyatt, *Thailand* (New Haven: Yale University Press, 1982), pp. 255–256.

134.   Wyatt, *Thailand*, pp. 250–252; see also B. J. Terwiel, *A History of Modern Thailand, 1767–1942* (St. Lucia, Queensland: University of Queensland Press, 1983), pp. 329–342.

trol over the release of news to the press to mobilize mass support for his policies of economic nationalism. At that time, Chinese non-citizens, an important community in Thailand, were remitting large sums to China and, spurred by the Sino-Japanese War of 1937, organizing in Thailand around Chinese nationalist issues. In an effort to weaken the role of Chinese middlemen in the economy and to create an indigenous, state-dependent Thai business class, the Phibun regime forbade non-citizens to hold key jobs, curtailed Chinese schools, and established state corporations to compete with Chinese firms. In 1939, Phibun renamed the country Thailand, embarked on a range of mass campaigns to promote patriotic symbolism and modernize Thai daily customs, and expanded military conscription and youth scouting groups.[135]

Primed by this campaign of nationalist public relations, Thailand's public was genuinely enthusiastic about the successful irredentist attack on the Vichy French territories. Militarily defeating a European power and reversing old humiliations gave Phibun a huge boost in public esteem.[136] Ever since 1932, Thailand's modernizing elite had groped for a way to generate authentic popular enthusiasm for their cause.[137] Their experiment with constitutionalism had produced only limited successes in that regard, and until 1938, had left a trail of largely ineffective, unstable regimes. Phibun's strategy of filling the empty forms of constitutionalism with nationalist content succeeded in energizing mass engagement with politics in a way that stabilized the regime. Many of the causal mechanisms at work in this phase of Thailand's incomplete democratization reflect those in our theory.

IRAQ IN THE PALESTINE WAR, 1948–49

Iraq's constitutional monarchy, torn by turbulent experiments with parliamentary government, played a catalytic role in pushing the shaky Arab states into war in 1948–49 to try to prevent the partition of Palestine and the creation of the Israeli state. In May 1948, 16,000 Iraqi troops joined four other Arab armies in attacking the new Israeli state.[138] Our

---

135. Wyatt, *Thailand*, pp. 253–255; David Van Praagh, *Thailand's Struggle for Democracy* (New York: Holmes and Meier, 1996), p. 45; David Elliott, *Thailand: Origins of Military Rule* (London: Zed, 1978), p. 87; and Likhit Dhiravegin, *Demi Democracy: The Evolution of the Thai Political System* (Singapore: Times Academic Press, 1992), p. 125.

136. Van Praagh, *Thailand's Struggle for Democracy*, p. 45; Terwiel, *A History of Modern Thailand*, pp. 344–346; and Wyatt, *Thailand*, pp. 255–256.

137. Wyatt, *Thailand*, pp. 246–247.

138. Michael Eppel, *The Palestine Conflict in the History of Modern Iraq* (London: Frank Cass, 1994), p. 190. Michael Clodfelter, *Warfare and Armed Conflicts*, 2d ed. (Jefferson,

database considers Iraq an incompletely democratizing initiator of the war, based on transitions from autocracy to a mixed regime as measured by constraints on the executive and the openness of executive recruitment. This case not only illustrates several of the causal mechanisms of our theory, but also shows the role of incomplete democratization in heightening a still vexatious conflict that has continued to bedevil the world for over half a century.

Interwar Iraq was a country with no coherent identity, tradition, or political institutions, undergoing the strains of socio-economic modernization and decolonization.[139] Under a British mandate, Iraq's 1924 constitution divided powers between the king and a parliament that was indirectly elected through electors chosen by universal manhood suffrage. After gaining independence in 1932, Iraq suffered a series of tribal rebellions, leadership struggles, and finally a coup by nationalist military officers, which triggered British reoccupation of the country from 1941 to 1945.[140]

Following World War II, the British encouraged the Regent Abd al-Ilah, ruling on behalf of the young King Faysal II, to liberalize the regime to enhance its popular legitimacy in the eyes of alienated urban middle classes who were attracted by nationalist and socialist doctrines. Press restrictions were removed, opposition parties were licensed, and electoral districts were redrawn to reflect population shifts to urban areas. However, the plan for political liberalization provoked resistance from established elites.[141] The Iraqi prime minister told a British diplomat that his government had "decided to allow political parties in order that it should become clear how harmful they are and their abolition be demanded."[142] Reflecting traditions of patronage politics in a still largely rural society, local notables dominated the parliament chosen in the election of 1946.[143]

N.C.: McFarland, 2002), p. 631, says that there were 10,000 Iraqis among the 55,000 Arabs deployed against the Israelis by October 1948.

139.   Quoted in Reeva Simon, *Iraq Between the Two World Wars: The Creation and Implementation of a Nationalist Ideology* (New York: Columbia University Press, 1986), pp. 3–4.

140.   Phebe Marr, *The Modern History of Iraq* (Boulder: Westview, 1985), pp. 55–93.

141.   Marr, *The Modern History of Iraq*, pp. 96–100; and Matthew Elliot, *"Independent Iraq": The Monarchy and British Influence, 1941–1958* (London: Tauris Academic Studies, 1996), p. 25.

142.   Elliot, *"Independent Iraq,"* p. 26.

143.   Marr, *The Modern History of Iraq*, p. 101; and Eppel, *The Palestine Conflict in the History of Modern Iraq*, p. 139.

Middle-class nationalists, though thinly represented in parliament, remained loud voices in public debate. Important in government service, in the military, in the economy, and potentially in the streets, these educated urbanites could not be ignored. To appease such critics, Iraqi diplomats took the most radical stance on the Palestine issue at the June 1946 meeting of the Arab League, gratuitously calling for a boycott of British and American trade that they knew the Saudis and Egyptians would have to veto.[144] Such public relations tactics became increasingly entrenched in 1947, as the new Iraqi Prime Minster, Salih Jabr, groped to find a rhetorical stance that would reconcile Iraq's diverse constituencies to his weakly institutionalized regime.

Jabr faced a general economic crisis, severe food shortages, and a shortfall of money for salaries of civil servants, a prime constituency for Arab nationalist groups.[145] Despite widespread malnutrition in the country, entrenched rural interests insisted on the right to export scarce grain for hard currency. The regent and the traditional ruling elites hoped that British economic and military aid would, as usual, help them weather the crisis and fend off burgeoning urban radicalism. In pursuit of that strategy, Jabr counted on early renegotiation of Iraq's treaty with Britain to eliminate the embarrassment of British air bases on Iraqi soil and to create a firmer basis for economic and political cooperation.[146]

For the nationalists, however, even an improved agreement with the former colonial overlord was anathema. To immunize themselves from nationalist objections, Jabr and other Iraqi elites relied on demagogy on the Palestine issue.[147] Previously a moderate on the Palestinian issue, Jabr converted to the rhetorical hard line to get ideological cover for renewal of the treaty with Britain. In August 1947, he broke precedent in calling for the use of the regular armies of Arab states, not just volunteers, to fight against the Jews in Palestine.[148] At the culmination of the debate over the British treaty in December 1947, Jabr falsely told the Iraqi parliament that Iraq and Transjordan were committed to a joint policy of creat-

---

144.   Bruce Maddy-Weitzman, *The Crystallization of the Arab State System, 1945–1954* (Syracuse: Syracuse University Press, 1993), p. 36.

145.   Eppel, *The Palestine Conflict in the History of Modern Iraq*, p. 167; and Marr, *The Modern History of Iraq*, p. 103.

146.   Eppel, *The Palestine Conflict in the History of Modern Iraq*, pp. 159, 162–163; and Marr, *The Modern History of Iraq*, pp. 101–102.

147.   Maddy-Weitzman, *The Crystallization of the Arab State System*, p. 49; and Eppel, *The Palestine Conflict in the History of Modern Iraq*, p. 143.

148.   Eppel, *The Palestine Conflict in the History of Modern Iraq*, pp. 164–166.

ing a unitary Arab state in all of Palestine.[149] However, amid a worsening of the economy and a shortfall of expected British aid, the strategy of nationalist demagogy on the Palestine issue failed to reconcile Iraqi nationalists to the renewal of the treaty with Britain. The signing of the treaty in January 1948 provoked a wave of student strikes, demonstrations, and denunciations from political parties, leading to Jabr's replacement by a politician who was untainted by association with the treaty.[150]

While Jabr's rhetoric on Palestine failed to achieve its intended consequences, its unintended consequences were profound. A British diplomat reported that "the Iraqi Government is now to some extent the victim of their own brave words, which the opposition is not slow to challenge them to make good."[151] In a vicious bidding war, the regent, the parliamentary notables, and the socialist parties now all competed with the nationalist opposition to adopt the most militant position on Palestine.[152] Since Iraq was not a front-line state, the costs of undermining the chances of compromise in Palestine were low compared to the domestic political costs of being outbid on the Arab nationalism issue.

This rhetoric reverberated not just within Iraq, but throughout the Arab world. Jabr's militant stance on Palestine at the October and November 1947 meetings of the Arab League helped to set off a bidding war with other Arab states.[153] Initially, a number of the Arab states had hoped that the Palestine issue could be resolved through compromise. Egypt felt it was too weak to embark on a war. The Syrians feared that even a victorious war led by the Transjordanian army might lead the Hashemite monarchy to swallow up their country as part of a Greater Palestine. In comparison, Iraq was consistently more militant than Egypt and Syria from 1946 to 1948 because its more democratic political system made it more sensitive to public opinion.[154] Only Iraq rejected the UN's call for a ceasefire in July 1948. To curry favor with the nationalist opposition, the Iraqi regime even authorized public demonstrations condemning conces-

---

149. Maddy-Weitzman, *The Crystallization of the Arab State System*, p. 57.

150. Eppel, *The Palestine Conflict in the History of Modern Iraq*, pp. 174–175; and Marr, *The Modern History of Iraq*, pp. 101–105.

151. Eppel, *The Palestine Conflict in the History of Modern Iraq*, p. 169.

152. Eppel, *The Palestine Conflict in the History of Modern Iraq*, pp. 141–142, 181, 193; Maddy-Weitzman, *The Crystallization of the Arab State System*, p. 56; and Marr, *The Modern History of Iraq*, p. 102.

153. Eppel, *The Palestine Conflict in the History of Modern Iraq*, p. 158.

154. Maddy-Weitzman, *The Crystallization of the Arab State System*, p. 78.

sions made by other member states of the Arab League.[155] For a time, the less democratic Egyptian and Syrian regimes had greater leeway than Iraq to resist popular pressure to adopt radical positions on Palestine.[156] However, as Iraqi rhetoric ratcheted up the expectations of the Arab public, Egypt's King Faruq began to worry that the establishment of a Jewish state would spark riots. Despite his worries about the state of his army, he began to hope for a successful war to restore his waning prestige.[157] In the echo chamber of popular Arab politics, Iraq's incompletely democratized regime led the way in adopting a demagogic strategy that increasingly tied the hands of less democratic Arab states that otherwise might have been able to resist such popular pressures.[158]

In short, the Iraqi case illustrates several of the mechanisms of our theory. In a state with weak institutions and heterogeneous political constituencies undergoing an incomplete democratic transition, new entrants into politics used nationalist doctrines of popular self-rule as a battering ram to gain access to political power. Established elites responded with nationalist outbidding in an attempt to legitimate their waning power.[159] Because of the mismatch between the boundaries of the Arab states and the wider Arab nation, Iraq's opportunistic rhetoric helped to catalyze similar bidding wars in other less democratized, initially less belligerent Arabs states. Thus, our theory not only explains Iraqi policy, but also sheds light on the origins of the war more generally.[160]

---

155.   Ibid., pp. 49, 56, 78.

156.   Ibid., p. 61.

157.   Eppel, *The Palestine Conflict in the History of Modern Iraq*, p. 185; and Maddy-Weitzman, *The Crystallization of the Arab State System*, p. 67.

158.   For general statements by scholars along these lines, see Maddy-Weitzman, *The Crystallization of the Arab State System*, p. 49; and Eppel, *The Palestine Conflict in the History of Modern Iraq*, p. 158. For a related argument, see Michael Barnett, *Dialogues in Arab Politics: Negotiations in Regional Order* (New York: Columbia University Press, 1998), pp. 87–91 and passim.

159.   For an argument expressed in almost exactly these terms, see Eppel, *The Palestine Conflict in the History of Modern Iraq*, p. 194.

160.   Our database records a false positive for Iraq as a democratizing initiator in the Iran-Iraq War of 1980. In 1979, Saddam Hussein was chosen by a two-thirds vote of the Revolutionary Command Council to succeed Ahmad Hasan Al-Bakr as President of Iraq. At the same time, plans were underway for non-competitive, universal suffrage elections to a National Assembly. These elections, the first in Iraq since the fall of the monarchy in 1958, were held in 1980. Although these developments did nothing to democratize the regime in any meaningful way, Polity codes this as a transition to democracy based on the openness of executive recruitment. Adam Przeworksi, Michael Alvarez, José Cheibub, and Fernando Limongi, *Democracy and Development: Political In-*

THE FALKLANDS WAR

In April 1982, the military junta ruling Argentina needed a military victory to increase its popularity on the eve of an expected democratic transition, and so they invaded the British-owned Falkland Islands (called the Malvinas by Argentines). When the British defeated the Argentine forces and reclaimed the islands, the junta fell from power and multiparty democracy returned to Argentina. On its face it seems, therefore, that the war came before democratization. Nonetheless, according to our database, Argentina was an incompletely democratizing initiator of the war, based on a transition from autocracy to a mixed regime as measured by the competitiveness of political participation, which occurred in the last two years of the junta. In fact, the junta's pattern of coalition politics, mobilization of nationalism through the newly freed press, and gambling for resurrection in the expectation of multiparty elections fits our theory well.

In 1981, the ruthless Argentine military junta led by General Jorge Videla, with its popularity waning because of the failure of its economic policies, transferred power to the more pluralistic regime of General Roberto Viola. Viola permitted labor unions and opposition political parties to organize openly, and allowed a dramatic increase in the freedom of the press. However, since liberal journalists had earlier been removed by Videla's regime, the newly widened discourse was dominated by nationalist voices supporting the Argentine government's claims on the islands and clamoring for their seizure. A consortium of political parties organized large public demonstrations, calling for early elections and for "the immediate restitution of the Malvinas."[161] Spurred by the dangers and opportunities of this situation, hard-line Army officers around General Leopoldo Galtieri sought to bolster the military's popularity through a nationalist prestige strategy centered on conquering the islands.[162] Align-

---

stitutions and Well-Being in the World, 1950–1990 (Cambridge: Cambridge University Press, 2000) code this as a transition from autocracy to "bureaucracy." Iraq attacked revolutionary Iran in 1980, because the Shi'a fundamentalist regime of Ayatollah Khomeini had weakened Iran's army in the short run, yet the revolutionary regime loomed as a long-term threat that might link up with Iraq's large Shi'a minority. These events have nothing to do with our theory. See Marr, The Modern History of Iraq, p. 231; and Magid Khadduri, The Gulf War: The Origins and Implications of the Iraq-Iran Conflict (New York: Oxford University Press, 1988), pp. 74–76.

161. Paul Mares, Violent Peace: Militarized Interstate Bargaining in Latin America (New York: Columbia University Press, 2001), pp. 152, 200.

162. Jack S. Levy and Lily Vakili, "Diversionary Action by Authoritarian Regimes," in Manus Midlarsky, ed., The Internationalization of Communal Strife (London: Routledge, 1992), pp. 118–146; Richard Ned Lebow, "Miscalculation in the South At-

ing with hardliners in the Navy against more moderate elements in the junta, Galtieri seized power as leader of the ruling junta and hurried to implement his plan in the face of the parties' demands for elections.[163]

Through a victory in the Falklands, Galtieri hoped "to create a new civil-military alliance that would guide the transition back to democracy and lead him to victory in the elections," says Paul Mares.[164] Counting on an electoral base in conservative and regional parties, Galtieri "publicized his net worth to demonstrate that he was not corrupt, promised to return his presidential salary to the Treasury, and began making appearances 'shaking hands with the elderly and kissing babies'."[165] One motive for this gamble for resurrection may have been to escape the demands of the Mothers of the Plaza de Mayo for information and justice regarding their thousands of children who were "disappeared" during Videla's "dirty war" against the opposition. The junta also hoped that a successful war would be a distraction from economic grievances. Two days before the invasion, ten thousand people demonstrated against the government as part of a general strike; a thousand were arrested. Shortly after the invasion, a quarter of a million people jammed the streets of Buenos Aires in support of the government's policy. Dissent virtually disappeared as political parties, organized labor, businesses, and religious organizations rallied to support the military.[166]

In short, despite the fact that the culmination of the democratic transition took place only after the war, this case supports our theory, and illustrates how a factionalized, partially liberalizing authoritarian regime

lantic: The Origins of the Falklands War," in Robert Jervis, et al., eds., *Psychology and Deterrence* (Baltimore, Md.: Johns Hopkins University Press, 1985), pp. 98–99; and David Pion-Berlin, "The Fall of Military Rule in Argentina: 1976–1983," *Journal of Interamerican Studies and World Affairs*, Vol. 27 (1985), pp. 382–407.

163. On the time pressure caused by party-sponsored demonstrations, see Paulo Nascimento, "War-Proneness and Peaceful Disposition in Democratizing States," Ph.D. dissertation, Columbia University, 2002.

164. Mares, *Violent Peace*, p. 152

165. Ibid., p. 152, citing Martin Honeywell and Jenny Pearce, *Falklands/Malvinas: Whose Crisis?* (London: Latin American Bureau, 1982), p. 80; and more generally, Andres Miguel Fontana, "Political Decision-Making by a Military Corporation: Argentina, 1976–1983," Ph.D. dissertation, University of Texas at Austin, 1987. See also A. C. Vacs, "Authoritarian Breakdown and Redemocratization in Argentina," in J. M. Malloy and M. A. Seligson, eds., *Authoritarians and Democrats: Regime Transition in Latin America* (Pittsburgh: University of Pittsburgh Press, 1987), chap. 2, especially p. 27.

166. Honeywell and Pearce, *Falklands/Malvinas*, p. 82; and Vacs, "Authoritarian Breakdown," pp. 28–29.

used belligerent nationalism as a key element of a strategy of gambling for resurrection in the face of pressures to democratize.

Completely Democratizing Initiators of Interstate War

A few of the above cases were coded as transitions to complete democracy as measured by the openness of executive recruitment: France, Guatemala, Serbia, and Thailand. However, since these cases were undergoing transitions from autocracy to mixed regimes on other dimensions, we discussed them in the context of incomplete democratization. (Except for highly democratized constitutional monarchies, it is common for countries to achieve high scores on the openness of executive recruitment before they do so on the other variables.)

Apart from such cases, there are only two cases of completely democratizing war initiators in our database, the United States in the Mexican War and Turkey in the Cyprus War. Pakistan in the Kargil War would also be in this category, but it is so recent that it is not included in the database (we discuss it in Chapter 8). There are, in addition, numerous cases of completely democratizing states initiating war against non-state actors, such as Britain's colonial wars after the Reform bills in the nineteenth century, or participating in interstate wars, but not initiating them. Here, however, we discuss only the two cases of completely democratizing war-initiators as measured by our most valid indicators, competitiveness of participation and constraints on the executive.

THE UNITED STATES IN THE MEXICAN WAR

The United States initiated the Mexican War in 1846 shortly after undergoing a transition to complete democracy, as measured by the competitiveness of political participation. The broadening of the franchise arguably contributed to the decision for war by empowering Jacksonian Democrats, including non-slave-holding farmers and artisans hungry to take over Mexican land.

In the years before the war, the Jacksonian revolution in American politics had reduced restrictions on suffrage and provided for the direct election of officials, especially in western states. This was the era in which elite-dominated electoral politics was supplanted by a mass-democratic, two-party system.[167] Riding this rising tide of popular participation in politics, the Jacksonian Democrat James Polk was elected president in 1846 on a platform calling for territorial expansion in Oregon at the ex-

---

167. Chilton Williamson, *American Suffrage: From Property to Democracy, 1760–1860* (Princeton: Princeton University Press, 1960).

pense of Britain and in Texas and California at that of Mexico. "The Jacksonian hunger for territory was the driving force behind U.S. aggressiveness," says John Owen in his study of the democratic peace in U.S. diplomatic history.[168] Well-established slaveholders, represented by John C. Calhoun, often opposed the war, despite the fact that it might add slave states to the Union. Likewise, the relatively elitist Whigs, drawing support from manufacturing interests, were reluctant to support the conflict. Public opinion in New England and the Northeast was opposed to war, especially among abolitionists. In contrast, territorial expansion, even at the price of war, had a powerful appeal to Polk's newly empowered populist constituency in the West and South.[169]

In this way, the expanded democratization of the Jacksonian revolution was a factor contributing to war. Nonetheless, it is debatable whether this case exemplifies the main causal mechanisms of our theory. A traditional view portrays the Jacksonian revolution as an authentic people's movement from below.[170] In this interpretation, Polk and the Jacksonian Democrats were largely responding to the understandable, aggressive demands of their constituency. If so, this would have little to do with the causal mechanisms of our theory. More recently, however, some historians have questioned the simple view of the Democratic Party as the haven of poor farmers and artisans. Rather, they stress the way that Democratic politicians manipulated egalitarian symbols and rhetoric in order to portray their party and its program as more populist than it really was. In this interpretation, Polk used expansionist and nationalist themes to revive the connection between the Democratic Party and its Jacksonian popular base, which had been badly damaged by the economic recession during Martin Van Buren's term as president. More generally, in this view, the Jacksonian expansionism of the 1840s was an effort to use the mission of a continental empire to renovate the party's identity, seize the ideological high ground of nationalism, and thus rise above America's regional and class divisions.[171]

---

168. John M. Owen, "Perceptions and the Limits of Liberal Peace: The Mexican-American and Spanish-American Wars," in Miriam Elman, ed., *Paths to Peace: Is Democracy the Answer?* (Cambridge, Mass.: MIT Press, 1997), quotation at p. 170. For his larger study, see Owen, *Liberal Peace, Liberal War* (Ithaca, N.Y.: Cornell University Press, 1997), pp. 113–124.

169. John H. Schroeder, *Mr. Polk's War: American Opposition and Dissent, 1846–1848* (Madison: University of Wisconsin Press, 1973), chaps. 1 and 2.

170. Arthur M. Schlesinger, Jr., *The Age of Jackson* (Boston: Little, Brown, 1945).

171. Thomas Hietala, *Manifest Design: Anxious Aggrandizement in Late Jacksonian America* (Ithaca, N.Y.: Cornell University Press, 1985), pp. 4–5, 8–9, 256–257.

Overall, it seems that Jacksonian democratization has a plausible link to the Mexican War. Still, it is important to remember that America was very powerful compared to Mexico and that the territories it won were extremely valuable. Any American regime, democratizing or not, would probably have taken these territories sooner or later, by force if necessary. Although we do not necessarily claim that this case strongly supports our theory nor manifests its main causal mechanisms, neither does it refute them.

THE TURKISH INVASION OF CYPRUS

Turkey's invasion of Cyprus in 1974 illustrates many of the causal mechanisms of our theory. During the 1960s, rapid but uneven economic growth widened the range of interest groups clamoring to participate in Turkish political life. As a result of a more liberal constitution introduced in 1961, the rise of left and right wing extremist groups polarized the party system. Throughout this episode of democratization, the fragile institutions of Turkish democracy struggled to hold together the country's highly fragmented political mosaic.[172] In the face of mounting violence and radicalization, a military junta temporarily seized power in 1971. Electoral democracy was restored in 1973. Polity codes this as a transition to complete democracy, based on the composite index and the constitutional constraints on the chief executive.

The improbable ruling coalition that emerged from the 1973 elections was forged between Bulent Ecevit's social-democratic party and Necmettin Erbakan's Islamicist party. The still-influential military distrusted both of these parties, the socialists for opposing the 1971 coup and the Islamicists for challenging the secular principles that underpinned the military's position in the Turkish state. Virtually the only points that this coalition-of-opposites held in common were a firmly nationalist stance toward the conflict between Greeks and Turks on the island of Cyprus and a desire to stand up to U.S. pressure on that issue. To the socialists, the Greeks were not only an ethnic rival, but also pawns of U.S. capitalist hegemony, a central theme of their electoral campaign. To the Islamicists, the Greeks represented Christendom. The military had been on the lookout for an opportune moment to take action on Cyprus ever since 1967, when U.S. pressure had deterred Prime Minister Suleiman Demirel from invading Cyprus. Demirel had fallen from power

---

172.   As we mentioned in Chapter 4, Gurr, Jaggers, and Moore, *Polity II*, measure the concentration of domestic authority on a scale that varies from 0 to 10. Recall that based on our sample, the mean value of this variable is 5.7. During this episode, the level of domestic concentration in Turkey was only 4.

largely as a consequence of that decision, so both Ecevit and Erbakan were alert to avoid repeating his mistake.

As the situation on Cyprus heated up to a crisis level again in 1974, the increasingly free press of newly democratic Turkey—much of which was allied with various political parties—gave vent to steady outpourings of nationalist sentiment. Under these conditions, Erbakan and Ecevit each knew that to soft-pedal the crisis would be to hand power to the other, or to the military. Thus, when Greek nationalists mounted a coup against the elected Cypriot regime as preparation for unification with Greece, the leaders of the new Turkish democracy had little choice but to defy world opinion by invading and occupying part of Cyprus, including its Turkish-inhabited areas.

This case, then, illustrates virtually all of the themes that are central to our theory: the widening and fragmentation of the political spectrum through democratization, the gap between participation and institutions, the autonomy of the military veto group, the truculence of the popular press, the nationalist outbidding of competing elites, and the use of nationalist prestige strategies to integrate highly diverse coalitions.[173]

A possible objection to our interpretation is that Turkey might have responded to the Greek nationalist coup by invading Cyprus even if it had had a different type of regime. The Greek nationalist coup installed as ruler of Cyprus a notorious warlord who had mounted attacks on Turkish enclaves. Under these circumstances, it would have required extraordinary patience for any Turkish regime to remain passive while the rights of its co-ethnics were being flouted by a militarily weaker neighboring state. And yet the invasion was costly for Turkey. The international community, though hardly endorsing the coup by the Greek nationalists, universally condemned Turkey's unilateral use of force and refused to recognize the Turkish mini-state that was installed by force of arms on the Turkish-held portion of the island. In light of these costs, it seems plausible that a fully consolidated Turkish democracy with stronger democratic institutions might have adopted very different tactics in response to the coup. Working with the United States and international organizations, such as NATO and the United Nations, Turkey might have succeeded in reversing the coup through diplomatic pressure on the Greek Cypriots and the military junta in Athens that backed them. In general, our argument is not that states interacting with a democratizing country never share some of the blame for war's onset, but rather that the

---

173. Fiona Adamson, "Democratization and the Domestic Sources of Foreign Policy: Turkey in the 1974 Cyprus Crisis," *Political Science Quarterly*, Vol. 116, No. 2 (Summer 2001), pp. 277–303.

process of democratization frequently renders the transitional country belligerent and hampers its ability to peacefully resolve disputes with its rivals.

A further complication was that Greek calculations were also affected by pressure for democratization. In 1967, the military had mounted a coup to forestall the impending consolidation of Greek democracy. By 1973, the junta was dividing into a hard-line faction and a group that favored a constitutional republic. Facing the danger of a possible return to democracy, the hard-liners gambled for resurrection by pressing for *enosis* (union) with Cyprus, arguing that this urgent national question justified the continuation of military rule. Like the case of Argentine aggression on the Falkland Islands, this was a conflict triggered in part by the fear of imminent democratization.[174]

The Democratizing Initiators: An Overall Assessment

Of the ten countries reviewed in this chapter, seven—France, Prussia/ Germany, Chile, Serbia, Iraq in 1948, Argentina, and Turkey—provide clear support for our theory and demonstrate in a robust way the presence of our causal mechanisms. Of these seven countries, three—France, Prussia/Germany, and Serbia—fought additional wars that were not coded by our database as initiated by a democratizing state, but that nonetheless manifested the same causal mechanisms and were part of a state's longer-term trajectory of democratization and war. Two cases (the United States in the Mexican War and Thailand in the Franco-Thai War) neither clearly support nor refute our theory. Four wars with ostensibly democratizing initiators are false positives: Guatemala's two wars, the Franco-Spanish War of 1823, and the Iran-Iraq War. Three of these four false positives were based on our crudest indicator of democratic transition, the openness of executive recruitment.

Setting aside the false positives, these cases illustrate the full range of causal mechanisms that our theory predicts, and they bear out our predictions about the conditions under which we expect to find them. Political institutions were extremely weak at the moment of transition in at least five of these cases: Chile, Serbia, Thailand, Iraq, and Turkey. In all of the countries, with the partial exception of Chile, the ruling elite used nationalist rhetoric to shore up its endangered legitimacy in ways that

---

174. P. Nikiforos Diamandouros, "Regime Change and the Prospects for Democracy in Greece: 1974–1973," in Guillermo O'Donnell, Philippe Schmitter, and Laurence Whitehead, eds., *Transitions from Authoritarian Rule: Southern Europe* (Baltimore: Johns Hopkins University Press, 1986), pp. 138–164.

heightened the risk of war. As predicted, ethnic nationalist themes—Serb, Turk, Thai, and Iraqi Arab—were particularly salient in the states with the weakest political institutions. Counterrevolutionary themes were prominent in countries with stronger administrative institutions: France, Prussia/Germany, and Argentina. In the United States, with strong participatory institutions, expansionist ideology took a largely civic nationalist form. Nationalist bidding wars occurred between elite groups for the competitive recruitment of mass supporters in all cases except Thailand, where the ruling party bid high on nationalism without the goad of other nationalist elite competitors. Four of these cases (France, Prussia/Germany, Iraq, and Argentina) involved gambling for resurrection, in the strict sense that the hard-pressed ruling group largely manufactured an issue on which to fight a popular war primarily to raise its domestic prestige. Nationalist media manipulation by the state or by nationalist political parties played a prominent role in France, Germany, Chile, Serbia, Thailand, Argentina, and Turkey.

Causal mechanisms involving pressure groups and coalition dynamics were also present in several cases. Logrolling among economic, military, and governmental elites led to more belligerent policies in Germany's "coalition of iron and rye," Argentina's junta, and Iraq's deals among rural elites, urban middle classes, and the monarchy. Weak brokerage of pluralistic politics by the state was a factor contributing to war in Germany, Serbia, and Turkey. In France, Prussia/Germany, and elsewhere, rulers with a precarious hold on power used nationalist one-upmanship to gain advantages over elite coalition partners. Single-issue interest groups wielded enormous influence in favor of war in a few of the cases: Chilean nitrate firms, the Argentine Army and Navy, and the German military and economic cartels. In several cases, cryptic and muddled political dynamics hindered the state's ability to send coherent, credible diplomatic signals (Chile, Germany), to send signals that represented its real views (Iraq), to retain diplomatic flexibility and dexterity (France, Turkey), or to perceive signals correctly (Argentina). In short, the majority of these cases of democratizing initiators manifest many of the mechanisms of our theory.

The strongest competing explanation for these cases is probably *Realpolitik* opportunism. Democratizing initiators won eight of the wars they started, and lost only three (France in 1870, Iraq in 1948–49, and Argentina in the Falklands). A few of the decisions to initiate war seem quite reasonable from a realist standpoint. Geopolitical incentives to attack were obvious for Thailand and the United States. Prussia profited handsomely from its war against Denmark and especially its war against Austria. Arguably, Turkey was goaded into attacking. However, some of the winners paid heavy economic or diplomatic prices, or wound up gaining little: France in the Roman Republic, Chile, Thailand, and Turkey. If we included wars in a larger series of conflicts involving a democratizing state, but which were not themselves coded as initiated by a democratizer, this would add two losers (France in Mexico, Germany in the World Wars), two more winners (France in Crimea, Prussia in 1870), and a mixed bag of Serbian wins, losses, and draws. Assessed as a whole, these wars were not so enticing or unavoidable that the decision to attack can be understood without taking into account other causes which, we argue, were the effects of democratization.

Finally, these cases reveal patterns that add insight on the questions of time lags and reversals of democratization. The database identifies cases of war initiation at various time lags after democratization. Four countries experienced wars one year after a transition as measured by at least one of the component indices: France in the Roman Republic, Argentina in the Falklands, Turkey in Cyprus, and the United States in Mexico. In only two cases, Serbia in 1912 and Thailand in 1940, did war begin more than five years after the transition. Two countries (Prussia under Bismarck and Thailand under Phibun) initiated wars after first democratizing and then undergoing a relapse into a more authoritarian mode of rule, in which rhetoric continued to stress populist themes. France under Napoleon III is similar, but even more complicated: the war against the Roman Republic was initiated in the democratizing phase, then three wars were fought in a pseudo-populist authoritarian phase, and the Franco-Prussian War was initiated in a second democratizing phase.[175]

In sum, the cases of democratizing war initiators examined in this chapter provide many examples of the expected causal mechanisms. Although a few cases turned out to be false positives, these are arguably more than balanced out by a number of relevant cases that were not counted in our statistical results as wars initiated by democratizing states. Tracing these causal processes has shown that our arguments may be relevant to some cases that were not identified as wars initiated by democratizers in our statistical tests, and to patterns that unfold over longer periods of time. To that end, the next chapter, which considers wars that are too recent to be included in the database, concludes with some further remarks on the developmental trajectories that war-prone democratizing states follow.

---

175. For some statistical results that indicate the dangers of this kind of back-and-forth transition, see Michael Ward and Kristian Gleditsch, "Democratizing for Peace," *American Political Science Review*, Vol. 92, No. 1 (March 1998), pp. 51–61.

Chapter 8

Tracing Trajectories of Democratization and War in the 1990s

In this chapter, we examine the six international wars that occurred between 1992 and 2000.[1] We find that the causal mechanisms of democratization specified in our theory were significant contributors to war in all of them: the Nagorno-Karabakh War between Armenia and Azerbaijan, the Ecuador-Peru conflict, the Ethiopia-Eritrea War, the Kargil War in the context of previous wars between India and Pakistan, the Kosovo War in the context of the breakup of Yugoslavia, and the recent Central African wars, beginning with the conflicts in Rwanda and Burundi. Some of these conflicts might stretch some definitions of interstate war, either because the international aspects of the conflict were intertwined with civil war or because there might have been too few battlefield deaths to be counted as a war. Nevertheless, an examination of these recent conflicts demonstrates the contemporary relevance of our argument. In the same spirit, we also briefly discuss Russia's recent wars in quasi-independent Chechnya, which were not technically international wars, but nonetheless may be explained using our theory.

These cases are intrinsically important as examples of contemporary war, and they are also challenging for our theory because of the rise of a large, powerful bloc of advanced democratic states that has tried to promote peaceful transitions to democracy. Scholars of the democratic peace have shown that the absence of militarized disputes between democracies and the tendency to form inter-democratic alliances is stronger since 1945 than before. This may be because the quality of democratic norms or institutions has risen since 1945, or because a cohort of power-

---

1. The last year covered in our database is 1992.

ful democratic states has set up a robust system of free trade, international organizations, and democratic polities that functions as a more reliable peace system than in earlier less-institutionalized relations among democracies.[2]

Since 1991, the relative power of this bloc of advanced democracies has been enhanced by the Soviet collapse. As a result of this strengthening of the democratic peace system, some scholars expect that states undergoing democratic transitions in intensely supportive neighborhoods of mature democratic states might be less likely to fight than states undergoing transitions in earlier eras, when rougher neighborhoods were more prevalent.[3] To address this prediction, we need to examine recent cases to determine whether our causal mechanisms remain relevant.

Several of the cases discussed in the present chapter reinforce the insight from Chapter 7 that the relationship between democratization and war should not be viewed simply as a short-run phenomenon. Democratization does not always or only link a single moment of transition to a single war. Rather, in many cases, incomplete democratization sets up a trajectory that affects the likelihood and pattern of a number of future conflicts. Political changes set in motion by the initial transition establish pathways that shape, for good or ill, the subsequent development of nationalist ideologies and international rivalries. Since the sequence of democratic developments affects the peacefulness of these trajectories, those in the international community who seek to promote democratic change need to pay attention to getting the sequence right. Trying and failing to democratize in adverse circumstances can have fateful, long-term consequences. After discussing the post-1991 cases in this chapter, we draw on this evidence in the concluding chapter to illustrate the various trajectories that failed democratization may follow.

The Nagorno-Karabakh War

Our database identifies an interstate war beginning in 1992 between the newly independent states of Armenia and Azerbaijan. Both of these

---

2.   Bruce Russett and John R. Oneal, *Triangulating Peace: Democracy, Interdependence, and International Organizations* (New York: Norton, 2001). In contrast, realists have argued that the period after 1945 is different mainly because the democracies banded together against the Soviet threat. See Joanne Gowa, *Ballots and Bullets: The Elusive Democratic Peace* (Princeton: Princeton University Press, 1999); and John Mearsheimer, *The Tragedy of Great Power Politics* (New York: Norton, 2001).

3.   Kristian S. Gleditsch and Michael D. Ward, "War and Peace in Space and Time: The Role of Democratization," *International Studies Quarterly*, Vol. 44, No. 1 (March 2000), pp. 1–29.

countries held reasonably free elections in the early 1990s. While it can be debated how well our theory's precise mechanisms capture the dynamics that fueled this conflict, democratization undoubtedly played a central causal role.

As Soviet power in the Caucasus began to unravel in the late 1980s, violence broke out in the Armenian-populated enclave of Nagorno-Karabakh, a part of the Soviet republic of Azerbaijan. In February 1988, the city council of Karabakh's capital city passed a resolution requesting that Karabakh become part of Armenia.[4] In response, Azerbaijanis, including refugees from ethnic violence in Karabakh, attacked Armenian neighborhoods adjacent to Baku, Azerbaijan's capital. During the spring of that year, hundreds of thousands of Armenians demonstrated in Yerevan, the capital of the Soviet Armenian republic, in support of the Karabakh Armenians' demand to secede from Azerbaijan.[5] Azerbaijanis were later expelled from their villages in Armenia.

As the conflict in Karabakh continued, Armenia and Azerbaijan became independent states in 1991 upon the breakup of the Soviet Union. The Armenian government, elected in a free and fair contest, officially took the position that Armenia itself was not a belligerent in the war, and that Karabakh should be independent of Azerbaijan but not formally joined to Armenia. However, Armenian fighters and supplies were fed into the Karabakh enclave through a corridor of conquered Azerbaijani territory, and Armenia's armed forces engaged Azerbaijani forces on other fronts, including the Azerbaijani exclave of Nakhichevan.[6] Armenian fighters returning to Armenia from the front received government pensions and played a large role in Armenian politics. In 1999, Robert Kocharian, the former leader of the Karabakh Armenians, was elected president of Armenia. Although this is included in our database as an interstate war, the Correlates of War Project has recently debated whether to reclassify it as an internationalized civil war.

When the war began, Armenia was a democracy as measured by the composite index and openness of executive recruitment, and a mixed regime as measured by constraints on the executive and competitiveness of political participation. Azerbaijan was a mixed regime based on every measure, except for the openness of executive recruitment, which indi-

4. Gerard Libaridian, *The Challenge of Statehood: Armenian Political Thinking since Independence* (Cambridge, Mass: Blue Crane, 1999), p. 5.

5. Stuart J. Kaufman, *Modern Hatreds: The Symbolic Politics of Ethnic War* (Ithaca, N.Y.: Cornell University Press, 2001), pp. 62–65.

6. Michael P. Croissant, *The Armenia-Azerbaijan Conflict* (Westport: Praeger, 1998), chaps. 2 and 4.

cates that it was a democracy. Armenia held competitive elections shortly after independence, electing as President Levon Ter-Petrossian, a leading figure in the main committee of activists on the Karabakh issue. In Azerbaijan, the only truly competitive election occurred in 1992, when the mass-based Popular Front demanded that the communist holdover government resign because of its ineffectual prosecution of the Karabakh War. The Popular Front's candidate was elected president in a relatively fair contest on a highly nationalist platform, only to be ousted the following year in a military coup that reinstalled communist-era strongman Heidar Aliyev.[7] Our database does not consider this to be a war of democratization, because these were new states created out of the autocratic Soviet Union, not existing states that became more democratic on the eve of the war. This technicality aside, however, there is no question that these fit the definition of incompletely democratizing states.

To what degree did democratization cause the war? And to what extent did the war conform to the mechanisms predicted by our theory?

A skeptic might argue that the war was caused not so much by democratization as by the anarchic conditions resulting from Mikhail Gorbachev's policy of perestroika and the security dilemma inherent in the demographic intermingling of Azeris and Armenians, who shared a history of conflict dating back at least as far as the 1905 Revolution.[8] The initial fighting in Karabakh arose out of merely local frictions: one of the triggering incidents was a dispute over the election of the head of a collective farm.[9] Viewed more broadly, the escalation of the conflict to include the whole of the Armenian and Azerbaijani societies was inextricably linked to their stalled democratic transitions. The huge demonstrations organized by the Karabakh Committee in Erevan in 1988 sought independence from Armenia for Karabakh. It also established Ter-Petrossian's group as a popular force that could lead Armenia toward independence from the Soviet Union and to democratic elections.

Nationalists and democrats insisted on putting the popular Karabakh issue at the center of Armenia's political agenda, whereas the communists sought unsuccessfully to play it down. Similarly, in Azerbaijan, the communist regime was loath to mobilize the energies of society to create a mass army to fight the Karabakh Armenians. Again, it was the national-

---

7. Jack Snyder, *From Voting to Violence: Democratization and Nationalist Conflict* (New York: Norton, 2000), pp. 226–229.

8. Kaufman, *Modern Hatreds*, pp. 47, 205, 221, considers the security dilemma in this context, but rejects it as a sufficient cause.

9. Croissant, *The Armenia-Azerbaijan Conflict*, p. 27.

ists of the Popular Front who pressed for the creation of a democratic state that would take the lead in mobilizing the nation to fight.

Thus, a strong case can be made that democratization widened and intensified the conflict. Nonetheless, there remains the question of the causal mechanisms linking democratization and the war. Some have argued that democratization simply unleashed the long-established nationalist attitudes of the masses, which were heightened by the circumstances of the Soviet collapse.[10] This holds true more for the Armenian side of the conflict than for the Azeris, whose nationalism remained weakly established. Armenian nationalism dates back to the genocides and other conflicts with the Turks (including Turkic-speaking Azeris) in the late nineteenth century, in 1905, and during World War I. This national identity was further crystallized during Armenia's period as an independent democratic republic from 1918 to 1920.[11] Consequently, it would be wrong to argue that nationalist elites created mass nationalist attitudes during the course of Armenia's democratic transition. Indeed, Ter-Petrossian consistently tried to dampen the more reckless forms of Armenian nationalism. He fell from power in 1999, largely because of his attempt to persuade his fellow Armenians to accept compromises that would end the war. In short, militant Armenian nationalism was to a substantial degree a "bottom-up" phenomenon. Nonetheless, Armenia's democratic elites were eager to ride this wave of nationalist sentiment into office. Ter-Petrossian and the Karabakh Committee organized the massive rallies in Yerevan in the realization that exploiting the Karabakh issue was a highly effective tactic for establishing their leadership of an independent and democratic Armenia.

The Ecuador-Peru Conflict

In 1981, Ecuador and Peru fought a skirmish in disputed territory over Ecuador's access to the Amazon River; some 200 soldiers died.[12] The skirmish took place shortly after both Ecuador and Peru made transitions

---

10.   See Kaufman, *Modern Hatreds*, pp. 60–62, on "mass-led mobilization"; see also S. Neil MacFarlane, "Democratization, Nationalism and Regional Security in the Southern Caucasus," *Government and Opposition*, Vol. 32, No. 3 (Summer 1997), pp. 399–420.

11.   Snyder, *From Voting to Violence*, p. 223.

12.   David R. Mares, *Violent Peace: Militarized Interstate Bargaining in Latin America* (New York: Columbia University Press, 2001), p. 167. In 1980, Peru's Polity score went from autocracy 7, democracy 0, to democracy 7, autocracy 0; in 1979, Ecuador's score went from autocracy 5, democracy 0, to democracy 9, autocracy 0. On this measure, see chapter 4 in this volume.

from autocracy to complete democracy. Over the next fourteen years, the two states engaged in nine militarized incidents in this region, culminating in a war in January 1995 that killed between 500 and 1,500 combatants.[13] During this period Ecuador remained a full democracy. Peru remained democratic through two changes of government until 1992, when President Alberto Fujimori dissolved the Congress in order to win the on-going civil war against the Sendero Luminoso Incan Marxist insurgency and to restructure the economy. Fujimori's move was widely popular, and a new democratic constitution was approved by plebiscite in 1993. Fujimori won re-election as president in April 1995, gaining 52 percent of the vote.[14]

These armed conflicts were the most recent in a series that extended back two centuries, including 32 militarized disputes in the twentieth century alone. Although none of these are coded as wars in our database, conflicts in 1829, 1859, and 1941 involved substantial Peruvian invasions of Ecuadoran coastal territory, including the major city of Guayaquil.[15] Like the clashes of 1981 and 1995, the invasions of 1829 and 1941 occurred shortly after Peruvian transitions to democracy. In 1829 the new constitutional regime in Peru had just undergone a shift from an autocracy score (*Autoc*) of 6 and a democracy score (*Democ*) of 1 to the reverse. The 1941 war came two years after the election of a civilian president in which the votes were relatively evenly divided between two candidates.[16] The war came nine years after a restoration of partial democracy in which Peru's autocracy score changed from 9 to 2, and its democracy score changed from 2 to 4.[17] Between 1950 and 1960, when Peru was comparatively democratic, there were nine militarized disputes, and there were none between 1968 and 1976 when it was a military dictatorship.

What explains the correlation between democratic transitions and the outbreak of armed violence in this dyad? The most common explanation offered by Ecuadorans is that new or hard-pressed elected Peruvian leaders trump up military showdowns in order to rally public opinion behind them and score easy prestige victories over the smaller Ecuadoran army.

---

13. Monica Herz and João Nogueira, *Ecuador vs. Peru: Peacemaking Amid Rivalry* (Boulder, Colo.: Lynne Rienner, 2002), p. 47; and Mares, *Violent Peace*, p. 168. The Correlates of War Project does not list this as a war.

14. Mares, *Violent Peace*, p. 185; and Herz and Nogueira, *Ecuador vs. Peru*, p. 76.

15. Herz and Nogueira, *Ecuador vs. Peru*, pp. 25–32.

16. Daniel M. Masterson, *Militarism and Politics in Latin America: Peru from Sánchez Cerro to Sendero Luminoso* (Westport, Conn.: Greenwood, 1991), p. 67.

17. For descriptions of these transitions, see ibid., chaps. 2 and 3.

For example, they claim that Fujimori created a pretext for war in January 1995 in order to improve his prospects in the upcoming April elections. However, since Fujimori was already very popular because of his decisive victory over the Sendero Luminoso, this argument seems insufficient in this case.[18] Nonetheless, the general idea is not farfetched. For example, the victory of Peru's civilian president, Manuel Prado, in the 1941 war helped establish his credentials with both the military and public, paving the way for a relatively successful period of rule.[19]

David Mares offers a similar but perhaps more plausible argument: elected leaders in both countries give their nationalistic but cost-conscious voters exactly the kinds of militarized disputes they want. He shows that public opinion in both countries opposes concessions on territorial issues, but the publics also want to avoid hugely costly wars, and that is exactly what they get when their leaders are accountable to the people.[20] This sounds plausible, but it raises the question of why the voters take such a hard line on seemingly unimportant issues of hinterland boundaries. To understand this, it is necessary to consider the history of the rivalry and its symbolic implications for national pride and civil-military relations.

In both countries, the military retains considerable autonomy and influence even in comparatively democratic periods. In part, this is because the possibility of a coup can rarely be discounted. In the 1941 war, the Peruvian army commander told President Prado that he would start a military revolt against the regime if Prado ordered him to rein in the offensive.[21] Even in democratic Ecuador in the 1980s and 1990s, the military had extraordinary autonomy. It remained more popular than the elected leaders, enjoyed a near monopoly on military information, and by law received an automatic share of the country's oil revenues. Civilians knew about military plans to strengthen outposts in the disputed region in the years before the 1995 war, but whether the government could have altered these plans if it had wanted is unclear.[22] Ecuador's improved military was eager for revenge after its humiliation in 1941, and sought to goad the Peruvians into attacking its strengthened positions.

Some political scientists have argued that militaries tend to exaggerate foreign threats and to favor more assertive policies toward external

---

18. Herz and Nogueira, *Ecuador vs. Peru*, p. 76.

19. Masterson, *Militarism and Politics in Latin America*, pp. 65, 73.

20. Mares, *Violent Peace*, pp. 175–181.

21. Masterson, *Militarism and Politics in Latin America*, p. 71.

22. Mares, *Violent Peace*, pp. 182–183.

enemies when civilians are in power, because this increases the organiza-tion's prestige and claim on resources.[23] When the military rules the state directly, it takes a larger view of priorities, and in any case, needs no external justifications to increase military budgets if it wants to. Inso-far as this is true, one of the reasons that states like Ecuador and Peru become more war-prone in democratizing phases may be that their au-tonomous militaries have increased incentives to act assertively toward neighbors.

All of these causal mechanisms, which are quite consistent with the logic of our theory, have some plausibility as explanations for the pattern of Ecuadoran and Peruvian rivalry, especially when they are considered jointly.

The Ethiopia-Eritrea War

Between May 1998 and December 2000, Ethiopia and Eritrea fought a bloody, World War I–style conflict with set-piece battles between en-trenched, conventional armies, producing over 50,000 casualties. For Eritrea, this was a nearly total war. Ethiopia's country of 60 million peo-ple fielded an army of 450,000; Eritrea's 3.2 million fielded 350,000. One-third of all of Eritrea's able-bodied adults (men and women) participated in the fighting, and almost a third of its national income was devoted to the war effort. Hundreds of thousands of people in both countries be-came refugees from the fighting.[24] The war began with an Eritrean offen-sive to seize disputed territory following a number of violent incidents, some of them instigated by the Ethiopians. After a long lull in the fight-ing, the Ethiopian army mounted offensives deep into Eritrean territory; thereafter the two sides agreed to a United Nations–supervised settlement.

When the war broke out, observers were mystified by its apparent senselessness. "The undeclared war between Eritrea and Ethiopia is a be-wildering study in contradictions," reported the *New York Times*. "It is a

---

23. Stanislav Andreski, "On the Peaceful Disposition of Military Dictatorships," *Journal of Strategic Studies*, Vol. 3, No. 3 (December 1980), pp. 3–10; and Stephen Van Evera, *Causes of War*, vol. 2 (Ithaca, N.Y.: Cornell University Press, forthcoming). See also Kurt Dassel, "Civilians, Soldiers, and Strife: Domestic Sources of Aggression," *International Security*, Vol. 23, No. 1 (Summer 1998), pp. 107–140; and Kurt Dassel and Eric Reinhardt, "Domestic Strife and the Initiation of Violence at Home and Abroad," *American Journal of Political Science*, Vol. 43, No. 1. (January 1999), pp. 56–85.

24. Tekeste Negash and Kjetil Tronvoll, *Brothers at War: Making Sense of the Eritrean-Ethiopian War* (Oxford: James Currey, 2000), pp. 1–2; and Stockholm Interna-tional Peace Research Institute, *SIPRI Yearbook*, 2001. We are grateful to Barbora Somogyiova and Adrienne LeBas for research assistance on this case.

war that both heads of state maintain they do not want, set off by a minor land dispute both sides agree could easily be settled by historians and cartographical experts. Yet neither Prime Minister Meles Zenawi of Ethiopia nor President Isaias Afewerki of Eritrea appears able to stop the bloodshed."[25]

The political movements headed by Meles and Isaias had cooperated in a civil war that overthrew Ethiopia's Marxist Dergue dictatorship in 1991. In that victory, Eritrea gained independence from Ethiopia, and the ethnic Tigrean minority that formed the core of Meles's fighters became the central component of Ethiopia's new government. Both regimes faced dilemmas of democratization in poorly institutionalized, ethnically divided states. Eritrea comprises large Christian and Muslim populations; Ethiopia's population includes Amhara, Tigreans, Oromo, and other ethnic groups.

Ethiopia's new regime embarked on an incomplete democratic transition, holding several elections at the regional and statewide levels during the 1990s. Under a new system of ethnic federalism, considerable autonomy was granted to regions dominated by the Tigreans (6 percent of the overall population of Ethiopia), the historically oppressed Oromo in southern Ethiopia (32 percent or more), and the formerly dominant Amhara (30 percent). At the level of the central state, Meles's Tigrayan People's Liberation Front broadened itself into the multi-ethnic Ethiopian Peoples Revolutionary Democratic Front (EPRDF), which won majorities in the elected national legislature, but kept intact much of the old Amhara-dominated bureaucracy. Some opposition parties boycotted the elections on the grounds that the use of government resources gave unfair advantages to the ruling party. According to Polity, by 1994 Ethiopia had undergone a transition from a complete autocracy under the Marxist Dergue to a mixed regime, with improvements in constraints on the executive and the competitiveness of participation. By 1998, Freedom House had increased Ethiopia's rating on political rights and on civil rights to level 4 ("partly free"), on par with such countries as Armenia, Russia, and Senegal.[26]

---

25.   James C. McKinley, Jr., "Eritrea-Ethiopia War: Unwanted but Unchecked," *New York Times*, June 12, 1998, p. A3.

26.   Adrian Karatnycky, ed., *Freedom in the World, 1998–99* (New York: Freedom House, 1999), pp. 182–184; Terrence Lyons, "Closing the Transition: The May 1995 Elections in Ethiopia," *Journal of Modern African Studies*, Vol. 34, No. 1 (March 1996), pp. 121–142; and John Harbeson, "Elections and Democratization in Post-Mengistu Ethiopia," in Krishna Kumar, ed., *Postconflict Elections, Democratization, and International Assistance* (Boulder, Colo.: Lynne Rienner, 1998), pp. 111–132.

In contrast, Eritrea's ruling organization, the Eritrean People's Liberation Front (EPLF), has held only one vote, a 1993 referendum on independence; it has banned opposition parties, and allows only the government newspaper to circulate. EPLF espouses an ideology of civic nationalism, which holds that the lowland Muslims and highland Christians that fought together in the liberation struggle jointly constitute Eritrea's territorially based nation. A statewide, grass-roots consultative process led to the drafting of a democratic constitution that was supposed to go into effect in 1998, but these plans were derailed by the war.[27] During the 1990s, Freedom House typically ranked Eritrea at level 4 or 5 in civil liberties and at level 6 in political rights ("not free"), descending to rock-bottom level 7 during the war in 1999–2000.[28]

Most scholars have argued that the war was caused by the difficulties that each side's strategy for preserving the unity of its multi-ethnic state posed for the other.[29] These troubled identity politics were complicated by the dynamics of Ethiopia's partial democracy and by the demand for democratization in Eritrea.

On the Eritrean side, the central problem is that the Christians and Muslims refrain from fighting each other only when they are jointly fighting an outsider, and sometimes not even then.[30] Cultural, economic, and administrative developments under Italian colonial rule from 1890 to World War II gave Eritrea an identity distinct from that of the Amhara-ruled Ethiopian kingdom of Haile Selassie, based in part on a multi-ethnic, partly urbanized working class.[31] Although Muslims and Christians worked together to help oust the Italians, after the war the Christian highlanders sought union with Ethiopia, while Muslim lowlanders opposed it; even the urban secularists soon became caught up in ethnic polarization.[32] A temporary British trusteeship ended in 1952, when Eritrea

---

27. Ruth Iyob, "The Eritrean Experiment: A Cautious Pragmatism?" *Journal of Modern African Studies,* Vol. 35, No. 4 (1997), pp. 647–673; and Iyob, "From Defiance to Democracy? Emergent Eritrea," in Jonathan Hyslop, ed., *African Democracy in the Era of Globalization* (Johannesburg: Witwatersrand University Press, 1999), pp. 252–288.

28. *Freedom in the World, 1999–2000,* pp. 182–184.

29. Kjetil Tronvoll, "Borders of Violence—Boundaries of Identity: Demarcating the Eritrean Nation-State," *Ethnic and Racial Studies,* Vol. 22, No. 6 (November 1999), pp. 1037–1060; Ruth Iyob, "The Ethiopian-Eritrean Conflict: Diasporic vs. Hegemonic States in the Horn of Africa, 1991–2000," *Journal of Modern African Studies,* Vol. 38, No. 4 (2000), pp. 659–682.

30. Tronvoll, "Borders of Violence," p. 1055.

31. Ibid., p. 1043.

32. Iyob, "Eritrean Experiment," p. 666.

was joined to Ethiopia in a federal arrangement that the Ethiopian regime soon turned into absolute rule. Two liberation groups subsequently fought for Eritrean independence: the Muslim-dominated Eritrean Liberation Front (ELF) and Isaias's more ethnically balanced EPLF. These groups fought each other as well as the Ethiopian state until 1982, when the ELF was defeated.[33]

The victory over the Dergue eliminated the common enemy that had given Eritrea's Christians and Muslims an incentive to cooperate. Fearing a return to past patterns of polarization, Isaias's EPLF banned opposition groups organized along religious or ethnic lines. An Ethiopian scholar argues that Eritrea's armed conflicts with Sudan in 1994, Yemen in 1995, and Djibouti in 1996 were motivated in part by the EPLF's view that "external wars [were] a necessary ingredient to keep Eritrea together."[34] More subtly, other scholars suggest that the Eritreans' forceful assertion of territorial claims against a variety of ethno-national foes helped to establish the identity of the unitary, civic-territorial state. Establishing territoriality rather than ethnicity as the overriding principle of national identity has been especially important on the border with Ethiopia, since the Christians who comprise over half of Eritrea's population are ethnically the same as the neighboring Tigreans in Ethiopia, with whom the EPLF cooperated in unseating the Dergue.

Eritrea's efforts to stress territoriality directly conflicted with Ethiopia's strategy of ethno-federalism, which created decentralized structures that politicized ethnicity. Some scholars argue that these antithetical principles of legitimacy lay at the root of the Eritrean-Ethiopian conflict.[35] Isaias himself made an argument about Ethiopian legitimacy that directly mirrors the claim that Ethiopians make about his own: "Ethiopia must always live in a state of war," he said, because of its government's strategy of "trying to divide the country into conflicting regions on ethnic and other grounds" in "a situation that is reminiscent of the one that existed in Yugoslavia. . . . Their presence in power depends on creating foreign problems. The border issue is just an excuse and another political reason."[36] Isaias may have believed that Ethiopia would be easy to defeat because of these internal divisions, but even the disadvantaged, disgrun-

33. Tronvoll, "Borders of Violence," p. 1043; and Iyob, "Eritrean Experiment," p. 667.

34. Medhane Tadesse, *The Eritrea-Ethiopian War* (Addis Ababa: Mega, 1999), p. 107.

35. Tronvoll, "Borders of Violence," pp. 1048–1056; and Iyob, "Ethiopian-Eritrean Conflict."

36. Interview with President Isaias Afewerki, *London al-Sharq al-Awsat*, September 17, 2000, translated by FBIS-Africa.

tled Oromo rallied to the Ethiopian cause against what they saw as Eritrean aggression, signing up for military service in substantial numbers.[37]

On the Ethiopian side, Meles's efforts to maintain good relations with his former Eritrean allies were complicated in the mid-1990s by economic conflicts of interest. Tigre sought to shut out Eritrean competitors to its newly developed industries, even while Ethiopia sought to maintain access to Eritrean ports. The formerly open border was closed, heightening the importance of defining boundaries. Tigrean hard-liners pushed Meles's regime to take a firm stand on these issues, leading to a showdown in March 1998 and the expulsion of some of Meles's foes from the EPRDF's Central Committee. Far from consolidating Meles's position, however, opponents began to question his patriotism, charging that he was more loyal to his former Eritrean comrades in arms, with whom he shared family ties, than to the Ethiopian people. Meanwhile, a ruthless government crackdown on student strikes in April killed over a hundred protesters, and Oromo dissatisfaction remained significant. Facing this confluence of challenges, Meles was in no position to make compromises when border disputes intensified in May. Instead, by pursuing a strategy of confrontation, he strengthened his position at least temporarily with a rally-'round-the-flag boost as a result of the war.[38] This reprieve was short-lived: after the peace settlement, the opposition improved its showing in the March 2001 election, and student strife reappeared.[39]

Assuming that this interpretation is correct, how important were incomplete democratization in Ethiopia and the fear of democratization in Eritrea as causes of the conflict? On the one hand, the case manifests a number of our theory's causal mechanisms: weakly institutionalized regimes hard-pressed to maintain diverse coalitions, influential constituencies demanding belligerent policies, governments using nationalist appeals against out-groups either to win support from key elements of the electorate or to forestall democratic accountability. On the other hand, the specter of electoral competition was not necessarily the worst of the prob-

---

37. Lara Santoro, "Why War is Spreading in Horn of Africa," *Christian Science Monitor*, July 22, 1999, p. 6.

38. Jean-Louis Peninou, "Guerre contre le terrorisme: un redéploiement stratégique dans la Corne de L'Afrique," *Le Monde Diplomatique* (December 2001), pp. 20–21; Peninou, "Ethiopie-Erythrée, une paix en trompe l'oeil," *Le Monde Diplomatique* (July 2000); Peninou, "Guerre Absurde entre l'Ethiopie et l'Erythrée," *Review of African Political Economy*, Vol. 25, No. 77 (September 1998), pp. 504–508; *Africa Confidential*, September 11, 1998; Negash and Tronvoll, *Brothers at War*, pp. 30–45; and Kjetil Tronvoll, *Ethiopia: A New Start* (London: Minority Rights Group International, 1999), p. 27.

39. "Meles and the Plotters," *Economist*, March 24, 2001, p. 54.

lems facing Meles or Isaias. Arguably, any weakly institutionalized, pluralistic regime facing the need to forge a coherent national identity and maintain domestic support under such circumstances might have found itself in conflict, electoral pressures or not.[40] In this sense, the gap between a high demand for political participation and weak institutions to accommodate those demands increased the chance of war. Incomplete democratization was a factor that complicated this problem.

The India-Pakistan Kargil War and Its Precursors

In 1999, Pakistani soldiers disguised as civilian volunteers launched an offensive into the remote Indian-held Kargil area of Kashmir, provoking Indian counterattacks that resulted in one thousand battle deaths. It seems most likely that the initiative for the attack came principally from the Pakistani military, though there is some dispute about how early Prime Minister Nawaz Sharif was brought into the planning process.[41] Strategic explanations for the attack stress Pakistan's frustration with the success of the Indian counterinsurgency in Kashmir, and Islamabad's exaggerated confidence in Pakistan's new nuclear deterrent as a lever to extract concessions from India in negotiation.[42] Such miscalculations reflected the fact that Pakistani civilian and military leaders were viewing their strategic options through the kaleidoscopic prism of a domestic political process that had been shaped for decades by endemic nationalist rivalry. In the turbulent democratizing politics of the 1990s, a militant policy in Kashmir backed by a nuclear ace-in-the-hole had become the common denominator of Pakistani politics and a potential trump card for any hard-pressed faction in the country's party and bureaucratic struggles.

Especially in Pakistan, the gap between demands for mass political participation and weak state institutions has repeatedly created incentives for both civilian and military politicians to play the nationalist card to gamble on establishing a base of mass legitimacy. The side effects of this political strategy have been repeated warfare since 1947 and the lock-

---

40. Emphasizing the effects of political instability rather than democratization per se in this case is Brenda M. Seaver, *Political Instability, Dual Transitions, and Militarized Interstate Conflict in the Post–Cold War Era* (Ph.D. Dissertation, University of California, Irvine, 2000).

41. Owen Bennett Jones, *Pakistan: Eye of the Storm* (New Haven: Yale University Press, 2002), pp. 90–104.

42. Sumit Ganguly, *Conflict Unending: India-Pakistan Tensions since 1947* (New York: Columbia University Press, 2001), pp. 121–123.

ing in of rivalry with India. Wars have typically come during moments in Pakistan of fitful democratization. The causal pathways that produced these wars illustrate some of the principal mechanisms in our theory.

After the British Raj ended with the partition of India and Pakistan in 1947, Kashmir became a post-colonial anomaly. Despite its Muslim majority, its Hindu maharaja and Hindu elite effectively rejected accession to Pakistan. Even many Muslims in central Kashmir were attracted by the prospect of land reform in Nehru's India and repelled by the dominance of reactionary landlords in Pakistan. After the Pakistani army came to the aid of Muslim tribal rebels, the maharaja and other Kashmiri leaders called for Indian military support and agreed to join India. When the fighting reached a stalemate, Kashmir was divided *de facto* along the Line of Control between India and Pakistan, with India asserting sovereignty over the majority-Muslim central valley. Thus, the initial fighting reflected the ambiguities of poorly institutionalized national identities and the tension between Pakistan's religious principle of national identity and India's secular principle.[43]

India, after partition, quickly consolidated a functioning democratic system of rule, taking advantage of its strong institutional foundations in the Congress Party, which had engineered the independence movement, and the central administrative and legal structures that were a legacy of the British Raj. Pakistan, however, had neither a firm institutional base nor, despite its Muslim rationale, a clear national identity. Pakistan occupied the geographical and institutional periphery of the Raj rather than its administrative centers. Its founding movement, the Muslim League, was weakly institutionalized compared to the Indian Congress. These institutions proved woefully inadequate to bind together a splintered society consisting of several major ethnolinguistic groups, separated by a thousand miles of Indian territory between the populous Bengali East and the ethnically diverse West, and dominated by tradition-minded landlords and by a military elite disproportionately tied to the West Pakistani region of Punjab. Pakistan's elected, revolving-door parliamentary governments failed to establish any coherent policy in the early 1950s. Hardly anyone expressed regret when General Ayub Khan established military rule in 1958.[44]

In an attempt to establish a source of democratic legitimacy outside of the divisive party system, Ayub created a system of locally elected but

---

43. Ibid., pp. 15–30.

44. Lawrence Ziring, *The Ayub Khan Era: Politics in Pakistan, 1958–1969* (Syracuse: Syracuse University Press, 1971), p. 11; and Ian Talbot, *Pakistan: A Modern History* (New York: St. Martin's, 1998), pp. 126–127.

government-nominated administrative boards that he dubbed Basic Democracies. These local officials were the electorate in indirect elections for a national legislature and the presidency. Samuel Huntington's classic 1968 book, *Political Order in Changing Societies*, praised Ayub as a "Solon" who had devised a promising system for filling the gap between weak state institutions and rising demands for mass political participation.[45] However, Ayub's system of managed democracy was subjected to constant criticism from regional politicians, jurists, and those who sought to bring back the party system. Ayub's opponent in the 1965 presidential election, Fatima Jinna, the widow of Pakistan's founder, attracted large crowds and over a third of the vote.[46]

Hard pressed to maintain a semblance of popular legitimacy, Ayub followed the lead of his ambitious Foreign Minister, Zulfikar Ali Bhutto, in using the Kashmir issue to generate popular enthusiasm for his presidency, a tactic facilitated by India's crackdown on the opposition in Kashmir. During the 1964–65 presidential election campaign, Bhutto promised "retaliatory steps to counter the Indian attempt to merge the occupied parts of Kashmir with India," and "results in the very short future."[47] He asserted that "Kashmir must be liberated if Pakistan is to have its full meaning."[48] The tactic was effective in the elections: while Ayub fared poorly in Bengal and Sindh, he amassed an adequate margin of victory in the Punjab, whose electorate cared intensely about the fate of nearby Kashmir.[49]

Rather than planning for war, Ayub may have thought initially that the tension between India and China following their recent war would give him an opportunity to bargain with New Delhi over the fate of Kashmir. However, Pakistani military intelligence units created the false impression, both in public and in governmental circles, that powerful Kashmiri resistance forces would rise up to join an insurgency to be touched off by infiltrating Pakistani commandos into the India-occupied sector.[50] Under the influence of false information and blowback from his

---

45. Samuel P. Huntington, *Political Order in Changing Societies* (New Haven: Yale University Press, 1968), pp. 250–251.

46. Ziring, *Ayub*, pp. 23–43; and Talbot, *Pakistan*, pp. 160–161.

47. Ziring, *Ayub*, p. 58; see also p. 50.

48. Lawrence Ziring, *Pakistan in the Twentieth Century* (Oxford: Oxford University Press, 1997), p. 277; see also pp. 276, 284, 287.

49. Ibid., p. 283.

50. Ibid., p. 287. Ganguly, *Conflict Unending*, pp. 31–50, stresses Pakistani leaders' excessive optimism about a false "window of opportunity" as the cause of the war, but

own government's domestic political rhetoric, Ayub approved the infiltration operation, which did not spark a Kashmiri uprising but did trigger a massive Indian counterattack into West Pakistan. Historian Ian Talbot concludes, "The normally cautious Ayub, perhaps because he wanted success in Kashmir to bolster his generally failing fortunes, nevertheless gambled on the . . . proposal."[51]

Saddled with an unpopular peace settlement following Pakistan's defeat in the 1965 war (the Tashkent Accord), Ayub found that his opponents were increasingly effective in playing the nationalist card against him. Sheikh Mujibur Rahman's Awami League demanded increased autonomy from a state that exploited the Bengalis in East Pakistan to raise capital for investment in West Pakistan. In the west, Bhutto resigned from the government to organize an opposition party that played on urban discontent and the Kashmir issue. Ironically, the relative success of Ayub's policies in increasing crop yields and urban industrial growth helped spur these popular movements: whereas Ayub's paternalist indirect democracy might have worked in a static society, the rising demand for political participation in a highly unequal and rapidly changing society swept him and his system away.[52] Facing this inexorable popular pressure, the military junta that succeeded Ayub allowed fully competitive multiparty elections in 1971.

This electoral competition led directly to another Indo-Pakistani war and to the breakup of Pakistan. The winner in the more populous east, and the prospective holder of an absolute majority in Pakistan's National Assembly, was Mujib's autonomy-seeking Awami League. The victorious party in the west was Bhutto's Pakistan People's Party, energized by a rising constituency of urban professionals who had been excluded from power under Ayub. Weak in party organization, the PPP had to rely on Bhutto's passionate oratory, which condemned Ayub's betrayal of Kashmir in the Tashkent peace accord and promised "a thousand years war with India."[53]

"Both Mujib and Bhutto were explosive orators" who "mustered passionate followings," says Lawrence Ziring. "Each rode a wave of history

---

does not examine in detail the domestic political origins of the urge to act or the bureaucratic and political origins of falsely optimistic estimates.

51. Talbot, *Pakistan*, p. 177.

52. Ibid., pp. 153–154.

53. Ibid., p. 198; and Saeed Shafqat, *Civil-Military Relations in Pakistan: From Zulfikar Ali Bhutto to Benazir Bhutto* (Boulder, Colo.: Westview Press, 1997), p. 58.

he could not control."[54] Nationalist rhetorical excesses and the weakness of the PPP's party discipline left little room for compromise over the Awami League's autonomy demands. Bhutto was hemmed in by the military's resistance to autonomy and by the ethnic splits within the PPP. He believed that playing the Kashmir card would help him to unify West Pakistanis around the PPP. Bhutto rejected Mujib's proposals on the grounds that Bengali autonomy would weaken Pakistan in its confrontation with India over Kashmir. Bhutto seized an opportunity to praise two young Kashmiris who hijacked an Indian airliner and forced it to land in West Pakistan. Mujib played into Bhutto's hands by condemning the action.[55] Moreover, as a Shi'a Muslim from the province of Sindh, in a state dominated by an officer corps that was mostly Punjabi and Sunni, Bhutto could establish his credibility by outbidding the nationalist military on the issue of national unity.[56] On the heels of this breakdown of democratic politics, the Pakistani military's bloody repression of the Bengali autonomy movement caused millions of refugees to flee into India, which invaded East Pakistan and supported the creation of the independent state of Bangladesh.

The 1971 war demonstrates three distinct causal mechanisms linking the early phase of democratization when institutions are weak to nationalist politics and war. The first mechanism is the tendency of elections in poorly institutionalized multinational states to polarize society along ethnic lines, creating the risk that internal violence will spill over into external war. The second mechanism is the tendency of weak democratizing regimes to appease hard-line veto groups, in this case the military and the Punjabis, by pursuing an uncompromising nationalist policy. The third mechanism, echoing Ayub's 1965 Kashmir strategy, is the attempt of the hard-pressed leader to rally support from a divided constituency by means of a nationalist confrontation with an external foe.

This legacy of nationalist rivalry and war became ingrained in the domestic political life of the fitfully democratizing Pakistani state. Its themes were routinely available to be deployed in political maneuvering, whether by civilians who needed to show their militancy or by military figures who needed to show their national populism. Although India's increased military superiority after 1971 dampened the risk of war, inter-

---

54. Ziring, *Pakistan*, p. 335.

55. Richard Sisson and Leo Rose, *War and Secession: Pakistan, India, and the Creation of Bangladesh* (Berkeley: University of California Press, 1990), pp. 75–76.

56. Talbot, *Pakistan*, pp. 198–204.

national rivalry remained a potent tool in Pakistani internal politics, even after Bhutto was deposed by General Zia ul-Haq. Whereas Bhutto's nationalist appeal had been largely secular, Zia sought popular legitimacy for military rule through the rhetoric of Islamic fundamentalism and alliance with militant Islamic groups dedicated to the liberation of Kashmir and Afghanistan. In this setting, militant Islamic ideology gained a foothold among the younger cohorts of the military, especially its Inter-Services Intelligence branch (ISI), which coordinated strategy with Islamic organizations.[57] Rather than showing loyalty to Zia and his circle, these militant pressure groups grumbled that the army's failure to dislodge Indian forces from Kashmir's contested Siachen Glacier proved that Pakistan's top brass were unprofessional and corrupt.[58] Despite fostering Islamic groups and sensibilities, India and Pakistan came close to war only once under the autocratic Zia—during India's Brasstacks maneuvers in 1986, which were a calculated attempt on the part of the Indian military commanders to intimidate Pakistan and deter it from aiding Sikh separatists.[59]

Following Zia's death in a 1988 air crash, the PPP, now headed by Bhutto's daughter, gained a plurality of seats in competitive multiparty elections and governed in coalition with the party of former refugees from the 1947 partition. During Benazir Bhutto's first term as prime minister in 1990, armed clashes broke out between Pakistani-supported insurgents and Indian forces in Kashmir; the Pakistani army mobilized some units near the border, and the two states seemed momentarily at the brink of war. What role did Pakistan's return to democratization play in this confrontation?

Initially, Bhutto seemed ready to moderate Indo-Pakistani relations. Preliminary talks with Indian Prime Minister Rajiv Gandhi seemed mildly promising. The United States believed that Bhutto might help rein in the Pakistani nuclear program, and the Pakistani military feared this might be true.[60] Despite this, Bhutto initially maintained good relations with the army commander, General Mirza Beg, since both shared a common interest in containing the growing influence of the ISI, which had been strengthened by its successful campaigns in Afghanistan. Disgrun-

57.   Shafqat, *Civil-Military Relations,* p. 207; Sumit Ganguly, *The Crisis in Kashmir* (Cambridge: Cambridge University Press, 1997), p. 77; Jessica Stern, "Pakistan's Jihad Culture," *Foreign Affairs,* Vol. 79, No. 6 (November/December 2000), pp. 115–126.

58.   Rizvi, *Military, State and Society,* p. 204.

59.   For background on these arguments, see Ganguly, *Conflict Unending,* pp. 85–88.

60.   Ziring, *Pakistan,* p. 527.

tled as a result of Afghanistan-related personnel decisions, the ISI bought off some PPP legislators and nearly unseated Bhutto in an October 1989 confidence vote. Adding to her difficulties, Bhutto then quarreled with Beg over the use of the army to suppress riots in her home province of Sindh. Meanwhile, the PPP's chief electoral rival, Nawaz Sharif's coalition of Islamic parties, held a lock on the government of Punjab, Pakistan's most important province. Politically and bureaucratically weakened, Bhutto had no possibility of checking the ISI-supported infiltration into Indian Kashmir, and even her most minimal peace gestures made the army distrustful. Tacking with the political wind, Bhutto revived her father's call for a thousand-year war to liberate Kashmir.[61] Under these circumstances, democracy meant little more than institutional anarchy in which various parties, bureaucracies, and informal groups of drug-runners and insurgents vied for the mantle of Islam and nationalism in confrontations with Pakistan's perceived rivals.

Proclaiming that Bhutto had lost the capacity to govern, Pakistan's president dissolved the National Assembly in 1990. Nawaz Sharif, bankrolled in part by the ISI with the army commander's approval, prevailed in new elections.[62] Although Sharif hewed to the military line on Kashmir and the nuclear program, his power was soon broken, too, in an ill-advised test of constitutional authority with the military-backed president. Benazir Bhutto was elected to head another coalition government in October 1993. In this second term, Bhutto learned to adhere closely to the militant position on the issues of Kashmir and nuclear weapons, which she linked in her rhetoric.[63] Despite Pakistan's efforts to stay in Washington's good graces by contributing troops to international peacekeeping efforts, the Clinton administration placed Pakistan on a "watch list" of potential terrorist states.[64] Looking back on this period, Bhutto later said that her main regret was that she made "relations with India hostage to the Kashmir issue" and used hawkish posturing to curry favor with the military.[65]

When corruption scandals and family squabbles drove Bhutto from

---

61.   Ganguly, *Conflict Unending*, pp. 92–93.

62.   Rizvi, *Military, State and Society*, p. 193.

63.   On the connection between Pakistani nuclear weapons and Kashmir, see Mario Carranza, "Rethinking India-Pakistan Nuclear Relations," *Asian Survey*, Vol. 36, No. 6 (June 1996), pp. 561–573.

64.   Ziring, *Pakistan*, pp. 552–554.

65.   Benazir Bhutto, "Pakistan's Regression to an Authoritarian Past," remarks to the Director's Forum, the Woodrow Wilson International Center for Scholars, Washington, D.C., May 25, 1999.

power a second time, Nawaz Sharif once again became prime minister. Gaining an absolute majority in the 1997 election, Sharif pushed through a constitutional amendment revoking the president's authority to dissolve the National Assembly. This change led the Polity database to code Pakistan as making a transition to full democracy. And yet, as Hasan-Askari Rizvi argues, "Pakistan faced a paradox. Sharif had accumulated more power than any previous prime minister since Pakistan began its transition to democracy in 1985. However, the government's ability to evoke voluntary support at the popular level was on the decline and it presided over a weak and fragmented polity."[66] Sharif's regime remained dogged by economic crisis, corruption, ethnic rioting, and international economic sanctions following Pakistan's 1998 nuclear test, which had been a direct response to India's nuclear explosion. In this context of endemic crisis and waning popularity, Sharif's move to replace the country's secular legal code with *shari'a* in 1998 was an attempt to shore up his popular support among the religious parties, the Kashmir liberation groups, and militant Islamic army factions, including those in the ISI.

Amid these turbulent democratizing politics in the 1990s, the use of force in Kashmir, underwritten by Pakistan's newly demonstrated nuclear capability, had become the common denominator of Pakistani politics and a tempting source of legitimacy for the country's political and bureaucratic factions. Leaders of the Pakistani military were frustrated by the success of Indian repression of the Kashmiri insurgency and unjustifiably confident that Pakistan's new nuclear deterrent would spur an international effort to negotiate a favorable settlement to avert escalation.[67] Consulting, at least loosely, with Nawaz Sharif, the military, disguised as volunteers, attacked the remote Kargil area of Kashmir in 1999.[68] Following the failure of the offensive, Sharif was ousted in a showdown with General Pervez Musharraf, the army chief who had overseen the Kargil operation.

Some of the same political dynamics have prevailed during Musharraf's period of military rule as they had under the elected governments of the 1990s. Despite U.S. pressure on Pakistan to curtail Islamic terrorists after the 2001 terrorist attacks in the United States and the subsequent war on the Afghan Taliban regime, Musharraf found it difficult to rein in the violent groups who were infiltrating Indian Kashmir. Even when India mobilized a million soldiers on the Pakistani frontier in 2002

---

66. Rizvi, *Military, State, and Society*, p. 231.

67. Ganguly, *Conflict Unending*, pp. 121–123.

68. Jones, *Pakistan: Eye of the Storm*, pp. 90–104.

in response to a Pakistani terrorist attack on India's parliament, Musharraf was slow to crack down on the responsible groups. In part, his reluctance reflected the entrenched position of the militant groups and their bureaucratic patrons in the ISI. In part, it also reflected the need to maintain a popular nationalist stance in anticipation of an eventual return to competitive democratic politics. Although extremist Islamic parties rarely garner more than 5 percent of the Pakistani vote, in a survey taken on October 11–12, 2001, 83 percent of Pakistanis told the Gallup poll that they supported the Taliban, and over half blamed Israel rather than Osama bin Laden for the terrorist attacks on the United States.[69] Surviving several assassination attempts that may have been mounted by militant groups, Musharraf tried to make Pakistan's international stance less provocative, meeting in January 2004 with Indian Prime Minister Atal Behari Vajpayee and investigating the transfer of nuclear weapons know-how to Iran. Nonetheless, the perverse, ingrained dynamics of incomplete democratization continued to complicate foreign-policy decision-making even when Pakistan was in the military-rule phase of its cycle of instability.

In short, the Pakistan case echoes a number of the causal mechanisms highlighted in our theory: the nationalistic appeal for support against foreign rivals to enhance domestic legitimacy, the need of weak regimes to appease militant veto groups, and the polarizing effect of elections in transitional societies where the boundaries of states and cultures are not congruent. This military struggle between two nuclear-armed, elected regimes is a particularly dramatic example of a broader danger that darkens the path toward enlargement of the democratic peace.

The Kosovo War

In 1999 the United States and NATO fought an intense bombing campaign throughout Serbia in response to Serbia's expulsion of several hundred thousand Albanians from the Serbian province of Kosovo and Serbian atrocities against the Kosovar population. Serbia had held various partially free, competitive elections during the 1990s, generally producing victories for nationalist candidates. Since the Serbian leader Slobodan Milosevic had initially risen to power through elections as the ostensible protector of Serbs against their Albanian ethnic foes, the tactical successes of armed Albanian separatists in 1998 had struck at the heart of Milosevic's popular legitimacy. In April 1998, Milosevic held a referendum on Kosovo in which 95 percent of Serb voters rejected "the participation of

---

69. Douglas Frantz, "Pakistani Police Kill 2 Protesters Near Airport Used by U.S. Planes," *New York Times*, October 15, 2001, p. B6.

foreign representatives in solving the Kosovo issue."[70] Since Milosevic and his ruling party would presumably need to face partially free competitive elections at some future date, his decision to expel the Kosovar Albanians might be seen as a form of gambling for resurrection in an incomplete democracy. As it turned out, Serbia lost the war and withdrew from Kosovo, and Milosevic fell from power after losing an election the following year.

Although this interpretation is plausible, it requires some speculation about the place of elections in Milosevic's calculations in the Kosovo War. However, establishing the central importance of democratization in the broader context of the origins of the wars of the Yugoslav breakup requires no speculation: the connection is clear.

Between the break-up of Yugoslavia in 1991 and the signing of the 1995 Dayton Accords providing for NATO troops in Bosnia, armed conflict and atrocities claimed some 200,000 lives in the former Yugoslavia and displaced over 2,500,000 people.[71] This outcome occurred in circumstances that, according to commonly accepted liberal theory, should have been quite promising: the power of the central Yugoslav state and the Yugoslav communist party was evaporating by the 1980s, giving rise to a more pluralistic political environment in most of the federal republics. Political and economic decentralization, which are widely advocated liberal prescriptions for authoritarian multi-ethnic societies, had been accelerating since the 1960s. Bureaucratic representation for all ethnic groups, rights for ethnic minorities to veto legislation, and resource transfers from richer to poorer ethnic groups and regions were standard practices.[72] As power was devolving to the various republics, politics was also becoming more competitive within the republics. By 1990, eighty-six political parties had formed, six of them in Serbia.[73] Ruling groups in all of the republics were facing open electoral competition from parties that ranged from ultranationalist to liberal. According to Freedom House, civil liberties and freedom of speech, though still far from perfect, had improved somewhat on the eve of the break-up.[74] During the 1980s, al-

70. Robert Thomas, *The Politics of Serbia in the 1990s* (New York: Columbia University Press, 1999), pp. 418–419.

71. Michael E. Brown, *The International Dimensions of Internal Conflict* (Cambridge, Mass.: MIT Press, 1996), pp. 4–6.

72. Sabrina Ramet, *Nationalism and Federalism in Yugoslavia, 1962–1991*, 2d ed. (Bloomington: Indiana University Press, 1992), p. 36.

73. Ramet, *Nationalism and Federalism*, p. 234.

74. Raymond Gastil, ed., *Freedom in the World, 1988–1989* (New York: Freedom

though journalists and intellectuals might still suffer for deviating from the views of the powerful, some of them were able to seize opportunities to take those risks. Socially, the enforced ethnic tolerance of the communist years had created an integrated, secular, urban culture in which the rate of inter-ethnic marriages reached as high as one-third among some groups. In short, according to standard liberal prescriptions, Yugoslavia should have been well positioned for peaceful democratization.

In fact, however, this combination of incipient democratization and political decentralization contributed to the rise of aggressive nationalism and led to the derailment of liberal reform. Impending democratization threatened the position of the communist elite, giving them an incentive to reposition themselves at the head of popular nationalist movements.

Though hard pressed by the dilemmas of economic reform and the need to attract support in a more open political system, communist elites were able to exploit the increasing powers of the ethnic republics in devising a strategy for political survival.[75] Milosevic was especially astute in exploiting this maneuvering room. In the early 1980s, he had served loyally under pragmatic, moderate Serbian party leaders such as Ivan Stambolic, the head of the Serb government in 1980–82 and president of Serbia in 1986. In the new circumstances, however, Milosevic saw that the nationalism issue could be exploited to reconcile popular politics with continued authoritarian leadership, while also presenting a chance to push aside less nimble leaders such as Stambolic.[76]

A 1986 "Memorandum on the Position of Serbia in Yugoslavia," signed by a large number of prestigious members of the Serbian Academy of Sciences, provided a formula for a nationalist pseudo-democracy that would play into Milosevic's hands. Decrying the constraints placed on Serbia by the constitutional rights accorded to non-Serbs in the Serbian provinces of Kosovo and Voivodina, the memorandum called for a

---

House, 1989), pp. 411–412; and R. Bruce McColm, ed., *Freedom in the World, 1989–90* (New York: Freedom House, 1990), pp. 272–274.

75. Susan Woodward, *Balkan Tragedy* (Washington, D.C.: Brookings, 1995), p. 15. Sabrina Ramet likewise places the rise of ethno-nationalist conflict in the context of collapsing authoritarian institutions and the rise of mass politics: "As the 1980s wore on, it became clear that the fragmentation of power engineered by Tito's quasi-confederal but one-party framework was producing institutional weakness and political chaos. Chaos, of course, creates maneuvering room and uncertainty—which give the sense of freedom. And this inevitably opened the door to greater political participation by large numbers of citizens, as one could predict on the basis of Samuel P. Huntington's classic work on political order." Ramet, *Nationalism and Federalism*, p. 214.

76. Branka Magas, *The Destruction of Yugoslavia* (London: Verso, 1993), pp. 194–197.

new constitution to provide for the sovereignty and self-determination of "the Serbian people," defined in terms of the ethnic nation, not in terms of democratic participation by individuals.[77] Elite groups, including communist-era parliamentarians and intellectuals, jumped on the nationalist bandwagon, and Milosevic replaced Stambolic in April 1987.[78]

Milosevic's trumpeting of wrongs done to Serbs in Kosovo proved especially popular with people who had previously taken no part in the political process, especially older, rural, less educated Serbs. These constituencies, who voted heavily for Milosevic's party in the 1990 Serbian elections, perceived little potential gain from market-oriented, westernizing, liberalizing reforms.[79] Even so, Milosevic was not the most extreme nationalist competing in the elections. Other parties campaigned on platforms of entirely abolishing the autonomy of the Hungarian-populated Voivodina and Albanian-populated Kosovo regions.[80] In Croatia, likewise, the campaign leading up to the April 1990 election featured an explosion of nationalist rhetoric. Surveys recorded a large increase in ethnic tension between Serbs and Croats during those months.[81] The nationalist strategy served not only to mobilize a base of popular support for threatened elites of the erstwhile one-party state, but also to demobilize support for their liberal foes. Whereas opponents of the communist regimes of Czechoslovakia and Hungary rallied effectively in the streets and in political committees, in Serbia the atmosphere of ethnic resentment made it easier to silence opponents of the regime as traitors to the Serb people.[82]

Less than six months after the first democratic elections, Yugoslavia was at war.[83] Slovenia and Croatia, failing to win Serbian agreement to their demands for greater autonomy, declared independence. The Serb-

---

77. Mihailo Crnobrnja, *The Yugoslav Drama* (Montreal: McGill–Queen's University Press, 1994), p. 98.

78. Woodward, *Balkan Tragedy*, pp. 92–93; and Magas, *Destruction of Yugoslavia*, p. 198.

79. Lenard J. Cohen, *Broken Bonds: The Disintegration of Yugoslavia* (Boulder, Colo.: Westview Press, 1993) p. 157; and Woodward, *Balkan Tragedy*, p. 93.

80. Ramet, *Nationalism and Federalism*, p. 235.

81. Lenard Cohen, "Embattled Democracy," in Karen Dawisha and Bruce Parrott, eds., *Politics, Power, and the Struggle for Democracy in South-East Europe* (Cambridge: Cambridge University Press, 1997), p. 80.

82. V. P. Gagnon, *The Myth of Ethnic War: Serbia and Croatia in the 1990s* (Ithaca, N.Y.: Cornell University Press, 2004).

83. Woodward, *Balkan Tragedy*, p. 17; see also Bogdan Denitch, *Ethnic Nationalism: The Tragic Death of Yugoslavia* (Minneapolis: University of Minnesota Press, 1994), pp. 42–48.

dominated Yugoslav army used force in an unsuccessful attempt to prevent this. In response, Serbs in Croatia's border regions planned a referendum on autonomy from Croatia, so the new Croatian state moved to supplant local police forces in Serb villages.[84] These Serbs, provided with military materiel by Milosevic and the Yugoslav army, battled to create their own state along Croatia's southern perimeter.

In short, many of the causal mechanisms we describe were on display during the outbreak of war in 1991. The nationalist politics forged in this episode of incomplete democratization structured the ideas, institutions, and coalitions that led to the Kosovo War in 1999. Even after Milosevic's fall from power, these tendencies in Serbia's transitional democracy were far from extinguished. In parliamentary elections in December 2003, the nationalist parties of two indicted war criminals, Milosevic and Vojislav Seselj, defeated Serbia's relatively liberal democratic ruling coalition by campaigning against meddling by The Hague war crimes tribunal in Serbian affairs. Once democratization starts off on the wrong foot, it can become extraordinarily difficult to turn it onto a more successful path.

The Central African War

Another candidate for inclusion in the list of recent international wars is what some Correlates of War Project researchers call the Central African War, involving Rwandan, Ugandan, Angolan, Zimbabwean, and other forces fighting in Congo after 1998. Human rights organizations estimate that millions of people have died from the direct or indirect effects of this conflict. The struggle arose out of the collapse of the Mobutu dictatorship in Zaire (now Congo), which was precipitated by fighting among Hutu militias fleeing from Rwanda after perpetrating the 1994 genocide, victorious Rwandan Tutsi forces, and Tutsi who had long been resident in Zaire, as well as other local forces. The renewed international fighting after 1998 had nothing to do with democracy. Nonetheless, the initial fighting between Hutu and Tutsi in 1993 in Burundi and in 1994 in Rwanda was sparked in part by international pressures to democratize, adopt constitutional power sharing, and increase freedom of speech.

DEMOCRATIZATION AND ETHNIC VIOLENCE IN BURUNDI
The free and fair election of Burundi's first Hutu president in June 1993 set the stage for the killing of many tens of thousands of Hutu and Tutsi.

---

84. Cohen, "Embattled Democracy," p. 82.

Pressure from international aid donors was one of the main reasons that the Tutsi-dominated ethnic minority government of Pierre Buyoya agreed to hold these risky elections. An October 1988 mission of World Bank officials to Burundi stressed the need for "transparency in the judicial process" and a reversal of prosecutions of open critics of the government. At the same time, the U.S. House of Representatives passed a resolution urging a comprehensive reassessment of aid policies in light of human rights abuses by the Burundian military.[85] The Buyoya government responded by developing plans for more extensive power sharing with the Hutu majority and for elections. By 1992, says Réné Lemarchand, the premier student of Burundian politics, "there was more freedom of expression and association than at any time since 1972."[86]

In early 1993, on the eve of the elections, non-governmental organizations descended on the Burundian capital of Bujumbura to facilitate the transition to democracy. The U.S.-based National Democratic Institute arrived to train election monitors. A Swedish think tank mounted a symposium on human rights and development. The African-American Institute, at the behest of Buyoya himself, held a conference on the role of the military in a democracy.[87] The financially dependent regime thus gave the international community what it sought.

Buyoya seems to have been surprised when the 85 percent–Hutu electorate turned his largely Tutsi regime out of office in favor of a moderate Hutu, Melchior Ndadaye. The Tutsi-dominated military, fearing that the elected government's power-sharing scheme would neutralize the army's ability to guarantee the security of the Tutsi minority, launched a coup to protect its monopoly of force, touching off a series of bloody reprisals and leaving the country on the brink of all-out civil war. This was hardly unforeseeable: indeed, even the pro-liberalization Lemarchand had warned on the eve of these events that "how the officer corps, an all-Tutsi preserve, may react to a large influx of Hutu recruits is anybody's guess."[88]

Despite the debacle caused by international efforts to promote pluralism and power-sharing in Burundi in 1993, the international community failed to recognize that such policies were dangerous. Continuing to pur-

---

85. Réné Lemarchand, *Burundi: Ethnocide as Discourse and Practice* (Cambridge: Cambridge University Press, 1994), p. 129.

86. Ibid., p. 176.

87. Ibid., p. 185.

88. Ibid., p. 187.

sue a similar strategy in Rwanda, they catalyzed an even bigger human rights disaster the following year.

POWER-SHARING AND PLURALISM AS PRECURSORS TO THE RWANDAN GENOCIDE

In Rwanda, as in Burundi, the pressures to democratize applied by the international donors that were the source of 60 percent of the Rwandan government's revenue played a central role in triggering ethnic slaughter. The authoritarian Hutu regime of Rwandan President Juvénal Habyarimana was hard pressed on every front in the late 1980s and early 1990s. Rwanda's economy was suffering from falling prices for coffee, the country's main export. Attacks by Tutsi rebels from bases in neighboring Uganda caused further economic disruptions. Even among Hutu, domestic opponents of the regime were calling for an increase in political pluralism. International aid donors exerted their influence on behalf of these demands.

Yielding to these pressures, Habyarimana abandoned the government's press monopoly in July 1990, leading to "an explosion in the number of newspapers and journals" published by anti-government groups.[89] "A vibrant press had been born almost overnight," says Gérard Prunier. However, the newly free press included not only voices of moderation, but also many Hutu extremist organs mounting a vituperative campaign against the Tutsi minority.[90] Moreover, Hutu extremists attached to the regime continued to monopolize the radio, a key asset among a population that was 60 percent illiterate.

Despite these limited concessions to political pluralism, pressure on the Habyarimana regime increased in the early 1990s. The Tutsi military threat intensified. Hutu opposition political parties called for democratic elections. International backers urged Habyarimana to accept a power-sharing accord with his Hutu opponents and with the armed Tutsi rebels. After a Tutsi rebel attack on the capital in 1993 was parried only with the help of French troops, Habyarimana had no alternative but to accept the internationally sponsored Arusha Accords, which provided for Tutsi participation in government and a Tutsi military unit to provide security for Tutsi politicians in the capital city of Kigali. If implemented, these accords

---

89. Africa Rights (Rakiya Omaar and Alex de Waal), *Rwanda: Death, Despair and Defiance* (London: Africa Rights, September 1994), p. 150.

90. Gérard Prunier, *The Rwanda Crisis: History of a Genocide* (New York: Columbia University Press, 1995), chap. 4, "Slouching towards Democracy," esp. pp. 131–133 and 157, on the low quality and extremism of these new entrants into public discourse.

would have excluded from the new joint Hutu-Tutsi government those Hutu extremist members of the Habyarimana regime who were mounting the hate campaign against the Tutsi.

As pressure for the implementation of the Arusha Accords increased in early 1994, the Hutu extremist faction seemed cornered. As part of the settlement, an international commission named certain highly-placed Hutu extremists who had been complicit in small-scale killings of Tutsi. "Individuals named were promised an amnesty," says Alex de Waal of Africa Rights, "but knew that their actions were under scrutiny," and so distrusted these guarantees. Human rights groups were active in this period of internationally-sponsored power-sharing and pluralization. "Rwanda had one of the most vigorous human-rights movements in Africa," says de Waal. "Six independent human rights organizations cooperated in exposing abuses by government and rebel forces." [91] Meanwhile, moderate Hutu from southern Rwanda, where "Hutu" and "Tutsi" people were racially almost indistinguishable from one another, began to mobilize politically against Hutu extremists in the government clique and their northern Rwanda social base.[92]

In this setting, the extremist clique around Habyarimana had every reason to fear democratization. However, the extremists still had powerful cards to play to avert the implementation of the Arusha Accords. To forestall a fall from power and judicial accountability, these officials developed the plan for a mass genocide. "The extremists' aim," says Africa Rights, "was for the entire Hutu populace to participate in the killing. That way, the blood of genocide would stain everybody. There could be no going back for the Hutu population."[93] To prepare the ideological terrain for the genocide, the extremists intensified their inflammatory media campaign, playing on Hutu fears of the former Tutsi elite.

But there was a flaw in this plan. Habyarimana, heavily dependent on foreign aid to prop up his system of official patronage, balked at implementing a bloodbath that he knew would cut him off from foreign

---

91. Alex de Waal, "The Genocidal State," *Times Literary Supplement*, July 1, 1994, pp. 3–4; see also Africa Rights, *Rwanda*, pp. 30–32.

92. Africa Rights, *Rwanda*, pp. 30–34, 44; Bruce D. Jones, "The Arusha Process," in Howard Adelman and Astri Suhrke, eds., *The Path of a Genocide: The Rwanda Crisis from Uganda to Zaire* (New Brunswick, N.J. : Transaction, 1999); and Alan J. Kuperman, "The Other Lesson of Rwanda: Mediators Sometimes Do More Damage Than Good," *SAIS Review*, Vol. 16, No. 1 (Winter–Spring 1996), pp. 221–240.

93. Africa Rights, *Rwanda*, p. v; see also pp. 568–596; Prunier, *The Rwanda Crisis*, p. 170; and Jones, "Arusha."

funds. The president's extremist allies in the military and security services had no such qualms. From January to March 1994, their unofficial journal *Kangura,* an example of the flowering of Rwandan media in the period of pluralism and incipient power-sharing, warned Habyarimana not to flinch from the destruction of the Tutsi.[94] Tutsi rebels shot down Habyarimana's plane in April 1994, upon returning from a meeting at Dar es Salaam where he had made renewed concessions to international donors, the United Nations, and the Organization of African Unity.[95] Both the Tutsi rebels and the Hutu extremists had good reasons to want to cut short any possible move toward moderation or democratization.

In short, although we do not claim that the Central African War is itself a war of incomplete democratization, this conflict was nonetheless set in motion by the misguided Burundian elections of 1993 and the rise of perverse pluralism in Rwanda in 1994, both under the aegis of international pro-democracy influences. The causal mechanism of ethnonationalist gambling for resurrection under conditions of incomplete democratization played a central role in intensifying these conflicts.

Russia's Wars in Chechnya

Russia's military and economic weakness since the collapse of the Soviet Union has made military adventures outside the boundaries of the former Soviet Union infeasible and unattractive. Nonetheless, Russia has used military force to intervene in the civil war between newly independent Georgia and Georgia's separatist Abkhazia region. Russia has also fought two wars in its own separatist region of Chechnya. Although the wars in Chechnya do not count as international wars, the second of these followed the granting of de facto independence, if not de jure sovereignty. Russia's turbulent, incomplete democratization after the collapse of the Soviet Union in 1991 provided a political impetus for the decisions for war in Chechnya.

Russian President Boris Yeltsin embarked on the First Chechen War (1994–96) at a time when the party of the nationalist anti-Semite Vladimir

---

94. Africa Rights, *Rwanda,* pp. 66–68.

95. De Waal, "The Genocidal State," p. 4; see also Jones, "Arusha." Some have speculated that militant Hutu were responsible for Habyarimana's death, but more recent evidence points to the Uganda-based Tutsi Rwandan Patriotic Front. See Prunier, *Rwanda Crisis,* pp. 213–229; and Stephen Smith, "L'enquête sur l'attentat qui fit basculer le Rwanda dans le genocide," *Le Monde,* March 9, 2004.

Zhirinovsky had just won a quarter of the seats in a Duma election, and polls showed that 70 percent of Russians were dissatisfied with Yeltsin's performance. Unable to assert his authority over a hostile parliament, recalcitrant regions, stubborn bureaucracies, and disaffected public opinion, Yeltsin saw a military crackdown on Chechen pretensions to sovereign independence as a potentially popular way to act decisively in the face of a deadlock of incomplete democratization. Russia specialist Michael McFaul went so far as to claim that "Yeltsin did not order his troops into Chechnya to save the Russian Federation. He moved against Chechnya to save his presidency."[96]

While this interpretation might be controversial for the First Chechen War, there is less doubt that Prime Minister Vladimir Putin mounted a second offensive against the still turbulent Chechen rebels in 1999 to try to gain sufficient popularity to succeed Yeltsin as president. The strategy worked as planned, because Russian casualties were kept lower than in the first war, and because the elections were held before it became clear that the invasion had not fully suppressed Chechen resistance.[97]

Although the Chechen conflicts were not international wars, they manifested a number of the causal mechanisms we have outlined: gambling for resurrection, nationalist bidding wars, and the resort to nationalist prestige strategies in order to govern amid the political stalemate of a weakly institutionalized semi-democracy. As McFaul has pointed out, however, the damage caused by democratization in a turbulent great power could have been much greater. One reason that predictions of a "Weimar Russia" have not been borne out, he says, is that the state elites and economic oligarchs who have been in control of Russia's bureaucracy, economy, and media have a stake in maintaining stable economic relations with the West.[98] Moreover, they have no incentive to risk their hold on the levers of power by encouraging mass nationalist mobilization. Although institutions were weak, the demand for mass participation was relatively low, and therefore the gap between them was not unmanageable. In short, our theory sheds light both on Russia's use of military force during its early phase of democratization and on the limits placed on those military adventures.

---

96.   Michael McFaul, "Eurasia Letter: Politics after Chechnya," *Foreign Policy,* No. 99 (Summer 1995), p. 110; and Snyder, *From Voting to Violence,* p. 236.

97.   On the initial popularity of the war, see Daniel Treisman, "Russia Renewed," *Foreign Affairs,* Vol. 81, No. 6 (November/December 2002), p. 70.

98.   Michael McFaul, "A Precarious Peace: Domestic Politics in the Making of Russian Foreign Policy," *International Security,* Vol. 22, No. 3 (Winter 1997–98), pp. 5–35.

Causal Mechanisms and Trajectories: Recent Cases

The cases reviewed in this chapter, like those reviewed in Chapter 7, manifest many of the causal mechanisms of our theory. They also reinforce the view that perverse patterns of internal politics and external rivalry tend to get locked in when the early phase of the transition goes awry. Nationalist patterns at any early stage of democratization are likely to exert a troublesome influence in subsequent reversals to autocracy, where aggressive nationalism acts as a populist cover for the return to autocracy, and in subsequent attempts to re-democratize, where aggressive nationalism remains highly available as a tool to retard or steer these developments.

CAUSAL MECHANISMS OF RECENT WARS OF DEMOCRATIZATION
At the most general level, there is little doubt that rising levels of political participation intersected with weak political institutions in ways that sharpened violent conflicts in the cases of democratization and war in the 1990s. In a few of these cases, however, it might be argued that the quasi-anarchy of weak institutions, rather than democratic electoral mobilization per se, was the main culprit. For example, Rwanda, which had a rising political pluralism but no elections, got into even worse trouble than Burundi, which had both. Similarly, Eritrea, which had no elections, was just as important an instigator of war as Ethiopia, which did. Moreover, although Armenia, Azerbaijan, Ecuador, Pakistan, Peru, and Yugoslavia had some free and fair elections in which nationalist candidates did well, it could be argued that the weakness of political institutions in these countries might have led to external frictions even in the absence of mass voting. Consequently, it is worthwhile to assess whether the more specific causal mechanisms of our theory were at work in these cases.

Nationalistic ideology was a blatant factor in all of these cases. Many of the types of nationalism discussed in our theory were well represented. As our theory predicts, weakly institutionalized democratizing politics in culturally diverse societies heightened ethnic nationalism in Armenia and Azerbaijan and produced hybrids of ethnic and counterrevolutionary nationalism in Serbia, Rwanda, and Burundi. Somewhat more surprisingly, civic territorial forms of nationalism were likewise implicated in several of the recent wars. This included the conflicts between India and Pakistan and between Eritrea and Ethiopia, where civic-territorial principles of loyalty to the state clashed with ethno-federal or religious ones. However, this category also included the conflicts between Peru and Ecuador, which were animated by civic-territorial claims to legitimacy on both sides. Although both Peru and Ecuador are not lacking in divisive ethnic politics internally, that was not the issue motivating their external war. Civic nationalism has hardly been a silver bullet for preventing conflict between today's democratizing states.

How can this finding be reconciled with the historical example of civic Britain and our theoretical argument that civic nationalisms tend to be more prudent than other types in their foreign strategies? A civic-territorial ideology does not obviate the need for strong participatory institutions. Civic nationalism arguably requires coherent institutions even more than other types, because loyalty, in this case, attaches precisely to participatory political institutions, not to substitutes such as culture or religion. Thus, successful experiments in civic nationalism need to follow nineteenth-century Britain's example in establishing institutions before unleashing mass political participation. Proper sequence is just as important for civic nationalisms as for other types.

Many of our more specific mechanisms were well represented in these recent cases. Nationalist media manipulation played a central role in the former Yugoslavia and in Rwanda. The ideas that were spread through hate broadcasts, while originally developed in the context of internal ethnic violence, later animated warfare and atrocities in these conflicts' subsequent international phases. This media blitz was a tactic in elites' larger strategy of gambling for resurrection with a program of ethno-nationalist violence in Serbia, Rwanda, and Burundi.

Logrolling and coalition politics pushed outcomes toward violence in several cases. In Pakistan, Musharraf's motive for pushing the Kargil offensive may have been to regain the nationalist prestige of the regular military in order to shore up its political legitimacy against the Islamic radicals in the ISI and against Nawaz Sharif's push for increased civilian authority. Arguably, neither Nawaz nor Musharraf would have wanted to confront India recklessly without these political motivations, while without the active backing of these high authorities, the ISI could not have acted on its own. In the case of Eritrea, prevailing scholarly wisdom holds that the conflict with Ethiopia was needed in part to hold together the ruling coalition of Christians and Muslims. In Ethiopia, the Tigrean pressure group in the ruling coalition had the power to discredit Meles if he had continued to resist taking a hard line with Eritrea. Similarly, weak brokerage by coalition leaders was a factor in several cases. Militant factions ousted more moderate ruling coalition leaders before, during, or after the fighting in Pakistan, Armenia, Rwanda, and Burundi.

Nationalist bidding wars pushed outcomes toward violence in several cases, including some in which top leaders had no intrinsic preference to escalate nationalist violence. In Pakistan, Benazir Bhutto and

Nawaz Sharif both engaged in diplomacy with India over Kashmir before they were pushed toward confrontational rhetoric by Islamic militants or the army. In Serbia, Milosevic was entirely opportunistic in using nationalism to outbid the reform communist leadership of Ivan Stambolic, and then he continued in that vein in order to avoid being outflanked on the nationalism issue by more extreme nationalist politicians such as Vojislav Seselj. These were not simply cases where the preferences of the median voter or the overwhelming power of the militant faction drove the moderate leader to cave in to the inevitable outcome. Rather, as in the German case discussed in Chapter 7, the interaction over time of the rhetoric of the ruling circles and other elite factions increased the militancy of prevailing discourse and of voter attitudes through the processes of blowback and lock-in.

We are more skeptical that the signaling handicaps of weakly democratizing states played an independent causal role in these recent cases. Our criterion here would be that all crucial actors clearly preferred some bargain to fighting the war, and that the inability to signal threats or promises clearly and credibly prevented that bargain from being struck. But in all these recent cases, there were essential actors who preferred fighting to any conceivable compromise. Commitments to these actors hemmed in other decision-makers who were caught in their own rhetoric or coalition logics. It was not mainly signaling problems that made Karabakh Armenians, Kosovar Albanians, the Ecuadoran and Pakistani militaries, and Isaias in Eritrea prefer fighting to any possible agreement, nor were signaling problems the main reason that other actors refused to give in to their demands without a fight.

Alternative Explanations

In Chapter 7, we found that Realpolitik emerged as the strongest alternative explanation for the wars initiated by democratizing states. While some of them launched foolhardy attacks, a number won the wars they started. In the recent wars of democratization, however, it is hard to say that their democratizing instigators became more secure, prosperous, or ideologically gratified as a result.

The weaker party played the major role in instigating a number of these conflicts: Pakistan in Kargil, Ecuador against Peru, Eritrea against Ethiopia. Serbia was initially the stronger party in the Yugoslav civil war, but it so overplayed its hand that external interventions left it in a weak position by the time it launched the ethnic cleansing campaign in Kosovo. Armenia turned out to be stronger militarily than Azerbaijan, but this was not foreseeable at the outset of the conflict, since Armenia's population was much smaller and its industrial potential less than Azerbaijan's.

Thus, it is not surprising that some incompletely democratizing instigators fared badly in these conflicts. Despite Pakistan's initial tactical success in its surprise incursion at high altitudes, Kargil was a debacle for Nawaz Sharif's regime, if not for Musharraf. Likewise, Serbia ultimately lost its nationalist wars and the regime collapsed. Eritrea lost the war that it played a large part in provoking, but Ethiopia was by far the more democratic of these two states, so while this counts against the Realpolitik view, it also does not offer support for our theory. Ecuador arguably achieved its political objectives, because militarily it fared better than the Peruvians had expected, and because the fighting induced the international community to broker a diplomatic settlement. The Karabakh Armenians achieved the objective of *de facto* political autonomy from Azerbaijan, but Armenia itself suffered terrible economic privation and political instability as a result of the war.

Another possible alternative explanation is that these wars of democratization were spurred not by elite-fostered nationalism but simply by longstanding mass nationalist attitudes. This is a plausible view for the Armenian case, and it was a factor that interacted with elite manipulation in the Serbian case. In the case of both Ecuador and Peru, as Paul Mares argues, their median voters got the low-cost, low-risk confrontation that they wanted. On balance, however, in few of these cases was public opinion so clearly in favor of costly nationalist violence that any institutional arrangements would have aggregated popular preferences in a way that supported that policy. In these poorly institutionalized settings, elite manipulation of political agendas, coalition dynamics, and media access skewed outcomes toward nationalist violence in ways that could not be predicted simply from pre-existing individual attitudes.[99]

A final alternative is that the more general problem of weak political institutions, not only in the context of incomplete democratization, is the central cause of most of these wars. We reject this view in part because our statistical results refute it: low domestic concentration of power does not predict war, apart from its interaction with incomplete democratization. Moreover, the Peru-Ecuador case varies enough over time that it permits a head-to-head test of these competing views. While both countries have had weak political institutions for their entire history, their propensity to fight wars and engage in militarized disputes had been much greater when one or both has been in a democratizing phase. Similarly,

---

99. See Kaufman, *Modern Hatreds*, on bottom-up and top-down dynamics as alternative paths to ethnic violence in the context of processes of symbolic politics.

Pakistan is chronically weak in its central state institutions, whether it is in an autocratic or a democratic phase, but it has confronted India in war mainly in the context of political maneuverings during incomplete democratizations. Conversely, in Central Africa, Hutu and Tutsi have been at loggerheads in situations of autocracy, incomplete democratization, and anarchy. We do not deny that institutional chaos can sometimes cause conflict even apart from democratization; we simply contend that this by itself cannot explain much of our findings.

Timing and Trajectories

Incomplete democratic transitions can play out in a variety of subsequent trajectories. An influential book on the emergence of democracy by Dietrich Rueschemeyer, Evelyne Stephens, and John Stephens stresses the sequence-dependency of these trajectories.[100] Choices and class alignments made in the early stages of democratization significantly affect the options that are available at later stages. Ideologies, capabilities, and enmities tend to get locked in cognitively and institutionally, so that a country's second experiment with transition is affected, for better or worse, by what happened the first time. This means that premature transitions that get a country off on the wrong foot may impair future chances for consolidation of democracy. Moreover, say these scholars, leaping ahead to "full democracy," but failing to consolidate it and falling back, removes the option of a gradual transition via "restricted democracy" at the next opportunity.[101]

We argued in Chapter 7 that wars launched by democratizing initiators often unfolded in an interconnected series, reflecting stubborn patterns of ideas and relationships. This is true also for the recent conflicts examined in the present chapter. The wars of democratization in the 1990s were all embedded in the legacy of earlier experiments with mass politics. Armenian and Serbian nationalism had their origins in the developing mass political consciousness of the late nineteenth and early twentieth centuries, including partially democratic episodes in those people's histories. Despite being submerged in multi-ethnic communist states for several decades, these identities and the rivalries bound up with them were lurking in the popular consciousness when these nations re-democratized during the collapse of communism. The Ecuador-Peru

---

100. Dietrich Rueschemeyer, Evelyne Huber Stephens, and John D. Stephens, *Capitalist Development and Democracy* (Chicago: University of Chicago, 1992), p. 32.

101. Ibid., pp. 207–208, 216.

clash was simply the latest in a series of wars of democratization stretching over two hundred years. The Kargil War made sense only in terms of the symbolic significance of the Kashmir issue in Pakistan's partially democratic politics as it had taken shape in the course of a series of earlier showdowns with India. Relations between Hutu and Tutsi in Central Africa reflected earlier colonial legacies and the attempted settling of scores in the incomplete democracy of the early post-colonial years in Rwanda and Burundi. Finally, the clash between Eritrea and Ethiopia also reflected the way that mass politics had been structured in earlier periods. By the 1990s, most places on the planet had previously undergone some degree of incomplete democratization that established a template of ideas, institutions, or alignments that, in turn, shaped the transformational options available in the new round of democratization.

In the concluding chapter, we return to the question of the possible trajectories that play out in the wake of incomplete democratizations. We also assess which sequences lead to the most violent and least violent outcomes.

Chapter 9

Conclusion: Sequencing the Transition for Peace

In this book, we have demonstrated the dangers that can arise when democratic transitions do not follow an auspicious sequence. Not only does an out-of-sequence transition run the risk of failing to culminate in consolidated democracy, but it also risks triggering intense nationalism and war. This is most likely to occur when a country's political institutions are especially weak at the outset of the transition from autocracy to a partially democratic regime, and when elites are threatened by democratization. The politics of democratizing states that initiate war are likely to exhibit at least some of the following characteristics: exclusionary nationalism, pressure-group politics, logrolled political bargains by elite factions, weak brokerage of political bargains by the ruling elite, contradictory and unconvincing signaling in foreign affairs, the use of aggressive foreign policies to gamble for domestic political resurrection, the use of media dominance to promote nationalist ideology, and a nationalist bidding war between old elites and rising mass groups. Our statistical results and process-tracing case studies provide strong support for the six hypotheses that we formulated at the end of Chapter 3.

Our findings have prescriptive implications for those instances where policymakers have some latitude about the timing and sequencing of a transition. In cases where the institutional requisites for successful consolidation are not yet in place, it is best to try to see that they are developed before encouraging mass political contestation. In cases where powerful potential spoilers are threatened by a democratic transition, it is best to find ways to assure them a soft landing under the anticipated democratic regime. While transitions do not necessarily have to proceed slowly, they do have to build on sound foundations and neutralize potential spoilers effectively through some combination of constraints and inducements.[1]

These prescriptions for the sequencing, tactics, and pacing of a transition are important for both the short run and the long run. In the short run, transitions that ignore them risk stalling and degenerating into the politics of war-prone nationalism. Over the longer term, a failed and violent transition may leave a legacy of nationalist ideology, militarized institutions, undemocratic rules, and foreign enmities that will hinder future democratic consolidation and raise the risk of war during subsequent attempts at transition.

In this concluding chapter, we first identify six alternative trajectories that could emerge from incomplete democratization. We note potential pitfalls and prescribe tactics to avoid them. Next, we explain that incomplete democratization increases the risk not only of international war but also of civil war, human rights abuses, and economic distortions. Finally, we discuss the implications of our findings for theories of democratic transition and for the democratic peace.

Trajectories Emerging from Incomplete Democratization

"Transitions matter because they generate fairly durable legacies that affect the posttransitional regime and politics," observe political scientists Gerardo Munck and Carol Leff. "The mode of transition affects the form of posttransitional regime and politics through its influence on the pattern of elite competition, on the institutional rules crafted during the transition, and on key actors' acceptance or rejection of the new rules of the game."[2] In particular, they warn, the long-term consequences of "backlash from the old elites" and "the loss of identity of the antiauthoritarian coalition" can "lead to the adoption of institutional rules that are not optimal for democratization" and "leave a legacy that hinders governability and democratic consolidation."[3]

Munck and Leff argue that, "the primary challenge [for theory] is to explain how modes of transition matter by specifying causal mechanisms

---

1. Nancy Bermeo, "Myths of Moderation: Confrontation and Conflict During Democracy Transition," in Lisa Anderson, ed., *Transitions to Democracy* (New York: Columbia University Press, 1999), pp. 120–140; and Stephen John Stedman, "Spoiler Problems in Peace Processes," *International Security*, Vol. 22, No. 2 (Fall 1997), pp. 5–53.

2. Gerardo L. Munck and Carol Skalnik Leff, "Modes of Transition and Democratization: South America and Eastern Europe in Comparative Perspective," in Anderson, ed., *Transitions to Democracy*, pp. 193–216, at 195.

3. Ibid., p. 210.

and the significance of these legacies."[4] Our research responds to the challenge that Munck and Leff lay out. In the following sections, we identify several trajectories that may emerge from incomplete democratization, and we discuss how the sequence of steps in the transition affects the likelihood of subsequent war and democratic consolidation.

REVERSION TO AUTOCRACY

An incompletely democratizing state may revert to autocracy. Our earliest statistical results suggested that reversals toward autocracy might be more peaceful than democratic transitions, but more war-prone than the absence of regime change.[5] However, the statistical results in Chapters 5 and 6, based on an improved research design and more sophisticated techniques, suggest that transitions leading to a coherent autocracy do not have a systematic influence on conflict.

Notwithstanding this overall pattern, some noteworthy cases suggest that belligerent nationalism can sometimes offer a popular ideological justification for a reversion to autocracy, especially when nationalism has been prominent in the semi-democratic period preceding the reversion. For example, Napoleonic France, Nazi Germany, and the militarist Japan of the 1930s provide anecdotal evidence that revolutionary or counterrevolutionary nationalist ideas could serve as the ideological underpinnings for a return to autocracy and, through a blowback process, fuel intense warfare even after the demise of democratization.[6]

The reversal of Japan's incomplete democratization of the 1920s is particularly instructive, showing the dangers of a reversion to autocracy in a great power with weak civic institutions. Japan's invasion of Manchuria in 1931 and its subsequent aggression in China and the Pacific were legacies of the crisis of Japan's incomplete democratization in the 1920s. During the 1920s, Japan had adopted universal manhood suffrage and gradually increased the democratic accountability of the state. Although the Polity database does not count this as a democratic transition, by the late 1920s Japan had developed a competitive two-party system, and elections determined who held the top government posts.[7] For a time it seemed that popular accountability was a factor working to constrain

---

4. Ibid., p. 195.

5. Edward D. Mansfield and Jack Snyder, "Democratization and the Danger of War," *International Security*, Vol. 20, No. 1 (Summer 1995), pp. 5–38.

6. Blowback occurs when manipulators are captured by their own propaganda; see Jack Snyder, *Myths of Empire* (Ithaca, N.Y.: Cornell University Press, 1991), pp. 41–42.

7. Masayo Ohara, *Democratization and Expansionism: Historical Lessons, Contemporary Challenges* (Westport, Conn.: Praeger, 2001).

the militaristic elements that were entrenched in the Army, which never-theless enjoyed considerable autonomy from civilian control. In 1928, for example, a government led by the imperialist Seyukai Party lost public support when it failed to rein in the Army, which had asserted that its as-sassination of a Chinese warlord was a strictly internal military matter. As a result, the Seyukai fell from power, and the more peace-oriented Minseito Party won the next election.[8]

However, the military retained extraordinary autonomy under the Meiji constitution. Military radicals chafed under the pacific policies of the democratic coalitions of the 1920s and developed an alternative ideol-ogy of populist militarism. Under the stresses of the Great Depression, military propaganda and the unauthorized military *fait accompli* in Man-churia maneuvered the public into abandoning the peace-oriented demo-cratic coalitions and instead increasing their support for the imperialist policies of the Seyukai Party and the Army militarists. The Japanese pub-lic—fed a diet of slanted information about the Manchurian invasion—was largely convinced by the Army's propaganda.[9] In the 1932 election, the Seyukai used a pro-imperialist platform, similar to the positions of the military expansionists, to defeat the Minseito, whose policies offered only hardship amidst a steep economic downturn.[10]

In sum, the weakness of Japan's democratic institutions, combined with the economic depression, gave the military the opportunity to con-vince the Japanese people to abandon liberal democracy in favor of a mil-itaristic empire ruled in the name of the Japanese people. This suggests that when a great power's military has the motive and opportunity to act as a spoiler, it is especially important for the international community to maintain a supportive economic and security environment during the most precarious stages of a democratic transition. One implication is that the United States should avoid disrupting trade relations with China while it is in the midst of a future transition to democracy.

During the 1990s, too, autocratizing states—such as Serbia and

---

8. Lesley Connors, *The Emperor's Adviser: Saionji Kinmchi and Pre-war Japanese Politics* (London: Oxford University Press, 1988), pp. 102, 107, 117–119; Peter Duus, *Party Ri-valry and Political Change in Taisho Japan* (Cambridge, Mass.: Harvard University Press, 1968); Robert Scalapino, "Elections and Political Modernization in Prewar Japan," in Robert Ward, ed., *Political Development in Modern Japan* (Princeton: Princeton Univer-sity Press, 1968), pp. 276–277; and Snyder, *Myths of Empire*, pp. 136–139.

9. Louise Young, *Japan's Total Empire: Manchuria and the Culture of Wartime Imperial-ism* (Berkeley: University of California Press, 1998), chapter on "War Fever: Imperial Jingoism and the Mass Media."

10. Scalapino, "Elections," pp. 279–280; and James Crowley, *Japan's Quest for Auton-omy* (Princeton: Princeton University Press, 1966), pp. 126, 171.

Eritrea—suffered from continued war. In the Pakistani case, such a transition led to a militarized dispute, if not actual war. Only in Azerbaijan did reautocratization coincide with the cessation of military conflict. Peru and Ecuador moved toward settling their long-running dispute while staying on their erratic trajectories toward democracy. These recent cases offer little support for those who would propose reversals to autocracy as the solution for the danger of wars in incomplete democratization. Although autocratization can sometimes take the steam out of nationalist politics, there is nonetheless a chance that the autocratic rulers will still seek to invoke nationalist justifications for their rule as a legacy of the populist politics of the failed transition. If so, the nationalist conflicts associated with those justifications are likely to continue.

STABLE MIXED REGIME

An incompletely democratizing state might become a stable anocracy or mixed regime. Generally, such states have a fairly strong administrative capacity and make some attempt to rule in the interest of the broad mass of the population. They operate on the basis of limited pluralism and partial accommodation of mass movements, but use bureaucratic repression when mass politics threatens to make excessive demands for political participation. Malaysia is an example of a stable anocracy that is close to the democratic end of the scale; Egypt has been closer to the autocratic end.

Our statistical results suggest that stable mixed regimes are not especially war-prone. They are not, however, necessarily born peaceful. Egypt had a rough start as a warlike mixed regime, but has become relatively peaceful. Malaysia emerged from a legacy of communist insurgency, conflict with neighboring Indonesia, and bloody ethnic rioting.

It is too early to tell whether the warring incomplete democratizers of the 1990s, such as Ethiopia, will become stable, peaceful mixed regimes. However, this is likely to depend on whether these governments are able to co-opt potential domestic opponents and to foster obedience to the state. Doing so will require the development of a stronger, more reliable administrative capacity. China could become a stable, peaceful mixed regime of this kind if its future transition is sequenced reasonably well. But where such administrative capacity is lacking, as in Pakistan, mixed regimes are likely to be unstable and warlike, prone to veer from autocracy to democracy and back, and prone to fight wars in all of these transitions.

Some kinds of stable mixed regimes seem to be good candidates for an eventual peaceful transition to full democracy. This would be the case for those that have established a firm basis for administrative rationality, a somewhat reliable rule of law, and strong economic growth. Brazil, for example, has made such a transition successfully. Malaysia might do so as well, although its multi-ethnicity, its history of ethnic strife, and the presence of militant Islamic movements raise a note of caution. The chances for an eventual peaceful transition to full democracy might be improved for a country that remains a stable mixed regime for an extended period of time, during which it could strengthen its administrative rationality and the rule of law. This raises the broader question of the consequences of gradual transitions to democracy.

GRADUAL TRANSITION TO DEMOCRACY

Some countries are so rich in social capital or so well endowed with relevant political institutions that they can move smoothly from autocracy to consolidated democracy, as Poland and Hungary did after the fall of Communism. Where this is impossible, however, questions remain about the speed of transitions to democracy. More specifically, what are the consequences of gradual transitions for consolidation and for peace, and what is the best route to these favorable outcomes?

Dietrich Rueschemeyer, Evelyne Huber Stephens, and John D. Stephens argue that elite-protecting pacts have helped promote the gradual consolidation of democracy in South America—for example, in Brazil and Chile.[11] Of the various forms of transitional democracy, they maintain that "restricted democracy"—which places various kinds of limitations on democratic participation or powers—is especially stable. In their view, restricted democracy—using what Guillermo O'Donnell and Philippe Schmitter refer to as "pacts"—functions well when it is based on a center-right coalition between the middle class and old ruling elites, with one or two strong parties, at least one of which defends elite interests; a low level of involvement by the military in politics; and a working class organized to articulate its interests but not to contend for power. In this way, the typical counterrevolutionary nationalist coalition may be forged without playing the nationalist card in a belligerent fashion. Eventually, the country may become sufficiently rich and institutionally developed so that democratization is a smooth and orderly process, as in Taiwan and South Korea.

This strategy can sometimes be effective in consolidating democracy. Because it protects elite interests, it removes their incentives to gamble for resurrection with nationalist violence. Nonetheless, Rueschemeyer, Stephens, and Stephens's own data reveal that various restricted democ-

---

11. Dietrich Rueschemeyer, Evelyne Huber Stephens, and John D. Stephens, *Capitalist Development and Democracy* (Chicago: University of Chicago Press, 1992), pp. 171, 205–208.

racies of this type have degenerated into "bureaucratic-authoritarianism," especially in the 1970s, when the strategy of import-substituting industrialization broke down in countries such as Argentina and Brazil.[12]

A generic problem with restricted democracy as a strategy of gradual consolidation is that the policies required to ensure the short-term stability of a restricted regime are sometimes antithetical to the policies needed to move toward the long-term consolidation of democracy. Joel Hellman's comparison of gradual versus rapid political and economic transitions in post-communist Eastern Europe shows that groups that benefit from the limited accountability that marks mixed (or anocratic) regimes have an incentive to stall democratic transitions at that point rather than continue the gradual building of democratic institutions.[13] Thus, the groups that dominate the restricted democracy may have incentives to use nationalist rhetoric to justify their continued privileges, to gamble on war to forestall political changes that would unseat them, or to re-autocratize the state under the cover of nationalist sloganeering. This was a common pattern in the cases that we discussed in Chapters 7 and 8. Russia's Second Chechen War seems to fit this pattern: Vladimir Putin used the war to maintain the constraints on Russia's democracy and to strengthen his power as president within it. This picture is complicated, however, by Putin's use of his heightened and arbitrary presidential powers to break the oligarchic cartels that had formed during the stalled transition, and to push forward market-oriented reforms.[14]

As this example implies, sometimes restrictions on democracy reflect not only the power of self-seeking anti-democratic groups, but also the nature of the tactics that any actor must use, even a reform-minded one, given the institutional landscape of a mixed regime. In the case of semidemocratic Malaysia, for example, Prime Minister Muhammad Mahathir might be seen either as a power-hungry political boss who arbitrarily restricts individual liberties or as an astute tactician pulling the necessary levers to contain ethnic factionalism and the rise of popular but anti-democratic Islamic parties. In short, mixed regimes undertaking gradual reform sometimes face a Catch-22: in undemocratic settings, building

---

12.   Ibid., table 5.1 on pp. 160–161. Note also the qualifications that Bermeo, "Myths of Moderation," offers to what she sees as the conventional wisdom among scholars of comparative politics in favor of gradualism.

13.   Joel S. Hellman, "Winners Take All: The Politics of Partial Reform in Post-communist Transitions," *World Politics*, Vol. 50, No. 2 (January 1998), pp. 203–234.

14.   Daniel Treisman, "Russia Renewed?" *Foreign Affairs*, Vol. 81, No. 6 (November/December 2002), pp. 58–72.

democratic institutions may require the use of undemocratic tactics, which hinder progress toward the ultimate goal.

RIVALS CYCLING BETWEEN DEMOCRATIZATION AND AUTOCRATIZATION

Some of the most war-prone countries in our sample repeatedly cycle between democratization and autocratization.[15] There have been sporadic wars and numerous militarized disputes involving Pakistan and India, Turkey (especially when its Greek rival was also cycling), Ecuador and Peru, and Argentina and various rivals, especially Chile.[16] Such cycling tends to institutionalize the political role of the military and sustains the expectations of international rivalry that make the nationalist card more plausible.[17] Furthermore, the military is threatened during the democratizing parts of the cycle, which can provoke the military to play the nationalist card in a gamble for resurrection, while civilian elites are threatened during transitions toward autocracy, which can prompt them to play the nationalist card preemptively.

Cycling happens, in part, because it has happened before. Premature democratization, lapsing due to the lack of adequate institutional supports, puts the state on a bad trajectory from which it cannot easily escape. The dismal track record shapes the expectations of both domestic and international actors, and the pattern of nationalism and war gets locked in.

David Mares, studying recent South American cases, argues that leaders keep these limited interstate rivalries from escalating out of control.[18] Costs are kept low and proportionate to the domestic political incentives. Disputes and wars between Ecuador and Peru, he found, generally came during the re-democratization phases, when the political need for nationalist popularity was greatest. The India-Pakistan rivalry, in which Pakistan cycles between democratic and military rule, has also tended to involve relatively low-cost conflicts except for the 1971 Bangla-

---

15. See also Michael Ward and Kristian Gleditsch, "Democratizing for Peace," *American Political Science Review*, Vol. 92, No. 1 (March 1998), pp. 51–61.

16. On militarized disputes involving these and other cases, see Edward D. Mansfield and Jack Snyder, "Incomplete Democratization and the Outbreak of Military Disputes," *International Studies Quarterly*, Vol. 46, No. 4 (December 2002), pp. 529–549.

17. Kristina Mani, "Democratization and Defense; Rethinking Rivalry in South America," Ph.D. dissertation in progress, Columbia University.

18. David R. Mares, *Violent Peace: Militarized Interstate Bargaining in Latin America* (New York: Columbia University Press, 2001).

desh crisis, which was primarily a function of internal Pakistani conflicts that spilled over into international rivalry.

DECISIVE DEFEAT IN WAR

Being humiliated in war (and especially being occupied by an adversary) is likely to affect the trajectory of democratization. Decisive defeat led to democratization in Germany and Japan after World War II, in France after the Franco-Prussian War, and in Argentina after the Falklands War.[19] Defeat may limit the extent to which leaders can use the nationalist card as an effective anti-democratic strategy. For example, the nationalist card was not played so vehemently by Greece after the 1974 Cyprus debacle, and was no longer credible as a barrier to democratic consolidation. But things do not always work this way. Germany's violent nationalism revived despite its defeat in World War I. Russian public opinion supported the Second Chechen War despite the reverses Russia suffered in the First Chechen War. Likewise, the Serbian regime—under pressure from its democratic opposition—went back on the nationalist offensive in Kosovo despite setbacks in Croatia and Bosnia. Even after the defeat in Kosovo, a surprising number of Serbians voted in the December 2003 parliamentary elections for the parties of the deposed and indicted Slobodan Milosevic and the even more extreme nationalist Vojislav Seselj. In these cases, nationalism was most discredited when the military defeat was decisive and seen as self-inflicted. The troubled U.S. occupation of Iraq demonstrates, however, that divisive ethnic and religious politics can arise despite the military defeat of the former authoritarian regime when credible institutional supports for democracy are lacking.

Sequence of Political Changes

A common theme underlying all of these trajectories is that there can be adverse foreign policy consequences when democratization gets off to a bad start. Countries that begin to democratize when they are too unsettled in their national identity, too threatening to declining elites, or too weakly institutionalized may develop politically along any of several dangerous trajectories. The best strategy for the international community, therefore, is to encourage a country to move forward with democratization step-by-step, by establishing the institutional preconditions for effective administration before expanding the scope of mass political participation. When missteps have already been made, however, a practical

---

19.   See, for example, John W. Dower, *Embracing Defeat: Japan in the Wake of World War II* (New York: Norton, 1999).

strategy must be devised in the world of the second-best. We take up this issue in further detail later.

The Effects of Incomplete Democratization on Civil War, Human Rights, and International Trade

This has been a book about the effects of democratization, especially incomplete democratization, on external war. However, the use of armed force abroad hardly exhausts the ill effects of poorly timed, poorly sequenced, and tactically misconceived democratic transitions. Numerous studies have found that mixed regimes or newly transitional regimes are also at a heightened risk of civil war or internal ethnic conflict.[20] Our case studies provide additional evidence: states undergoing incomplete democratization sometimes become involved in civil wars for the same reasons that, as we explained, they become involved in external wars.[21] From a prescriptive standpoint, it would seem that the same sequencing tactics that should reduce the risk of external war for democratizing countries should also reduce their risk of internal war.

The same properties of incomplete democratizers that give rise to both external and civil war also predispose such states to engage in atrocities and massive human rights violations. Genocides and other atrocities take place in autocracies, but our case studies show that they also take place in states undergoing incomplete democratization. These abuses can result from the ethnic nationalist politics stirred up in the early stages of the transition process in weakly institutionalized political systems where elites are threatened by the prospect of political change. Yugoslavia and Central Africa have been prominent recent cases.

In the wake of such atrocities, successor regimes and the international community often face the question of whether to punish past abuses and how to inoculate the country against their recurrence. The typical prescription of human rights activist groups, human rights lawyers, and international organizations emphasizes individual accountabil-

---

20. Daniel Esty, Jack Goldstone, Ted Robert Gurr, Barbara Harff, Marc Levy, Geoffrey Dalbeko, Pamela Surko, and Alan Unger, "State Failure Task Force Report: Phase II Findings," July 1998. See also James Fearon and David Laitin, "Ethnicity, Insurgency, and Civil War," *American Political Science Review*, Vol. 97, No. 1 (February 2003), pp. 75–90, esp. 84–85; and Snyder, *From Voting to Violence*. For some qualifications, see Ted Robert Gurr, *Peoples Versus States* (Washington, D.C.: U.S. Institute of Peace, 2000).

21. Nonetheless, our statistical findings presented in Chapters 5 and 6 show that civil war does not account for the strong correlation between incomplete democratization with weak institutions and external war.

ity through trials and through truth-telling about past misdeeds. In this view, trials and truth commissions demonstrate that impunity is at an end, symbolize the move toward the rule of law, facilitate a cathartic clearing of the air between the communities of perpetrators and victims, and thus psychologically underpin a transition to stable democracy.[22]

While such measures may be effective in some cases, our theory suggests that the institutional and political circumstances of the transitional country should be assessed carefully before moving down this path. Sometimes it may be necessary to give an amnesty to rights abusers in order to remove them from power and forge a political coalition that can create an effective rule-of-law state. Amnesties have been quite effective in reconciling heavily armed factions to the task of democratic consolidation in such complicated cases as El Salvador, Mozambique, and South Africa. An amnesty in Macedonia worked reasonably well to calm the armed conflict and prepare the way for political stabilization. In Afghanistan, political and military figures who had perpetrated mass atrocities in the recent past were among the main props of Hamid Karzai's reform coalition government that struggled to maintain political order after the ouster of the Taliban.[23] Our theory helps explain the need for and the success of such pragmatic policies aimed at neutralizing spoilers and building state institutions in troubled transitional countries.

Economic reform is an issue that has stimulated enormous attention on the part of social scientists, but virtually no attention has been paid to the effects of incomplete democratization on economic policy. The nationalist appeals that public officials in these countries use to consolidate power and generate public support often involve the rejection of liberal economic policies. Nationalists, for example, tend to oppose market-oriented reforms, such as commercial liberalization, that make domestic firms more vulnerable to foreign competition and increase the participation of foreigners in the economy.[24] Thus, there is ample reason to fear

---

22. An example of this view is that of the Director of Human Rights Watch, Kenneth Roth, "The Case for Universal Jurisdiction," *Foreign Affairs*, Vol. 80, No. 5 (September 2001), pp. 150–154.

23. Jack Snyder and Leslie Vinjamuri, "Trials and Errors: Principle and Pragmatism in Strategies of International Justice," *International Security*, Vol. 28, No. 3 (Winter 2003/04), pp. 5–44.

24. Joan M. Nelson, "The Politics of Economic Transformation: Is the Third World Experience Relevant in Eastern Europe?" *World Politics*, Vol. 45, No. 3 (April 1993), p. 443.

that economic reform will be inhibited in countries undergoing an incomplete democratic transition.[25]

Further, the fragility of democratizing regimes—especially those marked by a low level of domestic concentration of power—limits the ability of policymakers to undertake the economic reforms that would be facilitated by a strong and centralized state.[26] Such fragility also compels governments in new democracies to consolidate their power and build popular support or face the prospects of reversals of democratization, including the restoration of autocracy. Distributing economic favors to influential groups in society is one means of building support. Such favors are likely to involve economic policies that protect uncompetitive sectors of the economy and generate rents for elite groups that thrived under autocratic rule and pose a threat to a new democracy.[27] That democratizing regimes will need to generate the support of many groups within society suggests that protection may be relatively widespread. This, too, hobbles economic reform.

Compounding this tendency is the fact that democratization elicits demands for greater political participation and the reduction of central authority, both of which may be difficult to reconcile with economic reform programs that impose substantial costs on society.[28] Moreover, democratizing regimes often fail to develop the social welfare policies needed to buffer these costs.[29] Consequently, economic liberalization may create greater political pressure than democratizing regimes are able to bear.

Terrorism, Democratization, and Nation-Building

Promoting democratization has been a central theme of U.S. foreign policy during the administrations of Ronald Reagan, Bill Clinton, and

---

25. Edward D. Mansfield, "Democratization and Commercial Liberalization" (paper presented at the annual meeting of the American Political Science Association, San Francisco, 1996).

26. Stephan Haggard and Robert R. Kaufman, *The Political Economy of Democratic Transitions* (Princeton: Princeton University Press, 1995); and José Mariá Maravall, "Economic Reform and Democracy: The Myth of the Authoritarian Advantage," *Journal of Democracy*, Vol. 5, No. 4 (October 1994), pp. 17–31.

27. Haggard and Kaufman, *The Political Economy of Democratic Transitions*, pp. 152–159.

28. Nelson, "The Politics of Economic Transformation," pp. 433–463.

29. Luiz Carlos Bresser Pereira, José Maria Maravall, and Adam Przeworski, *Economic Reforms in New Democracies: A Social-Democratic Approach* (Cambridge: Cambridge University Press, 1993).

George W. Bush. Clinton argued that since democracies do not fight wars against each other, promoting democratization would promote peace. Bush has argued that transforming rogue states into democracies will strike a blow against terrorism. Although the United States has not waged its recent wars primarily to spread democracy, the extent of its success in establishing democracy in the aftermath of victory in Kosovo, Afghanistan, and Iraq has been viewed as one criterion for assessing the efficacy of these administrations' strategies. Under the Bush "Millennium Challenge" program, the level of U.S. aid is determined in part by a country's progress in reaching a variety of indicators of democratic institutionalization. The official *National Security Strategy of the United States*, not limiting U.S. democratization efforts to weak and manipulable states, portrays democratization as a key goal of America's policy of engagement with China.[30]

Such grand objectives might be taken as just so much empty rhetoric if it were not for America's overwhelming military dominance and economic influence throughout the world. As Stephen Krasner showed more than twenty-five years ago, during periods of unchecked American power, the United States tends to indulge its ideological predilections abroad, typically in ways that incur high costs and court failure.[31] After September 11, 2001, the perceived need for an assertive policy to counter terrorists and their presumed pariah-state co-conspirators reinforced these temptations. While some Bush administration figures stressed strategic reasons for using force abroad after September 11, the rhetoric of Bush himself and the *National Security Strategy* document placed the doctrine of preventive war in a political and ideological context in which creating "a balance of power that favors freedom" played a central legitimating role.[32]

However, terrorism stands in an ambiguous relation to democratization. Many terrorist movements claim to be fighting for national self-determination. Like most of the nationalist political entrepreneurs that we study in this book, terrorists typically purport to be seeking political sovereignty for the people, although not necessarily a government that is accountable to the people. Sometimes, as in Algeria in the 1950s and Pal-

---

30. Office of the President, *National Security Strategy of the United States*, September 2002, at <www.whitehouse.gov/nsc/nss.html>.

31. Stephen D. Krasner, *Defending the National Interest: Raw Materials Investments and U.S. Foreign Policy* (Princeton: Princeton University Press, 1978), p. 340.

32. George Bush, West Point speech, June 1, 2002; *National Security Strategy of the United States*; and Jack Snyder, "Imperial Temptations," *The National Interest*, No. 71 (Spring 2003), pp. 29–40.

estine today, these claims are widely credited by the people on whose be-half the terrorists purport to act. Indeed, in many parts of the Arab world, public opinion sympathizes with the goals of terrorists even when am-bivalent about their methods. Consequently, democratizing the Arab states is a major gamble in the war on terror.

Paradoxically, Osama bin Laden and American neo-conservatives are in agreement on one goal: that the Saudi monarchy should be swept away and replaced by a form of government that is more responsive to the Saudi people. The neo-conservatives want this because they see Saudi Arabia as an insidious breeding ground of terrorism.[33] In this view, the weak Saudi autocracy offers the worst of both worlds. On the one hand, it radicalizes the population by repressing individual liberties (an outcome that the Saudi people blame on the regime's protector, the United States). On the other hand, the autocracy appeases the discontent by indulging radicals' appetite for militant forms of Islam and doing little to prevent their financial support for foreign terrorism, which partially redirects dis-content toward Israel, the Christian West, and secular Arab targets. Bin Laden wants the Saudi regime overturned for much the same reasons. Where the neo-conservatives and bin Laden differ is on what they expect to happen if Saudi Arabia were to democratize. Bin Laden expects the founding of an Islamic state, whereas the neo-conservatives hope that Is-lamic mass radicalism would lose its popular appeal outside of the hot-house in which the royal regime nurtures it.

Who is right about the consequences of the rise of a more popular politics in Saudi Arabia and more generally in the Arab world?[34] Our study cannot answer this question, but our theory does suggest some key issues that bear heavily on the answer. First, we point to the dangers of the early phase of democratization in a region where Arab national iden-tity is mismatched with state boundaries. In Chapter 7, we saw how this played out in Iraq during the late 1940s, an episode that stimulated tur-bulence in Arab-Israeli relations that remains unabated. Second, we point to the risks of democratization in a state like Saudi Arabia that lacks a de-veloped infrastructure of impartial administration and legal institutions, let alone tools of representative government. Third, we point to the many potential spoilers and manipulators of democratization in the region. These include not only the elites of oil-rich states, which in principle

33.   Richard K. Herrmann, "George W. Bush's Foreign Policy," in Colin Campbell and Bert Rockman, eds., *The George W. Bush Presidency* (Washington, D.C.: CQ Press, 2004), pp. 191–225.

34.   On the feasibility of democratization in the Arab world, see John Waterbury, "Fortuitous Byproducts," in Anderson, ed., *Transitions to Democracy*, pp. 261–283.

might be swept aside if the United States withdrew its support, but also the rising elites of mass movements, such as the sectarian factions of Iraq.[35] In the winter of 2004, Iraq's Shi'a leaders rallied their supporters into the streets around the slogan "one man, one vote," in an effort to press the U.S. occupation authorities into holding early elections structured in such a way as to benefit the Shi'ite majority. The election held in January 2005 amid continuing Sunni terror attacks recorded extremely low turnout in the Sunni region. This left the Sunni minority underrepresented and raised questions about the legitimacy of the results.

Even if democratization succeeds in some Islamic countries, the result might be, perversely, to increase inducements for terror attacks. As Robert Pape has convincingly shown, the targets of suicide terrorists are almost exclusively democracies or partial democracies.[36] Whereas nondemocratic states can shrug off such attacks, states that are responsive to cost-sensitive publics often wind up making concessions on political issues of concern to the terrorists in order to reduce their exposure to costly attacks. Terrorists know this and rationally use terror to extract these concessions.

During George W. Bush's first presidential campaign, he called for "humility" in assessing the feasibility of American "nation-building" projects abroad. Notwithstanding the assertive rhetoric and policies of the Bush administration since September 11, 2001, elements of this wary stance have continued to influence U.S. policy. Ambitions for nation-building in Afghanistan, for example, have focused mainly on controlling the capital city, bargaining with local warlords, and very gradually constructing the beginnings of a professionalized national army. Even in Iraq, the United States has become extensively involved in varied tasks of nation-building mostly as unavoidable consequences of a conquest undertaken for strategic purposes, not primarily as a principled commitment to transforming a troubled country.

Our findings suggest that it is indeed wise to approach the task of promoting democracy abroad with a healthy dose of wary skepticism. Even for those who seek out this task on principled rather than strictly pragmatic grounds, it is important to remember that shortcuts on the road to democratic consolidation are often dangerous. Consolidation may

---

35.   For an extended assessment of the dangers of and prospects for democratization in Iraq that draws on our earlier arguments about democratization and war, see Daniel Byman, "Constructing a Democratic Iraq: Challenges and Opportunities," *International Security*, Vol. 28, No. 1 (Summer 2003), pp. 47–78.

36.   Robert Pape, "The Strategic Logic of Suicide Terrorism," *American Political Science Review*, Vol. 97, No. 3 (August 2003), pp. 343–362, esp. 349–350.

be especially hard in countries where previous lunges in the direction of democratization have already roiled politics. In an age of democratization, it is the rare country that has not yet undergone its first bout of mass political participation. The legacy of those earlier skirmishes has mobilized political cleavages based on ethnicity in most states that remain on the "to-do list" of democracy promoters.

This raises the question of how promoters of democratization in the international community should devise their tactics. Where voters and nascent mass parties include strong voices of moderation, and where a number of the preconditions of democracy are already in place, as in Singapore and perhaps Malaysia, the best approach may be gradually to circumscribe the powers of the residual forces that are resistant to a full democratic transition. Where these favorable conditions are largely absent, patient attention must be paid to putting in place the necessary building blocks of democracy, starting with the institutions of administrative rationality, and only later creating channels of democratic accountability to a mass public.

During this process of institution-building, it may be necessary to make state authorities directly accountable to international authorities, constraining the scope of political competition in internationally regulated electoral contests. Internationally occupied territories such as Kosovo, Bosnia, and East Timor are examples of this approach. Much harder are the cases, such as Indonesia, where international influence must be more indirect and far weaker. We cannot suggest a general blueprint for when and how to press such regimes to stay on a productive track toward democratic consolidation. In such instances, our rules about sequencing must be interpreted in light of the specific features of the case, especially the presence of potential spoilers and the availability of good candidates to organize a center-right coalition that has the means and motive to neutralize or reassure them.

Given the strategic and domestic political pressures on U.S. decision-makers, it may be unrealistic to count on the systematic implementation of a finely calibrated strategy of international influence. Humility about the ability of any outsider to re-engineer a country's political institutions is prudent, combined with the physician's reminder to "do no harm" in the process of such re-engineering.[37] However, it would be wrong to assume that the policies of international actors can make no difference in the outcome of democratic transitions. Studies of recent democratizations have shown the impact of a range of international fac-

---

37. Mary B. Anderson, *Do No Harm: How Aid Can Support Peace—Or War* (Boulder, Colo.: Lynne Rienner, 1999).

tors, such as global economic trends, the changing policies of the Catholic Church, the demonstration effect of the collapse of Communism, and the influence of regional organizations.[38]

Implications of our Findings for Theories of Democratization

Some theories of successful democratization focus on the preconditions that must be in place before democratic consolidation is likely to occur. For example, the arguments of Seymour Martin Lipset and more recently of Adam Przeworski explore the economic preconditions of democracy. Juan Linz and Alfred Stepan posit five preconditions of consolidation: a useable state bureaucracy, rule of law, autonomous political parties, a free and lively civil society, and an institutionalized economic society.[39] Rueschemeyer, Stephens, and Stephens stress the political inclusion of the working class. Dankwart Rustow and Arend Lijphart emphasize the resolution or management of ethnic or cultural divisions.[40] Our theory advances arguments about such "preconditions" in that we identify a syndrome of incomplete democratization and war in transitional regimes that lack the institutional infrastructure needed to manage the turbulent processes of increased political participation, especially in settings where unresolved issues of national identity can be exploited for antidemocratic purposes.

In contrast, "bargaining" theories of democratization focus on the strategic choices and alliances of political actors, especially political and economic elites, in shaping the trajectory of a transition. Philippe Schmitter, Guillermo O'Donnell, and Adam Przeworski, for example, show how these tactical choices affect the speed, success, and distributional outcomes of political openings.[41] Our theory advances arguments

---

38.   Samuel P. Huntington, *The Third Wave* (Norman: University of Oklahoma Press, 1991); Jeffry A. Frieden, *Debt, Development, and Democracy: Modern Political Economy and Latin America, 1965–1985* (Princeton: Princeton University Press, 1991); Renée de Nevers, *Comrades No More: The Seeds of Political Change in Eastern Europe* (Cambridge, Mass.: MIT Press, 2003); and Jon C. Pevehouse, "Democracy from the Outside In? International Organizations and Democratization," *International Organization*, Vol. 56, No. 3 (Summer 2002), pp. 515–550.

39.   Juan Linz and Alfred Stepan, *Problems of Democratic Transition and Consolidation* (Baltimore, Md.: The Johns Hopkins University Press, 1996).

40.   Dankwart Rustow, "Transitions to Democracy: Toward a Dynamic Model," *Comparative Politics*, Vol. 2, No. 2 (April 1970), pp. 337–363, reprinted in Anderson, ed., *Transitions to Democracy*, pp. 14–41.

41.   Adam Przeworski, *Democracy and the Market* (Cambridge: Cambridge University Press, 1991).

of this type insofar as we show how the mobilizing rhetoric and coalitional maneuvering of elites in transitional regimes affect both the outcome of the democratization process and also its side effects on war and peace.

Thus, like Przeworski, we find ourselves on both sides of the debate between proponents of "preconditions" theories and proponents of "bargaining" theories of transitions. In our view, favorable or unfavorable initial conditions in the realm of institutions and threats to established elite interests are preconditions that load the dice toward peace or war. At the same time, political choices and bargaining among factions, coalition leaders, and nationalist rabble-rousers shape how the game, thus structured, plays out.

Our methodology reflects this duality. Our statistical analysis is best suited to demonstrating the impact of institutional conditions on outcomes. Our case narratives are better suited to showing how the political process produced these outcomes through the specific mechanisms that we describe in our theory. We do not claim to have invented a theory of democratic transitions. Our purpose has been the narrower one of establishing and explaining the causal links connecting incomplete democratization in states with weak political institutions to war. Nonetheless, we do think that our two-tiered methodology may have some utility for scholars of transitions who want to join the preconditions branch of the literature with the bargaining approach.

Implications for the Democratic Peace

The finding that mature democracies never fight wars against each other is sometimes described as the best-established law in the field of international relations, even in all of political science.[42] Nonetheless, some have charged that even if this purported regularity actually exists, it is probably a coincidental side effect of Cold War power politics or the political interests of states.[43] Our research was not primarily designed to engage this debate. For the most part, our theory was deduced from the assumption that a variant of the institutional explanation for the democratic

---

42.   Jack S. Levy, "The Causes of War: A Review of Theories and Evidence," in Philip Tetlock, et al., eds., *Behavior, Society, and Nuclear War*, Vol. 1 (New York: Oxford University Press, 1989), p. 88.

43.   Joanne Gowa, *Ballots and Bullets: The Elusive Democratic Peace* (Princeton: Princeton University Press, 1999); and Erik Gartzke, "Preferences and the Democratic Peace," *International Studies Quarterly*, Vol. 44, No. 2 (June 2000), pp. 191–212.

peace is probably valid. Our findings are, for the most part, fully consistent with this view.

Indeed, our results might be seen as supporting the institutional account of the democratic peace, since we confirm its implied predictions for a different set of cases: those where the institutional preconditions for the democratic peace are absent, yet politics is significantly influenced by competition for votes. For the same reason, our results lend support to the arguments of Dan Reiter and Allan Stam and others, who argue that the war behavior of individual democracies, not just democratic pairs, differs from that of other regime types.[44]

Our previous work on democratization and war has sometimes been characterized as a criticism of the democratic peace. As we have tried to clarify in this book, however, we do not take issue in any substantial way with the democratic peace theory or most of the empirical support for it. We do, however, seek to introduce a note of caution into the policy prescriptions of those who would seek to use the democratic peace to justify an overly broad campaign of democracy promotion in the developing world that insufficiently reflects the specific local conditions. We favor promoting democracy, but the methods and pacing of doing so must take into account the variations in institutional and political starting points that we have highlighted. How best to fill in the potholes on the road to democratic consolidation is one of the most important tasks facing those who seek to foster peace.

---

44.   Dan Reiter and Allan C. Stam, *Democracies at War* (Princeton: Princeton University Press, 2002).

Appendix: Democratizing Countries that Experienced the Outbreak of External War, 1816–1992

	Composite Index		
Country	Year	Type of War	Type of Democratization
Spain	1823	Interstate	Incomplete
Austria-Hungary	1849	Interstate	Incomplete
Ottoman Empire	1877	Interstate	Incomplete
Great Britain	1882	Both*	Complete
Great Britain	1885	Extra-systemic	Complete
Ottoman Empire	1911	Interstate	Incomplete
Ottoman Empire	1912	Interstate	Incomplete
Ottoman Empire	1913	Interstate	Incomplete
Belgium	1914	Interstate	Complete
Yugoslavia	1941	Interstate	Incomplete
France	1947	Extra-systemic	Complete
Turkey	1950	Interstate	Complete
South Korea	1965	Interstate	Incomplete
Pakistan	1965	Interstate	Incomplete
Cambodia	1975	Interstate	Incomplete
Iran	1980	Interstate	Incomplete

* In 1882, Great Britain was involved in the outbreak of both an extra-systemic (British-Mahdi) and an interstate (Anglo-Egyptian) war.

Competitiveness of Political Participation

Country	Year	Type of War	Type of Democratization
United States	1846	Interstate	Complete
Austria-Hungary	1849	Interstate	Incomplete
Ottoman Empire	1877	Interstate	Incomplete
Spain	1895	Extra-systemic	Complete
Ottoman Empire	1911	Interstate	Incomplete
Ottoman Empire	1912	Interstate	Incomplete
Ottoman Empire	1913	Interstate	Incomplete
Yugoslavia	1941	Interstate	Complete
France	1947	Extra-systemic	Complete
Turkey	1950	Interstate	Complete
Pakistan	1965	Interstate	Complete
Cambodia	1975	Interstate	Incomplete
Iran	1980	Interstate	Incomplete
Argentina	1982	Interstate	Incomplete

Constraints on the Chief Executive

Country	Year	Type of War	Type of Democratization
Spain	1823	Interstate	Incomplete
Peru	1841	Extra-systemic	Incomplete
Prussia	1864	Interstate	Incomplete
Austria-Hungary	1864	Interstate	Incomplete
Austria-Hungary	1866	Interstate	Incomplete
Ottoman Empire	1877	Interstate	Incomplete
Chile	1879	Interstate	Incomplete
Ottoman Empire	1911	Interstate	Incomplete
Ottoman Empire	1912	Interstate	Incomplete
Ottoman Empire	1913	Interstate	Incomplete
Soviet Union	1919	Interstate	Incomplete
Yugoslavia	1941	Interstate	Incomplete
France	1947	Extra-systemic	Complete
Turkey	1950	Interstate	Complete
Soviet Union	1956	Interstate	Incomplete
South Korea	1965	Interstate	Incomplete
Pakistan	1965	Interstate	Incomplete
North Vietnam	1975	Interstate	Incomplete
Ethiopia	1976	Extra-systemic	Incomplete
Ethiopia	1977	Interstate	Incomplete
Ethiopia	1978	Extra-systemic	Incomplete
China	1979	Interstate	Incomplete
Iran	1980	Interstate	Incomplete
France	1991	Interstate	Complete

Openness of Executive Recruitment			
Country	Year	Type of War	Type of Democratization
Spain	1823	Interstate	Incomplete
Great Britain	1838	Extra-systemic	Complete
Great Britain	1839	Extra-systemic	Complete
Great Britain	1840	Extra-systemic	Complete
France	1849	Interstate	Complete
Prussia	1864	Interstate	Incomplete
Prussia	1866	Interstate	Incomplete
Ottoman Empire	1877	Interstate	Incomplete
El Salvador	1906	Interstate	Complete
El Salvador	1907	Interstate	Complete
Ottoman Empire	1911	Interstate	Incomplete
Ottoman Empire	1912	Interstate	Incomplete
Ottoman Empire	1913	Interstate	Incomplete
China	1918	Extra-systemic	Complete
Ethiopia	1951	Interstate	Complete
Egypt	1956	Interstate	Complete
Pakistan	1965	Interstate	Complete
Iran	1980	Interstate	Complete
Iraq	1980	Interstate	Complete

Note: The years given are those in which war broke out (t). In each case, democratization occurred over the preceding five-year interval (from t-6 to t-1).

Index of Persons

Index of Subjects

BCSIA Studies in International Security

Published by The MIT Press

Sean M. Lynn-Jones and Steven E. Miller, series editors
Karen Motley, executive editor
Belfer Center for Science and International Affairs (BCSIA)
John F. Kennedy School of Government, Harvard University

Agha, Hussein, Shai Feldman, Ahmad Khalidi, and Zeev Schiff, *Track-II Diplomacy: Lessons from the Middle East* (2003)

Allison, Graham T., Owen R. Coté, Jr., Richard A. Falkenrath, and Steven E. Miller, *Avoiding Nuclear Anarchy: Containing the Threat of Loose Russian Nuclear Weapons and Fissile Material* (1996)

Allison, Graham T., and Kalypso Nicolaïdis, eds., *The Greek Paradox: Promise vs. Performance* (1996)

Arbatov, Alexei, Abram Chayes, Antonia Handler Chayes, and Lara Olson, eds., *Managing Conflict in the Former Soviet Union: Russian and American Perspectives* (1997)

Bennett, Andrew, *Condemned to Repetition? The Rise, Fall, and Reprise of Soviet-Russian Military Interventionism, 1973–1996* (1999)

Blackwill, Robert D., and Michael Stürmer, eds., *Allies Divided: Transatlantic Policies for the Greater Middle East* (1997)

Blackwill, Robert D., and Paul Dibb, eds., *America's Asian Alliances* (2000)

Brom, Shlomo, and Yiftah Shapir, eds., *The Middle East Military Balance, 1999–2000* (1999)

Brom, Shlomo, and Yiftah Shapir, eds., *The Middle East Military Balance, 2001–2002* (2002)

Brown, Michael E., ed., *The International Dimensions of Internal Conflict* (1996)

Brown, Michael E., and Šumit Ganguly, eds., *Government Policies and Ethnic Relations in Asia and the Pacific* (1997)

Brown, Michael E., and Šumit Ganguly, eds., *Fighting Words: Language Policy and Ethnic Relations in Asia* (2003)

Carter, Ashton B., and John P. White, eds., *Keeping the Edge: Managing Defense for the Future* (2001)

de Nevers, Renée, *Comrades No More: The Seeds of Political Change in Eastern Europe* (2003)

Elman, Colin, and Miriam Fendius Elman, eds., *Bridges and Boundaries: Historians, Political Scientists, and the Study of International Relations* (2001)

Elman, Colin, and Miriam Fendius Elman, eds., *Progress in International Relations Theory: Appraising the Field* (2003)

Elman, Miriam Fendius, ed., *Paths to Peace: Is Democracy the Answer?* (1997)

Falkenrath, Richard A., *Shaping Europe's Military Order: The Origins and Consequences of the CFE Treaty* (1994)

Falkenrath, Richard A., Robert D. Newman, and Bradley A. Thayer, *America's Achilles' Heel: Nuclear, Biological, and Chemical Terrorism and Covert Attack* (1998)

Feaver, Peter D., and Richard H. Kohn, eds., *Soldiers and Civilians: The Civil-Military Gap and American National Security* (2001)

Feldman, Shai, *Nuclear Weapons and Arms Control in the Middle East* (1996)

Feldman, Shai, and Yiftah Shapir, eds., *The Middle East Military Balance 2000–2001* (2001)

Forsberg, Randall, ed., *The Arms Production Dilemma: Contraction and Restraint in the World Combat Aircraft Industry* (1994)

George, Alexander L., and Andrew Bennett, *Case Studies and Theory Development in the Social Sciences* (2005)

Hagerty, Devin T., *The Consequences of Nuclear Proliferation: Lessons from South Asia* (1998)

Heymann, Philip B., *Terrorism and America: A Commonsense Strategy for a Democratic Society* (1998)

Heymann, Philip B., *Terrorism, Freedom, and Security: Winning without War* (2003)

Heymann, Philip B., and Juliette N. Kayyem, *Protecting Liberty in an Age of Terror* (2005)

Howitt, Arnold M., and Robyn L. Pangi, eds., *Countering Terrorism: Dimensions of Preparedness* (2003)

Hudson, Valerie M., and Andrea M. den Boer, *Bare Branches: The Security Implications of Asia's Surplus Male Population* (2004)

Kayyem, Juliette N., and Robyn L. Pangi, eds., *First to Arrive: State and Local Responses to Terrorism* (2003)

Kokoshin, Andrei A., *Soviet Strategic Thought, 1917–91* (1998)

Lederberg, Joshua, ed., *Biological Weapons: Limiting the Threat* (1999)

Mansfield, Edward D., and Jack Snyder, *Electing to Fight: Why Emerging Democracies Go to War* (2005)

Martin, Lenore G., and Dimitris Keridis, eds., *The Future of Turkish Foreign Policy* (2004)

Shaffer, Brenda, *Borders and Brethren: Iran and the Challenge of Azerbaijani Identity* (2002)

Shields, John M., and William C. Potter, eds., *Dismantling the Cold War: U.S. and NIS Perspectives on the Nunn-Lugar Cooperative Threat Reduction Program* (1997)

Tucker, Jonathan B., ed., *Toxic Terror: Assessing Terrorist Use of Chemical and Biological Weapons* (2000)

Utgoff, Victor A., ed., *The Coming Crisis: Nuclear Proliferation, U.S. Interests, and World Order* (2000)

Williams, Cindy, ed., *Holding the Line: U.S. Defense Alternatives for the Early 21st Century* (2001)

Williams, Cindy, ed., *Filling the Ranks: Transforming the U.S. Military Personnel System* (2004)

The Robert and Renée Belfer Center for Science and International Affairs

Graham T. Allison, Director
John F. Kennedy School of Government
Harvard University
79 JFK Street, Cambridge MA 02138
Tel: (617) 495–1400; Fax: (617) 495–8963
http://www.ksg.harvard.edu/bcsia   bcsia_ksg@harvard.edu

The Belfer Center for Science and International Affairs (BCSIA) is the hub of research, teaching and training in international security affairs, environmental and resource issues, science and technology policy, human rights, and conflict studies at Harvard's John F. Kennedy School of Government. The Center's mission is to provide leadership in advancing policy-relevant knowledge about the most important challenges of international security and other critical issues where science, technology and international affairs intersect.

BCSIA's leadership begins with the recognition of science and technology as driving forces transforming international affairs. The Center integrates insights of social scientists, natural scientists, technologists, and practitioners with experience in government, diplomacy, the military, and business to address these challenges. The Center pursues its mission in four complementary research programs:

- The **International Security Program** (ISP) addresses the most pressing threats to U.S. national interests and international security.

- The **Environment and Natural Resources Program** (ENRP) is the locus of Harvard's interdisciplinary research on resource and environmental problems and policy responses.

- The **Science, Technology and Public Policy Program** (STPP) analyzes ways in which science and technology policy influence international security, resources, environment, and development, and such cross-cutting issues as technological innovation and information infrastructure.

- The **WPF Program on Intrastate Conflict, Conflict Prevention and Conflict Resolution** analyzes the causes of ethnic, religious, and other conflicts, and seeks to identify practical ways to prevent and limit such conflicts.

The heart of the Center is its resident research community of more than 140 scholars: Harvard faculty, analysts, practitioners, and each year a new, interdisciplinary group of research fellows. BCSIA sponsors frequent seminars, workshops and conferences, maintains a substantial specialized library, and publishes books, monographs, and discussion papers.

The Center's International Security Program, directed by Steven E. Miller, publishes the BCSIA Studies in International Security, and sponsors and edits the quarterly journal *International Security*.

The Center is supported by an endowment established with funds from Robert and Renée Belfer, the Ford Foundation and Harvard University, by foundation grants, by individual gifts, and by occasional government contracts.